Complete Arabic

Jack Smart and Frances Altorfer

For Mairi and Kirsty

The publisher has used its best endeavours to ensure that the URLs for external websites referred to in this book are correct and active at the time of going to press. However, the publisher and author have no responsibility for the websites and can make no guarantee that a site will remain live or that the content will remain relevant, decent or appropriate.

For UK order enquiries: please contact
Bookpoint Ltd, 130 Milton Park, Abingdon, Oxon OX14 4SB.
Telephone: +44 (0) 1235 827720. *Fax:* +44 (0) 1235 400454.
Lines are open 09.00–18.00, Monday to Saturday, with a 24-hour message answering service. Details about our titles and how to order are available at www.teachyourself.co.uk

For USA order enquiries: please contact
McGraw-Hill Customer Services,
PO Box 545, Blacklick, OH 43004-0545, USA.
Telephone: 1-800-722-4726. *Fax:* 1-614-755-5645.

For Canada order enquiries: please contact
McGraw-Hill Ryerson Ltd,
300 Water St, Whitby, Ontario L1N 9B6, Canada.
Telephone: 905 430 5000. *Fax:* 905 430 5020.

Long renowned as the authoritative source for self-guided learning – with more than 40 million copies sold worldwide – the *Teach Yourself* series includes over 300 titles in the fields of languages, crafts, hobbies, business, computing and education.

British Library Cataloguing in Publication Data:
a catalogue record for this title is available from the British Library.

Library of Congress Catalog Card Number: on file.

First published in UK 2001 by Hodder Education,
338 Euston Road, London, NW1 3BH.

First published in US 2001 by Contemporary Books,
a Division of the McGraw-Hill Companies, 1 Prudential Plaza,
130 East Randolph Street, Chicago, IL 60601 USA.

Previously published as *Teach Yourself Arabic*.
This edition published 2010.

Typeset by WorldAccent, London, England.

Printed in the United Kingdom for Hodder Education, a division of Hodder Headline, 338 Euston Road, London NW1 3BH.

Impression number	5
Year	2013 2012

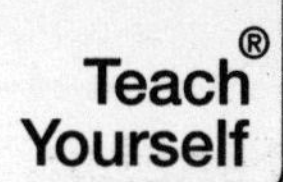

Complete Arabic

Jack Smart and Frances Altorfer

Acknowledgements

We would like to thank, first of all, H.H. Dr. Sheikh Sultan bin Muhammad al-Qasimi, Ruler of Sharjah, for his great generosity to us while we were collecting material for this book. Thanks also to Brian Pridham, Mike Pinder, Sharjah Television, Bob Coles and Ruth Butler at the Institute for Arab and Islamic Studies at Exeter University, and Frances Taylor, for helping us with realia and materials.

We are most grateful to Western Union for permission to use material.

Thanks are also due to Dorothea and Fred Altorfer, and to Lynne and Brent Noble, and Denise Mountford, for their generous help, and we couldn't have produced this edition without Kirsty and Mairi's contribution.

We are particularly grateful to our editors at Hodder & Stoughton, Sue Hart, Rebecca Green and Ginny Catmur, for their endless patience and understanding during the preparation of this book.

We would also like to thank Mr Jim Doran and H. Russell for their helpful comments on the earlier editions.

Contents

Meet the authors

The authors are both linguists of long experience, and are familiar with the Arab countries, their society, religion and culture.

Jack Smart has taught Arabic at university level for over thirty years, specialising in the learning of the language, his students ranging from beginners to candidates for a doctoral degree. He is familiar with the written language from its earliest pre-Islamic period to the present day, and has researched widely into spoken Arabic dialects, in several of which he is fluent. He has lived and worked in Egypt, Sudan and the Gulf countries, and has made short or extended visits and study trips to virtually all of the other Arab states.

Frances Altorfer has also lived in the Middle East. She knows several European languages as well as Swahili and Arabic, and has many years of experience of teaching languages, using the most up-to-date learning methods.

Working in partnership, Jack has provided the linguistic material, and Frances the teaching expertise. The result is, we are sure, a balanced self-teaching book with a broad scope, mainly linguistic, but also with useful sections on the Arabic and Islamic culture, in a clear and easily digestible format.

Only got a minute?

Arabic is spoken by over 200 million people in North Africa, the Arabian Peninsula and the Middle East, and in several other countries it is an official, albeit not universally spoken, language. Modern Standard Arabic (MSA) is the form used in writing and formal speech throughout the Arabic-speaking world (and what you will be learning in this course), enabling communication between speakers of the regional varieties, some of which are mutually incomprehensible. MSA is based on the 7th-century language of the Koran, the holy scripture of Islam. It has changed remarkably little since then. Indeed, if you know MSA, you will have far less difficulty reading the Koran than you would reading, say, *The Canterbury Tales* in 14th-century English!

Arabic is a Semitic language, an ancient group whose other main survivors are Hebrew and Ethiopian Amharic, and is written from right to left in cursive form, just like European handwriting. This means that letters are usually joined up. There are no capital letters.

Arabic has a reputation for being difficult, possibly because of its script. But in fact it is reasonably easy to write Arabic: its spelling is regular, unlike that of English (think of 'reading in Reading!'). Then of course some of the sounds of Arabic don't exist in English – but with practice these will become second nature. Finally, there is the difficulty that there are no cognates between English and Arabic, unlike, for example, English and German (think of 'garden' and *Garten*) or English and French ('possible' is the same in both languages). But there has been quite a lot of traffic between the two languages, with English adopting many Arabic words (e.g. 'safari', 'sherbet') and Arabic adopting many English ones (e.g. *bank*, *film*). Any difficulties can be overcome with application and perseverance, and we will help you all the way. You will find learning Arabic one of the most rewarding experiences you have ever undertaken.

5 Only got five minutes?

Your first Arabic words and phrases

Arabs think that Europeans can speak no Arabic and they are delighted if you make even a modest effort, so it is worth learning a few essential Arabic words and phrases right away, to get you going. The ones we have given are universally known throughout the Arabic-speaking world.

It would be helpful if you have a quick look at the pronunciation guide, so that you know to pronounce those letters that are different from ours. Keep a lookout for the accent sign ´ as this shows where the stress or emphasis lies in the word. Practise saying the words and phrases given a few times and, if you are in the company of Arabs, listen to how they pronounce things.

To make it easier for you to get started, we have given these in transliteration, that is, using the English alphabet, not the Arabic script that you will be learning once you begin working through the units.

Simple greetings

The universal greeting is **as-saláamu :aláykum**, which means *peace be upon you*, and the standard reply is **wa-:aláykum as-saláam,** which means *and peace upon you*.

Another common greeting is **áhlan!** or **áhlan wa-sáhlan!** This means *hello*, or *welcome*.

To say goodbye, say **má:a s-saláamah**, literally, *may you go in safety*.

The Arabs are very polite people and, no matter how busy they are, they regard the use of these greetings as essential, to be said before any other business is done, so it is well worth your while to keep practising them until you feel confident that you can understand them and use them without difficulty.

Arabic courtesies

To ask how someone is, say **kayf al-Haal?** or **kayf Háal-ak**, which, literally, means *how is the condition*, or *how is your condition?*

The reply, which you must make, however you are feeling!, is **al-Hámdu li-l-láah**, which means *praise be to God*.

To ask how the other person is, say **wa ánta?** This means *and you?* And the reply is also **al-Hámdu li-l-láah**.

Basic vocabulary

And now a few general words that you will find very useful to have in your vocabulary.

- *Yes* is **ná:am**, or, informally, **áywah**
- *No* is **laa'**.

You will often hear **Táyyib** meaning *OK*, which is universally understood. In Egypt, they say **kwáyyis**, which means *good*, and, in the Gulf states, they say **zayn**.

Lastly, you will need (and want) to be able to say **min fáDl-ak** for *please*, and **shúkran**, for *thank you*.

What kind of Arabic do Arabic speakers speak?

Arabic is what linguists call a *diglossic language* – this means that the language spoken in daily life differs from the written version and varies widely from country to country. A Gulf Arab would have difficulty taking part in a conversation between two Moroccans, for instance.

In modern everyday life in the Arab countries, Arabic dialects have replaced Standard Arabic for spoken communication, but they are all derived from Standard Arabic, so if you have a grounding in MSA, it will be easier to learn the modern local dialects that are based on it. MSA is also the lingua franca of the Arab world, and can be understood anywhere in conversation with educated speakers.

There are broadly speaking four groups of spoken dialect, which are:

1 *North African (including Morocco, Tunisia, Algeria and, to some extent, Libya)*
2 *Egyptian and Sudanese*
3 *Levantine (Syria, Jordan, the Palestinian Territories and the Lebanon)*
4 *Gulf Arabic, or the dialects of the Arabian Peninsula and Iraq.*

Egypt is the main producer of films and television in the Arabic-speaking world, so the Egyptian dialect is without doubt the most widely understood throughout the Arab world.

Everything that is written – with the minor exception of folk plays and cartoon captions – is expressed in Modern Standard Arabic.

Formal spoken announcements, such as political speeches and news broadcasts, are also in MSA and are universally understood by educated Arabs. This is the language that children learn at school and the one that you will learn in this book. So if you work through the units methodically, you should get to a level of proficiency that will enable you to read newspapers and listen to radio and television broadcasts, as well as to communicate with Arabic-speaking people all over the Arab world.

10 Only got 10 minutes?

Why learn Arabic?

Why do you want to learn Arabic? It could be one of several reasons: it may be that you are going to work in a country in which Arabic is the official language and you would like to be able to communicate with your business colleagues and local people and read such basic things as street signs, newspaper headings and so on. Or perhaps you want to be able to read the Koran in its original language. With this course, you will be learning Arabic at your own pace, beginning with simple dialogues and explanatory notes, but gradually the language you are learning will be taken up to a higher level. You will always be able to look back to check on what you have learned so far and at the end of the course you will find a summary of all key grammar points.

Your reason for wanting to learn Arabic may be because you intend to visit one of the Arabic-speaking countries as a tourist. Besides the wonderful pharaonic monuments in Egypt, the marvels of Roman and Arab civilisations extend across both North Africa and the Middle East.

If you already know some MSA, you will find it much easier to pick up the dialect of whichever Arabic-speaking country you happen to be in and you will have a good grounding in the basics of the language. All the dialects are ultimately based on MSA.

What kind of Arabic will you learn?

The Arabic taught in this book is the standard written language of more than 200 million inhabitants of mainly Arab states, ranging from Morocco to Iraq. It is the language of newspapers and Arabic literature and is usually called Modern Standard Arabic.

In addition to the native speakers, it is read and written by Muslims the world over as the language of religion. There are millions of Muslims in Pakistan, Afghanistan and in the Far East, in Malaysia and Indonesia. If you are a Muslim, you have to both read the Koran and pray in Arabic. Translations are only used for reference or to help with understanding the Arabic.

All the commentaries on the Holy Text and other literature on interpretation and rules for daily life are written in and have to be read in Arabic. And it is a matter of pride for Muslims that employing the language in this way means that Arabic is regarded as a prestige language.

In the same way that Welsh and Spanish and English use mostly the same letters and general script but are not closely related to one another, other languages of mainly Islamic countries, such as Persian (Farsi) and Urdu, and previously Turkish, also use adapted versions of the Arabic script, but are not linguistically related to Arabic. While Persian and Urdu are still written in slightly adapted forms of the Arabic alphabet, Turkish adopted a modified European alphabet in 1928. You will find that, if you already know some Arabic, you will often be able to get the gist of a newspaper article written in one of these languages. This is because they have borrowed many words from Arabic, due to a shared Islamic culture.

Writing Arabic

Many people are put off learning Arabic by the (apparently) difficult script. In fact, this is one of the most rewarding aspects of learning Arabic, since, once you have mastered the 28 letters of the alphabet, it is reasonably easy to write Arabic – the language has few of the spelling oddities of English, such as *write/right* or *cough/through*, for example.

Arabic – except in the Holy Koran and in ancient poetry – is always written omitting the short vowels, such as *a* in *hat* or *i* in *tin*. This is not as bizarre an arrangement as you might at first think, especially as, in English, we are nowadays actually used to this with text messaging (*txt msg*). These short vowels can be usually be predicted without too much difficulty as the number of word shapes in Arabic is limited.

The Arabic heritage

The Arabs began to study their language really quite early in their history, so the basics of grammar had been laid down already in the 8th century, which was also when the first dictionary was written.

Written Arabic has existed for about 12 centuries without any great amount of change. The west owes Arabic a major debt, as the language continued to carry the torch of classical learning while Europe entered the Dark Ages. Many pioneering Greek mathematical, medical and philosophical texts were translated by Arab writers and scientists. Had it not been for the efforts of these early scholars, the texts would have been lost to us completely. Much that we know of today in the fields of chemistry, medicine, astronomy and other branches of scientific endeavour comes from these Arab scholars.

Although they did not actually invent them, the Arabs also gave to the west what we call Arabic numerals, including the concept of *zero*, which derives from the Arabic **Sifr**. This is, perhaps, more obvious in the word *cipher*, which, when it was first used, meant the same thing.

Arabic has lent many words to the various European languages, most particularly to Spanish and Portuguese, as a result of the Arab occupation of the Iberian Peninsula, which lasted for over 700 years. There are also a surprising number in English: *magazine*, *calibre*, *algebra*, *arsenal* and *admiral*, for instance, all come from Arabic.

The Arabic word for *the* is **al-**, in Arabic script ال, which you can see in many borrowings, such as the English words *algebra*, mentioned earlier, and *algorithm*. Have you been to Granada in Spain? If you have, perhaps you visited the *Alhambra*? Here you can see another example of a borrowing with the Arabic word for *the* in it. Note that it is always joined on to the next word, so you never see it alone.

Arabic literature

Most popular Arabic literature that we are familiar with in the west tends to be confined to the *Arabian Nights*, a collection of tales that have come from many sources and that, interestingly, was not highly regarded in the Arab world until relatively recently, due to their popular folk origins. The poetry of Omar Khayyam is probably the piece of Middle Eastern literature next best known in the West – but the poet himself was, in fact, Persian and not an Arabic speaker! Furthermore, Arabic literature really begins with poetry in the pre-Islamic era. Before the 20th century, we find that there are no novels or drama at all.

The religion Muslims practise, Islam, technically prohibits the artistic representation of anything living, either plant or animal life. Although this proscription was ignored in many Muslim areas, it led to a highly developed art of calligraphy, which is readily visible in inscriptions on religious buildings and, indeed, in all walks of life in Arabic-speaking countries.

If you choose to learn Arabic, you will be able to deepen your knowledge about all these things – and more.

Introduction

Welcome to *Complete Arabic*!

The aims of the course

If you are an adult learner with no previous knowledge of Arabic and studying on your own, then this is the course for you. Perhaps you are taking up Arabic again after a break or perhaps you are intending to learn with the support of a class. Again, you will find this course very well suited to your purposes.

The language you will learn is based on the kind of material seen in Arabic newspapers and magazines or heard on radio and television news broadcasts. The main emphasis is on understanding Arabic, but we also aim to give you an idea of how the language works, so that you can create sentences of your own.

If you are working on your own, the audio recordings will be all the more important, as they will provide you with the essential opportunity to listen to Arabic and to speak it within a controlled framework. You should therefore try to get a copy of the audio recordings if you haven't already done so.

The structure of the course

This course contains:

- *a guide to Arabic script and pronunciation*
- *17 course units*
- *a reference section*
- *optional CDs*

How to use this course

All the important information that you need for the basic structures of Arabic are given in the first 10 units. The following 7 units introduce more advanced but essential structures, through texts and dialogues.

Statement of aims

At the beginning of each unit is a summary of what you can expect to learn by the end of that unit.

Presentation of new language

This is in the form of dialogues or texts introducing the new language, which are also recorded. These are followed by questions and phrase-matching exercises to help you check your comprehension. The answers to these and a translation of the texts are in the *Key* at the end of the book. New words are given in the order in which they appear, and they are followed where necessary by *Notes* (**al-mulaaHaDHáat** الملاحظات) which explain how the language works. The language is presented in manageable chunks, building carefully on what you have learned in earlier units. Throughout the course the texts and vocabulary are given both in Arabic script and in transliteration, that is, in English letters. Try to rely less on the transliteration as you progress through the units.

Key phrases (ta:biiráat ra'iisíyyah تعبيرات رئيسية)

To sum up what you have learned in the texts or dialogues, the **Key phrases** section will provide a valuable reference. These contain the main language elements of the unit and will help you when you come to the exercises.

Structures (taraakíib al-lughah تراكيب اللغة)

In this section the forms of the language are explained and illustrated. Main grammatical concepts have often been grouped together for ease of reference and they gradually build up to provide you with all the structures you need to read and write Arabic.

Cultural tips (ma:luumáat thaqaafíyyah معلومات ثقافية)

These highlight some of the social and cultural aspects of life in the Arab world.

Word shapes (awzáan al-kalimáat أوزان الكلمات)

This section will help you familiarise yourself with the way in which Arabic words are formed.

Practice (tamriináat تمرينات)

The **tamriináat** provide a variety of activities so that you can start using the new words and structures. Practice is graded so that activities which require mainly recognition come first. As you grow in confidence in manipulating language forms, you will be encouraged to write and speak the language yourself. The answers can be found at the end of the book, in the *Key*. Transcripts of listening comprehension exercises follow the *Key*.

Reference

The reference section contains a *Glossary of language terms*, a *Grammar summary* of the main structures of the Arabic language, and a set of *Verb tables*, so that every verb you come across in the book can be matched in the tables to a verb which works in the same way.

Selected *Arabic–English* and *English–Arabic* glossaries are provided so that you can look up words alphabetically and, finally, a *Grammar index* will enable you to look up specific points.

Study tips

Remember that the first step in learning a language is listening and understanding. Concentrate initially on that and then work on your writing skills, using the information in the units and, if possible, by listening to native speakers.

In using a course such as this, it is important to pace yourself, with a view to consolidating what you have learned before moving on. Due to the nature of the language, the units are of varying length and complexity. There is no need to attempt to absorb a whole unit in one sitting.

Our suggestion is that you concentrate on the texts first, with reference to the transcripts and the audio if you have it. This includes mastering the vocabulary as far as possible. The translations are there to help you if you get stuck. You should then look at the *Structures* section and make sure you understand how the language is working. Finally work through the exercises. These are based on the constructions explained in the unit and will help you consolidate what you have learned. Try to do each exercise before checking your work in the *Key*.

Hints for further study

This book covers all the main structures of Arabic and a reasonable amount of vocabulary.

If you want to dig deeper, you will first need a pair of dictionaries. The use of these has been discussed in the *Review unit*.

- *Arabic–English: Hans Wehr A* Dictionary of Modern Written Arabic *(edited by J. Milton Cowan) is an essential tool.*
- *English–Arabic: the best available is Munir Ba'albaki* Al-Mawrid, A Modern English–Arabic Dictionary. *This very comprehensive work was designed for use by native Arabic*

speakers and so, to select the correct word for a given context, some cross-referencing with Wehr may be necessary.

These two dictionaries are the best for the serious student, but there are others available.

There is a multitude of Arabic grammars on the market, of widely differing merits:

- *David Cowan,* Modern Literary Arabic *provides a concise look at the structures of written Arabic at a slightly deeper level than this book.*

Spoken Arabic varies widely from country to country, and you should choose from the wide selection of material available according to which country you intend to visit. Very roughly the Arabic dialects divide into the following groups: North Africa from Morocco to Libya; Egypt and the Sudan; the Lebanon, Jordan and Syria; Iraq and the Arabian Peninsula.

The Arabic of the last of these groups is probably the nearest to the written Arabic you will learn in this book and is covered by the present writers' *Complete Gulf Arabic* in the same series.

You can read and hear Arabic on the BBC News, CNN and al-Jazeera websites, although you should not expect to understand everything straight away. These websites give news items in small chunks, which are ideal pieces of 'real' Arabic.

Good luck! We hope you will enjoy learning Arabic!

Arabic script and pronunciation guide

1 Basic characteristics

The Arabic script looks difficult because it is so different from what we are used to. In fact, it is easy to master and, with one or two easily definable exceptions, all sounds are written as they are pronounced. There are no combinations of vowels (*diphthongs*) which result in a totally different sound, such as, for example, the English words *plough*, *dough*, *through*, *enough*.

Some important facts about the Arabic script:

- *Arabic is written from* right to left. *As a result of this, what we would regard as the back cover of a book, magazine or newspaper is, in fact, the front cover of an Arabic publication.*
- *Arabic script is always* joined, *or* cursive, *like English handwriting. There is no equivalent of the English text you are now reading, where all the letters have separate forms with spaces between them.*
- *There are no capital letters.*
- *The joining strokes between letters, called* ligatures, *have the effect of slightly altering the shape of the letters on either side. As a result, Arabic letters have varying forms, depending on whether they come at the beginning, in the middle or at the end of a word.*
- *A few letters do not join to the following letter.*
- *The three short vowels,* **a**, **i** *or* **u**, *as opposed to the long vowels* **aa**, **uu** *and* **ii**, *are not shown in the script. For example, the word* **bank** *(borrowed from English) is written* **b-n-k**. *This is not so much of a problem as you might think, since the*

number of shapes or forms which Arabic words take is limited. There is a system (not normally used in Modern Arabic) to show the short vowels, which is explained below. As almost all Modern Arabic is written without the short vowels, we have generally not included them in the Arabic script in this course, although the transliteration (pronunciation guide) given for all the Arabic vocabulary and structures will show you what they are. However, we have included the short vowels in the Arabic script in some places where it is especially helpful.

---

2 The alphabet

Because Arabic is a cursive script, we have given the *initial*, *medial* and *final* forms of each letter, used depending on where they occur in the word. A separate form has also been included, since some letters do not join to the one after them. If you look at the letters carefully you will see that there are really only two shapes, although four forms of the non-joining letters have been given.

The Arabic alphabet is given below in its traditional order. Letters which do not join to the following one are marked with an asterisk (*).

The term *final* in the table should be interpreted as meaning final after a joining letter. If the preceding letter is a non-joiner, the separate form will be used. If you look closely, you can see that final and separate letters are usually elongated in form or have a 'flourish' after them.

In most cases, the initial form of the letter can be regarded as the basic or nucleus form. For example, if you look at **baa'** (the second letter in the following list), you will see that its basic (initial) form is a small left-facing hook with a single dot below it. The medial form is more or less the same, with a ligature coming in from the right (remember Arabic reads from right to left). The final form is the same as the medial, with a little flourish to the left, at the end of the word, and the separate form is the same as the initial, but again with the flourish to the left. Study the letters bearing these features in mind, as many of them follow the same principle. Fuller descriptions and other hints on deciphering will be given in the units.

Here are the four shapes of **baa'** in enlarged type:

بـ	ـبـ	ـب	ب
initial	*medial*	*final*	*separate*

You will see that the nucleus is the hook with a dot under it (the initial form). The medial shape has joining strokes before and after the letter and the final form has an elongation or flourish.

The Arabic letters

Name	*Initial*	*Medial*	*Final*	*Separate*	*Pronunciation*
alif*	ا	ـا	ـا	ا	*see below*
baa'	بـ	ـبـ	ـب	ب	*b*
taa'	تـ	ـتـ	ـت	ت	*t*
thaa'	ثـ	ـثـ	ـث	ث	*th*
jiim	جـ	ـجـ	ـج	ج	*j*
Haa'	حـ	ـحـ	ـح	ح	*H*
khaa'	خـ	ـخـ	ـخ	خ	*kh*
daal*	د	ـد	ـد	د	*d*
dhaal*	ذ	ـذ	ـذ	ذ	*dh*
raa'*	ر	ـر	ـر	ر	*r*
zaay*	ز	ـز	ـز	ز	*z*
siin	سـ	ـسـ	ـس	س	*s*
shiin	شـ	ـشـ	ـش	ش	*sh*

Name	*Initial*	*Medial*	*Final*	*Separate*	*Pronunciation*
Saad	صـ	ـصـ	ـص	ص	*S*
Daad	ضـ	ـضـ	ـض	ض	*D*
Taa'	طـ	ـطـ	ـط	ط	*T*
DHaa'	ظـ	ـظـ	ـظ	ظ	*DH*
:ain	عـ	ـعـ	ـع	ع	*:*
ghain	غـ	ـغـ	ـغ	غ	*gh*
faa'	فـ	ـفـ	ـف	ف	*f*
qaaf	قـ	ـقـ	ـق	ق	*q*
kaaf	كـ	ـكـ	ـك	ك	*k*
laam	لـ	ـلـ	ـل	ل	*l*
miim	مـ	ـمـ	ـم	م	*m*
nuun	نـ	ـنـ	ـن	ن	*n*
haa'	هـ	ـهـ	ـه	ه	*h*
waaw*	و	ـو	ـو	و	*w*
yaa'	يـ	ـيـ	ـي	ي	*y*

There is one combination consonant **laam-alif**. This must be used when this series of letters occurs and it is a non-joiner:

Name	*Initial*	*Medial/Final*	*Separate*	*Pronunciation*
laam-alif	لا	ـلا	لا	*laa*

The **taa' marbuuTah**, referred to in this book as the 'hidden **-t**', is the Arabic feminine ending. As it only occurs at the end of words, it has only two forms: *final* (after joiners) and *separate* (after non-joiners). It is always preceded by a short **a** vowel:

Final	*Separate*
ـة	ة

If you look carefully at this letter, you will see that it is a **haa'** with the two dots above of the **taa'** added. It is normally ignored in speech, or rendered as a very weak **h**, but in certain combinations of words, it is pronounced as **t**. It has therefore been transcribed as **h** or **t** accordingly.

The **hamzah** is regarded by the Arabs as a supplementary sign, not as a letter of the alphabet. Its official pronunciation is a 'glottal stop' (as the *ts* in the Cockney pronunciation of *bottle*), and it has been transliterated by means of an apostrophe ('). It is sometimes omitted in speech, but should be shown in written Arabic, where it occurs either on its own, or written over an **alif**, **waaw** or **yaa'**. In the last case, the two dots under the **yaa'** are omitted. It can also occur written below an **alif**, but this is less common. The actual **hamzah** never joins to anything, but its 'supporting' letters take the form required by their position in the word:

	Initial	*Medial*	*Final*	*Separate*
independent		ء *in all cases*		
over **alif**	أ	ـأ	ـأ	أ
under **alif**	إ	*does not occur*		إ
over **waaw**	–	ـؤ	ـؤ	ؤ
over **yaa'**	–	ـئـ	ـئ	ئ

Note that, at the beginning of a word, **hamzah** is always written above or below **alif**.

The writing of the **hamzah** is a frequent source of spelling errors among native speakers and it is often omitted in print and writing.

In foreign loanwords the letter *p* is usually written as a **baa’** and the letter *v* is written either as **faa’** or with the Persian letter ڤ – a **faa’** with three dots above it instead of one.

Script Exercise 1

In the photograph below, which well-known international companies are sponsors of this racecourse?

---

3 Vowels

The letters of the Arabic alphabet are all regarded as consonants.

In Arabic writing, the short vowels are not usually marked except in children’s school textbooks, the Holy Koran and ancient classical poetry.

The long vowels are expressed by the three letters **alif, waaw** and **yaa’**. **Alif** almost always expresses the vowel **aa**, but **waaw** and

yaa' can also be consonantal **w** and **y** (as in English *wish* and *yes*).

The most important factors to consider in Arabic words are, first, the consonants and, second, the long vowels. It will not make much difference in most cases whether you pronounce a word with **a**, **u** or **i** (short vowels), but it is important to get the long vowels right. (See Section 8 for more details on vowels.)

---

4 Variations in handwriting

Think of the Arabic script as essentially handwriting (since it is always cursive, no matter how it is produced – by hand or on a computer). Since calligraphy is a highly developed art in the Arab world, there are more variations in the form of the letters than is the case in English.

The most common of these is that two dots above or below a letter are frequently combined into one dash, and three dots (which only occur above) into an inverted *v* like the French circumflex (ˆ). Here is an example showing **taa'** and **thaa'**:

Another common variation is the writing of **siin** (**s**) and **shiin** (**sh**) simply as long lines, ironing out their 'spikes', and often with a small hook below at the beginning:

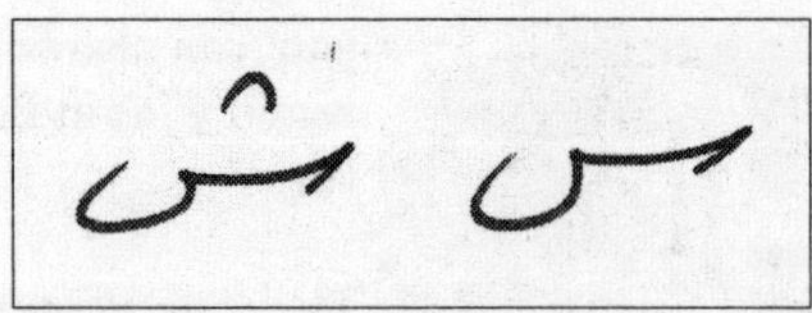

This occurs frequently in handwriting, signwriting and newspaper and advert headings – in fact, everywhere where the original copy has been prepared by a calligrapher rather than typeset.

Above all, Arabic writing is fun. Look at it as an art form!

5 Transliteration

Transliteration means expressing a language that uses a different writing system (like Arabic) in terms of symbols based on the Roman alphabet, usually for teaching purposes. There is no standard way of doing this and we have tried to keep the system used in this book as simple as possible.

The essential feature of a transliteration system is that it has to have a precise equivalent for every sound used in the target language. This differs from conventional spelling, e.g. in English the letter *s* has totally different sounds in the two words *loafs*, and *loaves*. Consider also that the same sound in the former can be spelled *ce*, e.g. *mince*. Transliteration systems have to iron out such discrepancies.

We have adapted the English alphabet, using capital letters to distinguish between Arabic sounds that seem related to speakers of English. For instance, Arabic has two sorts of *t*, which we have distinguished in this way: **rattab** means *arranged*, whereas **raTTab** means *moistened*. Consequently, you will not find capital letters used as they are conventionally, e.g. in personal and place names. (An exception has, however, been made in the case of **Al-laah** *God, Allah*.)

6 The Arabic sounds

CD1, TR01

We have divided the pronunciation table into three:

- *Group 1: Sounds that are more or less as in English.*
- *Group 2: Sounds that do not occur in English, but are found in other European languages with which you may be familiar.*
- *Group 3: Sounds that are specific to Arabic.*

Note: The letter **alif** has no sound of its own and is used only to express the long vowel **aa** and as a support for the **hamzah** (see the relevant sections below).

Group 1

b as in باب **baab** *door*

d as in درس **dars** *lesson*

dh as in ذلك **dháalik** *that*. Do not confuse this with the sound **th** (see below), as they convey entirely different meanings in Arabic (**dhawb** *melting*, **thawb** *a garment*).

f as in فلفل **fílfil** *pepper*

h as in هو **húwa** *he*, but never omitted in speech as it very often is in English (e.g. *vehement*). An exception is the common feminine ending -ah, see Section 2 above.

j as in جديد **jadíid** *new*

k as in كبير **kabíir** *big*

l mostly as in لا **laa** *not*, but sometimes has a duller sound, roughly as in English *alter*. This distinction is not meaningful in Arabic but depends on the surrounding consonants.

m as in ممكن **múmkin** *possible*

n as in نور **nuur** *light*

s as in سمسم **símsim** *sesame*, (it is never pronounced *z* as in *things*: see **z** below)

sh as in شريعة **sharíi:ah** *sharia* (Islamic law)

t as in تاجر **táajir** *merchant*

th as in ثلاثة **thaláthah** *three* (not as in *this*; see **dh** above)

w as in واحد **wáaHid** *one*

y as in يوم **yawm** *day*

z as in زوج **zawj** *husband* (sometimes spelled *s* in English, but in Arabic **s** and **z** never interchange; see also **th** and **dh**)

Group 2 🔊 CD1, TR02

r As in رجل **rájul** *man*. The Arabic **r** sound does not occur in standard English, but is familiar in dialect pronunciation. It is the trilled *r* of Scottish *very* ('*verry*'), and common in Italian and Spanish (*Parma*, *Barcelona*).

gh As in غرب **gharb** *west*. Near to the *r* of Parisian French. It is actually a more guttural scraping sound, and occurs in Dutch, e.g. *negen*. The Parisian *r* is near enough as an intermediate measure.

kh As in خارج **kháarij** *outside*. Roughly sound of *ch* in Scottish *loch* and *och aye*. Also familiar in German *doch* and (written *j*) in Spanish *José*.

Group 3 🔊 CD1, TR03

These sounds are particular to Arabic. To pronounce them requires practice and it is best to listen to native speakers if possible.

S, **T**, With the exception of **H** (see below), the capitalised **D**, consonants are pronounced in a way similar to their small **DH** letter versions **s**, **t**, **d** and **dh**, except that the tongue is depressed into a spoon shape and the pressure of air from the lungs increased. This gives a forceful and hollow sound, often referred to as *emphatic*. These sounds have a marked effect on surrounding vowels, making them sound more hollow. A rough (British) English equivalent is the difference in the *a* as in *Sam* and (with of course silent *p*) *psalm*. Examples are:

S as in صغير **Saghíir** *small*
T as in طالب **Táalib** *student*
D as in ضيف **Dayf** *guest*
DH as in ظهر **DHuhr** *noon*

: As in عمل **:ámal** *work*. We have a muscle in our throat which is never used except in vomiting. Think about that and pretend you are about to be sick. You will find that what is normally called gagging in English is actually a restriction in the deep part of the throat. If you begin to gag and then immediately relax the muscles in order to release the airstream from the lungs, you will have produced a perfect : (called **:ayn** in Arabic). This sound must be distinguished from the glottal stop **hamzah** as the difference affects the meaning. For instance, **:amal** means *work*, but **'amal** means *hope*.

H As in حج **Hajj** *pilgrimage*. Pronounced in exactly the same way as **:ayn**, except that, instead of completely closing the muscles referred to above, they are merely constricted and the air allowed to escape. The only time English speakers come near to a (weakish) **H** is when they breathe on their spectacle lenses before cleaning them. Both **:ayn** and **Haa'** should always be pronounced with the mouth fairly wide open (say '*ah*').

' As in أمل **'ámal** *hope* (not to be confused with **:ámal** *work* above). The **hamzah** occurs in English between words pronounced deliberately and emphatically (e.g. '*She [pause] is [pause] awful.*'), but is probably more familiar as the Cockney or Glaswegian pronunciation of *t* or *tt* as in *bottle*.

q As in قريب **qaríib** *near*. Officially pronounced as a 'back of the throat' English *c* or *k*. If you try to imitate the sound of a crow cawing you will not be far away. A rough equivalent is the difference in articulation of the letter *c* in (British) English *cam* and *calm*. *Note:* The symbol **q** has been chosen only for convenience: it has really nothing to do with the English combination *qu*.

Local variations

As with any language spoken over such a wide area, regional pronunciations occur. The versions given above are the officially correct ones, always used in reciting the Holy Koran, but local variants often slip into the pronunciation of politicians, radio and TV announcers etc. The most important of these affect the following letters:

th Many speakers in the north and west of the Arab world find this sound difficult to pronounce and render it as either **t** or **s**.

j In Egypt and a few other areas, this is rendered **g** as in *gold*. In the Lebanon, parts of Syria and Jordan, it sounds like the **j** of French *Jacques* (which is the same as the *s* in English *pleasure*).

dh Sometimes becomes **d** or **z** (see **th** above).

D Pronounced identically to **DH** in most of the eastern Arab world (Iraq, the Gulf and Saudi Arabia).

DH See **D** above. Additionally, in many urban parts of Egypt, the Lebanon, Syria and Jordan it often becomes a sort of emphatic **z**-sound.

q In informal speech, this is often pronounced as **g** in many parts of the Arab world. In the spoken Arabic of urban areas of Egypt, the Lebanon and Syria it is pronounced as a glottal stop (**hamzah**).

Insight

The above variants are given to help you avoid confusion when listening to 'live' Arabic in various parts of the Arab world. It is probably better to stick to the more formal values until your ear becomes attuned but if – as is highly recommended – you enlist the help of a native speaker, imitate his or her pronunciation.

---

7 Vowels

CD1, TR04

There are only three common vowels, all of which occur both long and short. These have been transcribed as follows:

a As in أوّل **áwwal** *first*

aa As in ثالث **tháalith** *third*, an elongated emphatic *a* as in the word *bad* in: '*You've been a* ***baad baad*** *boy!*' In juxtaposition with some of the consonants (mainly the capitalised ones **S, D, T, DH**, but also **q, gh** and sometimes **l** and **r**, it sounds more like the vowel in the English *palm*.

i As in اِبن **ibn** *son*

ii The long equivalent of **i**, as in كريم **kariim** *generous*

u As in مسلم **múslim** *muslim* (never as in *sup*)

uu As in محمود **maHmúud** *Mahmoud*

aw As in لون **lawn** *colour*

ay as in بيت **bayt** *house* like **ai** as in *bail* in informal situations)

oo As in تلفون **tilifóon** *telephone* or *home* as pronounced in Scotland – occurs in less formal speech and in some foreign loanwords.

8 Writing vowels and other signs

As short vowels are not normally written in Modern Arabic, it is better to become used to recognising Arabic words without them. However, the transliterated Arabic throughout this course will show you which short vowel should be pronounced and the short vowels are also sometimes included on the Arabic script where helpful to understanding the patterns of words.

All these signs are written above or below (as indicated) the consonant they *follow*. For instance, to express the word **kutiba**, you write the (Arabic) consonant **k** + the vowel sign for **u**, consonant **t** + the sign for **i**, **b** + the sign for **a**, like this:

As all three letters are joining letters, the **k** has the initial form, the **t** the medial form and the **b** the final form.

The long vowels are the same signs, but followed by **alif** for **aa**, **waaw** for **uu** and **yaa'** for **ii**. For example, if the above word had all three vowels long (**kuutiibaa** – an imaginary word, for purposes of illustration only), it would be written like this:

كُوتِيبَا

A similar means is used to express the diphthong vowels **aw** and **ay**, except that, as you would expect, the vowel sign preceding the و or ي is always **a**, for example:

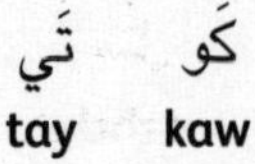

Zero vowel sign

When a consonant has no vowel after it, this is marked by writing a miniature circle (like a zero) above it; here above the **k**:

مَكْتَب

maktab

This sign is omitted at the end of words, in this case the **b**.

Doubled consonants

CD1, TR05

Doubled consonants (written in the transliteration as **bb, nn, ss,** etc.) are very important in Arabic, as they can change the meanings of words radically. They are only pronounced in English when they span two words, e.g. '*But Tim, my young friend…*' In Arabic, however, they must always be pronounced carefully, wherever they occur, with a slight hesitation between them. **mathal** means *a proverb*, **maththal** means *he acted*, *represented*.

In Arabic, the consonant is written once only, with the following sign (a little Arabic س **s** without the tail) above it, for example:

مَثَّل

maththal

The sign for the vowel following the doubled letter – here an **a** – is written above the doubling sign. As you have already learned, an **i** vowel is expressed by writing a short oblique stroke under the letter. However, by convention, when a letter already has the doubling sign, the stroke is put under the sign but actually above the letter.

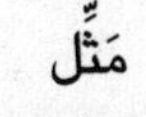

maththil

Other signs

The letter **alif** occasionally appears with a longer, curved stroke above it (similar to a stretched out Spanish *tilde* as in *cañon*). It is then pronounced as a **hamzah** (glottal stop) followed by a long **aa** vowel. An important word which you will meet often and should take pains to learn to write and pronounce correctly is the Arabic word for the Koran:

اَلْقُرْآن

al-qur'aan

Finally, a sign used on only a very few (but common) words is a vertical stroke above the preceding letter, often called the 'dagger alif'. This is simply a shorthand way of writing the long **aa** vowel. Another very important word in Arab culture is *God*, or *Allah*. Here the vertical stroke is written over the doubling sign. Pronounce this **alláah** with the stress on the second syllable. (It is usually uttered with the 'dark' **l**, i.e. an **l** pronounced with the tongue hollowed at the back of the upper teeth. This gives the **aa** a 'hollow' sound.)

اللّٰه

---

9 Irregular spellings

The letter **yaa'** occurs frequently at the end of words in Arabic. It is usually pronounced **-ii**, but also sometimes **-aa**. In the former case, it is usually written with two dots under it (ي) and in the latter, without them (ى), but this rule is not, unfortunately, always adhered to.

بَنَى

banaa

Note that in this case, the vowel preceding the **yaa'** is **a**. Words showing this characteristic will be explained as they occur.

The hybrid letter ة, the 'hidden t', is always preceded by **a** (ـَة) (see Section 2 above).

Important note: Both of these spellings can only occur at the end of a word. If any suffix is added to the word, they become ا and ت respectively. (This will be explained fully later in the book.)

10 One-letter words

By convention, Arabic words consisting only of one consonantal letter (and usually a short vowel) are joined to the following word. Thus **wa** (*and*) + **anta** (*you*) is written:

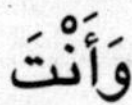

To make things clearer in transliteration, such words are separated by a hyphen: **wa-anta** in this book.

11 Stress

CD1, TR05, 00:32

The rules for stress in Arabic are complex and it is better to learn from the audio if you have it or by listening to native speakers.

One simple general rule, however, is that if a word contains a long vowel (**aa**, **uu**, etc.) the stress falls on this; and if there is more than one (long vowel), the stress falls on the one nearest the end of the word, e.g.:

مَكاتِب **makáatib** but مَكاتِيب **makaatíib**

The stress will be on the last long syllable before a vowel ending.

To help you, the stressed syllables of words have been marked with an acute accent: **á**, **áa**, etc. in the first few units so that you become used to where they occur.

12 Case endings

Classical Arabic had a set of three grammatical case endings for nouns and adjectives, but these are nowadays largely ignored in all but very formal speech such as Koranic recitation and ancient poetry.

The only one of these that concerns us is the so-called *indefinite accusative*, because this shows in the script. This is known as the *accusative marker*.

Its form is an **alif** attached to the end of the noun or adjective, technically with two slashes above the preceding consonant: ـًا. It is pronounced **-an**, e.g. كتاب **kitáab**, but with accusative marker كتابًا **kitáaban**. In practice, the two slashes before the **alif** are usually omitted: كتابا.

1

فلنبدأ fal-nábda'
Let's get started!

In this unit you will learn:

- ***how to greet people***
- ***how to make short descriptive phrases***
- ***about definites and indefinites***

---

1 السلام عليكم as-saláamu :aláy-kum

hello [lit., Peace be upon you]

CD1, TR06

In Arabic, it is extremely important to be able to greet people and to reply when someone greets you. Notice that each greeting has its own particular reply. If you have the recording, listen to these people greeting each other and see how they respond.

Simple greetings

السلام عليكم **as-saláamu :aláy-kum***	*hello* [lit., peace be upon you]
وعليكم السلام **wa- :aláy-kum as-saláam**	*hello (reply)* [lit., (and) upon you peace]

*This pronunciation is explained in Structures 1b below.

Exercise 1

Kamal is visiting an old friend, John, in his hotel in Cairo and Kamal speaks first. Practise saying each phrase, filling in the gaps. Remember to pronounce the stress on every word where it is shown.

a	*as-saláamu …, yaa John!*	السلام... يا جون!
b	*wa :aláy-kum …, yaa Kamáal!*	وعليكم... يا كمال!

Exercise 2

You are going to visit your Arabic-speaking friend Nadia. She welcomes you into her house. What do you say to her?

يا **yaa** *O*

(obligatory before anyone's name or title when addressing them)

---

2 صباح الخير SabáaH al-kháyr Good morning

CD1, TR07

Suad is about to begin teaching an Arabic course at the university in Cairo. First she greets a new student.

Su:áad	**SabáaH al-kháyr.**	سعاد صباح الخير.
Táalibah	**SabáaH an-núur.**	طالبة صباح النور.

طالبة، طالبات **Táalibah** (pl. **Taalibáat**) *female student*

Insight

The plurals of nouns and adjectives in Arabic do not follow a logical system, so it is better to learn them along with the singular from the beginning. They are given after the singular noun in the vocabulary, separated by a comma.

In Arabic, there is no word for *good afternoon*, so **masáa' al-kháyr** is used for both late afternoon and evening.

تعبيرات رئيسية **ta:biiráat ra'iisíyyah** (Key phrases)

CD1, TR08

How to wish someone good morning, evening

صباح الخير **SabáaH al-kháyr**	*good morning* [lit., morning (of) the goodness]
صباح النور **SabáaH an-núur**	*good morning (reply)* [lit., morning (of) the light]
مساء الخير **masáa' al-kháyr**	*good afternoon/good evening* [lit., evening (of) the goodness]
مساء النور **masáa' an-núur**	*good afternoon/good evening (reply)* [lit., evening (of) the light]

Exercise 3
Fill in the bubbles with the appropriate greetings.

Exercise 4

a *It is 11am and you go to the bank for cash. Greet the bank clerk.*

b *You are in a restaurant one evening and an acquaintance comes up and greets you. What would you say?*

c *Your partner comes home from work at 7pm. What does he/she say to you?*

d *You go into a shop in the market. Say hello to the shopkeeper.*

e *You see your neighbour in the street and she says hello to you. How would you reply?*

---

3 كيف حالك؟ kayfa Háal-ak? How are you?

🔊 CD1, TR09

Suad asks one of the students, Michael, how he is:

Su:áad	**káyfa Háal-ak?**	كيف حالك؟	سعاد
Michael	**al-Hámdu lil-láah.**	الحمد لله.	مايكل
Su:áad	**áhlan wa-sáhlan.**	أهلا وسهلا.	سعاد
Michael	**áhlan bi-ki. wa ánti, káyfa Háal-ik?**	أهلا بك. وأنت، كيف حالك؟	مايكل
Su:áad	**al-Hámdu lil-láah, bi-kháyr.**	الحمد لله، بخير.	سعاد

Insight

Note the spelling of **ahlan** and **sahlan** with a final **alif**. This is the accusative marker (see Unit 8).

تعبيرات رئيسية ta:biiráat ra'iisíyyah (Key phrases)

🔈 **CD1, TR10**

كيف حالك؟ **kayfa Háal-ak?**	*how are you? (to a man)* [lit., How [is] condition-your?]
كيف حالك؟ **kayfa Háal-ik?**	*how are you?* (to a woman)
الحمد لله **al-Hámdu lil-láah**	*praise [be] to God* (response to above)
أهلا وسهلا **áhlan wa-sáhlan**	*welcome*
أهلا بك **áhlan bi-k**	(reply to a man)
أهلا بك **áhlan bi-ki**	(reply to a woman)
وأنت؟ **wa-ánta/ánti**	*and you?* (sing. m./f.)
بخير **bi-khayr**	*well* adj. [lit., in well-being]

الملاحظات al-mulaaHaDHáat (Notes)

- **káyfa Háal-ak** *If you are speaking to a woman, you must say* **káyfa Háal-ik**, *although there is no difference in written Arabic. If you are talking a group of people, you must say* **káyfa Háal-kum** *(كيف حالكم).*
- **al-Hámdu lil-láah** *never changes and is used in many situations. Even if something unfortunate or unpleasant has happened, the devout Muslim must submit to the will of Allah and praise Him for what He has decreed.*

- **áhlan bi-k** *You must say* **áhlan bi-ki** *to a woman (same spelling) or* **áhlan bi-kum** (أهلا بكم) *to a group of people.*

Exercise 5

a *Mohammad is having a party and his English friend John arrives. Finish the sentence for Mohammad.*

káyfa ...? كيف ...؟

b *What does John reply?*

c *Fill in the missing words in the next exchange between Mohammed and John.*

– ... wa sáhlan ... وسهلا.

– áhlan .... أهلا ....

d *You meet some Arabic-speaking friends. How do you ask them how they are?*

e *An Arabic-speaking colleague comes into your office and you greet him. What do you say?*

---

4 What do they want?

الأهرام **al-ahráam *(The pyramids)***

CD1, TR11

Exercise 6

Some tourists are spending the day in Cairo. Listen to the recording or read the dialogues below and try to work out which picture belongs to each dialogue.

1

– **táaksi! al-ahráam, min faDl-ak!**	تاكسي! الأهرام من فضلك!
– **ná:am, ya sáyyid-i!**	نعم يا سيدي!

2

– **al-miSbáaH min fáDl-ak.**	المصباح من فضلك.
– **tafáDDal.**	تفضل.
– **shúkran.**	شكرا.

3

– **shaay wa-sandawíitsh minfáDl-ak.**	شاي، وسندويتش من فضلك.
– **shaay bi-súkkar?**	شاي بسكر؟
– **laa shúkran, bidúun súkkar.**	لا، شكرا، بدون سكر.
bi-kam háadhaa?	بكم هذا؟
– **thaláathah junayháat.**	ثلاثة جنيهات.

Exercise 7

Which dialogue takes place:

a *in a café beside the Nile?*
b *in Khan al-Khalili market?*
c *in Tahrir Square, in the centre of Cairo?*

Exercise 8

Find the words for the following items:

a *a tea with sugar*

b *the lamp*
c *the pyramids*
d *a sandwich*

معلومات ثقافية **ma:luumáat thaqaafíyyah** (Cultural tips)

People don't usually use terms like Mr and Mrs. In Egypt and some other northern Arab countries, people say **síidi** where we might say *sir*, but in other countries this term is reserved for certain classes of nobility. Its correct formal pronunciation is **sáyyidi**, but this does not show in the Arabic script.

Exercise 9

Which figure from the Arabian Nights is this?

علاء الدين والمصباح السحري
:aláa'ad-diin wa-l-miSbáaH as-síHrii

تعبيرات رئيسية **ta:biiráat ra'iisíyyah** (Key phrases)

CD1, TR12

تاكسي **táaksii** *taxi*

من فضلك **min fáDl-ak** *please*

نعم **ná:am** *yes*

مصباح **miSbáaH** *lamp*

تفضل **tafáDDal** *here you are, welcome*

شكرا shúkran	*thank you*
شاي shaay	*tea*
و wa-	*and*
لا laa	*no*
بـ bi-	*with*
سكر súkkar	*sugar*
بدون bi-dúun	*without*
بكم هذا؟ bi-kam háadha?	*how much is this?*
ثلاثة جنيهات thaláathah junayháat	*three pounds*
سحري síHrii	*magic*

تراكيب اللغة taraakíib al-lúghah (Structures)

1 Definite or indefinite?

It is important in Arabic to be able to distinguish between *definite* words and phrases and *indefinites*.

Indefinite words have *a* or *an* before them in English. There is no indefinite article, or word for *a* or *an*, in Arabic.

بيت bayt	*(a) house*
سندويتش sandawíitsh	*(a) sandwich*

There are three types of definite word in English:

1 *words that have the definite article – the house*
2 *proper nouns – Mohammed, Cairo, Egypt*
3 *pronouns such as he, I, you, etc.*

The definite article *the* never varies in writing, and is always ال **al-**. The hyphen shows that, in the Arabic script, **al-** is always attached to the following word.

البيت **al-bayt**	*the house*
الأهرام **al-ahráam**	*the pyramids*

There are two points of pronunciation:

1 *If the preceding word ends in a vowel or* **-ah**, *the* **a** *of* **al-** *is omitted in pronunciation, but kept in writing.*

CD1, TR13

Written	*Pronounced*
باب البيت	**baab al-bayt** *the door of the house* after a preceding consonant
في البيت	**fi l-bayt** *in the house* after a preceding vowel

2 *If the word to which* **al-** *is attached begins with one of the following consonants, the* **l** *of the* **al-** *is omitted in pronunciation and the following letter is doubled.*

t	*th*	*d*	*dh*	*r*	*z*	*s*	*sh*	*S*	*D*	*T*	*DH*	*l*	*n*
ت	ث	د	ذ	ر	ز	س	ش	ص	ض	ط	ظ	ل	ن

You are pronouncing the word properly if you make a small hesitation on the doubled letters.

Written	*Pronounced* after a consonant	after a vowel
الشمس	**ash-shams**	**sh-shams** *the sun*
النور	**an-nuur**	**n-nuur** *the light*
السندويتش	**as-sandwíitsh**	**s-sandwíitsh** *the sandwich*

Insight

An easy way to remember these letters is to pronounce them all out loud. With the slight exception of **sh**, you will notice that the tip of your tongue is contacting somewhere in the region of your front teeth or the gum above them – where the letter **l** is pronounced, which is why the assimilation occurs. No other Arabic consonants are pronounced in this area.

The Arabs call these the 'sun letters', simply because the word **shams** (شمس) *sun* begins with one of them. The remaining letters are called the 'moon letters', because **qamar** (قمر) *moon* does not begin with an assimilated letter.

Remember: The written form remains the same; it is only the pronunciation that varies. However, to help you, the assimilations have been represented in the transliteration.

Exercise 10

CD1, TR15

Listen to the following words on the recording, or study them carefully:

a الشاي　　　　*e* النور
b الأهرام　　　　*f* الكبير
c السلام　　　　*g* الصغير
d السندويتش

List those that begin with sun letters and those that begin with moon letters.

2 Nouns and adjectives

Arabic adjectives behave like nouns but:

a *they always follow the noun*
b *they must agree with the noun in definiteness and in gender*
c *additional adjectives are simply added after the first one with no punctuation or joining word. If the noun is definite, the adjectives must all be definite and have the definite article.*

Insight

It will be a great help when you are learning Arabic if you can come to look on nouns and adjectives as being virtually the same thing. This only happens in slightly archaic English in phrases such as *'the great and the good'*, *'the meek shall inherit the earth'*. More commonly we use the helping word 'one': *'Which dress do you prefer?'*, *'The blue one'*.

Arabic grammar will become easier if you mentally add the word *'one'* to Arabic adjectives, so that you are effectively equating them with nouns. In Arabic, the reply to the question above would have been simply *'The blue'*.

◀) CD1, TR15, 02:35

بيت صغير **bayt Saghiir**	*a small house = (a) house (a) small(-one)*

الولد الطويل **al-wálad aT-Tawíil**	*the tall boy = the-boy the-tall(-one)*
بريطانيا العظمى **briiTáanyaa l-:úDHma**	*Great Britain = Britain the-great (-one)*
كتاب كبير جديد **kitáab kabíir jadíid**	*a big new book = (a) book (a) big (-one) (a) new(-one)*
البنت الجميلة الصغيرة **al-bint al-jamíilah S-Saghíirah**	*the beautiful young girl = the-girl the-beautiful(-one) the-young(-one)*

بيت، بيوت **bayt**, **buyúut** *house*

صغير **Saghíir** *young* (person), *small* (thing)

ولد، أولاد **wálad**, **awláad** *boy* (pl. also *children*)

طويل **Tawíil** *tall* (person), *long* (thing)

كتاب، كتب **kitáab** (**kútub**) *book*

كبير **kabíir** *big*

جميل (جميلة) **jamíil** (f. **jamíilah**) *beautiful*

QUICK VOCAB

هرم كبير
háram kabíir
a big pyramid
(a) pyramid (a) big(-one)

هرم صغير
háram Saghíir
a small pyramid
(a) pyramid (a) small(-one)

Insight

إلى المركز التجاري

TO THE COMMERCIAL CENTRE

Some words end with a final ى (written without the two dots) which is pronounced **-a** (strictly **-aa**, but often shortened). إلى **ila(a)**, *to/towards* is an example of this.

تمرينات **tamriináat** (Practice)

Exercise 11

Listen again to the greetings at the beginning of the recording and repeat the phrases after the speakers. If you don't have the recording, read the dialogues several times until you are sure you are familiar with them.

Exercise 12

Match the following greetings with the appropriate reply.

i	السلام عليكم	*a*	شكرا
ii	مساء الخير	*b*	مساء النور
iii	كيف حالك؟	*c*	أهلا بك
iv	أهلا وسهلا	*d*	وعليكم السلام
v	تفضل!	*e*	الحمد لله

Exercise 13

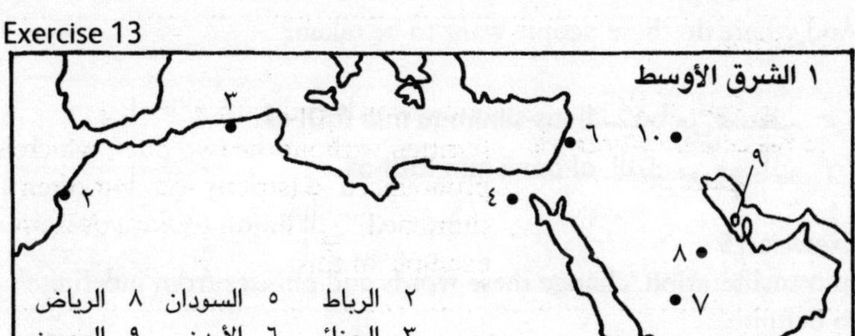

Match the Arabic words for the places in the Arab world in the above box with the transliterated words below and practise saying them.

a **ar-ribáaT**
b **al-jazáa'ir**
c **al-qáahirah**
d **ar-riyáaDH**
e **al-baHráyn**
f **baghdáad**
g **ash-shárq al-áwsaT**
h **as-sa:uudíyyah**
i **as-suudáan**
j **al-úrdunn**

Now work out the English names for the towns and countries.

Exercise 14

CD1, TR16

Listen to the recording or read the transliteration and work out what is being asked for in the café.

a قهوة من فضلك. **qáhwah min fáDl-ak.**
b ليمون من فضلك. **laymóon min fáDl-ak.**
c كوكاكولا صغيرة من فضلك. **kookakóola Saghíirah min fáDl-ak.**
d أيس كريم بالشوكولاتة من فضلك. **ays kriim bi-sh-shokoláatah min fáDl-ak.**

And where do these people want to be taken?

e السينما من فضلك. **as-síinimaa min fáDl-ak.**

f البنك من فضلك. **al-bank min fáDl-ak.**

Exercise 15

In transliteration, change these words and phrases from indefinite to definite.

a سندويتش **sandawíitsh**

b تلفون **tilifúun**

c بيت **bayt**

d طماطم **TamáaTim**

e سينما **síinima**

f بيرة صغيرة **bíirah Saghíirah**

g برجر كبير **bárgar kabíir**

h راديو جديد **ráadyo jadíid**

Exercise 16

See if you can match the words in Exercise 15 to the drawings below.

Exercise 17

Choose the correct adjective from the brackets to complete the phrases.

١ السينما (جديدة، الجديدة)	*1 the new cinema*
٢ بنت (صغيرة، الصغيرة)	*2 a small girl*
٣ كتاب (جميل، الجميل)	*3 a beautiful book*
٤ فيلم (طويل، الطويل)	*4 a long film*
٥ البيت الكبير (واسع، الواسع)	*5 the big roomy house*

واسع **wáasi:** *roomy, spacious*
كبير **kabíir** *big*

أوزان الكلمات awzáan al-kalimáat (Word shapes)

🔊 CD1, TR17

The large majority of Arabic words are built around a three-consonant root. It is conventional to express the first consonant of the root by **C¹** – i.e. first consonant – and later consonants as **C²** and **C³**. The vowels between are usually stated as they are (**a**, **i**, **u**, **aa**, **uu**, **ii** and so on) or, where they are variable, simply by **v**, meaning *vowel*.

The word pattern for this unit is **C¹a C²iiC³**, for example **kabiir**.

Insight

The word **kabíir** means *big* (*old* when applied to people). In Arabic, anything to do with the root **k-b-r** will have something to do with *bigness*, *large size* and so on. This is a very useful concept, noticed long ago by Arab philologists. Most dictionaries are still arranged according to these three-letter roots.

Here we have the three consonants **k-b-r**. In Arabic, they are fleshed out with long and short vowels. You can see that in the word **kabíir**, *big*, the first consonant of the root (**k**) has an **a** vowel after it and the second consonant (**b**) has a long **ii** after it. This is a very common pattern for adjectives in Arabic.

To help you feel the cadences of the Arabic sounds, an English equivalent (or one as near as possible) is given. Such words which are familiar to you will also help with the Arabic stress patterns.

Pattern	*Arabic example*	*Eng. sound-alike*
$C^1aC^2iiC^3$	كبير **kabíir** *big*	*marine*

It will help you greatly in learning Arabic if you learn and listen for these patterns.

Here are some more words to show the pattern:

1 صغير **Saghíir** *young* (person), *small* (thing)

2 طويل **Tawíil** *tall* (person), *long* (thing)

3 بعيد **ba:íid** *far, distant*

4 قريب **qaríib** *near*

5 جديد **jadíid** *new*

6 قديم **qadíim** *old* (things)

7 جميل **jamíil** *beautiful, handsome*

8 لطيف **laTíif** *pleasant, nice*

9 كريم **karíim** *noble, generous*

10 صحيح **SaHíiH** *correct, right*

Exercise 18

Write down the roots for the words above in Arabic or transliteration with hyphens between the letters.

Note: For this type of Exercise, use the *independent* forms of the letters in the Arabic script.

---

10 things you need to know

1. *Learn the common phrases of greetings as a whole, with their special replies:*
   as-salaamu :alaykum!
   wa-:alaykum as-salaam
2. *In the phrase* **kayfa Haalak** how are you?, *the* **-ak** *changes to* **-ik** *when you are speaking to a woman, and to* **-kum** *when speaking to more than one person.*
3. *The standard reply,* **al-Hamdu li-l-laah** Praise be to God, *never changes.*
4. *There is no word for* a *or* an *in Arabic.*
5. *The word for* the, **al**, *never changes in writing.*
6. *If a word begins with a Sun letter, the* **-l** *of the word* **al** *is omitted in speech, and the first letter of the word is doubled.*
7. *Nouns and adjectives are treated as the same thing in Arabic.*
8. *There is no general rule for forming plurals, so learn them when you learn the singular.*
9. *Adjectives always follow their nouns.*
10. *Most Arabic words are built around a three-consonant root.*

2

التفاصيل الشخصية

at-tafaaSíil ash-shakhSíyyah

Personal details

In this unit you will learn:

- ***how to ask someone's name and give your own name***
- ***how to say where you are from***
- ***how to construct simple sentences with 'is'/'are'***
- ***how to say 'there is'/'there are'***
- ***the numbers 1–10***

---

1 من أين أنت؟ min áyna ánta? Where are you from?

Suad introduces herself to the students, and asks one of them his name and where he is from.

CD1, TR18

Exercise 1
Listen to the conversation a first time.

a What is the woman's name?
b What is the man's name?

Exercise 2

Now listen again to the conversation.

a Where does the man come from?
b Where does the woman come from?

Now read the dialogue.

سعاد	حسنا. أنا اسمي سعاد. ما اسمك؟
مايكل	أنا اسمي مايكل.
سعاد	أهلا وسهلا يا مايكل. من أين أنت؟
مايكل	أنا من مانشستر في إنجلترا. وأنت؟
سعاد	أنا من الاسكندرية في مصر.

Exercise 3

Find the Arabic for:

a I'm from Manchester.
b And you?

حسنا **Hásanan** (note spelling) *well, right, OK*

من **min** *from*

في **fii** *in*

الاسكندرية **al-iskandaríyyah** *Alexandria*

2 مصر جميلة miSr jamíilah Egypt is beautiful

🔈 CD1, TR19

Suad tells her students a little about Egypt.

Exercise 4
Read or listen to the description and answer the questions.

a *What does Suad say about Cairo?*
b *Where is the Egyptian Museum?*
c *What does she recommend in the hotel?*

مصر جميلة جدا. القاهرة مدينة كبيرة، وهي قديمة جدا.
المتحف المصري في ميدان التحرير قريب من فندق النيل.
هناك مطعم ممتاز في فندق النيل في ميدان التحرير. وطبعا هناك
الأهرام في الجيزة.

Insight

Most, although not all, place names are regarded as feminine.

QUICK VOCAB

مصر **miSr** *Egypt*

جدا **jíddan** (note spelling) *very*

القاهرة **al-qáahirah** *Cairo*

مدينة **madíinah** *city*

و **wa** *and* (joined to next word)

هي **híya** *she, it* (f.)

قديمة **qadíimah** *old* [of things only] (f.)

المتحف المصري **al-mátHaf al-míSri** *The Egyptian Museum*

ميدان التحرير **maydáan at-taHríir** *Tahrir Square*

قريب من **qaríib min** *near to* [lit., *from*]

فندق النيل **fúnduq an-níil** *Nile Hotel*

هناك **hunáaka** *there is/are*

مطعم **máT:am** *restaurant*

ممتاز **mumtáaz** *excellent*

طبعا **Táb:an** (note spelling) *naturally, of course*

الأهرام **al-ahráam** *the pyramids*

الجيزة **al-jíizah** *Geezah*, a district of Cairo [in Egypt the letter ج is pronounced like *g* in *garden*]

QUICK VOCAB

---

3 رقم تلفونك كم؟ raqm tilifóon-ak kam? What's your telephone number?

CD1, TR20

After the class, some of the students want to arrange to meet up. They exchange telephone numbers. Look carefully at the Arabic numbers on page 44 then listen to the audio. Now answer the questions.

Exercise 5

a What is Zaki's telephone number?
b What is Marie's number?
c What is the Arabic for 'telephone number'?
d How would you say 'My telephone number is...'?

زكي	رقم تلفونك كم يا حامد؟
حامد	رقم تلفوني ٦٣٤٧٢١١. ورقم تلفونك أنت؟
زكي	رقم تلفوني ٦٢١٥٥٠٠. يا ماري، رقم تلفونك كم؟
ماري	رقم تلفوني ٦٢٠٧٥٨٩.

رقم تلفون **raqm tilifóon** *telephone number*

تعبيرات رئيسية **ta:biiráat ra'iisíyyah** (Key phrases)

🔊 CD1, TR21

In Arabic, some possessive pronouns, e.g. *your*, vary, according to whether you are speaking to a man, a woman or several people.

Asking people their name and telling them yours

ما اسمك؟ **maa ísm-ak/ísm-ik** (m./f.)?	*What is your name?*
اسمي... **ísm-i...**	*My name is ...*

Asking people where they are from and replying

من أين أنت؟ **min áyna ánta/ánti** (m./f.)?	*Where are you from?*

Saying you're from either a town or a country

أنا من الخرطوم **ána min al-kharTúum**	*I am from Khartoum*
أنا من لندن **ána min lándan**	*I am from London*
أنا من السودان **ána min as-suudáan**	*I am from Sudan*
أنا من فرنسا **ána min faránsa**	*I am from France*
أنا من ... **ána min...**	*I am from...*

The Arabic numbers 1–10

CD1, TR22

The numbers are given here in their spoken or colloquial forms. In strictly grammatical Arabic, the use of the numbers is complicated and so these forms are the ones nearly always used.

There are two main points to remember when writing Arabic numbers:

- *The numerals are written from left to right (the opposite direction of the script), for example:*

٦٢	٧٣١	٨٥٤	٧٥٩١	٤٠٠٢
62	*731*	*854*	*7591*	*4002*

- *The written forms given here are the standard ones used in most of the Arab world, but some countries (mainly in North Africa) use the same forms as we do (1, 2, 3, 4, etc.), and this tendency seems to be spreading.*

We call our numerical system 'Arabic' to distinguish it from Roman, but the forms of the numbers have changed slightly over time. Still, if you use a little imagination – and turn some of them through 90° – you should spot the similarities.

1	*2*	*3*	*4*	*5*	*6*	*7*	*8*	*9*	*10*
١	٢	٣	٤	٥	٦	٧	٨	٩	١٠

These are pronounced (colloquial form) as follows:

١	واحد	**wáaHid**	٦	ستّة	**síttah**
٢	اثنين	**ithnáyn**	٧	سبعة	**sáb:ah**
٣	ثلاثة	**thaláathah**	٨	ثمانية	**thamáanyah**
٤	أربعة	**árba:ah**	٩	تسعة	**tís:ah**
٥	خمسة	**khámsah**	١٠	عشرة	**:áshrah**

QUICK VOCAB

Zero is **Sifr** صفر, written as ٠.

تراكيب اللغة taraakíib al-lúghah (Structures)

1 How to say 'is' and 'are' in Arabic

There is no equivalent of the verb *to be* in the present tense in Arabic. Sentences which contain the words *is* or *are* in English are constructed in Arabic by putting together the following:

a any definite noun with an indefinite noun or adjective:

al-bayt kabíir
the house (is a) big(-one)

البيت كبير
The house is big

muHámmad mashghúul
Muhammad (is a) busy(-person)

محمد مشغول
Muhammad is busy

húwa mudíir
He (is a) director

هو مدير
He is a director

b a definite noun or a pronoun with a phrase beginning with a preposition:

ána min al-iskandaríyyah
I (am) from Alexandria

أنا من الاسكندرية
I am from Alexandria

bayrúut fii lubnáan
Beirut (is) in the Lebanon

بيروت في لبنان
Beirut is in the Lebanon

If a definite noun is put with a definite noun or adjective, a separating pronoun must be inserted, to make the meaning clear:

muHámmad húwa al-mudíir
Mohammed he (is) the director

محمد هو المدير
Mohammed is the director

Insight

Here is a summary of how to make definite and indefinite phrases and sentences in Arabic:

بيت كبير
bayt kabíir
a big house, lit. *(a) house (a) big(-one)*

البيت الكبير
al-bayt al-kabíir
the big house, lit. *the-house the-big(-one)*

البيت كبير
al-bayt kabíir
the house is big, lit. *the-house (is a) big-one*

ناصر هو الرئيس
náaSir húwa r-ra'íis
Nasser is the boss, lit. *Nasser he the-boss*

2 How to say 'there is', 'there are'

This is expressed in modern Arabic by starting the sentence with هناك **hunáaka**, *there*:

هناك مطعم في الميدان **hunáaka máT:am fi l-maydáan**	*there is a restaurant in the square*
هناك غرف كثيرة في الفندق **hunáaka ghúraf kathíirah fi l-fúnduq**	*there are many rooms in the hotel*

3 Personal pronouns

Personal pronouns are always definite, i.e. if you say *he* you are talking about one particular person.

These are the personal pronouns:

أنا **ána** *I*	نحن **náHnu** *we*
أنت **ánta** *you* (m.)	أنتم **ántum** *you* (m. pl.)
أنت **ánti** *you* (f.)	أنتن **antúnna** *you* (f. pl.)
هو **húwa** *he*	هم **hum** *they* (m. pl.)
هي **híya** *she*	هن **húnna** *they* (f. pl.)

Insight

The final **alif** of أنا **ana** is there to distinguish it from other similarly-spelled words. Pronounce it short, and accent the first syllable. (In fact most final **-aa** sounds in informal modern Arabic tend to be pronounced short.)

The male and female forms of *you* (singular) are identical in unvowelled writing. The context usually makes it clear which is intended.

Since all Arabic words are either masculine or feminine, English *it* must be translated as *he* or *she*, depending on the gender of the word:

الميدان كبير **al-maydáan kabíir**	*the square is big* (m.)
هو كبير **húwa kabíir**	*it is big*
السيارة صغيرة **as-sayyáarah Saghíirah**	*the car is small* (f.)
هي صغيرة **híya Saghíirah**	*it is small*

4 Asking questions in Arabic

There are several ways to ask questions in Arabic:

a by using a question word such as which?, what? or where?:

ما اسمك؟ **maa ísm-ak?**	*What is your name?*
من أين أنت؟ **min áyna ánta?**	*Where are you from?* [lit., *from where you?*]

b if no question word is present, **hal** *or* **'a** *must be placed at the beginning of the sentence, acting as a verbal question mark:*

هل محمد مشغول؟ **hal muHámmad mashghúul**	*Is Muhammad busy?* (?) Muhammad (is a) busy (-person)
أهو مشغول؟ **'a-húwa mashghúul**	*Is he busy?* (?) He (is a) busy (-person)

There is no precise rule about which to use, except that **a** is usually used with personal pronouns. Written question marks are also used in modern Arabic, in addition to these question words.

Arabic words which consist of only one letter plus a short vowel, such as أ or و, must not be written alone but are attached to the following word.

Insight: Pronunciation of al- after long vowel

When Arabic prepositions ending with a long vowel, such as **fii**, *in*, are placed before a word beginning with **al-**, *the*, the **a** of **al-** disappears and the vowel of the preposition is pronounced short:

في المدينة *in the city*

fii al-madíinah → fi l-madíinah

If the word begins with one of the 'sun letters' (see Unit 1) the doubling of the initial consonant still applies.

في السعودية *in Saudi Arabia*

fi s-sa:uudíyyah

Irregular spellings

Some of the most common prepositions (e.g. على **:álaa**, *on*, إلى **ílaa**, *to/towards*), have an irregular spelling of the final **aa** vowel which is written as a **yaa'** without the dots. This is also shortened before **al-** (see **fii** above).

أوزان الكلمات awzáan al-kalimáat (Word shapes)

CD1, TR23

The word pattern for this unit is: **C¹aaC²iC³**, for example, **báarid** بارد, which sounds like the English *calmish*.

This pattern expresses the idea of someone or something doing or carrying out the root meaning. In English, for nouns we use the suffix *-er* or a variant (*painter*, *actor*) and for adjectives we have *-ing*: a *going concern*, a *stunning performance*. This is another common pattern in adjectives. Again, the root of the word gives an idea of the meaning: ب–ر–د **b-r-d**, the root of the word has to do with *cold*, e.g.:

يبرد **yábrud**	*to be*, *to become cold* (verb)
بارد **báarid**	*cold* (adjective: not used for people)

عادل **:áadil** *just, upright**
لازم **láazim** *necessary*
ناشف **náashif** *dry*
كامل **káamil** *complete, perfect**
نافع **náafi:** *useful*
صالح **SáaliH** *doing right, upright, honest**
سالم **sáalim** *safe, sound**
*These words are also used for men's names in Arabic.

QUICK VOCAB

Exercise 6
Extract the roots from the above words.

تمرينات tamriináat (Practice)

Exercise 7
Change the indefinite noun/adjective phrases below into definite phrases.

e.g. كتاب كبير → الكتاب الكبير
kitaab kabiir → **al-kitaab al-kabiir**

a بيت صغير
b سيارة جميلة
c ولد طويل
d سكرتير جديد
e مدير مشغول

Exercise 8

Change the phrases in Exercise 7 into *is/are* sentences.

e.g. الكتاب الكبير ➔ الكتاب كبير

al-kitaab al-kabiir ➔ al-kitaab kabiir

Exercise 9

Now substitute a pronoun for the noun in the sentences in Exercise 8.

e.g. الكتاب كبير ➔ هو كبير

al-kitaab kabiir ➔ huwa kabiir

Exercise 10

Change the following statements into questions.

١ أنت من مصر.
٢ محمد في دبي.
٣ هي أمريكية.
٤ الكتاب جديد.
٥ يتكلم عربي.

QUICK VOCAB

دبي **dubáy** *Dubai*
يتكلم **yatakállam** *he speaks*
عربي **:árabi** *Arab, Arabic*

Exercise 11

Change the following questions into statements.

١ هل السيارة جديدة؟
٢ أهي مشغولة؟
٣ هل الفندق قريب من الأهرام؟
٤ هل محمد هنا؟
٥ أهو مشغول؟

سيارة **sayyáarah** *car*

هنا **húnaa** *here*

مشغول **mashghúul** *busy, occupied*

Exercise 12

CD1, TR24

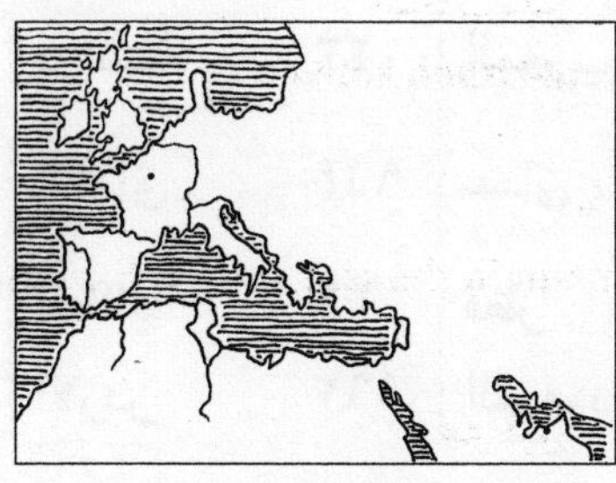

Where do you think the following people are from? Listen to the recording and repeat what they are saying.

١ أنا من تونس.
٢ أنا من لبنان.
٣ أنا من باريس.
٤ أنا من اسكتلاندا.
٥ أنا من أبو ظبي.
٦ أنا من ايطاليا.

Exercise 13

In the telephone directory, all the UAE airports are listed together. Which of the six airports below would you get if you dialled:

a *245555?*
b *448111?*
c *757611?*

1 *Abu Dhabi*
2 *Dubai*
3 *Sharjah*
4 *Ras al Khaimah*
5 *Fujairah*
6 *Al Ain*

مطارات الإمارات

• مطار أبو ظبي الدولي	٧٥٧٦١١
• مطار دبي الدولي	٢٤٥٥٥٥
• مطار الشارقة الدولي	٥٨١٠٠٠
• مطار رأس الخيمة الدولي	٤٤٨١١١
• مطار الفجيرة الدولي	٢٧٦٢٢٢
• مطار العين الدولي	٨٥٥٥٥٥

مطارات **maTáar, -áat** *airport*

Exercise 14

Here is a list of international dialling codes from a United Arab Emirates telephone directory.

٢٤٩	السودان	٩٦٥	الكويت	٢١٣	الجزائر
٩٦٣	سورية	٩٦١	لبنان	٩٧٣	البحرين
٢١٦	تونس	٢١٨	ليبيا	٢٠	مصر
٩٧١	الإمارات	٢١٢	المغرب	٠٣٣	فرانسا
٤٤	المملكة المتحدة	٩٦٨	عمان	٩٦٤	العراق
١	أمريكا	٩٧٤	قطر	٣٩	إيطاليا
٩٦٧	اليمن	٩٦٦	السعودية	٩٦٢	الأردن

What is the code for:

a *Bahrain?*
b *Egypt?*
c *America?*
d *Qatar?*
e *Saudi Arabia?*
f *Italy?*

---

10 things you need to know

1 *Numerals are written from left to right.*
2 *There is a growing trend to use western numerals.*
3 *There is no word for* is *or* are.
4 *To make a sentence expressing* is *or* are, *use a definite noun such as* the city *followed by an indefinite noun or adjective such as* beautiful.
5 There is, there are *are both expressed by* **hunaaka**.
6 *Some possessive pronouns such as* your, his, her, *vary depending on whether you are speaking to a man, a woman, or to several people.*

7 *When* **fii** in *is followed by* **al**, *its vowel is shortened to* **fi-** *and the* **a** *of* **al** *is omitted.*
8 *Questions that have no question word, like* where *or* who, *start with* **hal** *or* **a-**.
9 *Arabic words of only one letter plus a short vowel like* **wa** and *are written as part of the following word.*
10 *Some common words ending in the sound* **-aa** *are written for historical reasons with a final* **yaa'** *without the two dots.*

3

كيف تصف نفسك

kayfa taSif nafs-ak

How you describe yourself

In this unit you will learn:

- ***how to say your nationality***
- ***how to say which languages you speak***
- ***how to talk about more than one object***
- ***the names of some places around town***
- ***how to talk about professions***

---

1 أأنت سوداني؟ **'a-ánta suudáani?** Are you Sudanese?

🔊 CD1, TR25

Two of the students in Suad's class are asking each other where they come from.

Exercise 1
Listen to the recording or read the conversation and then answer the questions.

a What nationality is Zaki?
b What town does he come from?

حسام مرحبا. أأنت مصري؟
زكي لا، أنا سوداني من الخرطوم. وأنت؟
حسام أنا مصري من طنطا.
زكي أين طنطا؟
حسام طنطا قريبة من القاهرة.

مرحباً **márHaban** *welcome, hello*

طنطا **TánTaa** *Tanta* (a town in Egypt)

Exercise 2

CD1, TR26

The students at Suad's class begin to talk about their nationalities. Listen to the recording and work out where they all come from.

سعاد أنا مصرية، وأنت يا مايك؟
مايك أنا إنجليزي.
كايلي أنا أسترالية.
يونس أنا لبناني. أنا من بيروت.
ماري أنا فرنسية.

a Suad
b Mike
c Kylie
d Younis
e Marie

2 هل تتكلم انجليزي؟ hal tatakállam inglíizii?

Do you speak English?

🔊 **CD1, TR27**

On a flight to Jordan, Julie, an English girl, gets talking to one of the other passengers. Listen to the first part of the conversation several times and answer the questions.

Exercise 3

a *Which language does the passenger* not *speak?*

b *Which language* does *he speak?*

راكب	عن إذنك. من أين أنت؟
جولي	أنا من إنجلترا. وأنت؟
راكب	أنا من عمان. أنا أردني.
جولي	هل تتكلم إنجليزي؟
راكب	لا، مع الأسف، لا أتكلم إنجليزي. أتكلم عربي فقط
راكب	تتكلمين العربية بطلاقة!
جولي	لا، قليلة فقط

QUICK VOCAB

راكب **ráakib** *passenger*

عن إذنك **:an ídhn-ik** *excuse me, by your leave* (to a woman)

إنجلترا **ingiltárra** (with *g* as in *garden*) *England*

عمان **:ammáan** *Amman*

أردني **úrduni** *Jordanian*

تتكلم **tatakállam** *you speak* (to a man)

إنجليزي **inglíizi** *English*

مع الأسف **má:a l-ásaf** *I'm sorry* (lit., *with the-sorrow*)

لا **laa** *no, not*

أتكلم **atakállam** *I speak*

فقط **fáqaT** *only*

Exercise 4

Listen again and find the Arabic for the following:

a *Do you speak English?*
b *A little.*

Now listen to the second part of the dialogue.

QUICK VOCAB

تتكلمين **tatakallamíin** *you speak* (to a woman)

العربية **al-:arabíyyah** *Arabic, the Arabic language* (more formal than **:árabi**)

بطلاقة **bi-Taláaqah** *fluently*

قليلة **qalíilah** *a little, few* (f.)

Exercise 5

The passenger thinks Julie speaks good Arabic. True or false?

---

3 ما عملك؟ maa :ámal-ak? What's your occupation?

CD1, TR28

During the flight the passenger asks Julie what she does. Listen to the recording or read the text a few times.

Exercise 6

a *What does Julie do at the moment?*
b *Where does the passenger work?*

راكب ما عملك؟
جولي أنا طالبة في جامعة لندن. وأنت؟
راكب أنا طبيب في عمان.

ما عملك؟ **maa :ámal-ik** *what's your occupation?* (to a woman)

جامعة لندن **jáami:at lándan** *University (of) London*

طبيب **Tabíib** *doctor*

Exercise 7

Find the Arabic equivalent for:

a *What's your occupation?*
b *I am a doctor.*

الملاحظات **al-mulaaHaDHáat** (Notes)

Talking about your occupation

When you refer to a woman's profession in Arabic, add **-ah** (ة) to the masculine.

Masculine	*Feminine*	
طبيب **Tabíib**	طبيبة **Tabíibah**	*doctor*
طالب**Táalib**	طالبة	*student*
مدرس **mudárris**	مدرسة	*teacher*
مهندس **muhándis**	مهندسة	*engineer*
مدير **mudíir**	مديرة	*manager*
رئيس **ra'íis**	رئيسة	*boss*

محمد مدير **muHámmad mudíir** *Mohammed is a manager*

ليلى مدرسة **láylaa mudárrisah** *Leila is a teacher*

4 هل لندن مدينة كبيرة؟ hal lándan madíinah kabíirah?

Is London a big city?

🔊 **CD1, TR29**

The passenger asks Julie about London.

Exercise 8

Listen to the recording and answer the questions.

a Name one of the places Julie mentions in London.
b Which institution does the passenger ask her about?

راكب	هل لندن مدينة كبيرة؟
جولي	نعم، هي مدينة كبيرة جدا. هناك متاحف كبيرة كثيرة وجسور ومحلات.
راكب	أين الجامعة؟
جولي	هي في وسط المدينة، قريبة من المتحف البريطاني.

QUICK VOCAB

جداً **jíddan** *very*

متحف، متاحف **mátHaf**, (pl.) **matáaHif*** *museum*

كثيرة **kathíirah** *many, much* (f.)

جسر، جسور **jisr**, (pl.) **jusúur** *bridge*

محل، محلات **maHáll**, (pl.) **maHalláat** *shop, store*

جامعة **jáami:ah** *university*

وسط **wasT** or **wasaT** *middle*

كثير **kathíir** *much, many* (m.)

تعبيرات رئيسية ta:biiráat ra'iisíyyah (Key phrases)

CD1, TR30

Asking someone's nationality and replying

أأنت مصري؟ **a-ánta míSrii?** (m.)	*Are you Egyptian?*
أأنت مصرية؟ **a-ánti miSríyyah?** (f.)	
أنا سوداني **ána suudáanii** (m.)	*I am Sudanese*
أنا سودانية **ána suudaaníyyah** (f.)	

Asking whether people speak a language and replying

هل تتكلم/تتكلمين عربي؟	*Do you speak Arabic?*
hal tatakállam/tatakallamíin :árabi?	(to a man/woman)
أتكلم إنجليزي **atakállam ingliizi**	*I speak English*
لا أتكلم عربي **laa atakállam :árabi**	*I don't speak Arabic*
بطلاقة **bi-Taláaqah**	*fluently*
قليل **qalíil**	*a little*
يتكلم فرنساوي **yatakállam faransáawi***	*he speaks French*
تتكلم عربي **tatakállam :árabi**	*she speaks Arabic*

*This is a variant of **faránsi**, usually used when referring to the language.

Asking someone's occupation

ما عملك؟ **maa :ámal-ak?**	*What is your work?*
أنا طبيب **ána Tabíib**	*I am a doctor.*

تراكيب اللغة **taraakíib al-lúghah** (Structures)

1 Masculine and Feminine

All words in Arabic are either masculine or feminine in gender, as in French and Spanish. Where we use the word *it* in English for objects, Arabic uses *he* or *she* depending on the gender of the object:

المكتب نظيف **al-máktab naDHíif**	*the office is clean*
هو نظيف **húwa naDHíif**	*it is clean*
الجامعة بعيدة **al-jáami:ah ba:íidah**	*the university is far (away)*
هي بعيدة **híya ba:íidah**	*it is far (away)*

2 Feminine endings

There is no marker for masculine words, but most feminine words are marked by the ending ة.

This is pronounced as a weak **h** sound and is always preceded by an **a-** vowel, which is not written. The ending has been transcribed as **-ah** in this book.

Insight

A few Arabic words for female family members, for example أم **umm**, *mother*, have no feminine gender marker, but are naturally dealt with as feminine.

3 Agreement

Adjectives agree in gender, number and definiteness with the noun they are describing. This applies to the three types of construction you have already met: indefinite phrases, definite phrases and *is/are* sentences:

حقيبة ثقيلة **Haqíibah thaqíilah** *a heavy bag*

الميدان الكبير **al-maydáan al-kabíir** *the big square*

الغرفة وسخة **al-ghúrfah wásikhah** *the room is dirty*

Unless otherwise stated, you can assume that the feminine of any word is formed by adding ـة as shown above.

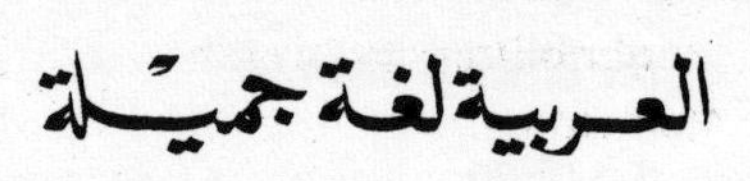

العربية لغة جميلة
al-:arabíyyah lúghah jamíilah
Arabic is a beautiful language

4 Nationality adjectives

To form a masculine adjective, add ـي (**-ii**) to the name of the place. To form a feminine adjective, add ـية (**-íyyah**):

مصر
miSr *Egypt*

مصري/ مصرية
míSrii/miSríyyah *Egyptian*

لبنان
lubnáan *Lebanon*

لبناني/ لبنانية
lubnáanii/lubnaaníyyah *Lebanese*

Insight

The final **-ii** of the masculine is technically **-iyy**, but this is not normally reflected in the pronunciation.

Where the name of a country ends in **-aa** or **-ah**, this is omitted:

بريطانيا
briiTáanya *Britain*

بريطاني/بريطانية
briiTáanii/briiTaaníyyah *British*

أمريكا
amríikaa *America*

أمريكي/أمريكية
amríikii/amriikíyyah *American*

مكة	مكي/مكية
mákkah *Mecca*	**mákki/makkíyyah** *Meccan*

Many Arabic place names have the word *the* (**al-**) in front of them, as in English *Canada*, but *the United States*. When this occurs, the Arabic **al-** is omitted from the nationality adjective:

المغرب	مغربي/مغربية
al-mághrib *Morocco*	**mághribii/maghribíyyah** *Moroccan*
الكويت	كويتي/كويتية
al-kuwáyt *Kuwait*	**kuwáytii/kuwaytíyyah** *Kuwaiti*

Note that some of these adjectives take slightly different forms from those given above, but these will be pointed out as we come to them.

5 More than one

There are no particular rules for forming Arabic plurals and they should be learned along with the singular, as they are given in the vocabulary. The word **al-** the does not change in the plural:

الغرفة **al-ghúrfah**	*the room*
الغرف **al-ghúraf**	*the rooms*

Insight

Arabic has a special formation for saying two of anything (see Unit 9).

6 Plurals of people and objects

Plurals of objects and abstracts are regarded in Arabic as feminine singular. So all adjectives agree by using their feminine singular and the pronoun **híya** *she* is used to refer to them:

كتب طويلة **kútub Tawíilah**	*long books*
الكتب الطويلة **al-kútub aT-Tawíilah**	*the long books*
الكتب طويلة **al-kútub Tawíilah**	*the books are long*
هي طويلة **híya Tawíilah**	*they are long*

7 Talking about one of something

The word for *one* is an adjective and therefore comes after its noun and agrees with it like any other adjective:

فندق واحد **fúnduq wáaHid**	*one hotel*
غرفة واحدة **ghúrfah wáHidah**	*one room*

8 The verb 'to speak'

Here are the singular present tense forms of the verb *to speak.*

أتكلم	**atakállam**	*I speak*
تتكلم	**tatakállam**	*you speak* (m.)
تتكلمين	**tatakallamíin**	*you speak* (f.)
يتكلم	**yatakállam**	*he speaks*
تتكلم	**tatakállam**	*she speaks*

Insight

Note that the *you* m. and *she* forms are identical.

هل يتكلم جون عربي؟ **hal yatakállam juun :árabi?**	*Does John speak Arabic?*
يتكلم عربي بطلاقة **yatakállam :árabi bi-Taláaqah**	*He speaks Arabic fluently*

أوزان الكلمات **awzáan al-kalimáat** (Word shapes)

🔈 CD1, TR31

The word pattern for this unit is **maC¹C²uuC³**, for example, **mashgúul** مشغول, which sounds like the English *Mam(e)luke*.

This word pattern expresses something or someone to which an action has been done, called a *passive participle* in English.

mamlúuk is an Arabic word meaning *owned*, as the Mam(e)luke rulers in Egypt originally were, having been brought in as soldier slaves.

An example of this pattern is **mashghúul**, coming from the root **sh-gh-l**, *work/occupation*; so **mashghúul** means *occupied/made to work*, i.e. *busy*.

The **ma-** never changes. It is a prefix and can be applied to any root, but is not part of it.

Here are some more examples:

مكتوم **maktúum**	*concealed*
مكتوب **maktúub**	*written*
مسموح **masmúuH**	*permitted*
ممنوع **mamnúu:**	*forbidden*
مبسوط **mabsúuT**	*contented, happy*
مفروض **mafrúuD**	*necessary, obligatory*

تمرينات tamriináat (Practice)

Exercise 9

CD1, TR32

Listen to the recording and work out which country these people say they come from. The countries are listed below.

a مرحبا، أنا مغربية **márHaban, ánaa maghribíyyah**
b صباح الخير، أنا أردني **SabáaH al-khayr, ána úrdunii**
c أهلا، أنا عماني **áhlan, ánaa :umáanii**
d مرحبا، أنا بحرينية **márHaban, ánaa baHrayníyyah**
e وأنا كويتي **wa-ánaa kuwáytii**

١ عمان   ٢ الأردن   ٣ الكويت   ٤ المغرب   ٥ البحرين

Exercise 10
How many of the countries below do you recognise? Match them with their corresponding nationality and language.

Country	*Nationality*	*Language*
a إيطاليا	*1* تونسي	*A* الأسبانية
b هولندا	*2* أسترالي	*B* العربية
c إسبانيا	*3* ألماني	*C* الهولندية
d أستراليا	*4* إيطالي	*D* الألمانية

e تونس	*5* فرنسي	*E* الإيطالية
f ألمانيا	*6* إسباني	*F* الفرنسية
g فرنسا	*7* هولندي	*G* الإنجليزية

Exercise 11

Michael is writing to an Arabic-speaking friend about someone he's met. Read this excerpt from his letter and answer the questions.

a *What is her name?*
b *Where does she come from?*

... اسمها سلمى وهي سورية من دمشق. تتكلم اللغة العربية والانجليزية والفرنسية. هي مدرسة.

Find the Arabic for the following expressions:

c *Her name is Salma.*
d *She speaks Arabic.*

Exercise 12

CD1, TR33

Read (or listen to) the following information about Martin Romano.

مارتن رومانو من أمريكا. هو طالب. يتكلم انجليزي و إيطالي بطلاقة وعربي قليلا.

Martin is registering with a college in Cairo for an evening class. The secretary asks him some questions about himself. Imagine that you are Martin. How would you answer the following questions?

◀ **CD1, TR33, 00:24**

السكرتيرة ما اسمك؟
مارتن
السكرتيرة ما جنسيتك؟
مارتن
السكرتيرة ما عملك؟
مارتن
السكرتيرة هل تتكلم عربي؟
مارتن
السكرتيرة تتكلم إنجليزي بطلاقة طبعا؟
مارتن
السكرتيرة وأية لغة غير الإنجليزية؟
مارتن

QUICK VOCAB

جنسية **jinsíyyah** *nationality*
أية **áyyah** *any*
غير **ghayr** *other than*
قليلاً **qalíilan** *slightly, a bit*

Exercise 13

Supply the correct adjective endings from the masculine form given in brackets.

١ السكرتيرة (مشغول)
٢ الأهرام (المصري) (مشهور)
٣ الفيلم (جديد)
٤ السيارة (الكبير) (أمريكي)
٥ سميرة طالبة (جديد)
٦ هل اللغة (الانجليزي) (نافع)؟

٧ هناك في دبي فنادق (جديد) (كثير)

٨ هناك في الميدان صيدلية (واحد)

٩ فاطمة بنت (سعيد)

QUICK VOCAB

مشهور **mashhúur** *famous*
نافع **náafi:** *useful*
فندق، فنادق **fúnduq, fanáadiq** *hotel*
صيدلية، ـات **Saydalíyyah, -aat** *pharmacy*
سعيد **sa:iid** *happy, joyful*

Exercise 14

What are the professions of these people? Write a sentence using a personal pronoun, as in the example.

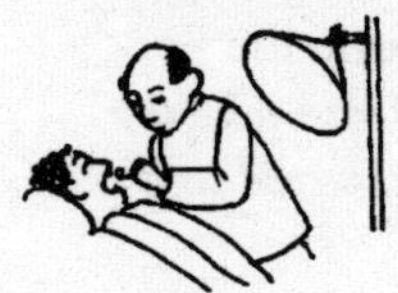

هو طبيب اسنان **húwa Tabíib asnáan**
He is a dentist

طبيب أسنان **Tabíib asnáan** dentist

10 things you need to know

1. *Definite nouns are nouns with* **-al** the, *names of people or places, and personal pronouns* I, you, she, they *and so on.*
2. *Indefinite nouns are nouns with* a *or* an.
3. *Adjectives must agree with their nouns in gender: masculine noun + masculine adjective.*
4. *They must also agree in definiteness and are made definite by adding* **al-** the.
5. *By far the most common feminine ending for nouns and adjectives is* **-ah** *written with a hybrid letter – an Arabic* **h** *with two dots above it. This is the only place where this letter is used.*
6. *Adjectives describing where you come from are formed by adding* **-ii** *(m.) and* **-iyyah** *(f.) to the place name.*
7. *If the place name has* **al-** the *(e.g.* **al-baHrayn***), this is omitted before adding the ending.*
8. *In Arabic, plurals of inanimate objects and abstracts* (stone, idea) *are regarded as feminine singular and take the appropriate agreement of adjectives, and are referred to by the pronoun* she, *not* they.
9. *The Arabic word* **waaHid** one *is an adjective and so must follow and agree with its noun.*
10. *The same set of prefixes is used for the present tense of all Arabic verbs, so you must learn these thoroughly.*

4

هذا وذلك
háadhaa wa-dháalik
This and that

In this unit you will learn:

- ***how to tell the time***
- ***how to ask about opening times***
- ***the days of the week***
- ***the numbers 11–20***
- ***how to form phrases and sentences with 'this', 'that', 'those', etc.***

---

1 أين المتاحف؟ áyna l-matáaHif?
Where are the museums?

CD1, TR34

Bridget and Jim Hayes are visiting Sharjah and an Arabic-speaking friend, Hassan, is showing them around. Today they plan to visit some of the new museums in the city.

Exercise 1
Listen to the recording several times. Then answer the questions.

a What does Hassan point out on the map first?

b *Why don't they want to go to the Natural History Museum?*
c *Which museum do they decide to visit eventually?*

حسن هذه خريطة الشارقة. هذه هي المدينة القديمة، وهذا سوق السمك.
جيم أين المتاحف؟
حسن هذه هي المتاحف، هنا وهنا. هذا هو متحف الفنون، وهذا هو متحف التاريخ الطبيعي في شارع المطار.
بريجت ذلك المتحف بعيد.
جيم نعم، هذا صحيح. انظري، متحف الحصن هنا في شارع البرج. هو متحف ممتاز، ومن الممكن أن نذهب إلى المدينة القديمة بعد ذلك.
بريجت حسنا. نذهب إلى متحف الحصن.

Exercise 2
Link the English phrases to their Arabic equivalents.

a *This is the Old Town.*
b *That museum is far away.*
c *That's true.*
d *Maybe we can go to the Old Town.*

١ من الممكن أن نذهب إلى المدينة القديمة.
٢ ذلك المتحف بعيد.
٣ هذا صحيح.
٤ هذه هي المدينة القديمة.

QUICK VOCAB

هذا/هذه **háadha/háadhih(i)** *this* (m./f.)
خريطة، خرائط **kharíiTah, kharáa'iT** *map*
الشارقة **ash-sháariqah** *Sharjah*
سوق، أسواق **suuq, aswáaq** *market*
سمك **sámak** *fish* (collective)
هنا **húnaa** *here*

تاريخ **taaríikh** *history*

طبيعي**Tabíi:ii** *natural*

فن، فنون **fann, funúun** *art*

شارع، شوارع **sháari:, shawáari:** *street, road*

ذلك **dháalik(a)** *that* (m.)

بعيد **ba:íid** *far away, distant*

صحيح **SaHíiH** *true*

انظري **únDHuri** *look!* (to a woman)

حصن، حصون **HiSn, HuSúun** *fort, fortress*

برج، أبراج **burj, abráaj** *tower*

من الممكن أن **min al-múmkin an** *maybe* (before a verb)

نذهب **nádhhab** *we go*

بعد **ba:d** *after*

QUICK VOCAB

Insight

The word **suuq** *market* is usually regarded as feminine.

---

2 يقفل الساعة كم؟ yáqfil as-sáa:ah kam?

What time does it close?

CD1, TR35

Hassan, Jim and Bridget arrive at the museum. They ask the attendant about opening hours.

First look at the section on asking the time, then listen to the audio a few times.

Exercise 3

a What times does the museum close for lunch?
b When does it open again?

c *What is the time now?*
d *What does the attendant give them?*

حسن	صباح الخير. المتحف يقفل الساعة كم؟
مسؤولة المتحف	صباح النور. يقفل الساعة واحدة ويفتح الساعة أربعة بعد الظهر.
بريجت	كم الساعة الآن؟
حسن	الساعة عشرة وربع.
بريجت	حسنا، عندنا وقت كثير.
مسؤولة المتحف	مرحبا، تفضلوا. هذا هو كتيّب عن المتحف.
حسن	شكرا.

Exercise 4
Link the English phrases to the appropriate Arabic.

1	*It closes.*	يفتح	١
2	*It opens.*	الساعة عشرة وربع.	٢
3	*What's the time?*	هذا هو كتيّب عن المتحف.	٣
4	*It's a quarter past ten.*	يقفل.	٤
5	*Welcome, come in.*	مرحبا، تفضلوا.	٥
6	*This is a brochure of the museum.*	الساعة كم؟	٦

QUICK VOCAB

يقفل **yáqfil** *he/it closes, shuts*
مسؤول، ـون **mas'úul, -uun** *official*
مسؤول المتحف **mas'úul al-mátHaf** *attendant, official of the museum*
ساعة، ـات **sáa:ah, -aat** *hour, time, watch, clock*
الساعة كم؟ **as-sáa:ah kam** *(at) what time?*
يفتح **yáftaH** *he/it opens*
ظهر **DHuhr** *noon*
بعد الظهر **ba:d aDH-DHuhr** *(in) the afternoon*
الآن **al-'áan** *now*

ربع **rub:** *quarter*

عشرة وربع **:áshrah wa-rub:** *quarter past ten*

عندنا **:índ-naa** *we have*

وقت، أوقات **waqt, awqáat** *time*

تفضلوا **tafáDDaluu** *come in, here you are* (pl.): used when inviting someone to come in, sit down, or when giving them something. The final **alif** is not pronounced.

كتيّب **kutáyyib** *booklet, brochure*

عن **:an** *about, concerning*

---

3 مواقيت المتحف mawaaqiit al-mátHaf

Museum opening times

Exercise 5

Read the notice for the museum opening times and answer the questions.

The days of the week are given in Key phrases below.

مواقيت المتحف	
يوم السبت	٩،٠٠ - ١٣،٠٠ و ١٧,٠٠ - ٢٠،٠٠
يوم الأحد	٩،٠٠ - ١٢،٠٠ و ١٧,٠٠ - ٢٠،٠٠
يوم الاثنين	إجازة
يوم الثلاثاء	٩،٠٠ - ١٣،٠٠ و ١٧,٠٠ - ٢٠،٠٠
يوم الأربعاء	٩،٠٠ - ١٣،٠٠ و ١٧,٠٠ - ٢٠،٠٠
	(الزيارة للنساء فقط)
يوم الخميس	٩،٠٠ - ١٣،٠٠ و ١٧,٠٠ - ٢٠،٠٠
يوم الجمعة	١٦،٣٠ - ٢٠،٣٠

a *When are women particularly welcome?*
b *Which day is the museum closed?*
c *When does the museum close on Friday evening?*
d *When does the museum usually open in the morning?*
e *On which day does the museum not open in the morning?*
f *How many days have the same opening times?*

QUICK VOCAB

مواقيت **mawaaqíit** *appointments, times* (of opening etc.)

إجازة **ijáazah** *holiday, vacation, closing day*

زيارة ـات **ziyáarah, -aat** *visit*

لـ **li-** *to, for*

نساء **nisáa:** *women*

للنساء **li-n-nisáa'** [lit., '*for the women*' (by convention, the **alif** of **al** is omitted after **li-**]

---

4 بكم...؟ bi-kam...?

How much does it cost?

They go to the admission desk to buy tickets.

Exercise 6

🔊 CD1, TR36

Listen to the recording and answer the questions.

a *How much does an adult ticket cost?*
b *How much does a child ticket cost?*
c *How much does Hassan have to pay?*

حسن	السلام عليكم.
مسؤولة المتحف	وعليكم السلام.
حسن	التذكرة بكم من فضلك؟
مسؤولة المتحف	البالغون بستة دراهم ، والأطفال بثلاثة دراهم.
حسن	ثلاث تذاكر بستة دراهم من فضلك.
مسؤولة المتحف	ثمانية عشر درهما من فضلك. شكرا.
	تفضلوا التذاكر.
حسن	شكرا.

Exercise 7

Link the English to the appropriate Arabic expressions.

a	*How much is a ticket, please?*	١	البالغون بستة دراهم.
b	*Adults are six dirhams.*	٢	ثلاث تذاكر بستة دراهم، من فضلك.
c	*Three six-dirham tickets, please.*	٣	تفضلوا التذاكر.
d	*Here are the tickets.*	٤	التذكرة بكم، من فضلك؟

QUICK VOCAB

مسؤولة المتحف **mas'úulat al-mátHaf** *museum* official (f.)

تذكرة، تذاكر **tádhkirah,tadháakir** *ticket*

بكم **bi-kám** *how much* [lit., *for how much*]

بالغون **baalighúun** *adults*

درهم، دراهم **dírham, daráahim** *dirham* (unit of currency)

طفل، أطفال **Tifl, aTfáal** *child*

ثمانية عشر **thamániyat* :ashar** *eighteen*

(* Feminine ending pronounced **-at**. See Unit 5.)

تعبيرات رئيسية **ta:biiráat ra'iisíyyah** (Key phrases)

Asking and telling the time **CD1, TR37**

الساعة كم؟ **as-sáa:ah kam?**	*What time is it?*
الساعة واحدة **as-sáa:ah wáaHidah**	*It's one o'clock*
الساعة اثنين وربع/إلا ربع **as-sáa:ah ithnáyn wa-rub:/íllaa rub:**	*It's quarter past/quarter to two*
الساعة ثلاثة و/إلا ثلث **as-sáa:ah thaláathah wa/ íllaa thulth**	*It's twenty past/to three*
الساعة عشرة ونصف **as-sáa:ah :áshrah wa-níSf**	*It's half past ten*

Times of day **CD1, TR38**

If it is not clear from the context whether the hour referred to is am or pm, Arabic has a set of words to indicate periods of the day which may be placed after stating the time:

الصبح **aS-SúbH**	*morning, forenoon*
الظهر **aDH-DHúhr**	*around noon*
بعد الظهر **ba:d aDH-DHúhr**	*afternoon*
العصر **al-:áSr**	*late afternoon* (about 4 pm)
المساء **al-masáa'**	*evening*
الليل **al-layl**	*night*
الساعة تسعة الصبح **as-sáa:ah tís:ah aS-SubH**	*nine o'clock in the morning*

الساعة سبعة المساء **as-sáa:ah sáb:ah al-masáa'**	*seven o'clock at night*

Asking about opening times 🔊 **CD1, TR39**

يفتح/يقفل الساعة كم؟ **yáftaH/yáqfil as-sáa:ah kam**	*What time does it open/close?*
يفتح/يقفل الساعة سبعة **yáftaH/yáqfil as-sáa:ah sáb:ah**	*It opens/closes at seven o'clock*

The days of the week 🔊 **CD1, TR40**

يوم الأحد **yawm al-áHad**	*Sunday*
يوم الاثنين **yawm al-ithnayn**	*Monday*
يوم الثلاثاء **yawm ath-thalaatháa'**	*Tuesday*
يوم الأربعاء **yawm al-arbi:áa'**	*Wednesday*
يوم الخميس **yawm al-khamíis**	*Thursday*
يوم الجمعة **yawm al-júm:ah**	*Friday*
يوم السبت **yawm as-sabt**	*Saturday*

Sometimes the word **yawm** is omitted:

الغد الأحد **al-ghad al-áHad**	*tomorrow is Sunday*

More time-related words 🔊 **CD1, TR41**

اليوم **al-yawm**	*today*
الغد **al-ghad**	*tomorrow*
أمس **ams**	*yesterday*
بعد الغد **ba:d al-ghad**	*the day after tomorrow*
أمس الأول **ams al-áwwal**	*the day before yesterday*

قبل ثلاثة أيام **qabl thaláathat ayyáam** — *three days ago*

بعد أربعة أيام **ba:d arba:at ayyáam** — *in four days*

Asking the price of something **CD1, TR42**

التذكرة بكم؟ **at-tádhkirah bi-kám?** — *How much is a ticket?*

هذا بكم؟ **háadhaa bi-kám?** — *How much is this?*

هذا بخمسة دراهم **háadha bi-khámsah daráahim** — *This is five dirhams*

بكم تلك المجلة؟ **bi-kám tílka l-majállah?** — *How much is that magazine?*

هي بدينار واحد **híya bi-diináar wáaHid** — *It is one dinar*

تراكيب اللغة taraakíib al-lúghah (Structures)

1 Demonstratives

The words *this*, *that*, etc. are called demonstratives. In English, they behave in two ways.

- *as an adjective:* this book is expensive. *The word this describes which book we mean.*
- *as a pronoun:* that was an excellent film. *Here the word that represents a noun (the film).*

Insight

It will help you in the use of the Arabic demonstratives if you bear in mind that, in Arabic, they are *always* pronouns and never adjectives. Arabic really says *this* (object, person) *the-big* (thing, one).

Singular		
masc.	هذا المتحف **háadhaa l-mátHaf**	*this museum*
fem.	هذه الخريطة **háadhihi l-kharíiTah**	*this map*
masc.	ذلك الشارع **dháalika sh-sháari:**	*that street*
fem.	تلك المدينة **tílka l-madíinah**	*that town*
Plural		
	هؤلاء الأولاد/البنات **haa'uláa'i l-awláad/ l-banáat**	*these boys/girls*
	أولائك البنات **uuláa'ika l-banáat**	*those girls*

Insight

There is no difference between masculine and feminine in the plural words for *these* and *those*.

Agreement

Demonstratives agree with their noun in gender:

háadhaa l-mátHaf هذا المتحف

this(thing) the-museum *this museum* (m.)

háadhihi l-madíinah هذه المدينة

this(thing) the-town *this town* (f.)

Adjectives

Adjectives come after their nouns in the usual way:

háadha l-maktab al-jadíid هذا المكتب الجديد

this(thing) the-office the-new(one) *this new office*

háadhihi l-jaríidah t-tuunisíyyah هذه الجريدة التونسية

this(thing) the-newspaper the-Tunisian(one) *this Tunisian newspaper*

Demonstrative sentences with indefinites

háadhaa kitáab هذا كتاب

this(thing) [is] book *this is a book*

háadhihi sayyáarah هذه سيارة

this (thing) [is] car *this is a car*

dháalika qálam jadíid ذلك قلم جديد

that(thing) [is] pen new(one) *that is a new pen*

tílka jaríidah yawmíyyah تلك جريدة يومية

that (thing) [is] newspaper daily(one) *that is a daily newspaper*

Demonstrative sentences with definites

The pronoun agreeing with the subject noun is always put between the demonstrative and the rest of the sentence. This is necessary, as otherwise, we would get a definite phrase (see Unit 1):

háadhaa sh-sháari: هذا الشارع

this the-street *this street*

háadhaa húwa sh-sháari: هذا هو الشارع

this(thing) he [is] the-street *this is the street*

tílka híya l-bint تلك هي البنت

that(person) she [is] the-girl *that's the girl*

The same procedure is often followed with names of people or places:

háadhaa húwa muHámmad هذا هو محمد

this(person) he Muhammad *this is Muhammad*

These/those with people:

haa'uláa'i l-awláad هؤلاء الأولاد

these boys

uuláa'ika l-banáat أولائك البنات

those girls

Insight

Remember that since plurals of inanimate objects are regarded in Arabic as being feminine singular, the demonstrative used is feminine singular and the pronoun used for *they* is actually *she*:

tílka híya l-kútub al-:arabíyyah تلك هي الكتب العربية

These(things) they [are] the-books the-Arabic *These are the Arabic books*

Spelling and pronunciation

a *Note that* **háadhaa, haadhíhi** *and* **dháalika** *are nominally spelled with the dagger* **alif** *for the first long* **a** *(see page 16). This is usually omitted in print, but a normal* **alif** cannot *be used.*

b *Although spelled long, the final vowel of* **háadhaa** *is usually pronounced short.*

c *When these words – or any word ending in a vowel – come before* **al-**, *the, the* **a** *of the latter is omitted:*

هذا المتحف	**háadhaa l-matHaf**
تلك المدرسة الكبيرة	**tilka l-mádrasah l-kabíirah**

d *When* **dháalika** *comes at the end of a sentence, its final* **a** *is usually omitted.*

2 Telling the time

Insight

The way of telling the time in Standard Arabic is complicated and used only in the most formal situations. For this reason, the following section is given in the more common colloquial (transliterated) form, without Arabic script, except for the main terms.

as-sáa:ah wáaHidah
it's one o'clock

as-sáa:ah ithnáyn wa-rúb:
the hour is two and a quarter

as-sáa:ah thaláathah ílla thulth
the hour is three less a third [of an hour], *20 minutes*

as-sáa:ah iHdá:shar waa-niSf
the hour is eleven and a half

Note that:

a *one o'clock, and in some dialects two o'clock, use the feminine form of the numeral (***wáaHidah, ithnáyn/thintáyn***)*

b *three o'clock to ten o'clock inclusive use the independent form ending in* **-ah**

c *for eleven and twelve o'clock there is only one possible form*

d **niSf**, *half, is often pronounced* **nuSS**

e *for the English past, Arabic uses* **wa-** و*, and*

as-sáa:ah iHdá:shar wa-rúb: *quarter past eleven*

f *for the English to, Arabic uses* **ílla** إلا*, except for, less*

as-sáa:ah thaláathah ílla rúb: *quarter to three*

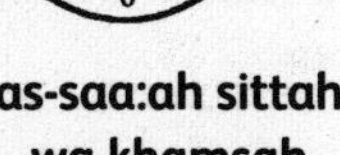

as-saa:ah sittah wa khamsah

as-saa:ah waaHidah wa nuSS

as-saa:ah arba:ah illa thulth

Twenty-five past and *twenty-five to* the hour are expressed in Arabic as 'the hour and a half less five' and 'the hour and a half and five' respectively:

as-sáa:ah khámsah wa-niSf ílla khámsah *twenty five past five*

as-sáa:ah khámsah wa-niSf wa-khámsah *twenty five to six*

More formally (and less commonly) all times can be stated using the preceding hour plus the number of minutes:

as-sáa:ah :ásharah wa khámsah wa-arba:íin daqíiqah *10:45*

دقيقة دقائق **daqíiqah, daqáa'iq** *minute*

This is the method used by speaking clocks and other automats, and also sometimes on official radio and television announcements. These, however, use the literary Arabic forms of the numbers, which differ significantly.

3 Saying 'at' a particular time

Arabic requires no additional word, so **as-saa:ah khamsah** can mean *(it is) five o'clock* or *at five o' clock.*

4 Numbers 11–20

CD1, TR43

The numbers are given here in the colloquial form as they were in Unit 2.

11 iHdá:shar	**16 sittá:shar**
12 ithná:shar	**17 sab:atá:shar**
13 thalaathtá:shar	**18 thamantá:shar**
14 arba:atá:shar	**19 tis:atá:shar**
15 khamsatá:shar	**20 :ishríin**

Note the common element (equivalent to English *-teen*) **á:shar**, which is a slightly altered form of the written **:áshar.**

Agreement with nouns

a *In written Arabic, the numbers must agree with their nouns in gender.*

b *With the numbers 11–99 inclusive, the noun is in the accusative* singular. *This is shown on most nouns without an* **-ah** *ending by the alif accusative marker and pronounced* **-an** *in formal speech (see Script and Pronunciation).*

أربعة عشر كتابا **arba:atá:shar kitáaban** *14 books, but*

خمسة عشر تذكرة **khamastá:shar tádhkirah** *15 tickets*

c *In Arabic, the noun is plural* only *after the numerals 3–10 inclusive.*

خمسة بيوت **khámsah buyúut** *five houses*

Talking about *two* of anything requires a special ending known as the dual. This is dealt with in Unit 14.

5 Asking the price of something

Here Arabic uses the preposition **bi-**:

هذا بكم؟ **háadhaa bi-kám?**	*How much is this?*
هذا بخمسة دراهم **háadha bi-khámsah daráahim**	*This is five dirhams*
بكم تلك المجلة؟ **bi-kám tílka l-majállah?**	*How much is that magazine?*
هي بدينار واحد **híya bi-diináar wáaHid**	*It is one dinar*

أوزان الكلمات **awzáan al-kalimáat** (Word shapes)

CD1, TR44

The word pattern for this unit is **maC¹C²aC³**, for example, **máktab** مكتب *office*, *desk*, which sounds like the English *madman*.

This shape usually represents a place where the action of the root takes place.

The root **k-t-b** refers to *writing*, so **máktab** means *a desk* or *an office*, i.e. a place where you write.

Sometimes this pattern adds a feminine ending **-ah**. Thus, from the root **d-r-s** to do with *studying*, we have **mádrasah** مدرسة, meaning a place of study, i.e. *a school*. Occasionally, the two forms exist side by side:

مكتب **máktab** *office*

مكتبة **máktabah** *library, bookshop*

Other examples:

مدخل **mádkhal** *entrance*

مخرج **mákhraj** *exit*

متحف **mátHaf** *museum*

ملعب **mál:ab** *playing field*

مسرح **másraH** *theatre*

مسبح **másbaH** *swimming pool*

مقبرة **máqbarah** *cemetery*

تمرينات **tamriináat** (Practice)

Exercise 8

🔊 CD1, TR45

Listen to the times of day on the recording or read the transcript and look at the times below. Decide in each case what the correct time is.

a	**as-sáa:ah wáaHidah wa-niSf**	*a*	*1:15, 1:20 or 1:30?*
b	**as-sáa:ah sáb:ah ílla khámsah**	*b*	*6:25, 6:35 or 6:55?*
c	**as-sáa:ah :ásharah wa-rub:**	*c*	*10:15, 10:30 or 10:45?*
d	**as-sáa:ah khámsah**	*d*	*4:55, 5:00 or 5:05?*
e	**as-sáa:ah tís:ah aS-SubH**	*e*	*9:00am or 9:00pm?*

Exercise 9

CD1, TR46

Ask what time it is and say the time shown on the clock. Listen to the recording or read the transcript to see if you are right.

Example:

as-sáa:ah kam?	*What time is it?*
as-sáa:ah thamáanyah	*It is eight o' clock*

Exercise 10

Do you remember the days of the week? See if you can fill in the gaps in these sentences in Arabic.

١ اليوم .... الثلاثاء

٢ الغد ....

٣ كان .... يوم الاثنين

٤ كان أمس الأول ....

٥ .... يوم الخميس

٦ .... بعد ثلاثة أيام

كان **kaan(a)** *was* (see Unit 8)

Exercise 11

Your Arabic-speaking friend is showing you some photographs of his home and family. Choose the correct demonstrative:

١ هذا/هذه هو البيت الجديد.

٢ هذا/هذه هي الأشجار في الحديقة.

٣ أولائك/ذلك هم الأولاد.

٤ هذا/هذه هي فاطمة.

٥ أولائك/تلك هم الجيران.

٦ ذلك/تلك هي القوارب في البحر.

QUICK VOCAB

شجرة، أشجار **shájarah, ashjáar** *tree*

حديقة، حدائق **Hadíiqah, Hadáa'iq** *garden, park*

جار، جيران **jaar, jiiráan** *neighbour*

قارب، قوارب **qáarib, qawáarib** *(small) boat*

بحر، بحار **baHr, biHáar** *sea, large river*

Exercise 12

Write out the following dates in English in numerical fashion, e.g. 10/6/1989 (day/month/year). Watch the direction of writing!

١ ٣ \ ١٢ \ ١٩٥٢

٢ ١٩ \ ١١ \ ١٩٦٧

٣ ١ \ ١ \ ٢٠٠٠

٤ ٢٨ \ ٢ \ ١٩٩٠

٥ ١٧ \ ٤ \ ١٨٣٦

Exercise 13

You want to buy tickets for a performance at the National Theatre in Kuwait. Fill in your side of the dialogue, guided by the translation below.

أنت	
كاتب	مساء النور.
أنت	
كاتب	التذكرة بأربعة دنانير.
أنت	
كاتب	١٦ دينارا من فضلك.
أنت	
كاتب	شكرا.
أنت	
كاتب	يفتح الساعة سبعة، والمسرحية تبتدئ الساعة سبعة ونصف.
أنت	

1 *Say good evening*
2 *Ask how much a ticket costs*
3 *Ask for four tickets*
4 *Offer the ticket clerk your money*
5 *Ask the ticket clerk when the theatre opens*
6 *Say thank you*

مسرح مسارح **másraH, masáariH*** *theatre*

دينار دنانير **diináar, danaaníir*** *dinar* (unit of currency)

مسرحية، ـات **masraHíyyah, -aat** *play* (theatrical)

تبتدئ **tabtádi'** *she/it begins*

Now answer the following questions.

a How much does a ticket cost?
b When does the theatre open?
c When does the play begin?

Exercise 14

Write out the following times in transliteration and practise saying them out loud.

a	٦:٣٥	*f*	٥:٣٠
b	٨:١٠	*g*	١:١٥
c	٩:٢٥	*h*	١٢:٥٥
d	٧:٠٠	*i*	٣:٢٠
e	٣:٤٥	*j*	١٠:٠٥

---

10 things you need to know

1 *The demonstratives* this, that, these *and* those *are regarded not as adjectives, but as pronouns, i.e. they imply the word* thing *or* person *after them. An awareness of this is important in Arabic sentences.*
2 *If you want to say* this is, these are, *you must put the appropriate pronoun between the demonstrative and the noun, so* that's the girl *would be* **tilka hiya al-bint** that [person] she [is] the girl. **tilka al-bint** *would simply mean* that girl.
3 *Demonstratives with a long* **-aa** *in the first syllable like* **haadhaa** *must be written without the conventional* **alif** *to indicate the long vowel. In theory, there should be a dagger* **alif** *above the first letter, but this is usually omitted.*
4 *The method of telling the time is given in spoken form, as the technically correct forms are complicated and rarely used except for in the most formal circumstances.*
5 *To say* the time is ... o'clock, *you only need to say* **as-saa:ah...** *followed by the number of the hour. There is no need for a word to express* at, *so to say* at six o'clock *is just* **as-saa:ah sittah.**

5

بيتنا بيتكم
báyt-naa báyt-kum
Our house is your house

In this unit you will learn:

- ***how to talk about your family***
- ***how to say who things belong to***
- ***how to describe them***
- ***the numbers 21–100***

---

1 هذه هي زوجتي háadhihi híya záwjat-ii
This is my wife

🔊 CD2, TR01

Hamed has invited his English friend, Tom, to his flat in Cairo for dinner. The whole family is there, so Tom has the chance to meet them all.

Exercise 1
Listen to the dialogue and answer the following questions.

a Who does Hamed introduce to Tom first?
b How old is Tamiim?

c *How old is their daughter?*
d *Are Tom's children older or younger than Hamed's?*

حامد	تفضل يا توم!
توم	شكرا يا حامد.
حامد	هذه هي زوجتي سلمى. سلمى، هذا توم، من المكتب.
توم	مساء الخير يا سلمى، كيف حالك؟
سلمى	بخير الحمد لله. أهلا وسهلا. و كيف حالك أنت؟
توم	الحمد لله. هذه هدية لك!
سلمى	شكرا يا توم. هذا والدي، وهذه والدتي... وهذا ابننا تميم. تفضل، اجلس.
توم	تميم كم عمره؟
سلمى	عمره ١٥ سنة، وبنتنا فريدة عمرها ١٢ سنة.
حامد	أولادك أنت، كم عمرهم، يا توم؟
توم	أولادنا صغار - ابننا عمره ٥ سنوات، وبنتنا عمرها ٣ سنوات.

Exercise 2
Find the Arabic for:

a *This is my father.*
b *Please sit down.*
c *This is our son.*
d *How old are your children?*
e *Our daughter is three years old.*

QUICK VOCAB

زوجة **záwjah** *wife*

زوجتي **záwjat-ii** *my wife* (see below for possessive pronouns)

لك **lá-ki** *for you* (to a woman)

تفضل **tafáDDal** *come in* (to a man)

هدية، هدايا **hadíyyah, hadáayaa** *present, gift*

والد **wáalid** *father*

والدة **wáalidah** *mother*

ابن، أبناء **ibn, abnáa'** *son*

QUICK VOCAB

اجلس **íjlis** *sit down!* (to a man)

كم عمره **kam :úmr-uh** *how old is he?*

سنة، سنوات **sánah, sanawáat** *year*

بنت، بنات **bint, banáat** *girl, daughter*

صغار **Sigháar** *young, small* (pl.)

معلومات ثقافية ma:luumáat thaqaafíyyah (Cultural tips)

Within the framework of the Islamic way of life, customs vary widely in the Arab world. For example, in the more conservative areas, a man visiting a family will never see any of the women and should not even ask about them. However, in more liberal countries, he can behave much as he would in a European country. It is best to err on the safe side until you are sure of your ground, taking your cue from your hosts.

In very traditional areas, if a man is invited with his wife, she may be taken to the women's quarters on arrival and be entertained and fed with the women, while her husband stays with the men. She will be reunited with her husband when they leave.

تعبيرات رئيسية ta:biiráat ra'iisíyyah (Key phrases)

Introducing people

هذا توم **háadha Tom**	*This is Tom* (for a man)
هذه هي زوجتي، سلمى **háadhihi híya záwjat-ii, sálma**	*This is my wife, Salma* (for a woman)

Asking people how they are and saying how you are

كيف حالك **káyfa Háal-ak** *How are you?* (to a man)

káyfa Háal-ik (to a woman)

Note: Arabic spelling is the same.

أنا بخير الحمد لله *I'm well, praise be to God*

ána bi-kháyr, al-Hámdu li-Láah

Welcoming people to your home

تفضل، تفضلي **tafáDDal, tafáDDali** *Come in!* (to a man/woman)

اجلس، اجلسي **íjlis, íjlisii** *Sit down!* (man/woman)

Asking and saying how old someone is

تميم كم عمره؟ *How old is Tamim?*

tamíim kam :umr-uh [lit., how much his-life]

عمره ٨ سنوات **:umr-uh 8 sanawáat** *He is eight years old*

Members of the family

والد/أب **wáalid/ab***	*father*
والدة/أم **wáalidah/umm**	*mother*
ابن، ابناء **ibn, abnáa'**	*son*
بنت، بنات **bint, banáat**	*daughter, girl*
أولاد **awláad**	*boys, children*
أخ، إخوان/إخوة **akh, ikhwáan/íkhwah**	*brother*
أخت، أخوات **ukht, akhawáat**	*sister*
زوج **zawj**	*husband*

زوجة **záwjah** *wife*

عم/خال **:ámm/kháal** *uncle*

Insight

Arabic distinguishes here. **:ámm** is your father's brother, **kháal** is your mother's brother.

عمة/خالة **:ámmah/kháalah**	*aunt* (see note above)
جد **jadd**	*grandfather*
جدة **jáddah**	*grandmother*
ابن عم/خال **ibn :amm/khaal**	(male) *cousin* (father's/mother's side)
بنت عم/خال **bint :amm/khaal**	(female) *cousin*

Insight

The words **akh**, *brother*, and **ab**, *father*, are irregular nouns (see Unit 17 for details). They take a long vowel (usually **uu**) before most of the possessive pronouns given later in this lesson. For *father*, you can also use the regular **wáalid**, but for *brother*, there is no alternative.

Numbers 21–100

CD2, TR02

Exercise 3

Listen to the recording and repeat each number as you hear it and fill in the blanks with the missing numbers.

....	**44/٤٤**		**20/٢٠**
khamsíin	**50/٥٠**	**wáaHid wa-:ishríin**	**21/٢١**
wáaHid wa-khamsíin	**51/٥١**	**ithnáyn wa-:ishríin**	**22/٢٢**

thaláathah wa-:ishríin 23/٢٣

árba:ah wa-:ishríin 24/٢٤

khámsah wa-:ishríin 25/٢٥

síttah wa-:ishríin 26/٢٦

sab:ah wa-:ishríin 27/٢٧

thamáaniyah wa-:ishríin 28/٢٨

tís:ah wa-:ishríin 29/٢٩

thalaathíin 30/٣٠

wáaHid wa-thalaathíin 31/٣١

.... 33/٣٣

arba:íin ....

ithnáyn wa-arba:íin 42/٤٢

.... 57/٥٧

sittíin 60/٦٠

thaláathah wa-sittíin 63/٦٣

.... 68/٦٨

sab:íin 70/٧٠

.... 76/٧٦

thamaaníin 80/٨٠

.... 85/٨٥

tis:íin 90/٩٠

.... 99/٩٩

míiyah 100/١٠٠

Insight

Don't forget that these numbers take a *singular* noun. Look at the section on Numbers 11–20 in Unit 4.

Tens with units

Units are placed before the tens:

٢٣/23 thaláathah wa-:ishríin	*three and twenty*
٦٥/65 khámsah wa-sittíin	*five and sixty*

Insight: Pronunciation

The tens have a slightly different written form ending in **-uun** ـون in some contexts, but they are universally pronounced with the **-iin** ending in everyday speech. They are easy to remember, as, with the exception of *twenty*, they closely resemble the equivalent unit numbers, with the addition of **-iin**.

تراكيب اللغة **taraakíib al-lúghah** (Structures)

1 Possessive pronouns

Possessives describe who or what something belongs to. English expresses this in several ways:

This is my shirt.

This shirt is mine.

This shirt belongs to me.

There are several points to note in Arabic:

a *Written Arabic has only one way to express the possessive, using the equivalents of English* my, your, his, etc. *We call these words possessive pronouns. There is no equivalent in Arabic of the English* mine, yours, etc. *In Arabic, these pronouns are suffixes, which are joined on to the object that is possessed:*

their house becomes in Arabic بيتهم **báyt-hum** *house-their*

this is my car becomes هذه سيارتي **háadhihi sayyáarat-i** *this(-one) [is] car-my (see below for spelling)*

b *Arabic distinguishes, in the case of* his *and* her, your *and* their *(but not* my *or* our*), whether the owner of the thing is a man or a woman. In the following list (and throughout this book), some of these possessive pronouns are given in a slightly simplified form, much as they are used in spoken Arabic.*

c *Since they are suffixes, the Arabic script versions of these pronouns have been given here as if they were joined to a word ending in a joining letter.*

Singular	*Plural*
ـي **-ii** *my*	ـنا **-na(a)** *our*
ـك **-ak** *your* (m.)	ـكم **-kum** *your* (m.)
ـك **-ik** *your* (f.)	ـكن **kúnna** *your* (f.)
ـه **-uh** *his*	ـهم **-hum** *their* (m.)
ـها **-ha(a)** *her*	ـهن **-húnna** *their* (f.)

Pronunciation

1 **-haa** *and* **-naa** *are generally pronounced short, although written with long vowels.*

2 *There are the following changes in pronunciation that are not reflected in the Arabic script:*

After words ending in long vowels or **-ay:**

- **-ii**, *my, becomes* **-ya.**
  يداي **yadáa-ya** *my hands* (**yadaa** *hands)*
- **-ak** *and* **-uh** *lose their vowels:*
  يداك، يداه **yadáa-k, yadáa-h**
- **-ik** *becomes* **-ki**
  يداك **yadáa-ki**

When preceded by **i, ii** *or* **ay:**

- **-hum** *and* **-hunna** *change to* **-him** *and* **-hinna:**
  مبانيهم **mabaaníi-him** *their buildings*

The hidden **t**

You will remember that ـة is the most common feminine ending in Arabic and is written with a hybrid letter, a cross between **h** and **t.** If a possessive pronoun suffix is added to a feminine word, the ـة **h** changes into an ordinary ـتـ **t:**

السيارة الجديدة	-the-car the new-one
as-sayyáarah l-jadíidah	*the new car*

6 *Times up to half past the hour are expressed by naming the hour followed by* **wa-**, and, *and the number of minutes or fraction of the hour.*

7 *Times after half past the hour are expressed by naming the following hour plus* **illa**, except for, *and the minutes or fractions of the hour.*

8 Twenty-five past *and* twenty-five to *the hour are exceptions, for which you should see the main text.*

9 *The numbers from 11–29 and in fact to 99 are given in spoken form for the same reasons as above.*

10 *The numbers from 11–99 are followed by the noun in the singular form and the special accusative marker where appropriate.*

سيارته الجديدة	car-his the new-one
sayyáarat-uh al-jadíidah	*his new car*

Definites

All Arabic possessives are regarded as definite and follow the agreement rules for definites. This is because if you say *my book*, you are referring to one specific book (see Unit 3).

a-háadha báyt-ak?	[?]This(thing) house-your?
أهذا بيتك؟	*Is this your house?*

ná:am, háadha báyt-ii	نعم، هذا بيتي
Yes, this(thing) house-my	*Yes, this is my house*

a-haadhíhi sayyaarát-haa?	This(thing) car-her?
أهذه سيارتها؟	*Is this her car?*

laa, láysat haadhíhi sayyaarát-haa	لا، ليست هذه سيارتها
No, is-not this(thing) car-her	*No, this is not her car*

ليست **láysat** *is not* (f.)

أوزان الكلمات **awzáan al-kalimáat** (Word shapes)

CD2, TR03

The pattern for this unit is **$C^1uC^2úuC^3$**, for example, **buyúut** بيوت *houses*, which sounds like the English *to lose*.

This shape usually represents one of two things:

a *the plural of simple nouns whose singular shape is* **$C^1vC^2C^3$**: **b-y-t** *singular* **bayt** *house* ➔ *plural* **buyúut** *houses:*

فلس/فلوس **fils/fulúus** *piastre, small unit of currency*

شعب/شعوب **sha:b/shu:úub** *people, folk*

b *nouns expressing the action of a verb – usually formed in English by adding the ending -ing (e.g. do* ➔ *doing, think* ➔ *thinking). In English we call this a verbal noun:*

دخول **dukhúul** *from* **d-kh-l** *enter, meaning entering, entrance*

خروج **khurúuj** *from* **kh-r-j** *exiting, leaving; the act of going out*

Note that, as is the case with many shapes, **CuCúuC** cannot be formed from every noun or verb root. The benefit of learning the shapes is in recognition, not formation. However, any noun which you come across in this form will be either a plural or a verbal noun.

تمرينات tamriináat (Practice)

Exercise 4

Put the following numbers into numerical order:

٦٧ ٣١ ٥٨ ٩٦ ٢٤ ٨٨ ٤٢ ٥٣ ٢٨ ١٤

Exercise 5

CD2, TR04

You are planning a camping trip with some Arab friends and see the following advertisement in an Arabic paper. You want to tell your friends about it. Read aloud the prices of the items below several times. Then listen to the recording to check that you were correct and write the prices in English.

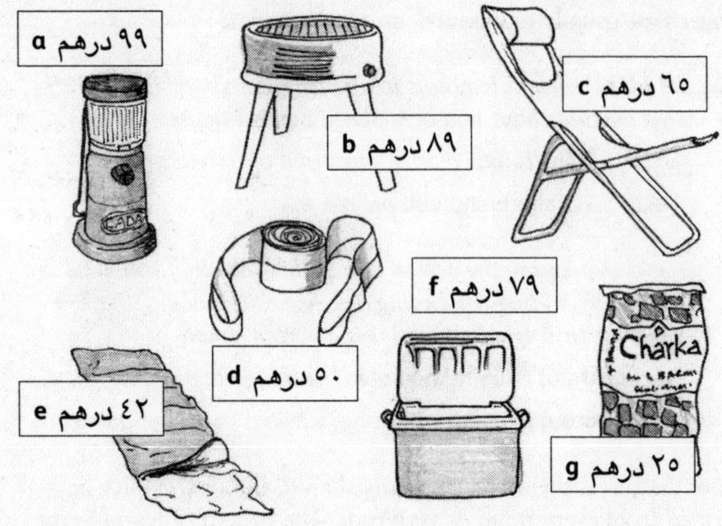

Exercise 6

You have invited an Arab friend and her husband for dinner. Match the English phrases with the appropriate Arabic ones:

a *Please come in.*
b *This is my husband.*
c *How are you?*
d *This is a present for you.*
e *Sit down*
f *Welcome*

١ هذا هو زوجي.
٢ أهلا وسهلا.
٣ كيف حالك؟
٤ تفضل.
٥ اجلس.
٦ هذه هدية لك.

Exercise 7

Fill in the gaps with a possessive, using the correct suffix endings. The first one has been done for you.

١ قميص .... وسخ. (قميصك وسخ.)
٢ والدة .... إيطالية.
٣ هرم .... هو الكبير.

٤ هذه أخت .... مريم.

٥ ليست هذه السيارة سيارة ....

٦ أهذا مكتب .... الجديد؟

٧ جد .... من تونس.

٨ أين حقائب ....؟

1 *Your shirt is dirty!*
2 *My mother is Italian.*
3 *My pyramid is the big one.*
4 *This is my sister, Miriam.*
5 *This car is not mine.*
6 *Is this his new office?*
7 *Their grandfather is from Tunis.*
8 *Where are our suitcases?*

قميص قمصان **qamíiS, qumSáan** *shirt*
وسخ **wásikh** *dirty*
حقيبة، حقائب **Haqíibah, Haqáa'ib** *bag, suitcase*

Exercise 8
Study the family tree below, then answer the questions in Arabic:

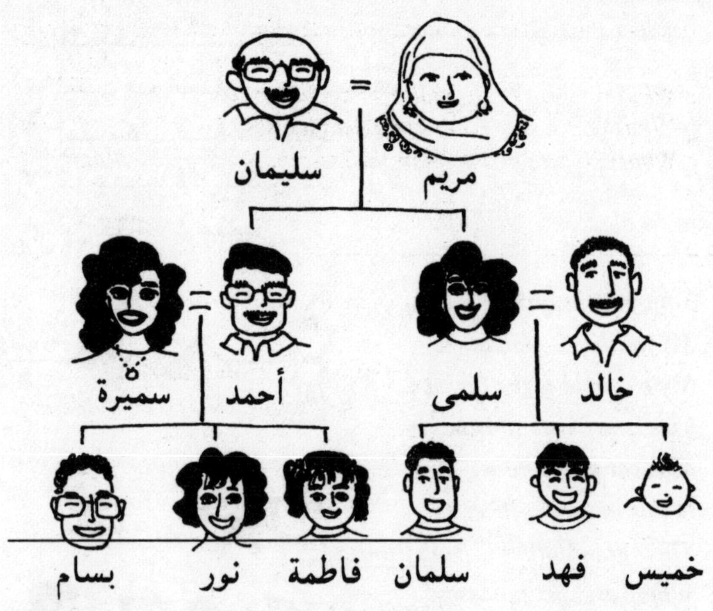

i *Imagine that you are Salma, and answer the questions.*

Example: من أخوك **man akhúu-ki** *Who is your brother?*

Answer: أخي أحمد **ákh-ii áHmad** *My brother is Ahmed.*

من **man** *who?*

a Who is your husband?; b Who is your mother?;
c Who are your children?

ii *What relation are the following people to Ahmed?*

Example: سميرة **samíirah**

Answer: هي زوجته **híya záwjat-uh** *She is his wife.*

a Bassam; b Fatima; c Suleiman; d Salma

iii Answer the following questions in Arabic.

a What relation is Fatimah to Fahad?;
b What relation is Khalid to Bassam?;
c What relation is Suleiman to Bassam, Noor and Fatima?

---

10 things you need to know

1 *With the exception of the number 20,* **:ishríin**, *the Arabic numeral tens are formed from the unit words by removing the* **-ah** *ending and adding* **-iin**.
2 *In Arabic, units are placed before the tens, as in* five-and-twenty, *like the blackbirds in the pie of the nursery rhyme.*
3 *Remember that the counted noun is in the singular, with the accusative marker if necessary.*
4 *In describing who or what belongs to someone or something, English uses a possessive pronoun such as* his, my, our. *Arabic uses a pronoun suffix, added to the end of the word, so* my house *becomes* **bayt-ii** house-my.
5 *Nouns with these pronoun suffixes are regarded as definite, since we are talking of a specific person or thing, and adjectives describing them must have the definite article* **al** the.
6 *The common feminine noun and adjective ending* **-ah** ـة *is written with a hybrid letter* **-h** ـه *and the two dots of a* **-t** ت. *This is called the 'hidden* **t**'.
7 *When a possessive pronoun suffix is added, the ending is written as and pronounced as a* **-t** ـتـ *which is then followed by the suffix ending.* Her car *is* **sayyaarat-haa** سيارتها. *This is why it is called the 'hidden* **t**'.
8 *If you want to say something* is not, *use the special verb* **laysa** *before a masculine noun.*
9 *Use* **laysat** *before a feminine noun.*
10 *The words* **akh** brother *and* **ab** father *take a long* **-uu** *before all the possessive suffixes except* **-ii** my, *as in* **abuu-haa** her father *and* **akh-ii** my brother.

6

أين وسط المدينة؟
áyna wásT al-madíinah?
Where is the town centre?

In this unit you will learn:

- ***to give simple directions***
- ***about more places in town and their location***
- ***to say what belongs to whom***

---

1 أين وسط المدينة من فضلك

áyna wásT al-madíinah, min fáDl-ak

Where is the town centre, please?

CD2, TR05

Andy Fraser, a Scot working in Jordan, has to go to a small town near Amman to visit a client. He stops a passer-by to ask directions.

Exercise 1

Listen to the recording once, then answer these questions.

a What does Andy say to get the man's attention?

b Is the first thing Andy has to look out for:

i a mosque?

ii traffic lights?

iii King Hussein Street?

c In which direction should he turn at the traffic lights?

Listen to the recording again.

d How far should he go along the street?

e What is the office next to?

f Is the car park:

i on the left?

ii on the right?

iii behind the office?

Now read the dialogue.

أندي	عن إذنك! أين وسط المدينة؟
الرجل	على طول. إلى أين تذهب؟
أندي	أذهب إلى مكتب علي المبروك. هل تعرفه؟ هذه هي خريطة المدينة.
الرجل	نعم، أعرفه. خلني أفكر. نعم هو هنا. بعد الجامع الكبير لف شمال عند الإشارة. هذا شارع الملك حسين. إذهب على طول حوالي ١٠٠ متر.
أندي	نعم، أنا فاهم.
الرجل	مكتب علي المبروك على اليمين، بجانب محطة البنزين، أمام سينما البلازا
أندي	نعم، أشكرك. هل هناك موقف للسيارات؟
الرجل	نعم، هناك موقف كبير للسيارات وراء مكتب علي المبروك.
أندي	شكرا جزيلا!
الرجل	عفوا!

Exercise 2

Link the English phrases with the equivalent Arabic expressions:

a	*excuse me*	أنا فاهم	١
b	*straight ahead*	على طول	٢
c	*let me think*	لف شمال	٣
d	*turn left*	هل هناك موقف للسيارات؟	٤
e	*on the right*	خلني أفكر	٥
f	*I understand*	على اليمين	٦
g	*Is there a car park there?*	عن إذنك	٧

QUICK VOCAB

عن إذنك **:an ídhn-ak** *excuse me* [lit., by your leave]

وسط **wásT** *centre* (of town, etc.)

مدينة، مدن **madíinah, múdun** *town, city*

رجل، رجال **rájul, rijáal** *man*

على طول **:ála Tuul** *straight ahead*

تذهب **tádh-hab** *you go* (to a man)

أذهب **ádh-hab** *I go*

مكتب، مكاتب **máktab, makáatib** *office*

تعرفه **tá:raf-uh** *you* (m.) *know it/him*

أعرفه **á:raf-uh** *I know it/him*

خلني أفكر **khallí-nii ufákkir** *let me think*

جامع، جوامع **jáami:, jawáami:** *main mosque*

لف **liff** *turn!* (to a man)

شمال **shamáal** *left* (side)

عند **:ind** *at*

إشارة، ـــات **isháarah, -aat** *(traffic) signal*

ملك، ملوك **málik, mulúuk** *king*

إذهب **ídh-hab** *go!* (to a man)

حوالي **Hawáalii** *approximately, about*

متر، أمتار **mitr, amtáar** *metre*

فاهم **fáahim** *understanding*

يمين **yamíin** *right* (side)

بجانب **bi-jáanib** *next to, beside*

محطة، ـــات **maHáTTah, -aat** *station*

بنزين **banzíin** *petrol*

أمام **amáam** *in front of*

سينما ، سينمات **síinamaa, siinamáat** *cinema*

أشكرك **ashkúr-ak** *thank you* [lit. I thank you: to a man]

موقف، مواقف **máwqif, mawáaqif** *stopping, parking place*

وراء **waráa'** *behind*

شكرا جزيلا **shúkran jazíilan** *thank you very much*; *many thanks*

عفوا **:áfwan** *you're welcome*

QUICK VOCAB

---

2 في المدينة fi l-madíinah
In the town

CD2, TR06

Look at the town map on the following page and read through the names of all the places.

Then listen to the recording to hear how they are pronounced.

1 سوق الذهب **suuq adh-dháhab** *gold market*
2 مطعم **máT:am** *restaurant*
3 فندق **fúnduq** *hotel*
4 محطة الباص **maHáTTat al-báaS** *bus station*
5 الخور **al-khawr** *the creek*
6 سوق السمك **suuq as-sámak** *fish market*
7 مركز الشرطة **márkaz ash-shúrTah** *police station*
8 بنك الشارقة **bank as-sháariqah** *Bank of Sharjah*

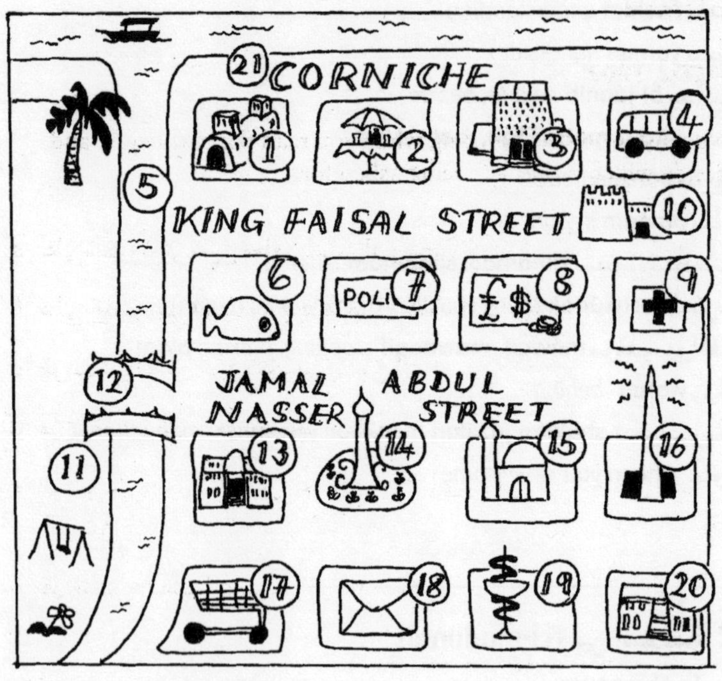

9 مستشفى **mustáshfaa** *hospital*
10 الحصن القديم **al-HiSn al-qadíim** *the old fort*
11 حديقة **Hadíiqah** *park, garden*
12 جسر **jisr** *bridge*
13 البلدية **al-baladíyyah** *town hall*
14 ميدان **maydáan** *square*
15 جامع **jáami:** *mosque*
16 برج الاتصالات **burj al-ittiSáalaat** *communications tower*
17 سوبرماركت **suubarmáarkit** *supermarket*
18 مكتب البريد **máktab al-baríid** *post office*
19 صيدلية **Saydalíyyah** *pharmacy*
20 مركز التسوق **márkaz at-tasáwwuq** *shopping centre*
21 الكورنيش **al-koorníish** *the Corniche*

Exercise 3

🔊 **CD2, TR07**

Now listen to the recording while you read the text below and decide which places are being asked for.

a على الكورنيش، بين مطعم شهرزاد ومحطة الباص

b على اليمين في الميدان، بجانب برج الاتصالات

c قريب من الخور، بين الجسر وسوق الذ هب

d بين السوبرماركت وصيدلية ابن سينا

e اذهب على طول في شارع جمال عبد الناصر وهو على الشمال بعد الجسر.

f في شارع الملك فيصل، وراء المستشفى

تعبيرات رئيسية **ta:biiráat ra'iisíyyah** (Key phrases)

Asking and giving simple directions

أين الفندق؟ **áyna l-fúnduq**	*Where is the hotel?*
لف يمين **liff yamíin**	*Turn right*
اذهب على طول **ídh-hab :ála Tuul**	*Go straight ahead*
على اليمين **:ála l-yamíin**	*On the right*
بجانب مكتب البريد **bi-jáanib máktab al-baríid**	*Beside, next to the post office*
أمام محطة الباص **amáama maHáTTat al-baaS**	*Opposite, in front of the bus station*
وراء البنك **waráa' al-bank**	*Behind the bank*

بين الصيدلية ومحطة البنزين **báyna aS-Saydalíyyah wa-maHáTTat al-banzíin**	*Between the pharmacy and the petrol station*
بعد الجسر **ba:d al-jisr**	*After the bridge*

تراكيب اللغة **taraakíib al-lúghah** (Structures)

1 Possessives with two nouns

Possessive constructions have two elements: the possessor, or owner, and the thing possessed, or property. In 'the doctor's car' the doctor is the *owner* and the car is the *property*.

Owner (of)	*Property*
The doctor's	car

The most usual way to say this in English is by the use of an apostrophe s: 's, as above, in which case the order is *owner* before *property*. However, sometimes we use the word *of* and reverse the order:

Property	*(of)*	*Owner*
The title	of	the book
The Dogs	of	War

Arabic is similar to the above, except that:

a no word for of *is used*

b The first possessed noun (title, Dogs*)* never *has the definite article* **al-**. *So the normal form in Arabic looks like this:*

noun without **al-**	*followed by*	*noun with al-*
máktab		**al-mudíir**
office		(of) *the manager*
(the possessed object)		(the owner/possessor)

al-maktab al-mudíir does not make sense to an Arab.

c If the first (possessed) noun has the feminine ending ـة *this is pronounced* **-t** *but – unlike with the possessive pronouns in Unit 5 – does not change its form when written. This is because it is still at the end of a word.*

سيارة محمد **sayyáarat muHámmad** *Mohammed's car*

Insight

The second element of a possessive may also be a proper name.

Saydalíyyat sáarah
Sarah's pharmacy

d With the exception of the demonstratives this, that, *etc, no word may be inserted between the two nouns, so any additional words such as adjectives have to come at the end (see also below).*

Insight

Possessives are frequently used in Arabic to associate two concepts that English would express in another way.

márkaz ash-shúrTah	مركز الشرطة
station [lit., centre] (of) the-police	*the police station*
maHáTTat al-baaS	محطة الباص
station (of) the-bus	*the bus station*

2 Proper names

You will remember that all proper names are regarded as definite, whether or not they begin with the definite article **al-**, *the*, such as القاهرة **al-qáahirah**, *Cairo*. In either case they refer to a specific person or place.

بيت أحمد **bayt áHmad**	*Ahmed's house*
جامعة القاهرة **jáami:at al-qáahirah**	*University of Cairo, Cairo University*

3 Simple sentences

The formula *definite + indefinite* gives a simple sentence in Arabic (see Unit 2) implying the word *is/are* in English. Since nearly all possessive constructions are by nature definite (see above), you can use them in the same way. The last part of the sentence can be a simple adjective (e.g. *Muhammad's house is big*), but can also be a phrase with a preposition (using words such as *in*, *under*, *on*, etc.), telling you where something is located:

jáami:at al-qáahirah kabíirah	جامعة القاهرة كبيرة
university (of)(the) Cairo (is) big	*Cairo University is big*
bayt muHámmad qaríib	بيت محمد قريب
house (of) muHammad (is) near	*Muhammad's house is near*
bayt muHámmad fii wásT al-madíinah	بيت محمد في وسط المدينة
house (of) muHammad (is) in (the) centre (of) the-town	*Muhammad's house is in the centre of town*

4 Word order and adjectives

Because nothing except the demonstratives can come between the two parts of a possessive, any other words introduced into the sentence must be placed elsewhere.

If any adjectives are applied to either of the terms in a possessive construction, these must come at the end. The possessive construction must not be split up.

If both possessive terms are of the same gender, it will strike you that these adjectives placed at the end of the phrase might describe either of the possessive terms. However, the context usually makes everything clear:

wazíir ad-daakhilíyyah al-jadíid	وزير الداخلية الجديد
minister (of) the-interior the-new	*the new minister of the interior*
wizáarat al-:adl al-jadíidah	وزارة العدل الجديدة
ministry (of) the-justice the-new	*the new ministry of justice*
kútub al-ustáadh al-jadíidah	كتب الأستاذ الجديدة
books (of) the-professor the-new	*the professor's new books*

Insight

Ministries, embassies and government departments usually have the possessive construction, with the hidden **-t**. وزارة **wizáarah**, *ministry* is derived from وزير **wazíir**, *minister*, and is the origin of the English word *vizier*:

وزارة السياحة **wizáarat as-siyáaHah**	*the ministry of tourism*
وزارة التعليم قريبة من الميدان **wizáarat at-ta:líim qaríibah min al-maydáan**	*the ministry of education is near the square*
دائرة المرور **dáa'irat al-murúur**	*the traffic department*

If the name of a country is mentioned, place the nationality adjective after the noun, in which case there is no hidden **-t**.

Insight

سفارة **sifáarah**, *embassy* comes from سفير **safíir**, *ambassador* (which is derived in turn from **sáfar** *travel*, the origin of the word *safari*).

السفارة البريطانية **as-sifáarah al-briiTaaníyyah**	*the British embassy*
السفارة الامريكية **as-sifáarah al-amriikíyyah**	*the American embassy*

5 Demonstratives with possessives

Demonstratives (*this*, *that*, *those*, etc.) are the only words that can go between the two terms of a possessive:

a If the this word applies to the second (possessor) word, it goes between, usually taking the form: noun without **al-** *+ this + noun with* **al-***:*

qálam háadhaa t-tilmíidh قلم هذا التلميذ
pen (of) this(person) the-pupil *this pupil's pen*

b) If the this word applies to the first (possessed) word, it comes at the end: noun without **al-** *+ noun with* **al-** *+ this:*

sayyáarat al-mudíir haadhíhi سيارة المدير هذه
car (of) the-manager this (one) *this car of the manager's*

In both cases, the demonstrative must agree in gender with the word to which it applies.

أوزان الكلمات awzáan al-kalimáat (Word shapes)

CD2, TR08

The word pattern for this unit is **C¹iC²aaC³ah**, for example, **wizáarah** وزارة, *ministry*, which sounds like the English *banana*.

This type of noun is usually derived from a word of the **CaCíiC** shape (see Unit 1), which refers to a man. Its meaning is the place in which he operates. Thus, as we have seen above, a وزير **wazíir**, *minister*, operates from a وزارة **wizáarah**, *ministry*, and a سفير **safíir**, *ambassador*, from a سفارة **sifáarah**, *embassy*.

Insight

In the Gulf, the Emirates (**imaaráat**, plural of إمارة **imáarah**) are so named because they were each originally ruled by an أمير **amíir**, *emir/prince*.

The shape is also used for some nouns derived from verbs, e.g. كتابة **kitáabah**, *writing*, and قراءة **qiráa'ah**, *reading*.

تمرينات tamriináat (Practice)

Exercise 4

Fit the two words together to make places found around an Arab city.

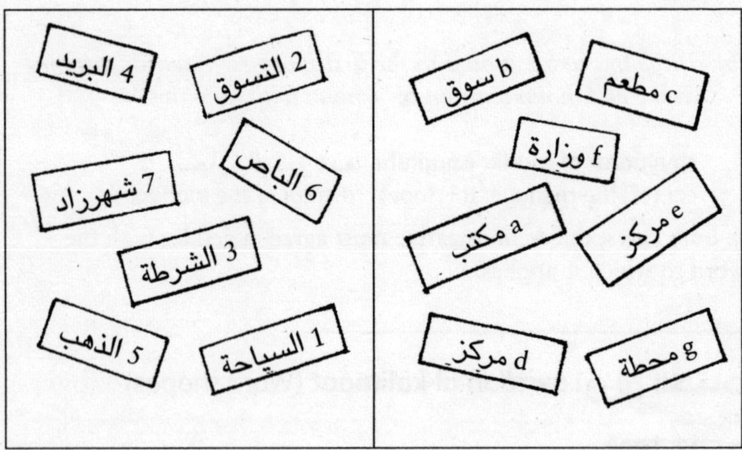

Exercise 5

🔈 CD2, TR09

Ask where the following places are. Check your answers with the recording or the transcript:

a *the town hall*
b *the police station*
c *al-Bustan shopping centre*
d *King Faisal Street*
e *Sheherazade restaurant*

Exercise 6

🔊 CD2, TR10

Now look at the town map in Dialogue 2 and imagine that you are walking down the street and someone asks you the way. Give directions to the places in Exercise 5, using the Key phrases on page 112 to help you. Possible answers are given on the recording or transcript.

Exercise 7
Combine a noun from each column, to form a possessive construction.

Example: *boy – bicycle*

عجلة الولد **:ajalat al-walad** *the boy's bicycle*

عجلة، ـــات **:ájalah, -aat** *bicycle*

a bank – manager
b town – centre
c country – capital
d company – office
e Rashid – sister

عاصمة، عواصم **:áaSimah, :awáaSim*** *capital* (political)
شركة، ـــات **shárikah, -aat** *company* (commercial)
بلد، بلاد/بلدان **balad, biláad/buldáan** *country, nation*

Exercise 8
Now make *is/are* sentences from the words below, making sure that the adjectives agree.

Example: *watch – Faisal – new* ➔ ساعة فيصل جديدة
(Faisal's watch is new)

1 *streets – Abu Dhabi – wide*
2 *University – Cairo – big*
3 *gardens – palace – beautiful*
4 *rooms – apartment – spacious*
5 *cuisine – Morocco – delicious*
6 *shops – market – small*

QUICK VOCAB

عريض **:ariiD** *wide*
قصر، قصور **qaSr, quSúur** *palace*
غرفة، غرف **ghúrfah, ghúraf** *room*
شقة، شقق **sháqqah, shíqaq** *flat, apartment*
واسع **wáasi:** *roomy, spacious*
طبيخ **Tabíikh** *cooking, cuisine*
لذيذ **ladhíidh** *delicious, tasty*
دكان، دكاكين **dukkáan, dakaakíin** *small shop, stall*

Exercise 9
Saalim's mother is trying to tidy up the boys' bedroom and she asks Saalim what belongs to him and what to his brother Tamim. Complete the sentences using the correct possessive construction.

Example:
أهذا قميصك؟ لا، هذا قميص تميم.
Is this your shirt? No, it's Tamim's shirt.

a أهذا حزامك؟ نعم هذا ...
b أهذه جواربك؟ لا، هذه ...
c أذلك منديلك؟ نعم، ذلك ...
d أهذه نظارتك؟ نعم، هذه ...
e أهذا بنطلونك؟ لا، هذا ...

10 things you need to know

1 *In English, there are two possible ways to express possession. We can use an 's, or the word* of, *for example,* Salim's house *and* the door of the house.

2 *Arabic possessives resemble the* 'door of the house' *type, with the possessed object coming first and the possessor coming second.*

3 *There is no word for* of.

4 *The first word must not have* **al-** *the, so* 'the door of the house' *is* **bab al-bayt**, *literally* 'door the-house'.

5 *No word other than the demonstratives* this, that, *etc. can come in between the two elements, e.g.* **bab haadhaa al-bayt** the door of this house.

6 *Don't forget that the property comes before the owner.*

7 *Remember that all possessive constructions are regarded as definite, for the logical reason that e.g.* my book *refers to a single specific book (mine, and nobody else's).*

8 *Proper names are regarded as definite, whether they have the word* **al-** *or not, because they are again referring to a specific person or place, as in* **al-kuwayt** Kuwait, **baghdaad** Baghdad.

9 *Whether something is definite or indefinite is very important in Arabic, e.g. because of agreement of adjectives, and subjects of* is/are *sentences are definite.*

10 *To summarise, the definites are words with* the, *proper nouns which are always spelled with a capital letter in English, possessive phrases regarded as a whole unit, and pronouns* I, you, *etc.*

7

ماذا فعلت؟
máadhaa fa:ált?
What did you do?

In this unit you will learn:

- ***how to talk about things that happened in the past***
- ***about means of transport***
- ***about Arabic verbs***
- ***how to say 'me', 'him', 'them', etc.***

1 أخي فهد ákhii fahd

My brother, Fahd

CD2, TR11

Samira, a Kuwaiti girl, writes to a friend to tell her about her brother who was working abroad.

Exercise 1

Listen to the recording while you read the letter and say whether the following are true or false:

a Her brother went to Amman in May.
b He wrote to Samira every week.
c He returned to Kuwait in September.

سافر إلى عمان في شهر مارس وعمل في مكتب شركته في الأردن. سكن عند عمي. كتبنا له رسالة كل أسبوع. رجع إلى الكويت في شهر سبتمبر.

Exercise 2

Link the English phrases with the equivalent Arabic:

a	*He worked in the office.*	سكن عند عمي.	١
b	*He stayed with my uncle.*	كتبنا له رسالة كل أسبوع.	٢
c	*We wrote him a letter every week.*	عمل في المكتب.	٣

QUICK VOCAB

سافر **sáafara** *to travel*

شهر، شهور/أشهر **shahr, shuhúur/ásh-hur** *month*

مارس **maars** *March*

عمل **:ámila** *to work, do*

سكن **sákana** *to reside, live*

رسالة، رسائل **risáalah, rasáa'il** *letter, message*

كل **kull** *every, each*

أسبوع أسابيع **usbúu: asaabíi:** *week*

رجع **rája:a** *to return, come/go back*

سبتمبر **sabtámbar** *September**

*A full list of the Christian and Islamic months is given in Unit 11.

2 ماذا فعلت أمس؟ máadhaa fa:ált ams?

What did you do yesterday?

CD2, TR12

Zaki, a student at the college in Cairo, asks Sonya, an English friend, what she did the day before.

Exercise 3

Listen to the conversation, and answer the questions.

a *How did Sonya go to Ahmed's house?*
b *Who lives with Ahmed and his wife?*
c *Do they live in:*
i Zamalek? *ii Maadi?* *iii Helwan?*

Listen to the recording again.

d *Did they eat:*
i breakfast? *ii lunch?* *iii dinner?*
e *Who cooked the meal?*
f *Did they have:*
i Arabic coffee? *ii Turkish coffee?* *iii American coffee?*
g *Did Sonya get home:*
i by taxi? *ii by bus?* *iii by car?*

زكي	ماذا فعلت أمس؟
سونية	أمس ذهبت إلى بيت أحمد
زكي	كيف ذهبت إلى هناك؟
سونية	ذهبت بالتاكسي. هو وعائلته يسكنون في الزمالك.
زكي	ماذا فعلتم؟
سونية	قابلت والده ووالدته وأخواته. طبخت والدته الغداء. بعد الغداء شربنا قهوة عربية.
زكي	وهل أعجبتك؟
سونية	نعم، هي لذيذة.
زكي	هل رجعت بالتاكسي؟
سونية	لا، ما رجعت بالتاكسي. أحمد وصلني إلى البيت في سيارته.

Link the English phrases with the Arabic equivalents.

١	كيف ذهبت إلى هناك؟	*h*	*yesterday*
٢	هل أعجبتك؟	*i*	*How did you go there?*
٣	وصلني إلى البيت.	*j*	*I went by taxi*
٤	أمس	*k*	*Did you like it?*
٥	ذهبت بالتاكسي.	*l*	*He gave me a lift home*

QUICK VOCAB

فعل **fá:ala** *to do*

ذهب **dháhaba** *to go*

عائلة، ـات **:áa'ilah, -aat** *family*

يسكنون **yaskunúun** *they live, reside, stay*

قابل **qáabala** *to meet, encounter*

طبخ **Tábakha** *to cook*

غداء **ghadáa'** *lunch*

شرب **shármba** *to drink*

قهوة **qáhwah** *coffee*

هل أعجبتك **hal a:jábat-ik** *did you* (f.) *like it* (f.)*?*

ما **maa** *not*

وصل **wáSSala** *to transport, take, give a lift*

تعبيرات رئيسية **ta:biiráat ra'iisíyyah** (Key phrases)

Talking about how you travelled

He travelled to Jeddah… سافر إلى جدة...:

by car	بالسيارة
by plane	بالطائرة
by bus/coach	بالباص
by train	بالقطار
by taxi	بالتاكسي
by ship	بالسفينة

Further expressions of time

I met him… قابلته:

last night	أمس بالليل
last week/month	الأسبوع/الشهر الماضي
last year	السنة الماضية
three years ago	قبل ثلاث سنوات
in 1995	في سنة ١٩٩٥
a week/month ago	قبل أسبوع/شهر
a year ago	قبل سنة

تراكيب اللغة **taraakíib al-lúghah** (Structures)

1 The Arabic verb: general

The Arabic verb differs from the English verb in two ways:

a *It has only two tenses (i.e. ways to express when an action took place):*
- *the* past *tense is used for all* completed *actions*
- *the* present *tense is used for all actions* not yet complete.

b *Most verbs can be reduced to a* past stem *and a* present stem *and a standard set of prefixes and suffixes can be added to these stems to form meaningful words.*

Arabic verbs fit into a limited number of categories, but there are virtually no truly irregular verbs in Arabic – apparent irregularities can usually be explained by the occurrence of the weak letters **waaw** and **yaa'** as one of the letters in the stem. (For further details, see Verb tables.)

Insight

There is no Arabic equivalent of the English infinitive *to do*, *to speak*, etc. Instead, Arabic verbs are given in the *he* form of the past tense, because this part is the simplest form of the verb, with no written suffixes or prefixes. It often also constitutes the past stem, from which which all other parts of the past tense can be formed.

So when we give a verb as, for example, **kátaba**, *to write*, the part we give actually means *he wrote*.

In the box below, we have given the suffix endings separated by a hyphen from the past stem of the verb **kátaba** so that you can learn them more easily. The verb **kátaba** belongs to Type **S-I** in the Verb tables. The root **k-t-b** indicates *writing*.

Note: study the following in conjunction with the S section of the Verb tables, which contains further information.

2 Past tense

Singular	*Plural*
كتب **kátab(a)** *he wrote*	كتبوا **kátab-uu** *they* (m.) *wrote*
كتبت **kátab-at** *she wrote*	كتبن **katáb-na** *they* (f.) *wrote*
كتبت **katáb-t(a)** *you* (m.) *wrote*	كتبتم **katáb-tum** *you* (m.) *wrote*
كتبت **katáb-ti** *you* (f.) *wrote*	كتبتن **katab-túnna** *you* (f.) *wrote*
كتبت **katáb-t(u)** *I wrote*	كتبنا **katáb-na(a)** *we wrote*

Note: the final vowels in brackets are usually omitted in informal speech.

Here is a list of some commonly used verbs. Remember that these are all in the *he* form of the past tense and, in the past tense, they can all be formed in the same way as **kátaba**.

Note: some verbs must be used in conjunction with a preposition. This is given after the verb.

لذهب **dháhaba** *go*
سافر **sáafara** *travel*
وصل **wáSala** *arrive*
رجع **rája:a** *return, go back*
عمل **:ámila** *do, work*
تفرج على **tafárraja :álaa**
watch, spectate

خبر **khábbara** *tell, inform*
قابل **qáabala** *meet*
غسل **ghásala** *wash*
غادر **gháadara** *leave, depart*
كلم **kállama** *speak to*
وجد **wájada** *find*
قرأ **qára'a** *read*

فعل **fá:ala** *do, act*

ركب **rákiba** *ride*

سكن **sákana** *live, reside*

أكل **'ákala** *eat*

شرب **sháriba** *drink*

لعب **lá:iba** *play*

طبخ **Tábakha** *cook*

شاهد **sháahada** *see, look at*

وضع **wáDa:a** *put, place*

قرأ **qára'a** *read*

رقص **ráqaSa** *dance*

دخل **dákhala** *enter*

خرج **kháraja** *go out (of)*

كسر **kásara** *break*

تأخر **ta'ákhkhara** *be late*

فتح **fátaHa** *open*

قفل **qáfala** *close*

Insight: Noun and pronoun subjects

The subject of a verb is the person or thing which performs the action. It is important in Arabic to distinguish between noun and pronoun subjects.

1 Verbs with pronoun subjects

When you say *they arrived*, *he said*, *it opened*, you are using a pronoun subject and the suffix ending of the verb indicates who or what the subject is. The separate pronouns, which you learned in Unit 2, are not normally used with verbs, except for emphasis:

waSalat min al-maghrib ams She-arrived from Morocco yesterday	وصلت من المغرب أمس *She arrived from Morocco yesterday*
saafara ila r-ribaaT al-usbuu: al-maaDii He-travelled to Rabat last week	سافر إلى الرباط الأسبوع الماضي *He travelled to Rabat last week*

2 Verbs with noun subjects

When the subject of a sentence is specified by means of a noun (*the workmen arrived, Ahmed said*):

a *the verb usually comes first, followed by the subject*

b the verb is always in the he *or* she *form, no matter what the subject.*

In English, we usually say who or what we are talking about (the subject), then go on to say what the subject did (the verb) and follow this with any other information such as who or what he did it to, where and when he did it (the object or predicate), so that the word order is usually *subject–verb–the rest*:

Subject	*Verb*	*Object/predicate*
The man	wrote	the letter.

The normal word order in Arabic is *verb–subject–the rest.*

Verb	*Subject*	*Object/predicate*
كتب الرجل الرسالة		
kataba	**r-rajul**	**ar-risaalah**
wrote(-he)	*the man*	*the letter*
سافرت المدرسة مع تلامذتها		
saafarat	**al-mudarrisah**	**ma:a talaamidhat-haa**
travelled (-she)	*the teacher*	*with her students*
وصلت الطائرة الصبح		
waSalat	**aT-Taa'irah**	**S-SubH**
arrived (-she)	*the plane*	*in the morning*
دخل الوزراء القصر		
dakhala	**l-wuzaraa'**	**al-qaSr**
entered (-he)	*the ministers*	*the palace*

The fact that the verb in these cases is either in the *he* or *she* form, i.e. always singular, never plural, should be noted carefully. Remember that the plural of things (inanimate objects or abstracts) is regarded as feminine *singular*, so that the rule for verbs which precede their subjects looks like this:

Subject	Example	Verb
One or more male human beings; singular inanimate noun of m. gender	*man, boys, book*	*he* form
one or more female human beings; singular inanimate noun of f. gender; plural of inanimate noun of either gender	*woman, girls, car, books, cars*	*she* form

3 Saying 'not'

To negate something that happened in the past, the word **maa,** *not* can be placed before the verb:

maa sharibt al-qahwah ما شربت القهوة

Not I-drank the-coffee *I didn't drink the coffee*

Exercise 4
Turn the following sentences into negatives:

a *The aeroplane was late* تأخرت الطائرة

b *The workmen spoke to the boss* كلم العمال الرئيس

c *I ate the bread* أكلت الخبز

QUICK VOCAB

طائرة، ـات **Táa'irah, -aat** *aeroplane*

عامل، عمال **:áamil, :ummáal** *workman*

رئيس، رؤساء **ra'íis, ru'asáa'** *boss, chief*

خبز **khubz** *bread*

4 Sentences in which the verb comes after the subject

The *verb–subject–rest* word order given above is the most common in Arabic, but it is possible to have verbs that come after their subjects. This occurs most frequently in sentences with more than one verb, e.g. *The workmen arrived on the site and started to dig the foundations.*

If a sentence starting with a noun subject has more than one verb, the first one comes before the noun subject and obeys the *he/she* form agreement rule above, and any subsequent verb comes *after* the subject and must agree with it completely, in number (singular or plural) and gender (male or female).

So if the subject refers to men, the second and any subsequent verbs must end in **-uu** (masculine plural). If it refers to women, it must end in **-na** (feminine plural). The plural of things, regarded as feminine singular, will have the ending **-at** on both verbs:

وصل العمال وصلحوا الباب **wáSala l-:ummaal wa-SallaHuu l-baab**	*The workmen arrived and mended the door*
دخلت البنات الغرفة وشربن القهوة **dakhalat al-banaat al-ghurfah wa-sharibna l-qahwah**	*The girls entered the room and drank the coffee*
وقعت الكتب من الرف وأصابت المدرس **waqa:at al-kutub min ar-raff wa-aSaabat al-mudarris**	*The books fell from the shelf and struck the teacher*

وقع **wáqa:a** *to fall*

رف، رفوف **raff, rufúuf** *shelf*

أصاب **aSáaba** *to hit, strike*

5 'It', 'him', 'me' – object pronouns

To say *me*, *it*, *them*, Arabic uses – with one exception – the same pronoun suffixes as the possessive pronoun suffixes that mean *my*, *his*, *our* (see Unit 5).

They are added to the verb to express the object of the sentence, to which the action of the verb is applied:

Singular	*Plural*
ني **-nii** *me*	ـنا **-naa** *us*
ـك **-ak** *you* (to a man)	ـكم **-kum** *you* (to men)
ـك **-ik** *your* (to a woman)	ـكن **-kúnna** *you* (to women)
ـه **-uh** *him*	ـهم **-hum** *them* (men)
ـها **-haa** *her*	ـهن **-húnna** *them* (women)

Insight

As the above table shows, the only one that differs is the suffix for *me*, which is ـني **-nii** after verbs (as opposed to ـي **-ii** after other types of word).

خبرني ناصر *Nasser told me*
khabbara-nii naaSir

كلمته أمس *I spoke to him yesterday*
kallamt-uh ams

قابلناهم في السوق *We met them in the souq*
qaabalnaa-hum fi s-suuq

When **-ak** and **-uh** come after a vowel, they are reduced to **-k** and **-h** respectively and **-ik** becomes **-ki**. This is another example of elision:

شاهدناك **shaahadnáa-k/ki** *We saw you* (m./f.)

شربوه **sharibúu-h** *They* (m.) *drank it*

Insight

The masculine plural ending **-uu** is written with a 'silent' **alif** at the end (ـوا – see Verb tables). This is omitted when any suffix is joined on to the verb.

Pronunciation – elision

Here are some more conventions of Arabic pronunciation. They will help to polish your Arabic.

1 Definition of elision

Elision usually means in Arabic that a preceding vowel swallows up a following one.

al- *the* becomes **l-** after vowels:

صلحوا الباب **SállaHuu l-baab** *They repaired the gate*

Elision also occurs with the sun letters (see Unit 1):

صلحوا السيارة **SállaHuu s-sayyáarah** *They repaired the car*

2 Elision of fii

When the word **fii**, *in*, precedes **al-**, *the*, the **a** of **al-** omitted and the vowel of **fii** is shortened to make **fi**. Technically, this applies to all words ending in long vowels, but it is most noticeable with **fii**:

في البيت **fi l-bayt** *in the house*

3 Initial i

Standard Arabic does not allow words to begin with two consonants like English does (e.g. *trip*, *blank*). Instead it adds an

i- vowel prefix (in Arabic, expressed by an **alif** with an **i** vowel below it). In practice, however, this vowel sign is rarely written:

اِجتماع **ijtimáa:**	meeting

When this vowel is preceded by a word ending in a vowel, the **i** vowel is elided: واجتماع **wa-ijtimáa:**, *and (a) meeting*, is pronounced **wa-jtimaa:**. This is a refinement in pronunciation and it will do no harm if you fail to observe it meticulously.

Insight

Some words beginning with **alif** use this to carry a radical **hamzah** (i.e. one which is part of the root) and this should *not* be elided. This kind of **hamzah** is quite often – but not always – marked in print and we have tried to follow the Arab convention:

أكل **ákala**	*he ate*
أمير **amíir**	*prince, Emir*
أخذ **ákhadha**	*he took*

أوزان الكلمات **awzáan al-kalimáat** (Word shapes)

CD2, TR13

The word pattern for this unit is **taC¹áaC²uC³**, for example, **ta:áawun** تعاون *cooperation*, which sounds like the English *to our one*.

More examples are:

تكاتب **takáatub**	*correspondence, writing to each other*
تفاهم **tafáahum**	*mutual understanding*

تضامن **taDáamun** *solidarity*

تبادل **tabáadul** *exchange, exchanging*

If you look at the nature of the meaning of all these nouns, you will see that they all carry the idea of doing something with someone else.

تمرينات tamriináat (Practice)

Exercise 5

How did Mohammed travel to Cairo? Match the Arabic phrases to the pictures .

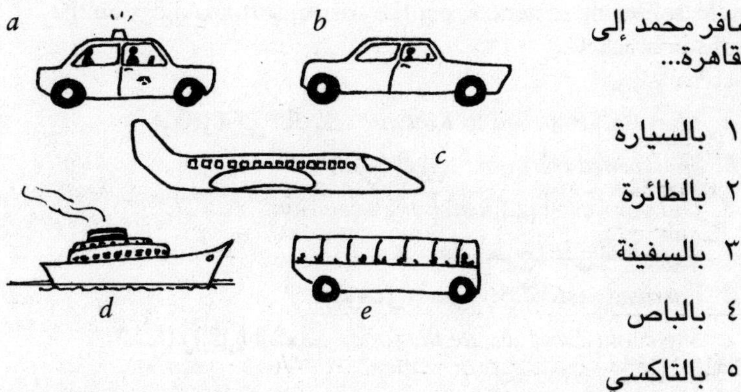

سافر محمد إلى القاهرة...

١ بالسيارة

٢ بالطائرة

٣ بالسفينة

٤ بالباص

٥ بالتاكسي

Exercise 6

Who did what? Match the Arabic to the English sentences.

a	*We read the newspapers.*	دخلنا الغرفة.	١
b	*She put her bag on the table.*	وجدت المفاتيح في جيبي.	٢
c	*We entered the room.*	وضعت حقيبتها على المائدة.	٣
d	*You* (m. sing.) *wrote a letter.*	وصلوا إلى مطار البحرين.	٤
e	*He lived in London.*	خرجتن من الفندق.	٥

f *You* (f. pl.) *came out of the hotel.* ٦ كتبت رسالة.

g *I found the keys in my pocket.* ٧ سكن في لندن.

h *They* (m.) *arrived at Bahrain Airport.* ٨ قرأنا الجرائد.

QUICK VOCAB

مفتاح، مفاتيح **miftáaH, mafaatíiH** *key*

جيب، جيوب **jayb, juyúub** *pocket*

مائدة، موائد **máa'ida, mawáa'id** *table*

جريدة، جرائد **jaríidah, jaráa'id** *newspaper*

Exercise 7

In the following sentences, put the correct suffix endings on the verbs in brackets.

a *They* (m.) *travelled to Kuwait.* **(سافر)** إلى الكويت.

b *She opened the door.* **(فتح.)** الباب.

c *Did you* (m. sing.) *watch the television?*

هل **(تفرج)** على التلفزيون؟

d *I arrived yesterday.* **(وصل.)** أمس.

e *She cooked and we ate the food.* **(طبخ)** و**(أكل)** الطعام.

Exercise 8

Jim went on holiday to Egypt.

a *Match the drawings with the sentences below.*

b *Write his postcard home for him, putting the verbs in brackets in the* I-*form.*

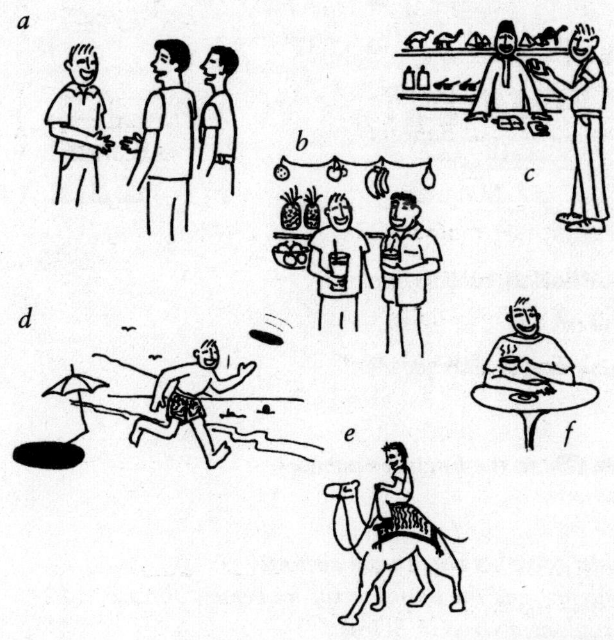

١ (لعب) على الشاطئ
٢ (قابل) شبابا مصريين
٣ (جلس) في الكافيتريا
٤ (ركب) جملا
٥ (شرب) عصيرا
٦ (ذهب) إلى السوق

شاطئ **sháaTi'** *shore, beach*
جمل، جمال **jámal, jimáal** *camel*
شاب، شباب **shaabb, shabáab** *youth/young person*
كافيتريا **kaafitírya** *cafeteria/café*
عصير **:aSíir** *juice*

QUICK VOCAB

Exercise 9

Alter the underlined nouns in the following sentences to object pronouns.

Example: *I met the manager.* → *I met him.*

قابلت المدير. → قابلته.

١ كتبت الرسالة

٢ أكلت التفاحة

٣ كلم الرجال

٤ سألت السؤال

٥ غسلن القمصان

٦ قابل فاطمة في عمان

تفاحة، تفاح **tufáaHah, tufáaH** *apple*

سأل **sá'ala** *to ask*

سؤال، أسئلة **su'áal, ás'ilah** *question*

Exercise 10

Match the Arabic to the English sentences:

a *My wife cooked the food.*
b *The driver took his boss to the airport.*
c *The students read the books in the university library.*
d *The aeroplane arrived in Beirut.*
e *The secretaries drank coffee every day.*

١ قرأ الطلاب الكتب في مكتبة الجامعة.

٢ شربت السكرتيرات قهوة كل يوم.

٣ طبخت زوجتي الطعام.

٤ وصل السائق رئيسه إلى المطار.

٥ وصلت الطائرة إلى بيروت.

سائق، ـون/ساقة **sáa'iq, -úun/sáaqah** *driver*

Exercise 11

Read the passage below and fill the gaps with the correct form of the past tense of the appropriate verb chosen from those in the box below the passage.

ــــــ بيل وميري والأولاد من لندن ــــــ إلى دبي في شهر مارس سنة ٢٠١٠ هناك لمدة أسبوع. ــــــ في شقة كبيرة قريبة من البحر، وــــــ ناسا كثيرين من الإمارات. يوم الاثنين ــــــ بيل تنس، وــــــ ميري إلى الشاطئ. يوم الثلاثاء ــــــ إلى بيت صديقهم منصور، وــــــ لهم زوجته طعاما عربيا.

ذهبت	ووصلوا	سكنوا	سافر	ذهبوا
قابلوا	طبخت	قعدوا	لعب	

قعد **qá:ada** *to stay, remain, sit*

لمدة... **li-múddat...** *for the period of...*

ناس **naas** *people*

تنس **tánis** *tennis*

صديق، أصدقاء **Sadíiq, aSdiqáa'** *friend*

لهم **lá-hum** *for them*

Exercise 12

The following sentences all have the verb (bold type) before the subject. Rewrite them with the verb after the subject, paying attention to the correct agreement.

Example:

رجع المدراء من الاجتماع. ← المدراء رجعوا من الاجتماع.

١ سافر محمد إلى القاهرة.

٢ رجع الأولاد من المدرسة.

٣ حضر المهندسون المؤتمر.

٤ طبخت البنات طعاما عربيا.

٥ وقعت الصحون من المائدة.

QUICK VOCAB

حضر **HáDara** *attend, be present*

مؤتمر، ـات **mu'támar, -áat** *conference*

صحن، صحون **SaHn, SuHúun** *dish*

10 things you need to know

1 *Arabic has only two real tenses, the past and the present. The past tense is used for completed actions, for example,* I spoke, I have spoken, *and the present tense is used for actions that are not yet completed, as in* I speak, I am speaking.

2 *English has many irregular verbs such as* do, did, done. *Arabic has virtually no irregular verbs, but has many different types. The Verb tables at the end of this book are given to help with these.*

3 *All past tenses have the same suffix endings, so it is important to learn these thoroughly.*

4 *There is no equivalent to the English infinitive such as* to speak, to do, *and by convention Arabic verbs are given in the* he- *form of the past tense. This is because it is the simplest form of the verb, with no prefixes or suffixes.*

5 *As with the pronouns, you must remember to distinguish gender in all but the first person (*I *and* we*) forms of the verb.*

6 *In sentences with pronoun subjects, e.g.* you knew, I ate, *the pronoun is usually omitted, because the verb suffix makes it clear who has carried out the action.*

7 *The past tense is negated by using the word* **maa** *before the verb.*

8 *In sentences with noun subjects, e.g.* the women arrived, *the verb precedes the subject and is always in the masculine or feminine singular* **waSalat an-nisaa'**.

9 *If a sentence has two verbs, e.g.* the women arrived and sat down, *the first verb is as above and the second must agree in full* **waSalat an-nisaa' wa-jalasna**.

10 *If the object of a verb is a pronoun,* I saw him, *the same pronoun suffixes are used as for the possessives, except that* **-ii** my *becomes* **-nii** me.

8

كان يا ما كان
kaan yaa maa kaan
Once upon a time

In this unit you will learn:

- ***how to say 'was'/'were'***
- ***how to say 'is/are not'***
- ***how to describe what something was like***
- ***how to say 'became'***
- ***a new type of 'is'/'are' sentence***
- ***how to say you had done something***

---

1 كان يا ما كان kaan yaa maa kaan
Once upon a time

CD2, TR14

In *The Arabian Nights*, or ألف ليلة وليلة **alf laylah wa-laylah** (lit., *a thousand nights and a night*), Princess Sheherazade kept the Sultan from executing her when, for 1001 nights, she told him one tale after another, always ending at an exciting point of the story, so that he had to let her live to tell the rest of the tale the next night.

This is how she introduced the stories of Sindbad the Sailor.

Exercise 1

Listen to the recording of the first part of the introduction below, and answer the questions:

a *Was the porter called:*
i Harun al-Rashid? *ii al-Hindbad?* *iii Sindbad?*
b *Where was the porter going?*
c *Why did he stop?*
d *Did he stop beside:*
i a house *ii a door* *iii a market*
e *What did he ask the servant?*

Now read the beginning of the story.

في أيام الخليفة هارون الرشيد كان في بغداد حمال فقير اسمه الهندباد. وفي يوم من الأيام كان الهندباد هذا يحمل حملا ثقيلا إلى بيت تاجر في السوق. وكان ذلك في الصيف وكانت حرارة الشمس شديدة جدا. وأصبح الهندباد تعبانا وعطشانا. فوقف في الطريق عند باب قصر فخم للاستراحة من عمله. ووضع حمله على الأرض وجلس. وبينما هو جالس هكذا سمع موسيقى جميلة منبعثة من داخل القصر. وكان هناك خادم واقف أمام باب القصر، فسأله الهندباد: من صاحب هذا القصر الفخم؟

Exercise 2

Link the English phrases with the appropriate Arabic expressions:

a *beautiful music*
b *the heat of the sun was very strong*
c *that was in the summer*
d *in the days of the Caliph Harun al-Rashid*
e *in front of the gate of the palace*
f *al-Hindbad became tired*

١ كان ذلك في الصيف

٢ أمام باب القصر

٣ في أيام الخليفة هارون الرشيد

٤ أصبح الهندباد تعبانا

٥ موسيقى جميلة

٦ كانت حرارة الشمس شديدة جدا

QUICK VOCAB

خليفة، خلفاء **khalíifah, khulafáa'** *caliph*, head of the Islamic state (obviously m., despite its ending)
حمال، ـون **Hammáal, -uun** *porter*
فقير، فقراء **faqíir, fuqaráa'** *poor, poor person*
في يوم من الأيام **fii yawm min al-ayyáam** *one day* [lit., 'in a day of the days']
كان ... يحمل **káana ... yáHmil** *he was carrying*
حمل، أحمال **Himl, aHmáal** *load, burden*
ثقيل **thaqíil** *heavy*
تاجر، تجار **táajir, tujjáar** *merchant*
صيف **Sayf** *summer*
حرارة **Haráarah** *heat*
شمس **shams** *sun* (f.)
شديد **shadíid** *strong, mighty*
أصبح **áSbaHa** *become*
تعبان **ta:báan** *tired*
عطشان **:aTsháan** *thirsty*
وقف **wáqafa** *stop, stand*
طريق، طرق **Taríiq, Túruq** *road, way*
باب، أبواب **baab, abwáab** *gate, door*
فخم **fakhm** *magnificent*
للاستراحة **li-l-istiráaHah** *in order to rest* [lit., 'for the resting']
عمل، أعمال **:ámal, a:máal** *work, job, business*
الأرض **al-árD** *the ground, the earth* (f.)

QUICK VOCAB

جلس **jálasa** *sit, sit down*
بينما **báynamaa** *while*
جالس **jáalis** *sitting, seated*
كـ **ka-** *like* (joined to following word)
سمع **sámi:a** *hear, listen*
موسيقى **muusíiqaa** *music* (f.)
منبعث **munbá:ith** *emanating*
داخل **dáakhil** *inside, the inside of something*
خادم، خدام **kháadim, khuddáam** *servant*
واقف **wáaqif** *standing, stationary*
صاحب، أصحاب **SáaHib, aS-Háab** *owner, master;* also sometimes *friend*

---

2 السندباد البحري as-sindibaad al-baHrii

Sindbad the Sailor

CD2, TR15

Exercise 3

Who could own this magnificent palace? Listen to the rest of the story and answer the questions below:

a *Why was the servant astonished?*
b *Had the sailor travelled:*
i for seven years? *ii the seven seas?* *iii to seven countries?*
c *Did the porter become sad because:*
i Sindbad was rich and he was poor?
ii the servant told him to leave?
iii he was hungry?
d *Who was with Sindbad:*
i a group of servants? *ii his wife?* *iii a group of people?*

e *Did Sindbad give him:*
i gold? *ii food?* *iii drink?*
f *What had he ordered his servants to do?*

Listen to the story again, looking at the Quick Vocab on page 150.

وقال له الخادم: إنه قصر السندباد البحري. قال الحمال: ومن هو؟ فدهش الخادم وقال: أنت ساكن في بغداد وما سمعت عن السندباد البحري؟ قال الهندباد: لا. قال الخادم: هو الذي سافر في البحار السبعة وشاهد عجائب الدنيا كلها. فعند ذلك أصبح الحمال حزينا وسأل نفسه قال: لماذا السندباد هذا غني، وأنا لست غنيا؟ وسمع السندباد هذا الكلام من داخل القصر وأرسل خادما آخر إلى الباب. وخرج هذا الخادم من باب القصر وكلم الهندباد وقال: تعال معي. فتبعه الحمال إلى داخل القصر وشاهد هناك رجلا طويلا جالسا في وسط جماعة من الناس، وكان هذا الرجل السندباد. وقال البحري للحمال: مرحبا، أهلا وسهلا. وأجلسه بجانبه وقدم له أنواعا كثيرة من الأكل اللذيذ. وبعد ذلك خبره عن رحلاته العجيبة، وكان السندباد قد أمر خدامه بنقل حمل الهندباد إلى بيت التاجر.

Exercise 4

Link the English phrases with the appropriate Arabic expressions:

a	*he said*	تعال معي	١
b	*(Indeed) it is the palace of Sindbad the Sailor*	سافر في البحار السبعة	٢
c	*He has travelled the seven seas*	خبره عن رحلاته العجيبة	٣
d	*I am not rich*	إنه قصر السندباد البحري	٤
e	*Come with me*	كان قد أمر خدامه	٥
f	*Greetings and welcome!*	قال	٦
g	*He told him about his amazing voyages*	مرحبا، أهلا وسهلا	٧
h	*he had ordered his servants*	أنا لست غنيا	٨

QUICK VOCAB

قال (له) **qáala (lá-hu)** *he said* (to him)

إنه **ínn-uh** *it is…* (see grammar section below)

من؟ **man** *who?*

دهش **dáhisha** *be surprised, astonished*

ساكن **sáakin** *living, residing*

الذي **alládhii** *who, the one who*

البحار السبعة **al-biHáar as-sáb:ah** *the seven seas*

عجيبة، عجائب **:ajíibah, :ajáa'ib** (object of) *wonder*

الدنيا **ad-dúnya(a)** *the world* (f.)

كلها **kúll-haa** *all of them*

حزين **Hazíin** *sad*

نفسه **náfs-uh** *himself*

لماذا؟ **li-máadha(a)** *why*

غني، أغنياء **ghánii, aghniyáa'** *rich, rich person*

لست **lástu** *I am not* (see grammar section below)

كلام **kaláam** *speech*

أرسل **ársala** *send*

آخر **áakhar** *other*

تعال **ta:áala** *come!*

مع **má:a** *(along) with*

تبع **tábi:a** *follow*

جماعة، ـات **jamáa:ah, -aat** *group, gathering*

انسان، ناس **insáan, naas** *human being;* pl. = people

أجلس **ájlasa** *seat, cause to sit down*

قدم **qáddama** *offer, present with*

نوع، أنواع **naw:, anwáa:** *kind, sort, type*

أكل **akl** *things to eat, food*

رحلة، ـات **ríHlah, -aat** *journey, voyage*

عجيب **:ajíib** *wonderful*

أمر **ámara** *order, command* (بـ **bi-** something)

كان قد أمر **káana qad ámara** *he had ordered*

(for **qad** see grammar section)

نقل **naql** *transport, transportation*

تعبيرات رئيسية ta:biiráat ra'iisíyyah (Key phrases)

Describing someone or something

كان ممثلا مشهورا *He was a famous actor*
kaana mumaththilan mash-huuran

كانت تعبانة جدا بعد الرحلة *She was very tired after the journey*
kaanat ta:baanah jiddan ba:d ar-riHlah

كان شعرها أسود *Her hair was black*
kaana sha:r-haa aswad

(**aswad**, *black* does not take the accusative marker. See below and Unit 16.)

Talking about where something was

كان المفتاح في جيبه *The key was in his pocket*
kaana l-miftaaH fii jayb-uh

كانت الجرائد على المائدة *The papers were on the table*
kaanat al-jaraa'id :ala -l-maa'ida

Talking about what someone or something is not

ليس الفندق كبيرا *The hotel is not large*
laysa al-funduq kabiiran

لست مريضا **lastu mariiDan** *I am not ill*

Talking about what you had done in the past

هل كنت قد شاهدت الفيلم من قبل؟ **hal kunta qad shaahadta l-fiilm min qabl?** — *Had you seen the film before?*

كنا قد وقفنا وجلسنا **kunna qad waqafnaa wa-jalasnaa** — *We had stopped and sat down*

تراكيب اللغة **taraakíib al-lúghah** (Structures)

1 Saying 'was' and 'were'

Arabic does not use a verb for *is/are*, but when you talk about the past, the verb **kaana** for *was/were* is necessary.

This verb differs slightly from the past tense verbs that you have met in that it has two stems (**kaan-** and **kun-**). The endings are the standard past tense suffixes used on all Arabic verbs (see the verb tables at the end of the book).

Singular			*Plural*		
he was	كان	**kaana**	*they* (m.) *were*	كانوا	**kaan-uu**
she was	كانت	**kaan-at**	*they* (f.) *were*	كن	**kun-na**
you (m.) *were*	كنت	**kun-t(a)**	*you* (m.) *were*	كنتم	**kun-tum**
you (f.) *were*	كنت	**kun-ti**	*you* (f.) *were*	كنتن	**kun-tunna**
I was	كنت	**kun-t(u)**	*we were*	كنا	**kun-naa**

a The final vowels in brackets can be omitted in informal speech (see page 131).
b The stem **kaan-** *is used in the he, she and they* (m.) *forms, and the stem* **kun-** *for the rest. It may help you to remember*

them if you notice that the shortened **kun-** *stem is used before suffixes which begin with a consonant.* **kaana** *is a type* **Mw-I** *verb: see Verb tables.*

Insight

Since the last letter of the root of this verb is **n**, the usual shorthand spellings with the doubling sign is used when the suffix also begins with an **n** (كن **kunna** – *they (f.) were*, and كنا **kunnaa** – *we were*).

كنا في تونس في الصيف **kunnaa fii tuunis fi S-Sayf**	*We were in Tunisia in the summer*

Word order

The verb **kaana** usually comes first in the sentence, and the normal rules of agreement given in the previous unit apply:

kaana jamaal :abd an-naaSir qaa'idan :aDHiiman (he-)was jamaal :abd an-naaSir (a) leader (a) great-one	كان جمال عبد الناصر قائدا عظيما *Jamaal Abd al-Nasir was a great leader*
kaana l-mudiir mashghuulan (he-)was the-manager busy	كان المدير مشغولا *The manager was busy*
kunt(u) mariiDan I-was ill	كنت مريضا *I was ill*
kaanat al-mumaththilah mash-huurah she-was the actress famous	كانت الممثلة مشهورة *The actress was famous*
kaanat al-buyuut qadiimah she-was the-houses old	كانت البيوت قديمة *The houses were old*

2 The accusative marker

Formal Arabic has a set of (usually) three varying noun endings, which show the part played by a word in a sentence, similar to case endings in Latin or German. The words *he*, *him* and *his* show these cases in English:

1 Nominative	*2 Accusative*	*3 Genitive*
he	*him*	*his*

Insight

Most of these endings are only vowel marks which are omitted in modern written Arabic, and for the sake of simplification we have not included them in this book.

The only case ending appearing in print in contemporary written Arabic – except for a few special types of noun – is the *accusative* case.

How to form the accusative

This ending only affects the spelling of indefinite unsuffixed nouns or adjectives. The full form is actually ـًا (pronounced **-an**), but only the **alif** is usually written after the noun/adjective.

Unsuffixed in this context normally means that the noun or adjective does not have the feminine ending ـة (**-ah**). Nouns and adjectives that have this ending never add the **alif**. The examples above illustrate this point.

NOTE

a *You may think that we could have said simply masculine nouns take the extra* **alif**, *but there are feminine nouns that do not have the* ـة *(*-**ah**) *ending and these have to obey the* **alif** *law.*

For example, أم **umm**, mother, *is clearly feminine, but has no* ـة *(-ah) ending. Its accusative indefinite is therefore* أما **umman**. *There is also a handful of nouns signifying men that have the feminine ending, such as* خليفة **khaliifa**, caliph, *in the text above. These are obviously regarded as masculine, but do not take the* **alif** *because of the presence of the* ـة *(*-**ah**) *ending.*

b *A minority of Arabic unsuffixed nouns and adjectives do not add the* **alif**. *The commonest of these are the main colours, as well as some forms of the internal plural and many proper nouns. From this unit on, these are marked in the vocabulary secctions with an asterisk(*), and also appear like this in the glossaries at the end of the book:*

كان الكلب أبيض **kaana l-kalb abyaD**	*The dog was white*
قرأنا جرائد كثيرة أمس **qara'naa jaraa'id kathiirah ams**	*We read many newspapers yesterday*
قابلنا أحمد في السوق **qaabalnaa aHmad fi s-suuq**	*We met Ahmed in the souq*

When to use the accusative

In Arabic, the accusative is used in four instances:

1 *When the second noun is the object of the sentence, i.e. the thing or person the verb applies to:*

شاهدوا قصرا فخما **shaahaduu qaSran fakhman**	*They saw a magnificent castle*

2 *After the verbs* **kaana** *was, were,* **laysa** *is not, are not,* **aSbaHa** *to become, and a few other similar verbs*.*

Note: **laysa** *alone can also take an alternative construction using the preposition* **bi-** *which does not take the accusative:*

لست غنيا/لست بغني **lastu ghaniyyan/lastu bi-ghanii**	*I am not rich*

3 *In some common expressions and adverbs, when the ending is most commonly heard in spoken Arabic:*

أهلا وسهلا **ahlan wa sahlan** *hello, greetings*

مرحبا **marHaban** *welcome*

شكرا **shukran** *thanks*

جدا **jiddan** *very*

أبدا **abadan** *never*

طبعا **Tab:an** *naturally*

4 *After certain short words, known as particles, such as* **inna** *and* **anna**** (see Section 6 below).*

The Arabs refer to these words as '*kaana** *and her sisters' and '***inna** *and her sisters'.*

3 Saying where something was

kaana can be used before prepositions (words that tell you where something is) and such sentences are the same as the those verbless sentences in the present, except that **kaana** is put at the beginning (and obeys the agreement rules given in Unit 7):

kaana qalam-ii fii jayb-ii	كان قلمي في جيبي
(he-)was pen-my in pocket-my	*My pen was in my pocket*

4 How to say 'is/are not'

The word **maa**, *not*, is used before normal verbs (see Units 7 and 10) and can also be used before **kaana** in a past tense sentence.

Insight

To negate *is/are* sentences, the verb **laysa** is used. This verb is unique in Arabic, as it is only used in what looks like the past tense, with past tense suffixes, but the meaning is actually present.

Like **kaana** it has two stems (**lays-** and **las-**). As with **kaan-/kun-** you will see that in both verbs the first stem is used for the *he*, *she* and *they* (m.) parts, and the second stem with the rest.

Remember that, although it looks like a past tense, it means *isn't/aren't*.

Singular			*Plural*		
he isn't	ليس	**lays-a**	*they* (m.) *aren't*	ليسوا	**lays-uu**
she isn't	ليست	**lays-at**	*they* (f.) *aren't*	لسن	**las-na**
you (m.) *aren't*	لست	**las-t(a)**	*you* (m.) *aren't*	لستم	**las-tum**
you (f.) *aren't*	لست	**las-ti**	*you* (f.) *aren't*	لستن	**las-tunna**
I am not	لست	**las-t(u)**	*we aren't*	لسنا	**las-naa**

laysa l-walad mujtahidan — ليس الولد مجتهدا

(he-)is-not the boy diligent — *The boy is not diligent*

Accusative marker

laysa requires the accusative marker in the same way as **kaana.** (But see also alternative construction with **bi-** described above.)

5 How to say **to become**

There are several verbs in Arabic meaning *to become* but أصبح **aSbaHa** is by far the most common. Like **kaana** and **laysa**, it requires the accusative marker on unsuffixed indefinites, but it has only one stem **aSbaH-**.

Insight

The initial **hamzah** of **aSbaH** is never elided, so if you say *and he became* it is **wa-aSbaHa**, *not* **wa-SbaH**.

aSbaHa l-walad mariiDan أصبح الولد مريضا
he-became the-boy ill *The boy became ill*

aSbaHat al-bint mariiDah أصبحت البنت مريضة
she-became the-girl ill *The girl became ill*

بنت **bint** is an example of a feminine noun without the suffix ـة. However, the adjective **mariiDah** still has to have the suffix, as it refers to a female.

These verbs have all been dealt with together here as they share the common feature of using the accusative marker on what is not a direct object.

6 Sentences with 'inna' *and* 'anna'

Insight

The particle **inna**, though frequently used, is virtually meaningless. However, it is translated in this book where necessary as *indeed*, just to show it is there (older Arabic-teaching manuals use the biblical *verily*).

inna is usually used with *is/are* sentences which require no verb in Arabic. When they are followed by an indefinite unsuffixed noun – usually the name of a person or place – this noun takes the accusative marker **-an** and this time it is the first noun in the sentence which has the accusative marker (unlike **kaana**, **laysa** and **aSbaHa** sentences where it is attached to the second noun):

inna muHammadan :aamil mujtahid إن محمدا عامل مجتهد
indeed Muhammad worker hard *Muhammad is a hard worker*

anna is the conjunction *that* and follows the same rules as **inna**.

Insight

The Muslim Confession of Faith as heard from the minarets every prayer time is a good example of the use of **anna:**

أشهد ألا إله إلا الله وأن محمدا رسول الله

ash-hadu allaa ilaaha illa l-laah wa-anna muHammadan rasuulu l-laah*

It is usually translated as '*I witness that there is no god but Allah, and that Muhammed is His apostle.*'

*The transliteration here reflects the Classical Arabic pronunciation. **allaa** is a contraction of **an-laa** *that not*, *no*.

inna and **anna** with pronouns

Since **inna** requires an accusative after it, it has to use the suffixed pronouns (given in Unit 7):

إنه خبر جيد — *(Indeed) it is good news*

inna-h khabar jayyid

إنها بنت لطيفة — *(Indeed) she is a pleasant girl*

inna-haa bint laTiifah

Summary of the Arabic sentence

These are the four types of Arabic sentence:

1 *Is/are* sentences with no verb: *(the) X [is/are] Y*

السندباد رجل غني — *Sindbad is a rich man*

as-sindibaad rajul ghanii

2 Sentences with a verb (other than the **kaana** group below): *verb X Y*

شرب محمد الشاي — *Mohammed drank the tea*

shariba muHammad ash-shaay

3 Sentences with **kaan**, **aSbaHa** and **laysa**

The second term of the sentence is accusative, marked with an **alif** when required:

kaana/aSbaHa/laysa (*the*) X Y accusative

كان الهندباد فقيرا **kaana l-hindibaad faqiiran**	*Hindbad was poor*

4 Sentences introduced by **inna** and its associates.

The first term of the sentence is accusative, marked as appropriate:

inna *(the) X accusative [is/are] Y*

إن حسنا تلميذ مجتهد **inna Hasanan tilmiidh mujtahid**	*Indeed Hassan is a hard-working pupil*

Remember:

a *The accusative marker is only written after words which do not have* **al-** *the in front of them. It is not used after words with a suffix such as the feminine ending* **-ah** *or that are one of the minority of such words which never take the accusative marker (noted with an asterisk as they occur).*

b *The negative verb* **laysa**, *is/are not, is past in form, but present in meaning.*

7 How to say 'had done something'

Although there are only two tenses in Arabic, past and present, the verb **kaana** can be used to express the meaning of *had done something*, called the *pluperfect* tense in English.

The little word **qad** is commonly introduced between the subject and the main verb. It emphasises that the action has been well and truly completed, that it is over and done with.

The word order is as follows:

1 *The he or she form of* **kaana** *(because it always precedes its noun – see Unit 7).*
2 *The subject of the sentence (i.e. who is doing the action) if this is stated. If it is a pronoun (he, we, etc) it will be implicit in the verb (see Unit 7).*
3 *The word* **qad** *(optional).*
4 *The fully-agreeing part of the main verb (i.e. the action that had been carried out) It is fully agreeing because it comes after its subject (see Unit 7).*
5 *Any other information (when, where it happened, etc.):*

kaana l-mudiir waSal yawm as-sabt	كان المدير وصل يوم السبت
he-was the-manager he-arrived day the-Saturday	*The manager had arrived on Saturday*
kaanuu qad saafaruu ila l-hind min qabl	كانوا قد سافروا إلى الهند من قبل
they-were **qad** they-travelled to the-India from before	*They had travelled to India before*

أوزان الكلمات **awzáan al-kalimáat** (Word shapes)

CD2, TR16

The word pattern for this unit is **C¹aC²C²aaC³**, for example, **Haddáad** حداد *blacksmith*, which sounds like the English *had Dad* (as in *had Dad known…*).

This is a formation often used for trades. In the Sindbad story we have حمال **Hammaal,** *porter*, from the root **H-m-l,** *carrying.*

Haddaad comes from حديد **Hadiid,** *iron*. Other examples are:

نجار **najjaar**	*carpenter*
خباز **khabbaaz**	*baker*

بناء **bannaa'**	*builder*
خياط **khayyaaT**	*tailor*

This type of word takes the ـون **-uun** plural.

It is really an intensive form of **CaaCiC** (see Unit 2), in that it expresses the idea that somebody is always, habitually or professionally performing the action of the root.

The feminine ending **-ah** is often added to this word shape either to indicate a female member of the trade or profession, e.g. خياطة **khayyaaTah** *tailoress*, *seamstress*, or a machine:

دبابة **dabbaabah**	*a (military) tank* [lit., a crawling machine, from the root **d-b-b** *crawling*]
غسالة **ghassaalah**	*washing machine* (from root **gh-s-l** *washing*)
سيارة **sayyaarah**	*car* [lit., going-machine]
عصارة **:aSSáarah**	*juicer*
دباسة **dabbáasah**	*stapler*

These take the plural ـات **-aat**.

تمرينات **tamriináat** (Practice)

Exercise 5

Fill in the gaps in the following sentences with the appropriate form of **kaana**. Don't forget to add the accusative marker where necessary.

١ الآن درجة الحرارة ٣٥.
الصبح .... ١٨.

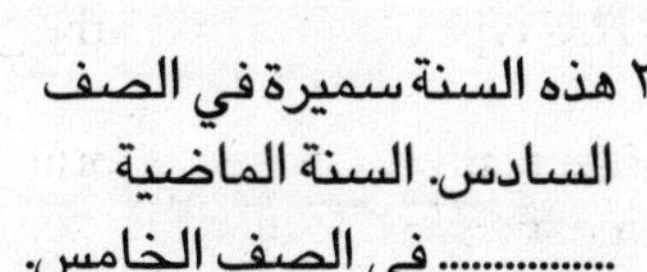

٢ هذه السنة سميرة في الصف
السادس. السنة الماضية
.... في الصف الخامس.

٣ الآن الأولاد طوال، في سنة ١٩٩٠
.... قصارا.

٤ اليوم حامد سعيد، أمس ....
حزينا.

أمس

اليوم

QUICK VOCAB

الآن **al-áan** *now*

درجة، ـات **dárajah, -aat** *step, degree*

درجة الحرارة **dárajat al-Haráarah** *temperature* [lit., degree of heat]

صف، صفوف **Saff, Sufúuf** *class* (in school)

سادس **sáadis** *sixth*

خامس **kháamis** *fifth*

طويل طوال **Tawíil, Tiwáal** *long, tall*

قصير قصار **qaSíir, qiSáar** *short*

سعيد، سعداء **sa:íid, su:adáa'*** *happy, joyful*

* This asterisk indicates that the word does not add **alif** in the accusative. See section 2.

Exercise 6

Write the sentences below in the past tense, remembering to put the accusative marker where necessary (see page 154).

Example: *Mahmoud is unhappy* ➔ *Mahmoud was unhappy*

محمود حزين ➔ كان محمود حزينا

١ ذلك الطعام لذيذ.
٢ حدائق الفندق واسعة.
٣ شركتنا مشهورة في الخليج.
٤ عمر الشريف ممثل مصري.
٥ الأولاد سعداء.

ممثل، ـون **mumáththil, -uun** *actor, representative*

Exercise 7

Where are they? Mahmoud and his wife Salma and their son Hamad and daughters Faridah and Sarah are staying at a hotel in Abu Dhabi. They have left a note at the desk to say where they can be found if friends or colleagues want to contact them. Answer the questions below in Arabic, using **laysa** and the accusative marker where necessary:

Example: *Is Salma in the Palm Court café?*
No, she is not at the Palm Court café.

هل سلمى في مقهى النخيل؟
لا، ليست في مقهى النخيل

١ هل الساعة ١٠,٣٠ الصبح؟
٢ هل محمود في البهو؟
٣ هل سلمى في مطعم البستان؟
٤ هل سلمى وفريدة وسارة في المسبح؟
٥ هل محمود في مركز الأعمال؟
٦ هل سلمى في ملعب الجولف؟
٧ هل أرقام الغرف ٥١١، ٥١٢ و٥١٣؟
٨ هل الأولاد في ملعب التنس؟

Where are you? أين أنت؟

Name:	الاسم: ....محمود صالح....	
Date:	التاريخ:	
Room number:	رقم الغرفة: ٥١٤/٥١٥/٥١٦	
Time:	الساعة: ....١١:١٠....	

AL-BUSTAN RESTAURANT		☐	مطعم البستان
PALM COURT CAFÉ		☐	مقهى النخيل
LOBBY		☐	البهو
BUSINESS CENTRE	محمود	☑	مركز رجال الأعمال
CLUB HOUSE		☐	النادي
SWIMMING POOL		☐	المسبح
TENNIS COURT		☑	حمد وفريدة وسارة ملعب التنس
GOLF COURSE	سلمى	☑	ملعب الجولف

بهو **bahw** *(hotel) lobby*

بستان **bustáan** *orchard*

مسبح، مسابح **másbaH, masáabiH*** *swimming pool*

أعمال **a:máal** (pl.) *business, affairs, works*

ملعب، ملاعب **mál:ab, maláa:ib*** *pitch, court, course*

QUICK VOCAB

Exercise 8

An Arabic proverb says:

الفهد منقط والنمر مخطط

A leopard can't change his spots
[lit., 'the leopard is spotted and the tiger is striped']

QUICK VOCAB

فهد، فهود **fahd, fuhúud** *leopard*

نمر، نمور **námir, numúur** *tiger*

منقط **munáqqaT** *spotted*

مخطط **mukháTTaT** *striped*

What is wrong with these two? Change the sentence below into the negative to make sense.

الفهد مخطط والنمر منقط

Exercise 9
Change the following sentences into the negative, using the verb **laysa**:

١ علي طالب كسلان.
٢ أنا تعبان بعد رحلتي.
٣ الفنادق الكبيرة في وسط المدينة.
٤ هي مشهورة جدا.
٥ الطبيب مشغول في المستشفى.
٦ هذه القصة من ألف ليلة وليلة طويلة جدا.

QUICK VOCAB

كسلان **kasláan** *lazy*

مشغول **mashghúul** *busy*

مستشفى، مستشفيات **mustáshfaa, mustashfayáat** *hospital*

قصة، قصص **qíSSah, qíSaS** *story, tale*

Exercise 10
Change the sentences below into the pluperfect tense:

Example: وجد الهنداباد قصر السندباد.
كان الهنداباد (قد) وجد قصر السندباد.

Note: The use of **qad** is optional. Watch out for the agreement of the main verb which comes after its subject in the pluperfect.

١ روت شهرزاد قصة جديدة كل ليلة.
٢ خبر البحري الحمال عن رحلاته العجيبة.
٣ الفنادق الكبيرة في وسط المدينة.
٤ تبعته الخادمات الى داخل القصر.
٥ أكل الناس الأكل اللذيذ.

روت **ráwat** *she told*

خادمة، ـات **kháadimah, -aat** (female) *servant*

10 things you need to know

1. *While present tense* is, are *sentences have no verb, past tense* was, were *sentences use the verb* **kaana.**
2. *This verb* **kaana** *affects the following word, putting it into the accusative, as in colloquial English I* see him.
3. *Words with the feminine ending* **-ah** *do not mark the accusative.*
4. *Most other words mark the accusative by adding an* **alif** *to the end of the word, which is pronounced* **-an**. *The adjective describing someone or something must show the accusative marker too.*
5. *However, a significant number of words do not show this* **alif**. *These are marked in the glossaries with an asterisk*.*
6. *The accusative is also required after* **laysa** is/are not, **aSbaHa** to become, *and certain small words or particles such as* **inna** *or* **anna**, *as in* **aSbaHa l-hindibaad ta:baanan wa-:aTshaanan** became-Hindbad-tired-and-thirsty.
7. *The particles* **:inna** indeed *and* **:anna** that *frequently occur with pronouns.* **innahu qaSr as-sindibaad** indeed it is the palace of Sindbad *and* **qaalat ana-haa** she said that she...
8. *Since an accusative is required, the suffix and not the independent pronouns is used.*
9. To say someone had done something, *Arabic uses the past tense of the verb* **kaana** *followed by the (optional) word* **qad**, *then the main verb in the past tense.* **kaanuu qad saafaruu** they had travelled.
10. *The word* **qad** *has no real meaning, but is used to emphasise that the action is in the past.*

9

أكثر من واحد
akthar min waaHid
More than one

In this unit you will learn:

- ***how to look for a job in the paper***
- ***how to look for a flat or a house***
- ***how to talk about more than one person or thing***
- ***how to say 'these'/'those'***
- ***how to talk about two people or things***

1 وظائف شاغرة waDHáa'if sháaghirah
Situations vacant

Arabic newspapers carry classified advertisements, with all the usual sections for *Situations vacant*, *For sale*, *To let* and so on. When you are reading them, concentrate on picking out the key words and learn to recognise words such as *Wanted* and *For rent*.

Read through the Key phrases, then look at the job advertisements below and answer the questions. You don't need to understand every word.

Exercise 1

You are an experienced hairdresser looking for a job in Dubai. Which of these three jobs would suit you best?

i

وظائف شاغرة

كوافيرة درجة اولى براتب مغر
لصالون كبير في الشارقة

ii

مطلوب كوافيرة ذات خبرة لتسريح
الشعر والمنكير والباديكر بالعين

iii

مطلوب كوافيرة درجة اولى
لصالون راق بدبي

Exercise 2

Which picture is most appropriate for each of the job advertisements below?

i

ii

iii

a

مدربة للرشاقة والايروبيك لمركز
رياضي ت:٦٥١٣٩

b

مطلوب كهربائي سيارات
ومكيفات بالعين
ت٠٣/٧٢١٢٨٨٤ -
٣٦١١٩

c

مطلوب فني أجهزة الكترونية
لتصليح هواتف متحركة فاكس
٧٤٧٥١

Exercise 3

What people are wanted for the jobs advertised on page 171? Match the people to the jobs.

1 *labourers and builders*

2 *French teacher*

3 *manageress for a ladies' fashion shop*

4 *pharmacist*

5 *secretary (male or female)*

6 *employees for a restaurant*

7 *salesmen and saleswomen*

8 *saleswoman for a shoe shop*

i

مطلوب صيدلانية للعمل في صيدلية بعجمان مرخصة من وزارة الصحة
ت:١٨٢٦٠

ii

مطلوب بائعة لمحل احذية نسائي بدبي لديها خبرة ٣ سنوات
ت:٧٧١٧٣

iii

مدرس لغة فرنسية مؤهل لمدرسة هندية ت٢٧٦٠٠
ف٢٧٦٠٦

iv

v

مطلوب موظفات لمطعم بالعين
ت٤٦٣٢٤

vi

مندوبات مبيعات ذوات خبرة مع رخصة سواقة راتب ٥٠٠٠ - ٦٠٠٠ الرجاء ارسال السيرة الذاتية على فاكس ٩١٨٥٥ لعناية المهندس حسام

vii

مطلوب
مديرة
لمحل أزياء نسائي بدبي
خبرة وإجادة اللغة الانجليزية
نقال: ٤٤٠٥٩
فاكس: ٣١٩٣

viii

عمال + بنائيين الاتصال
٩١٥٥١

ix

مندوب مبيعات خبرة في اجهزة التبريد والتكييف لاتقل عن خمس سنوات في الامارات مع لغة انجليزية وعربية ارسال السيرة الذاتية على الفاكس
٣٩٩٢١

x

Exercise 4

Which of the advertisements on page 171 require:

1 *some previous experience?*
2 *a driving licence?*
3 *a knowledge of English?*

Exercise 5

Name any three requirements applicants need for this position as a sales representative.

مطلوب لشركة تجارية رائدة في دبي

مندوبو مبيعات

على المتقدمين أن يكون لديهم :

• خبرة ٣ سنوات على الأقل في مبيعات المواد الغذائية داخل الإمارات

• يجيد اللغة الانجليزية • إقامة صالحة للتحويل

• العمر بين ٢٤ و ٢٨ عاما • يحمل رخصة قيادة إماراتية

الرجاء ارسال السيرة الذاتية الى المدير الاداري فاكس رقم ٢٦٥٢٠

2 للإيجار li-l-iijáar For rent

Read through the Key phrases to familiarise yourself with the new vocabulary, then answer the questions.

Exercise 6

Match the Arabic abbreviations to the English words:

a	*room, bedroom*	ت	١
b	*bathroom*	ش	٢
c	*telephone*	غ	٣

d *fax* — ٤ ح
e *Post Office (PO) Box No.* — ٥ ف
f *street* — ٦ ص ب

Exercise 7

You are looking for accommodation. Read the advertisements and answer the questions below.

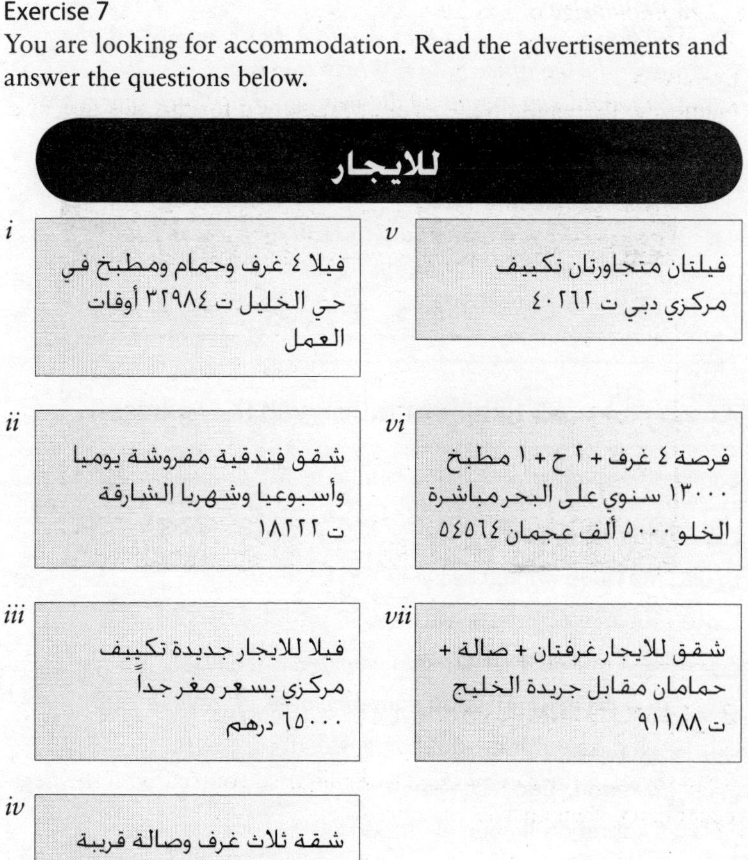

a *You want to rent somewhere for your large family. Which place has the most bedrooms and bathrooms?*
b *You are looking for two villas close to each other for your firm. Are there any which would be suitable?*
c *You want to rent a villa for just a few weeks. Is there anything available?*
d *You have found a villa that you like, but can only call the owner during office hours. Which one is it?*
e *You would like to rent a villa near a park. Which one could you choose?*
f *You work for the al-Khaleej newspaper. Which flat would be most convenient for you?*
g *Where could you find a villa to rent, which is not too expensive, with air conditioning if possible?*

تعبيرات رئيسية **ta:biiráat ra'iisíyyah** (Key phrases)

Looking for a job

QUICK VOCAB

طلب **Tálaba** *seek, want*

مطلوب **maTlúub** *wanted, required*

وظيفة، وظائف **waDHiifah, waDHáa'if*** *job, situation*

موظف، ـون **muwáDHDHaf, -úun** *employee, official* (m.)

موظفة، ـات **muwáDHDHafah, -áat** *employee, official* (f.)

كوافيرة، ـات **kwaafíirah, -áat** *hairdresser* (f.), *coiffeuse*

فني، ـون **fánnii, -úun** *technician*

كهربائي **kahrabáa'ii, -úun** *electrician*

مدربة، ـات **mudárribah, -áat** *trainer* (f.)

بناء، ـون **bannáa', -uun** *builder*

صيدلانية، ـات **Saydalaaníyyah, -áat** *pharmacist* (f.)

سكرتيرة، ـات **sikritáyrah, -áat** *secretary*

مندوب مبيعات، مندوبو مبيعات **mandúub mabii:áat, manduubúu mabii:áat** *sales representative* (**mumáththil** is also used instead of **mandúub**)

بائع، ـون **báa'i:, -úun** *salesman*

بائعة، ـات **báa'i:ah, -áat** *saleswoman*

مبيع، ـات **mabíi:, -áat** *selling, sales*

مكيف، ـات **mukáyyif, -áat** *air conditioner*

محل، ـات **maHáll, -áat** *(big) shop, store*

أحذية **aHdhíyyah** *footwear*

خبرة **khíbrah** *experience*

رخصة سواقة **rúkhSat siwáaqah** *driving licence*

إقامة **iqáamah** *residence; residence permit*

صالح **SáaliH** *valid*; (of people) *upright*

معرفة **má:rifah** *knowledge*

راتب **ráatib** *salary*

مغر(ي) **múghrii** *attractive, tempting*

(for the spelling of this kind of adjective, see Unit 17)

سيرة ذاتية **síirah dhaatíyyah** *CV; resumé*

لعناية... **li-:ináayat...** *for the attention of...*

على الأقل **:ála l-aqáll** *at least*

Looking for accommodation

للإيجار **li-l-iijáar** *for rent*

مفروش **mafrúush** *furnished*

فيلا، فيلل **fíilla, fíilal** *villa*

تكييف **takyíif** *air conditioning*

مركزي **márkazii** *central*

غرفة، غرف **ghúrfah, ghúraf** *room, bedroom*

صالة **Sáalah** *sitting room, lounge*

حمام، ـات **Hammáam, -aat** *bathroom*

QUICK VOCAB

QUICK VOCAB

QUICK VOCAB

دش **dushsh** *shower*

مطبخ **máTbakh** *kitchen*

سعر، أسعار **si:r, as:áar** *price*

متجاور **mutajáawir** *adjacent, neighbouring, next to each other*

مباشرة الخلو **mubáasharat al-khalw** *for immediate occupation*

أوقات العمل **awqáat al-:ámal** *working/office hours*

فاكس **faaks** *fax*

صندوق بريد **Sandúuq baríid** *PO Box*

تراكيب اللغة **taraakíib al-lúghah** (Structures)

1 Talking about more than one of anything

a *Arabic plural formations are not often predictable, so they must be learned along with their singulars.*
b *In Arabic, the plural of inanimate objects or abstracts is treated in all respects as a feminine singular, so verbs and adjectives must be in the feminine singular form.*
c *In English, the word 'plural' refers to more than one (i.e. 1+). However, Arabic has a special form for two of anything, called the dual, so the plural in Arabic refers to more than two (2+).*

Plurals of nouns
There are three ways to form the plural in Arabic:

1 *The external or suffix masculine plural.*
2 *The external feminine/neuter plural.*
3 *The internal plural.*

1 THE EXTERNAL OR SUFFIX MASCULINE PLURAL
Add the suffix ـون **-uun** to the singular noun. For the accusative form (see page 154), add ـين **-iin** to the singular.

This kind of plural can only be used on words which indicate male human beings, as opposed to females and things/abstracts. The common exception to this is سنة pl. سنون (**sanah, sinuun**) year, and even this word has an alternative plural (سنوات **sanawáat**):

HaDar al-mudarrisuun al-mu'tamar حضر المدرسون المؤتمر
he-attended the-teachers the-conference *The teachers attended the conference*

hum muqaawiluun هم مقاولون
they contractors *They are contractors*

kaana l-muhandisuun miSriyyiin كان المهندسون مصريين
he-was the-engineers Egyptians *The engineers were Egyptian*

aSbaHuu muHaasibíin أصبحوا محاسبين
they-became accountants *They became accountants*

2 THE EXTERNAL FEMININE/NEUTER PLURAL

Drop the ـة (if there is one) and add ـات **-aat** to the singular word. This can be applied to words indicating females or things/abstracts and there is no special accusative form:

waSalat aT-Taalibaat yawm al-jum:ah وصلت الطالبات يوم الجمعة
she-arrived the-[female]students day the-Friday *The (female) students arrived on Friday*

aSbaHna mudarrisaat أصبحن مدرسات
they (f)-became teachers *They became teachers*

a-antunna mumarriDaat? أأنتن ممرضات؟
(?)-you (f.) nurses? *Are you nurses?*

ta:allam-naa kull al-kalimaat تعلمنا كل الكلمات
we-learned all the-words *We learned all the words*

3 THE INTERNAL PLURAL

This is formed by altering the internal vowelling of the word (like English *foot* ➔ *feet*). Some words also add prefixes and/or suffixes.

The internal plural is used mainly for males and things/abstracts, rarely for females. There is no general relationship between the singular word shape and the plural word shape.

Some words indicating males form a plural with the feminine ending, e.g. طالب، طلبة **Táalib, Tálabah**, *male student*. (This word also illustrates the fact that some words have alternative plurals, in this case طلاب **Tulláab**.) Such plurals are still regarded as masculine.

Tip: the Arabic internal plural system cannot generally handle words consisting of more than four consonants, excluding suffixes such as ـة **-ah**, but counting doubled consonants as two. It is therefore likely that 'short' words will take an internal plural, but this is not a rule:

dakhala r-rijaal al-ghurfah
he-entered the-men the-room

دخل الرجال الغرفة
The men entered the room

naHnu :ummaal fii sharikat as-sayyaaraat
we workers in company (of) the-cars

نحن عمال في شركة السيارت
We are workers in the car company

al-kutub :alaa l-maa'ida
the-books on the-table

الكتب على المائدة
The books are on the table

Insight: Plurals of adjectives

It is a good idea to think of adjectives in Arabic as another class of noun. They have the same choice as nouns in forming their plurals:

- *-uun or -aat ending*
- *internal plurals, which which must be learned with their singulars.*

If no adjective plural is given in the vocabulary, use the suffixed plurals according to the rules below. Internal plurals are given for those adjectives that have them.

Noun	Adjective plural form
male human beings	internal plural if it has one, otherwise + **-uun**
female human beings	+ **-aat**
things/abstracts	+ **-ah** (f. singular)

These rules hold for nearly all adjectives with a few common exceptions, mainly relating to the primary colours (see Unit 16)

Common adjectives with internal plural forms

Adjective	Meaning	Male plural form
كسلان **kasláan**	*lazy*	كسالى **kasáalaa**
نشيط **nashíiT**	*active*	نشاط **nisháaT**
كبير **kabíir**	*big*	كبار **kibáar**
صغير **Saghíir**	*small*	صغار **Sigháar**
نحيف **naHíif**	*thin*	نحاف **niHáaf**
سمين **samíin**	*fat*	سمان **simáan**
طويل **Tawíil**	*tall*	طوال **Tiwáal**
قصير **qaSíir**	*short*	قصار **qiSáar**
ذكي **dhákii**	*clever*	أذكياء **adhkiyáa'***
غبي **ghábii**	*stupid*	أغبياء **aghbiyáa'***
سعيد **sa:íid**	*happy*	سعداء **su:adáa'***
حزين **Hazíin**	*sad*	حزناء **Huzanáa'***
غريب **gharíib**	*strange*	غرباء **ghurabáa'***
أجنبي **ájnabii**	*foreign*	أجانب **ajáanib***

عظيم :aDHíim	*great, mighty*	**عظماء :uDHamáa'***
جديد jadíid	*new*	**جدد júdud**

Note: many of these plurals – marked with * – do not take the accusative marker. This applies to the plural only, not the singular as well.

Insight

The plural of things in Arabic is regarded in all respects as feminine singular for the sake of grammatical agreement. Here are a few more mixed examples:

al-awlaad Tiwaal	الأولاد طوال
the-boys talls	*The boys are tall*
aT-Talabah mujtahiduun	الطلبة مجتهدون
the-students diligents	*The students are diligent*
al-mumaththilaat al-jadiidaat	الممثلات الجديدات
the-actresses the-new(ones)	*the new actresses*
al-buyuut al-qadiimah	البيوت القديمة
the-houses the-old(one)	*the old houses*

2 هؤلاء **haa'uláa'(i)..., أولائك uuláa'ik(a)...** ***(these..., those...)***

You have already learned the demonstrative pronouns هذا/هذه, *this*, and ذلك/تلك, *that* (see Unit 4), to describe singular words which are either masculine or feminine in gender.

Insight

Because plurals of things/abstracts in Arabic are regarded as feminine singular, all verbs, adjectives and pronouns relating to them must be feminine singular.

When speaking of plural male/female human beings, use the forms هؤلاء **haa'ulaa'(i)**, *these*, and أولائك **uulaa'ik(a)**, *those*, respectively. The final vowels are often missed out in informal situations.

With these plural forms, there is no distinction for gender, so both of them can apply to either males or females:

haa'ulaa'i T-Talabah HaaDiruun these the-students presents	هؤلاء الطلبة حاضرون *These students are present*
uulaa'ika l-banaat jamiilaat those the-girls beautifuls	أولائك البنات جميلات *Those girls are beautiful*
tilka l-buyuut kabiirah that the-houses big	تلك البيوت كبيرة *Those houses are big*

3 Talking about two people or things

Insight

Arabic has a special way of talking about two of anything, called the dual. This is obligatory in use for both people and things (i.e. you cannot use the plural).

Formation of the dual

a *If the noun does not have the feminine ending* **-ah**, *add the suffix* **-aan** *to the singular. This changes to* **-ayn** *when an accusative marker is required:*

al-waladaan Tawiilaan the(2)-boys tall (x2)	الولدان طويلان *The two boys are tall*
kaana l-waladaan Tawiilayn he-was the(2)-boys tall(x2)	كان الولدان طويلين *The two boys were tall*

This applies to the vast majority of nouns and adjectives.

b *If the noun has the* **-ah** *ending of the feminine singular, this changes to* **-at** *(spelled with an ordinary* ت*) and the suffix* **-aan/-ayn** *is added to it:*

as-sayyaarataan kabiirataan السيارتان كبيرتان
the(2)-cars big(x2) *The two cars are big*

kaanat as-sayyaarataan kabiiratayn كانت السيارتان كبيرتين
she-was the(2)-cars big(x2) *The two cars were big*

Since Arabic has this dual form for two, it is not usually necessary to insert the numeral word (see Unit 2).

(As with the masculine plural ending ـون/ـين **-uun/-iin** the final ن of the dual is omitted if the word constitutes the first term of a possessive construction. See Unit 14.)

DUAL PRONOUNS

Arabic does not need to distinguish between *one* and *two* for the person who is speaking, so where English says *we two*, Arabic says simply *we*, but *you two*, أنتما **antumaa** (both m. and f.):

antumaa ta:baanaan أنتما تعبانان
you-two tired(x2) *You two are tired*

they two هما **humaa** (both m. and f.):

humaa mashhuuraan هما مشهوران
they-two famous(x2) *They two are famous*

In practice, the dual is not common, except when speaking about things that always come in pairs like hands, feet, etc.

يدان **yadáan** *(two) hands*
رجلان **rijláan** *(two) feet*
أذنان **udhnáan** *(two) ears*
عينان **:aynáan** *(two) eyes*

Note: these words – and indeed all parts of the body that occur in pairs – are feminine.

There are also special dual markers for the verb. These are given in the Verb tables, but they occur so rarely that they need only to be noted at this stage.

أوزان الكلمات **awzáan al-kalimáat** (Word shapes)

CD2, TR17

The word pattern for this unit is **muC¹aC²C²iC³**, for example, **mudárris** مُدَرِّس *teacher*, which sounds like the English *molasses*.

This shape indicates the person or thing carrying out the action of Verb form II (see Table S-II), grammatically known as the active participle. The verb دَرَّس **dárrasa** means to teach, so مُدَرِّس is a *teaching person*, i.e. *teacher*. This shape is also often used to indicate trades or professions (see Word shapes in Unit 8).

A similar shape with an **a**-vowel instead of an **i**-vowel after the middle radical is also common. This is the passive participle, i.e. the person or thing to which the action of the verb has been applied. An example of this is مُوَظَّف **muwáDHDHaf**, *official*, *employee*. This comes from the verb وَظَّف **waDHDHafa**, *to appoint to an official position*, *to employ*.

All these words can be made feminine by the addition of the ending ة **-ah**. The male versions take the plural suffix ـون, and the females ـات.

Insight

Remember that the point of learning word shapes is to be able to read and know something about Arabic words. It is not always possible to get an exact English sound-alike, but the pattern is usually easy to imitate. Say them aloud one after another until they become familiar.

مدرس **mudárris**	*teacher*
مدرب **mudárrib**	*trainer*
ممثل **mumáththil**	*representative, actor*
محرر **muHárrir**	*editor*
مفتش **mufáttish**	*inspector*
ممرض **mumárriD**	*(male) nurse*
منجم **munájjim**	*astrologer*
مؤذن **mu'ádhdhin**	*muezzin*

تمرينات **tamriinάat** (Practice)

CD2, TR18

Exercise 8

Listen to the recording or read the text below of four people describing where they live.

Then try to identify which person lives in which of the flats or houses described below:

a *A villa with four bedrooms and two bathrooms, two living rooms and a kitchen.*
b *A small villa with three bedrooms, living room, bathroom and kitchen.*
c *A flat with one room and salon.*
d *A two-bedroomed apartment with living room.*

١ أسكن في شقة صغيرة قريبة من وسط المدينة، فيها غرفة واحدة وصالة وحمام ومطبخ.

٢ نسكن في شقة جديدة. فيها غرفتان، واحدة لي أنا وزوجي وواحدة للأولاد، وصالة.

٣ نسكن في فيلا قريبة من البحر. هي جميلة جدا.عندنا أربع غرف وحمامان وصالتان وهناك مطبخ طبعا.

٤ نسكن في فيلا، فيلا صغيرة. هناك ثلاث غرف وصالة وحمام ومطبخ.

Exercise 9

Write the correct form of plural for the adjectives in brackets.

١ بناتك (جميل)

٢ هولاء الأولاد (ذكي)

٣ القمصان (مخطط)

٤ قرأنا الجرائد (الإنجليزي)

٥ البنوك (مقفول) بعد الظهر

٦ الرجال (المصري) (نشيط)

Exercise 10

Change the underlined nouns, adjectives or pronouns in the following sentences into the correct plural form.

Example: *I bought a shirt last week.*
I bought three shirts last week.

اشتريت قميصا الأسبوع الماضي.
اشتريت ثلاثة قمصان الأسبوع الماضي.

١ وجدنا مطعما جيدا في القاهرة.

٢ حضر المدير الاجتماع.

٣ هل أنت جوعان؟

٤ السكرتيرة مشغولة.

٥ بنتها طالبة في الجامعة.

٦ هو ممثل كويتي.

٧ كان الفيلم طويل.

QUICK VOCAB

اشتريت **ishtaráyt** *I bought*

قميص، قمصان **qamíiS, qumSáan** *shirt*

جيد **jáyyid** *of good quality*

جوعان، جوعى **jaw:áan*, jáw:aa*** *hungry*

Exercise 11

Now change these whole sentences into the plural. Remember that verbs *preceding* their nouns remain singular, and that the **-uun/-iin** plural ending must show the correct case:

١ وصل العامل الجديد.

٢ أين الكتاب الفرنسي؟

٣ وجدته المدرسة على الرف.

٤ أصبح الولد سمينا.

٥ خرج الضيف من الفندق.

سمين، سمان **samíin, simáan** *fat* (adj.)

ضيف، ضيوف **Dayf, Duyúuf** *guest*

Exercise 12

Choose the correct ending for each of the sentences below.

١ هذه الشقق قريبة...

٢ هؤلاء نساء نحيفات...

٣ هذه الجرائد يومية...

٤ هؤلاء الطلبة اللبنانيون كثيرون...

a ولكن أولائك الطلبة المصريين قليلون.

b ولكن أولائك نساء سمينات.

c ولكن هذه الشقق بعيدة.

d ولكن هذه الجرائد أسبوعية.

ولكن **waláakin, walaakínna** *but*
(the latter behaves like إن **inna**. See Unit 8)
نساء **nisáa'*** *women* (pl.)

Exercise 13
Put the following sentences into the dual. (You can leave the verbs in the singular as they come before the noun.)

1	*The office is closed.*	المكتب مقفول.	١
2	*The technician is not present.*	ليس الفني حاضرا.	٢
3	*The bathroom is spacious.*	الحمام واسع.	٣
4	*The employee worked in the ministry.*	عمل الموظف في الوزارة.	٤
5	*The manageress spoke to the workman.*	كلمت المديرة العامل.	٥

Exercise 14

CD2, TR19

Read (and if you have the recording, listen to) the following information about John Barker:

جون باركر انجليزي. عمره ٣٢ سنة. هو متزوج. يتكلم عربي. له خبرة ٥
سنوات في المبيعات في الإمارات. لديه رخصة سواقة وإقامة في الإمارات.

John is looking for a job as a salesperson in Abu Dhabi and wants to register at an employment agency. He needs to fill in an application form.

Imagine that you are John, and fill out the application form for him. A possible reply is in the Key to the exercises.

١ الاسم الكامل..

٢ العمر ....

٣ الجنسية..

٤ أعزب/متزوج..

٥ العنوان...

٦ رقم التلفون ....

٧ اللغات ....

٨ هل لديك رخصة سواقة صالحة؟ ....

٩ هل لديك رخصة إقامة صالحة في الإمارات؟ ....

١٠ خبرة ....

كامل **káamil** *complete, whole*

جنسية، ـات **jinsíyyah, -aat** *nationality*

أعزب **á:zab*** *bachelor, single*

متزوج **mutazáwwaj** *married*

عنوان، عناوين **:unwáan, :anaawíin*** *address*

لديك **ladáy-k** *you have* [lit., 'with you; in your possession']

QUICK VOCAB

---

10 things you need to know

1 *Arabic plurals should be learned along with the singular form as there is no reliable formula for making the plural.*

2 *Plurals of inanimate objects and abstracts are regarded as feminine singular, and verbs and adjectives must agree accordingly.*

3 *The plural in Arabic is only used for more than two things (there is a special form called the dual used when talking about two of anything). There are three ways to form it.*

4 *The masculine suffix or external plural is only used for male human beings.*

5 *The feminine suffix or external plural is used for female human beings and some inanimates.*

6 *The internal plural is formed by changing the internal vowelling of the word and sometimes adding prefixes and/or suffixes.*

7 *As a rule of thumb, the internal plural is used for males and inanimates.*

8 *Adjectives can form their plurals in the same three ways as nouns, but remember that those describing inanimates are feminine singular, regardless of what form of plural the noun takes.*

9 *The use of the special dual form is obligatory when talking about two of anything.*

10 *With duals, because the meaning is obvious, no word for two is necessary unless for special emphasis.*

10

ماذا تعمل؟
maadhaa ta:mal?
What do you do?

In this unit you will learn:

- ***to say what you do every day***
- ***to talk about your interests***
- ***to say what you like or dislike***
- ***to say what you will do in the future***
- ***more about 'not'***

---

1 ماذا تعمل كل يوم؟ maadhaa ta:mal kull yawm?
What do you do every day?

CD2, TR20

A women's magazine has sent Fawzia to interview Kamal, the sales manager of a local business. She asks him about what he does during the day. Listen to or read the interview several times, each time concentrating on a different point. Then answer the questions.

Exercise 1

a What does Kamal always eat in the morning?
b Does he telephone his
i son? ii daughter? iii mother?

c *Does he read reports for*
i 2–3 hours? *ii 3–4 hours?* *iii 4–5 hours?*

d *Did he learn to use a computer*
i at school? *ii at college?* *iii at work?*

e *With whom does he sit in the afternoon?*

f *How often does he meet the employees?*

فوزية ماذا تأكل الصبح؟
كمال آكل الفواكه دائما، وأحيانا خبزا وجبنة وأشرب قهوة. وعادة أتكلم مع ابني بالتلفون. هو يعيش في أمريكا.
فوزية وماذا تعمل بعد ذلك؟
كمال أذهب إلى المكتب. السائق يوصلني الساعة ٨,٣٠ وأتكلم معه في السيارة عن أخبار اليوم.
فوزية وبعد ذلك؟
كمال السكرتيرة تطبع لي رسائل وأنا أقرأ التقارير المالية. هذا يستغرق ساعتين، ثلاث ساعات.
فوزية هل تستخدم الآلة الحاسبة؟
كمال نعم، طبعا. تعلمت استخدام الآلة الحاسبة في كلية التجارة.
فوزية وماذا تعمل بعد الظهر؟
كمال بعد الظهر أجلس مع المدير العام ونناقش شؤون الشركة، وأحضر اجتماعات يومية مع الموظفين.

Exercise 2

Now read the interview again. Link the English phrases to the corresponding Arabic expressions:

a	*I drink coffee.*	هو يعيش في أمريكا.	١
b	*He lives in America.*	نناقش شؤون الشركة.	٢
c	*I talk with him in the car.*	أشرب قهوة.	٣
d	*And what do you do in the afternoon?*	وماذا تعمل بعد الظهر؟	٤
e	*We discuss company affairs.*	أتكلم معه في السيارة.	٥

أكل، يأكل **ákala, yá'kul [S-I u]** *eat*[1]

فاكهة، فواكه **fáakihah, fawáakih*** *fruit*

خبز **khubz** *bread*

جبنة **júbnah** *cheese*

شرب، يشرب **shároba, yáshrab [S-I a]** *drink*

تكلم، يتكلم **takállama, yatakállam [S-V]** *speak*

عاش، يعيش **:aash, ya:íish [My-I]** *live*

عمل، يعمل **:ámila, yá:mal [S-I a]** *do, work*

ذهب، يذهب **dháhaba, yádh-hab [S-I a]** *go*

سائق، ـون **sáa'iq, -úun** *driver*

وصل، يوصل **wáSSala, yuwáSSil [S-II]** *connect, transport*

خبر، أخبار **khábar, akhbáar** *news*

طبع، يطبع **Tába:a, yáTba: [S-I a]** *print, type*

قرأ، يقرأ **qára'a, yáqra' [S-I a]** *read*

تقرير، تقارير **taqríir, taqaaríir*** *report*

مالي **máalii** *financial*

استغرق، يستغرق **istághraqa, yastághriq [S-X]** *take, use up, occupy* (of time)

استخدم، يستخدم **istákhdama, yastákhdim [S-X]** use

آلة حاسبة **áalah Háasibah** *computer*[2]

تعلم، يتعلم **ta:állama, yata:állam [S-V]** *learn*

استخدام **istikhdáam** *use, employment*

كلية، ـات **kullíyyah, -aat** *college, faculty*

تجارة **tijáarah** *trade, commerce*

جلس، يجلس **jálasa, yájlis [S-I i]** *sit*

عام **:aamm** *general*

ناقش، يناقش **náaqasha, yunáaqish [S-III]** *discuss*

شأن، شؤون **sha'n, shu'úun** *matter, affair*

حضر، يحضر **HáDara, yáHDur [S-I u]** *attend*

1 أكل **aakul** *I eat*. Note spelling here. This sign over the **alif** (called **maddah**) is always used when (theoretically) two **hamzahs** come together or a **hamzah** is followed by a long **a**-vowel (e.g. in the word for *computer* in the next note).
2 آلة حاسبة **aalah Haasibah** *computer*. This coinage – literally meaning *counting machine* – seems to have met with fairly general acceptance, although كمبيوتر **kambyuutir** is also common.

---

2 ماذا تعمل في أوقات الفراغ؟
maadhaa ta:mal fii awqaat al-faraagh?
What do you do in your free time?

CD2, TR21

Ruhiyyah and Hisham al-Musallam, on business from Jordan, are discussing with Ali, a Sudanese business contact, what they do in their free time.

Exercise 3
Listen to the discussion and answer the questions:

a *What does Hisham not play any more?*
b *What do he and Ali have in common?*
c *Who likes to watch Egyptian television serials?*
d *What does Ruhiyyah invite Ali to do this evening?*
e *Who is the most active:*
i Hisham? ii Ruhiyyah? iii Ali?

علي	ماذا تفعل في أوقات الفراغ يا هشام؟
هشام	ألعب الجولف وأسبح. لما كنا عائشين في عمان، كنت ألعب التنس، لكن الآن لا ألعب. أقرأ كثيرا.
علي	أنا أقرأ كثيرا كذلك. أحب الشعر الحديث. هل تحبين الشعر يا روحية؟
روحية	لا، أنا أفضل الروايات. أتفرج على التلفزيون كثيرا، وأحب المسلسلات المصرية
علي	أنا لا أحبها
هشام	ولا أنا. أكرهها فعلا. أفضل البرامج الثقافية أو الرياضة، لكن روحية لا تحب الرياضة.
روحية	ولكننا نحب السينما نحن الاثنان. سوف نذهب إلى السينما في المساء. ستجيء معنا يا علي؟

Exercise 4
Read the dialogue again and link the English phrases with the appropriate Arabic expressions:

a I used to play tennis.	١ كنت ألعب التنس.
b Do you like poetry?	٢ سوف نذهب إلى السينما.
c I prefer novels.	٣ روحية لا تحب الرياضة.
d Ruhiyyah doesn't like sport.	٤ هل تحبين الشعر؟
e We are going to the cinema.	٥ أفضل الروايات.

QUICK VOCAB

فعل، يفعل **fá:ala, yáf:al [S-I a]** *do*
أوقات الفراغ **áwqaat al-faráagh** *free time*
لعب، يلعب **lá:iba, yál:ab [S-I a]** *play*
عائش **:áa'ish** *living*
سبح، يسبح **sábaHa, yásbaH [S-I a]** *swim*
جولف **guulf** *golf*
الآن **al-áan** *now*
كذلك **ka-dháalik** *also, too* [lit., 'like that']

شعر **shi:r** *poetry*
حديث **Hadíith** *new, modern*
أحب، يحب **aHábba, yuHíbb [D-IV]** *like, love*
فضل، يفضل **fáDDala, yufáDDil [S-II]** *prefer*
رواية، ـات **riwáayah, -áat** *novel, story*
تفرج، يتفرج على **tafárraja, yatafárraj :ala [S-V]** *watch, look at*
مسلسل، ـات **musálsal, -áat** *serial, series*
ولا **wá-laa** *and not, nor*
كره، يكره **káriha, yákrah [S-I a]** *hate*
فعلا **fí:lan** *really, actually, in fact*
برنامج، برامج **barnáamij, baráamij*** *programme*
ثقافي **thaqáafii** *cultural*
رياضة **riyáaDah** *sport, sports*
جاء، يجيء **jáa'a, yajíi' [My-I]** *come*

QUICK VOCAB

تعبيرات رئيسية ta:biiráat ra'iisíyyah (Key phrases)

Asking what others do and saying what you do

ماذا تأكل الصبح؟	*What do you eat in the morning?*
ماذا تعمل بعد الظهر؟	*What do you do in the afternoon?*
هل تقرأ كثيرا؟	*Do you read a lot?*
أذهب إلى المكتب	*I go to the office*
آكل الفواكه دائما	*I always eat fruit*
أشرب قهوة كثيرا	*I drink coffee a lot*
ألعب تنس/ جولف	*I play tennis/golf*
أسبح	*I swim*

Asking what others like and saying what you like to do

ماذا تحب أن تفعل في أوقات الفراغ؟	*What do you like to do in your free time?*
أحب التلفزيون	*I like television*
هي لا تحب كرة القدم	*She doesn't like football*
نكره برامج الرياضة	*We hate sports programmes*

تحب أن تفعل **tuHíbb an táf:al** *you like to do* [lit. you like that you do]

كرة القدم **kúrat al-qádam** *football*

تراكيب اللغة **taraakíib al-lúghah** (Structures)

1 Talking about things in the present

Insight

This unit contains an overview of the Arabic verb system, placed here for ease of reference. Do not try to absorb all this information at once, as you will have ample opportunity to revise and consolidate your knowledge in future units. The overview should be studied in conjunction with Unit 7, which deals with the past tense and, in particular, with the Verb tables at the back of the book.

1 How to form the present tense

Look at the present tense column of Table 1 in the Verb tables. You will see that the present tense is formed from a stem (whose vowels usually differ from those of the past stem), to which are added prefixes for all parts, plus suffixes for certain parts.

With only a few exceptions (see below), the same set of prefixes and suffixes apply to every Arabic verb, so it is obviously important to learn them thoroughly from the beginning.

Here is the present tense of *to write* in transliterated form, without the dual forms, which occur rarely and can be learned later. The stem is given in bold type:

Singular	*Plural*
ya**ktub** *he writes, is writing*	ya**ktub**uun *they* (m.) *write*
ta**ktub** *she writes*	ya**ktub**na *they* (f.) *write*
ta**ktub** *you* (m.) *write*	ta**ktub**uun *you* (m) *write*
ta**ktub**iin *you* (f.) *write*	ta**ktub**na *you* (f.) *write*
a**ktub** *I write*	na**ktub** *we write*

Insight

To help you remember, here are some pointers

Prefixes:

- *The you forms all have the prefix* **ta-**, *which is similar to the* **t** *in the pronouns* **anta**, **anti**, *etc.*
- *All the third person forms have the prefix* **ya-** *with the exception of the feminine singular.*
- *The I form has* **a-**; *the pronoun is* **anaa**.
- *The we form has* **na-**; *the pronoun is* **naHnu**.

Suffixes:

- *The you (f. sing.) has suffix* **-iin** *to distinguish it from the masculine.*
- *The they and you (m. pl.) have the external plural suffix* **-uun**.
- *The they and you (f. pl.) have the suffix* **-na**.

2 Vowelling of the prefixes

In the types of stem that we have marked II, III and IV (see Verb tables), the vowel of all the prefixes changes to **u** (**yu-**, **tu-**, **u-**, etc.)

3 The present stem

In this unit, both tenses of the verb are given in Arabic script and transliteration in the *he* form, plus the verb type in square brackets [S-III, Mw-I, etc.] to enable you to look them up in the verb tables.

Example:

	Past	Present	Type	Meaning
فضل، يفضل	**faDDala**	**yufaDDil**	[S-II]	*prefer*

In subsequent units, verbs will be given as follows and you should refer to the appropriate verb table to identify all the parts of the verb.

Past Ar.	Past trans.	Type	Meaning
فضل	**faDDala**	[S-II]	*prefer*

4 Type S-I verbs

Type S-I verbs are the only ones in which the vowel on the middle radical is not predictable. In both tenses, it can be any of the three Arabic vowels, **a**, **i** or **u**.

Since these vowels are never written in Modern Arabic, they have to be learned. In this book, they are given in the following form:

Past Ar.	Past Trans.	Type	Meaning
كتب	**kataba**	[S-I u]	*write*

This should be interpreted as follows:

a *The Arabic gives the three root letters.*
b *The transliterated past identifies the middle radical vowel –*

here **a** *(***kataba***). Note: the vowel on the first radical is* always **a** *in the past tense and this radical has no vowel in the present.*

c *The verb type (here, S-I) directs you to the appropriate verb table.*

d *The vowel given after the verb type (here,* **u***) is the middle radical vowel in the present stem (***ktub***).*

The following scheme of things usually prevails, but there are always exceptions.

Past stem	*Vowel on C^2*	➔	*Vowel on C^2*	*Present stem*
CaCaC	a	➔	u or i	**CCuC**
kataba *to write*				**ktub**
CaCiC	i	➔	a	**CCaC**
fahima *to understand*				**fham**
CaCuC	u	➔	u	**CCuC**
kabura *to be big*				**kbur**

Most S-I verbs are of the **CaCaC ➔ CCu/iC** type. There are quite a few **CaCiC ➔ CCaC** types, but **CaCuC ➔ CCuC** is rare and usually indicates a state of being or becoming something.

Insight

You will usually still be understood if you get these vowels wrong, so don't worry too much about them at this stage.

5 Other types of verb

Type D-I and type Fw-I verbs also have variable vowellings, which will be indicated in the same way.

All other types of verb (including S-II to X) fortunately have standard vowellings for both stems, so reference to the appropriate verb table will provide all parts automatically.

These will be explained as they are introduced, with reference to the Verb tables, but there are some general pointers which you can learn about now.

You know already that there are no really irregular verbs in Arabic, with the exception of **laysa** (see Unit 8). The same prefixes and suffixes are used for all verbs, but some verbs have two stems, in one or both of the tenses.

An example of this is the verb **kaana** (see Unit 8), which has the two past stems **kaan-** and **kun-**. This type of verb is usually known as a hollow verb and is the subject of Table Mw-I. Although it should not be used in *is/are* sentences, **kaana** has a 'present' tense, used in certain contexts to express doubt or uncertainty. This also has two stems: **kuun-** and **kun-**. Again refer to Table Mw-I.

6 Function of the present tense

Arabic has only two simple tenses, the past and the present. Just as the past tense serves for *did*, *has done*, the present tense fulfils the functions of *does*, *is doing* and, in questions, *does do*, as in *Does he live here?* Common sense will tell you how to translate from Arabic:

يعيشون في شقة كبيرة في أبو ظبي

ya:iishuun fii shaqqah kabiirah fii abuu DHabi

they-live in apartment big in Abu Dhabi

They live in a big apartment in Abu Dhabi

تنشر الحكومة الإحصائيات في أول الشهر

tanshur al-Hukuumah al-iHSaa'iyaat fii awwal ash-shahr

she-publishes the-government the-statistics in first the-month

The government publishes the statistics at the beginning of the month

ماذا تأكل في الصباح؟

maadhaa ta'kul fi S-SabaaH?

what you-eat in the-morning

What do you eat in the morning?

7 The past continuous

The past continuous is what we call a verb phrase such as *was studying*, *used to study*, and so on.

In Arabic this is expressed with the aid of the verb **kaana** (type Mw-I), in the same way as the *had done* type verb explained in Unit 8, except that the main verb this time is in the present tense.

In all other respects, including agreement and word order, this tense behaves like its sister in Unit 8.

kaana + present tense verb	= past continuous *was studying*
kaana + past tense verb	= pluperfect *had studied*

كانت فاطمة تدرس في جامعة لندن

kaanat faaTimah tadrus fii jaami:at landan

she-was Fatimah she-studies in university [of] London

Fatimah was studying at the University of London

كنا نذهب إلى السوق كل يوم

kunnaa nadhhab ilaa s-suuq kull yawm

we-were we-go to the-market every day

We used to go to the market every day

8 Talking about what you will do in the future

There is no future tense in Arabic.

Actions that have not yet happened are expressed by placing the word سوف **sawfa** or the prefix سـ **sa-** before a present tense verb. Since it consists of only one Arabic letter, **sa-** is joined to the word that follows it. These are called future markers (noted in literal translations as [future]):

سوف يصل الوزير غدا

sawfa yaSil al-waziir ghadan
[future] he-arrives the-minister tomorrow
The minister will arrive tomorrow

سأسافر الأسبوع القادم

sa-usaafir al-usbuu: al-qaadim
[future] – I-travel the-week the-coming
I shall travel next week

وصل، يصل **wáSala, yáSil** [Fw-I i] *to arrive*

9 The complete *not*

Arabic has several ways of expressing *not* which must be used in different contexts.

Negative	*Context*	*Formation*
ليس **laysa***	*is/are* sentences	second noun/adjective, if indefinite, has accusative marker
لا **laa**	present verb	verb takes normal form
ما **maa**	past verb	verb in the past tense
لن **lan**	future verb	**sa-/sawfa** omitted, and verb in the subjunctive**
لم **lam**	past actions	verb in the present jussive** form, but with past meaning

* Unlike the other negatives, **laysa** is actually a verb and has to be used accordingly. (See Unit 8.)

** For these terms see later in this unit.

a **laysa** *is used for negating* is/are *sentences:*

laysa r-rajul kabiiran ليس الرجل كبيرا

is-not the-man old *The man is not old*

b **maa** *negates a past verb:*

maa saafarat ila l-maghrib ما سافرت إلى المغرب

not she-travelled to the-Morocco *She did not go to Morocco*

c **laa** *negates sentences with a present tense verb:*

laa ya:rafuun al-lughah l-faransiyyah لا يعرفون اللغة الفرنسية

They (m.) *don't know French*

not they-know the-language the-French

d **lan** *negates the future. The* **sa-** *or* **sawfa** *future marker is omitted when* **lan** *is used.*

lan taSilii qabl aDH-DHuhr لن تصلي قبل الظهر

not you-will-arrive before the-noon *You* (f. sing.) *will not arrive before noon*

e **lam** *negates verbs which refer to the past, although, as will be discussed below, the actual verb used is a form of the present.*

lam ya'kuluu l-laHm لم يأكلوا اللحم

not they-ate the-meat *They didn't eat the meat*

maa + past verb and **lam** + present verb convey exactly the same meaning. In literary Arabic, the latter construction is considered more elegant.

10 Altered forms of the present verb

If you look carefully at examples d) and e) above, you will note that the verbs used are slightly different from those you have learned (they have no final ن for example).

Historically, in addition to the normal form, Arabic had two so-called moods of the present (not the past) tense, called the *subjunctive* and the *jussive* respectively.

These altered forms must be used after certain words in Arabic. Two of these are **lan**, which requires the subjunctive, and **lam**, which requires the jussive.

Fortunately, for many verbs, the subjunctive and the jussive are identical in writing. They are given in full in Verb Table 1 on page 399 but, for convenience, here are the parts that show a difference. Other parts of the verb remain unchanged.

Verbs which show further deviations will be explained as they occur:

تكتبين **taktubiin** *you write* (f. sing.) ➔ **taktubii** تكتبي

يكتبون **yaktubuun** *they write* (m. pl.) ➔ **yaktubuu** يكتبوا

تكتبون **taktubuun** *you write* (m. pl.) ➔ **taktubuu** تكتبوا

The Arabs call this 'the omission of the **nuun**'.

Insight

An unpronounced **alif** is added at the end. You will remember that the same thing happened in the past tense. In fact, it is a convention that any verb which has a **-uu** suffix adds this redundant letter. Nobody knows why.

Remember to use these forms after both **lan** and **lam**.

11 Prepositions and pronoun suffixes

Prepositions tell you where something is in relation to something else, such as *on*, *behind*, *in*, etc.

However, in both English and Arabic, they often form an essential part of what are known as phrasal verbs. English examples of phrasal verbs are *call up*, *call on*, *call in*, all essentially different meanings derived from the simple verb *call*.

In Arabic, for instance, you don't 'need something', you 'need *towards* something'.

Here are some examples:

احتاج، يحتاج إلى **iHtaaja, yaHtaaj ilaa [Mw-VIII]** *to need something*

احتفل، يحتفل بـ **iHtafala, yahtafil bi- [S-VIII]** *to celebrate something*

رغب، يرغب في **raghiba, yarghab fii [S-I a]** *to want, desire something*

رحب، يرحب بـ **raHHaba bi- [S-II]** *to welcome someone*

Prepositions required after verbs are given in the vocabularies.

When prepositions are used with pronouns (*towards him*, *by her*, and so on), they use the same possessive pronouns suffixes as are used with nouns (see Unit 5):

كتابها **kitaab-ha** *her book*
منها **min-ha** *from her*

PRONUNCIATION

Some Arabic prepositions alter slightly when they are attached to a suffix and some of them affect certain suffixes:

i Prepositions ending in **-a** *lose the* **-a** *with the suffix* **-ii**, *me:*

ma:a with + **-ii** *me* = معي **ma:ii** *with me*

ii Prepositions ending in **-n** *double this with the suffix* **-ii**:
min *from* + **-ii** *me* = مني **minn-ii** *from me*

akhadhuu l-jariidah min-nii أخذوا الجريدة منّي

they-took the-newspaper from-me	*They took the newspaper from me*

(Note: This is different from منّا **min-naa**, *from us, where one* **n** *belongs to the suffix.)*

iii *After long vowels and* **-ay**, **-ii** *me is pronounced* **-ya**:

فيّ **fiiya** (or **fiyya**)	*in me*
عليّ **:alayya**	*on me*

iv *After* **-i**, **-ii** *or* **-ay**, **-hu**, **-hum** *and* **-hunna** *change* **-u** *to* **-i** *(not visible in the written form):*

فيه **fii-hi**	*in him*
بهم **bi-him**	*with them*

v *Prepositions ending in long* **-aa** *written as a* **-y** *without dots* *(see page 16)* *change their endings into* **-ay**:

إلى **ilaa**, *towards becomes* إليـ **ilay-**: إليكم **ilay-kum**, *towards you*

على **:alaa**, *on becomes* عليـ **:alay-**: علينا **:alay-naa**, *on us*

yaD-Hak :alay-naa	يضحك علينا
he-laughs on-us	*He's laughing at us*

vi لـ **li-**, *to, for becomes* **la-** *before all the suffixes except* **-ii** *(see i) above). This change is again not apparent in the written form:*

لهم **la-hum** *for them*

sa-adfa: la-haa l-mablagh al-maDbuuT	سأدفع لها المبلغ المضبوط
(future)I-pay to-her the-sum the-exact	*I'll pay her the exact amount*

Insight

li-, as a one letter word (see Arabic script and pronunciation guide) is attached to the word after it. If this has **al-** *the*, the **alif** is omitted:

للولد **li-l-walad** — *for the boy*

In addition, if the noun itself begins with **laam**, the doubling sign is used

للّغة **li-l-lughah** — *to the language*

أوزان الكلمات awzáan al-kalimáat (Word shapes)

CD2, TR22

The word pattern for this unit is **C¹uC²aC³áa'***, for example, **wuzaráa'** وزراء *ministers*, which sounds like the English *to a rat* (Cockney/Glaswegian pron. of the *t* as a glottal stop).

This shape is mainly used for the plural of certain male human beings that have the singular shape **CaCiiC**. In fact, it is relatively safe to guess plurals of such nouns using this shape. It does not take the accusative marker:

سفراء **sufaráa'*** from سفير **safíir**	*ambassador*
أمير، أمراء **amíir, umaráa'***	*prince, emir*
وزير، وزراء **wazíir, wuzaráa'***	*minister*
مدير، مدراء **mudíir, mudaráa'***	*director, manager*

It is also used with some adjectives of the same shape:

سعيد، سعداء **sa:iid, su:adáa'***	*happy, joyful*

and some nouns with the singular shape **CaaCiC**:

شاعر، شعراء **sháa:ir, shu:aráa'*** *poet*

تمرينات **tamriináat** (Practice)

Exercise 5

Nafisah plays tennis and enjoys going to the cinema and swimming. She would like to make friends with someone who has the same interests as she does. She sees the following entries in the newspaper. Who has most in common with her?

كن صديقي **kun Sadiiq-ii!** *Be my friend!*

لعب، ألعاب **la:b, al:áab** *playing, game*

هواية، ـات **hawáayah, -áat** *hobby*

سباحة **sibáaHah** *swimming*

Exercise 6

Change the following sentences into the negative, using one of the words in the box below. Use each word only once:

١ هذا الجمل قبيح.
٢ البيوت رخيصة في الرياض.
٣ سوف نسافر إلى الهند في الشهر القادم.
٤ ذهبنا إلى المسبح يوم الجمعة.
٥ أختي تعمل في صيدلية.
٦ درس صالح في أمريكا.

لم	لا	ليست	لن	ليس	ما

جمل، جمال **jámal, jimáal** *camel*

قبيح **qabíiH** *ugly*

الهند **al-hind** *India*

درس، يدرس **dárasa, yádrus [S-I u]** *study*

Exercise 7

Fill the gaps using the prepositions from the box below:

١ المدير يدفع ....ـها راتبا شهريا.

٢ ستسافر..............ـه في الطائرة.

٣ هل تضحك ....ـنا؟

٤ أخذت الجريدة ....ـي.

٥ أهذا كتاب جيد؟ زوجتي تحتاج ....ـه.

إلى	على	ل	مع	من

Exercise 8

Hameed is an active person. Make up complete sentences about him, saying what his sports are and what he likes and dislikes and using the information in the table below. The first one is done for you.

حميد يلعب كرة. *Hameed plays football*

يلعب	يحب	لا يحب	يكره
كرة	تنس	القراءة	السينما
سكواش	السباحة	الكتب	التلفزيون

Exercise 9

The verbs in brackets in the following sentences are all in the *he* form. Referring to the translation below, substitute the correct present tense forms:

١ الأولاد القطريون (يتعلم) اللغة الانجليزية في المدرسة الثانوية.

٢ (يتصل) بأمها كل يوم.

٣ (يشرب) شاي عند رجوعنا من العمل.

٤ (يكتب) رسالة إلى صديقتي نورة.

٥ الموظف يريد أن (يكلمـ)ـنا فورا.

٦ هل (يعرف) ذلك الرجل؟

٧ (يقفل) الصيدليات الساعة ٦.

٨ سوف (يصل) إلى نيو يورك يوم الخميس.

٩ كانت البنات (يلعب) مع أولاد الجيران.

١٠ كان محمود وإخوانه (يكسب) كثيرا في الكويت.

Translation:

1 *Qatari children learn English in secondary school.*
2 *She telephones her mother every day.*
3 *We drink tea on our return from work.*
4 *I am writing a letter to my friend Nourah.*

5 *The official wants to talk to us immediately.*
6 *Do you (fem. sing.) know that man?*
7 *The pharmacies close at six o'clock.*
8 *They (fem.) will arrive in New York on Thursday.*
9 *The girls used to play with the neighbours' children.*
10 *Mahmoud and his brothers used to earn a lot in Kuwait.*

Exercise 10

Change the following past tense verbs (in brackets) into the present tense:

١ (سأل) سكرتيره سؤالا.
٢ (حملت) البنت القهوة إلى الصالة.
٣ (فحص) الطبيب عيون المريض.
٤ صاحب الدكان (قدم) لنا شاي.
٥ ما (فهمت) هذا الكتاب.
٦ إلى أين (ذهبت)؟

Translation:

1 *He asked his (male) secretary a question.*
2 *The girl carried the coffee to the living room.*
3 *The doctor examined the eyes of the patient.*
4 *The shopkeeper offered us tea.*
5 *I didn't understand this book.*
6 *Where did you (m. sing.) go?*

فحص **fáHaSa, yáfHaS [S-I a]** *to examine*

مريض، مرضى **maríiD, márDaa*** (adj.) *ill*; (noun) *patient*

Exercise 11

Read the article below about the Dubai Shopping Festival and answer the following questions:

a *When does it take place?*
b *Why do so many people come to the festival?*
c *Name two of the attractions.*
d *Where is the firework display held?*

يقام مهرجان دبي للتسوق في
شهر مارس ويحضر الناس
بالآلاف من الإمارات والعالم
كله إلى دبي ليستفيدوا من
التنزيلات الكبيرة في أسعار
البضائع في المراكز التجارية
والأسواق. وإضافة إلى ذلك
تقدم الشركات جوائز قيمة
في سحوبات منها سيارات
وكيلوغرامات ذهب. وهناك
أيضا فعاليات ثقافية، وفنية
ورياضية مثل سباق الخيول
وعروض فخمة من الألعاب
النارية فوق خور دبي المشهور.

QUICK VOCAB

يقام **yuqáam** *is held, takes place* (passive verb)

مهرجان، ـات **mahrajáan, -áat** *festival*

تسوق **tasáwwuq** *shopping*

استفاد، يستفيد **istafáada, yastafíid [My-X]** *benefit*

تنزيل، ـات **tánzíil, -áat** *lowering, reduction*

سعر، أسعار **si:r, as:áar** *price*

بضائع **baDáa'i:*** *goods, merchandise*

إضافة إلى ذلك **iDáafatan ílaa dháalik** *in addition to that*

قدم، يقدم **qáddama, yuqáddim [S-II]** *offer, present*

جائزة، جوائز **jáa'izah, jawáa'iz*** *prize, reward*

قيم **qáyyim** *valuable*

سحب، سحوبات **saHb, suHuubáat** *lottery*

ذهب **dháhab** *gold*

أيضا **áyDan** *also*

فعالية، ـات **fa:aalíyyah, -aat** *activity, event*

فني **fánnii** *artistic; technical*

رياضي **riyáaDii** *sporting*

مثل **mithl** *like*

سباق **sibáaq** *racing*

خيل/خيول **khayl/khuyúul** *horses* (both with plural meaning)

عرض، عروض **:arD, :urúuD** *show, display*
ألعاب نارية **al:áab naaríyyah** *fireworks*
فوق **fawq(a)** *above, over*

10 things you need to know

1 *The basic present tense of the verb is used to express all actions that are incomplete, e.g.* he eats, is eating.
2 *There is one exception to this, which is when it is preceded by the negative word* **lam** not. *This changes its meaning to the past.*
3 *The present tense is formed by adding a fixed set of prefixes to the present stem of the verb, along with suffixes for the* you *and* they *plural forms.*
4 *To form the past continuous* (he was going) *or habitual* (he used to go to work by bus), *use the past of the verb* **kaana** *followed by the present tense of the main verb.*
5 *To express the future, use the present tense preceded by the future marker* **sawfa** *or its abbreviated form* **sa-** *written as a prefix.*
6 *Three new words for* not *are used with the present tense.* **laa** *negates a present action.*
7 **lan** *negates a future action (the* **sawfa** *or* **sa-** *being in this case omitted).*
8 **lam** *is used with a special form of the present tense and has the effect of changing its meaning to the past. (Alternatively,* **maa** *with the past tense can be used, but this is considered to be less stylish and is frowned on by purists.)*
9 *Formal Arabic has two additional variants of the present tense, called the subjunctive and the jussive. In many verbs these are indistinguishable in writing from the normal present, except in the masculine plural* you *and* they *forms, where the final* **nuun** *is omitted and an unpronounced* **alif** *put in its place if no other suffix is present.*
10 *Certain prepositions change their pronunciation before certain pronoun suffixes. These should be learned carefully.*

11

الأعياد الإسلامية
al-a:yaad al-islaamiyyah
Islamic festivals

In this unit you will learn:

- ***about the main Islamic festivals***
- ***special greetings used on festival days***
- ***the Islamic calendar***
- ***how to say 'what?'/'where?'/'who?'***
- ***how to say 'to have'***

Introduction

The emphasis of the book changes slightly from this unit onwards. Units 1–10 contain all the essential basics of Modern Standard Arabic, so now we can go on to more advanced and realistic texts and dialogues. These use more complex sentence structures, so make sure you have mastered the principles given in Units 1–10 before going on. Individual words can be looked up in the vocabulary after the texts. However, it is less easy to refer back to half-absorbed constructions, so some revision now will pay dividends later.

The Arabic texts and dialogues will be given as they would appear in a modern book or newspaper, that is, with only occasional vowelling. Only a literal word-for-word translation of the texts will be given in the Key to the exercises to help you to concentrate on the Arabic structures. You should try to convert this into normal English.

Major new grammatical features are given in special sections just as before and minor points and reminders of things already dealt with are given in the notes after the texts.

Insight

Where there is no realistic alternative, data that have to be learned mechanically (for instance, parts of the verb) can be referred to in the tables at the back of the book. We suggest that, while you refer to these as much as possible, you should not allow yourself to become discouraged if you can't take them all in at once. Rather keep coming back to them as you work through the units.

الأعياد الإسلامية al-a:yaad al-islaamiyyah

Islamic festivals

CD2, TR23

Jack and Fran, visiting Egypt during the month of Ramadan, ask their friend Ahmed about Islamic festivals.

Exercise 1

Look carefully through the new words before you begin. Listen to the recording or read the dialogue several times, and answer the questions:

a *How many festivals do all Muslims celebrate?*
b *Which month comes before the first festival?*
c *What should people abstain from during the month of Ramadan?*

Exercise 2

Listen to the recording again and answer these questions:

a *The great festival of the pilgrimage begins:*
i on the first day   ii on the last day   iii in the middle

b *People travel:*
i to Mecca   ii to Medina   iii from Mecca

c *They visit:*
i the Kaabah   ii the mosque

d *How do they celebrate the festival?*

e *Which Muslim celebration resembles a Christian festival?*

جاك   كم عيدا عند المسلمين؟
أحمد   الأعياد المهمّة عندنا إثنان.
فران   وما هما؟
أحمد   الأوّل هو العيد الصغير واسمه عيد الفطر.
جاك   وفي أيّ شهر هو؟
أحمد   العيد الصغير في أوّل يوم من شهر شوال.
فران   وما مناسبته؟
أحمد   مناسبته أنّ شهر شوال يعقب شهر رمضان الكريم، وهو شهر الصوم عند المسلمين.
جاك   وما معنى الصوم عندكم؟
أحمد   الصوم معناه أنّ الناس لا يأكلون ولا يشربون في النهار. هذا هو معنى الصوم.
فران   وما هو العيد الآخر؟
أحمد   هو العيد الكبير أو عيد الأضحى.
جاك   وما مناسبته؟
أحمد   مناسبته الحجّ وهو يبدأ في آخر يوم من أيّام الحج. والحج معناه أنّ الناس يسافرون الى مكّة المكرّمة ويزورون الكعبة.
فران   وكيف يحتفلون بهذا العيد؟
أحمد   هم يذبحون فيه ذبائح.
جاك   وما هي الذبيحة؟

أحمد	الذبيحة هي خروف يذبحونه ويأكلونه في نهاية الحج. وهذا عادة عند المسلمين.
فران	فأعيادكم اثنان فقط إذا؟
أحمد	لا، في بعض الأقطار يحتفلون بعيد ثالث.
جاك	وما هو؟
أحمد	هو مولد النبي، صلّى اللّه عليه وسلّم، في شهر ربيع الأوّل.
فران	نعم، هذا مثل عيد الميلاد عندنا نحن المسيحيّين.

Exercise 3

Read the text again, referring to the notes below and link the English phrases with the equivalent Arabic expressions:

a	*We have two important festivals.*	في أوّل يوم من شهر شوال.	١
b	*Which month is it in?*	كيف يحتفلون بهذا العيد؟	٢
c	*The first day of the month of Shawal.*	فأعيادكم اثنان فقط إذا؟	٣
d	*What do you mean by fasting?*	ما معنى الصوم عندكم؟	٤
e	*People don't eat or drink in the daytime.*	هذا مثل عيد الميلاد عندنا نحن المسيحيّين.	٥
f	*How do they celebrate this festival?*	الأعياد المهمّة عندنا إثنان.	٦
g	*What is the sacrifice?*	هذا عادة عند المسلمين.	٧
h	*It is a custom among the Muslims.*	الناس لا يأكلون ولا يشربون في النهار.	٨
i	*So you only have two festivals?*	ما هي الذبيحة؟	٩
i	*This is like our Christian Christmas.*	في أيّ شهر هو؟	١٠

QUICK VOCAB

عيد، أعياد **:iid, a:yáad** *festival; anniversary*
مسلم، ـون **múslim, -uun** *Muslim*
مهم **muhímm** *important*
فطر **fiTr** *breaking of a fast*
شوال **shawwáal** name of an Islamic month (see list later in this unit)
مناسبة، ـات **munáasabah, -aat** *occasion*
عقب **:áqaba S-1 u** *come after, follow*
كريم، كرام **karíim, kiráam** *noble, generous* (here used as an honorific adjective for the month of Ramadan, often translated as *holy*)
صوم **Sawm** *fast, fasting*
معنى **má:naa*** *meaning*
نهار **naháar** *daytime, hours of daylight*
آخر **áakhar*** (f. أخرى **úkhraa***) *other*
عيد الأضحى **:iid al-áD-Haa** *Festival of the Sacrifice* (see below)
الحج **al-Hajj** *the pilgrimage*
آخر **áakhir** *last* (of something)
يوم، أيّام **yawm, ayyáam** *day*
مكّة المكرّمة **mákkah l-mukárramah** *Holy (City of) Mecca*
زار **záara Mw-I** *visit*
الكعبة **al-ká:bah** *the Kaabah* (Holy Shrine in Mecca)
احتفل بـ **iHtáfala bi- [S-VIII]** *celebrate*
ذبح **dhábaHa S-I a** *slaughter*
ذبيحة، ذبائح **dhabíiHah, dhabáa'iH*** *sacrificial animal*
خروف، خرفان **kharúuf, khirfáan** *sheep*
نهاية **niháayah** *end*
عادة، ـات **:áadah, -aat** *custom, habit*
إذا **ídhan** *so, therefore*
بعض **ba:D** *some, part of something*
قطر، أقطار **quTr, aqTáar** *region, zone, area*
ثالث **tháalith** *third* (adj.)

مولد النبي **máwlid an-nábii** (festival of) *the Prophet's Birthday*

صلّى اللّه عليه وسلّم **Sállaa l-Láahu :aláy-hi wa-sállam** *Prayers and Peace be upon Him* (said after mentioning the name of the Prophet)

مثل **mithl** like

عيد الميلاد **:iid al-miiláad** *Christmas*

مسيحي، ـون **masíiHii, -uun** *Christian*

QUICK VOCAB

الملاحظات al-mulaaHaDHáat (Notes)

- **kam** *how many. This word takes the singular of the noun, which is also marked with the accusative ending* **-an** *if there is no other suffix (see Unit 8).*
- **muslimiin.** *The masculine plural ending* **-uun** *becomes* **-iin** *after all prepositions (in this case* **:ind**) *and also when the noun is the possessing item of a possessive construction (see Unit 14). For* **:ind** *expressing to have, see later in this unit.*
- *Note the dual pronoun* **humaa** *they-two for two things or persons (see Unit 9).*
- **awwal yawm** *the first day. The adjective* **awwal** *first can be used in the normal way, but frequently precedes its noun which then does not have* **al-** *the.*
- **shahr shawwaal** *is a possessive construction* (the month of Shawwal), *so the word* **shahr** *cannot have* **al-**.
- **anna** *that (conjunction), like* **inna** *(Unit 8), is always followed by a noun showing the accusative marker if applicable, or a pronoun suffix.*
- معناه **ma:naa-h** *its meaning. Words ending in* **-aa** *but written with* ى *change this to* **alif** *when anything is added.* ى *can only exist as the final letter of an Arabic word or word combination, the same as* ة *(which becomes* ت *when anything is added).*
- *The verbs eat and drink are in their full plural agreeing forms because they come after their subject* **an-naas** *the people (see Unit 7).*
- **aakhir** *last behaves in the same way as* **awwal**. *See above.*
- **yazuuruun** *they visit. This kind of verb, called a hollow verb*

by the Arabs, has two stems for both present and past tenses. This one is vowelled like **kaana**, *but there are two other vowel patterns. Study these in Tables* **Mw, My** *and* **Ma** *and you can always refer back to them in the future. Like all verbs, these occur usually in the* he *or* she *forms (because of the agreement rules) so are often recognizable from their long* **aa** *vowel in the past. In the present tense, the long vowel is (order of statistical frequency)* **uu, ii** *or (infrequently)* **aa**.

- **fii-h**. *The use of prepositions in both English and Arabic is very idiomatic and therefore unpredictable. We would say* on it, *but the Arabs say* in it. *A similar idiosyncracy in English would be: on Tuesday, but in March.*
- **kharuuf yadhbaHuun-uh** a sheep that they slaughter. *English would supply the word* that, *and ignore the ending* **-uh** *on the verb. See section on relative clauses in Unit 13.*
- **haadhaa :aadah** this is a custom. *You will recognise this as an* is/are *sentence. The* **haadhaa** *does not agree with the feminine noun, as it refers back to the preceding sentence as a whole.*
- **faqaT** only. *This word always follows what it refers to.*
- **yaHtafiluun** they celebrate. *The verb is plural here, because no subject is stated, it being the* they *implied within the verb.*
- **naHnu** we *is for emphasis or contrast here.*

تعبيرات رئيسية **ta:biiráat ra'iisíyyah** (Key phrases)

What to say at feast times and birthdays

The most universal greeting at festival times:

عيد مبارك **:iid mubaarak** *Blessed festival*

The reply:

الله يبارك فيك

Al-laah yubaarik fii-k (**fii-ki** to a woman, **fii-kum** to several people)

God bless you

A greeting which can be used for any annual occasion such as a birthday:

كل عام وأنت بخير

kull :aam w-anta bi-khayr (f. **anti**, pl. **antum**)

Every year and [may] you [be] well, many happy returns

The reply:

وأنت بخير

wa anta/anti/antum bi-khayr

And [may] you [be] well

Cards are often sent, usually bearing one of the congratulatory phrases given above.

معلومات ثقافية ma:luumáat thaqaafíyyah (Cultural tips)

The main religious festivals celebrated by all Muslims, regardless of sect or country of origin, are as follows.

عيد الفطر :iid al-fiTr *(or 'Lesser Bairam', at the end of Ramadan)*

Date: 1st of Shawwal (see 'The Islamic calendar', below).

This is a holiday of about three days, marking the end of the fast of the month of Ramadan, during which Muslims allow nothing to pass their lips (food, drink, smoke) between sunrise and sunset.

On the first day of the feast there are special prayers in the mosque and the rest of the holiday is traditionally spent visiting family and friends, offering congratulations and making up for lost time with large feasts. Children usually receive gifts of money and new clothes.

As you can imagine, total abstention from food and drink during the daytime in Ramadan causes considerable hardship. Working hours are reduced, but you will find that people tend to be listless. Lack of sleep is another problem, as a sustaining meal has to be prepared and consumed before the dawn deadline. If you are in a Muslim country during Ramadan, it is polite to show consideration by not eating or drinking in front of local people.

عيد الأضحى **:iid al-aD-Haa** ***(or 'Korban Bairam')***

Date: 10th of Dhuu l-Hijjah (see calendar).

This is the major feast of Islam and again merits a holiday of several days. Even for those not on the pilgrimage, a large feast is in order, those who can afford it slaughtering (usually) a sheep and sharing it with the family, often giving some of the meat to the poor. The richer and more important you are, the bigger the feast that is expected. Members of the family visit each other's houses, offering congratulations, and again gifts are made to the children.

مولد النبي **mawlid an-nabii** ***'Prophet's Birthday'***

Date: 12th of Rabii: al-awwal (see calendar).

The Prophet Muhammad's Birthday is often just called **al-mawlid.** Although not officially prescribed by Islam, this is celebrated in varying local forms in many parts of the Arab world.

Muslims of the Shi'ah persuasion have additional festivals of their own.

The Islamic calendar

Although nowadays it is only used in most countries for religious purposes (such as festival dates), you should be familiar with the Islamic calendar.

The Islamic date is calculated from the date of the Prophet Muhammad's flight (in Arabic, **hijrah**) from Mecca to Medinah, which took place on 16 July 622 AD. For this reason, Islamic dates are specified as هجري **hijrii**, often abbreviated to هـ. The English abbreviation is AH.

Apart from starting more than six centuries later than the western calendar, the Islamic year consists of 12 lunar months, adding up to only 354 days. Consequently, the years are not synchronised with our solar calendar, so festivals creep forward according to our dating system. For instance, in 2000 AD (1420–21 هـ) Ramadan started on about 5 December.

Insight

For most secular transactions, Arabic versions of the western month names are used. The Arabs call the AD year ميلادي **miilaadii** *pertaining to the birth* (i.e. of Christ), abbreviated to م.

٢٠٠٠م — ١٤٢٠هـ

Below is a table for the two sets of months. For the reasons given above, these do not, of course, correspond except in the order in which they come.

Western calendar	*Islamic calendar*
يناير **yanaayir**	محرم **muHarram**
فبراير **fabraayir**	صفر **Safar**
مارَس **maaris**	ربيع الأول **rabii: al-awwal**
أَبريل **abriil**	ربيع الثاني **rabii: ath-thaanii**
مايو **maayuu**	جمادى الأولى **jumaada l-uulaa**
يونيو **yuunyuu**	جمادى الآخرة **jumaada l-aakhirah**
يوليو **yuulyuu**	رجب **rajab**
أغسطس **aghusTus**	شَعْبان **sha:baan**
سبتمبر **sabtambar**	رمضان **ramaDaan**
أُكتوبر **uktuubir**	شوال **shawwaal**
نوفمبر **nuufambar**	ذو القعدة **dhuu l-qa:dah**
ديسمبر **diisambar**	ذو الحجة **dhuu l-Hijjah**

Insight

There is a third set of month names, starting, surprisingly, with **kaanuun ath-thaani** '*the second Kanoon*', used mainly in the Syria–Iraq region and you should try to learn these if you are going to that area.

تراكيب اللغة **taraakíib al-lúghah** (Structures)

1 Question words

These question words differ from the question markers هل **hal** and أ **a** given in Unit 2, which merely turn statements into *yes/no* questions. The words referred to here are more specific.

What?

There are two words for *what*: ما **maa** is used before nouns and subject pronouns:

ما هو؟	*What [is] it (he)?*
ما هذا؟	*What [is] this?*
ما اسمه؟	*What [is] his/its name?*

ماذا **maadhaa** is used before verbs:

ماذا أكلوا؟	*What they ate? (What did they eat?)*
ماذا يحمل؟	*What he-carries? (What is he carrying?)*

Insight

ما is a very versatile word in Arabic and its meaning depends on the context. You have already seen it meaning not in Units 7 and 10 and it has other usages too.

Note also the common construction in the text:

ما هي الذبيحة؟	*What [is] she the-sacrifice-animal?*

We would say *What is a sacrifice animal?*

Who?

من **man** is used before both nouns and verbs. In unvowelled Arabic, this looks identical to **min**, *from*. You have to decide from the context, which does not usually present any difficulty:

من هم؟ *Who [are] they?*

من فتح الباب؟ *Who he-opened the-door?*
Who opened the door?

Also note:

من هو المدير؟ *Who he [is] the-manager?*
Who is the manager?

Which?

أيّ **ayy** (m.), أيّة **ayyah** (f.). This is followed by a singular noun without **al-** and agrees with it in gender:

أيّ رجل؟ *Which man?*

أيّة بنت؟ *Which girl?*

How many?

كم **kam**. This is followed by a singular noun, which requires the accusative marker **-an**, unless it has a feminine ending:

كم عيدا؟ *How many festivals?*

كم سيّارة؟ *How many cars?*

How?

كيْف **kayf(a)** is used before nouns and verbs. The final **-a** is often omitted:

كيف سافرت؟ *How you-travelled?*

كيف حالك؟ *How [is] condition-your?* (i.e. *How are you?* – a very common greeting)

Where?

أَين **ayna**. Note that when **ayna** means *where to?* and *where from?* it is preceded by إلى to and من from respectively:

أين المتحف؟ *Where [is] the-museum?*

إلى أين تذهب؟	*To where you-go?*
من أين حضروا؟	*From where they-came?*

When?

متى **mataa** usually used with vèrbs:

متى وصلتم؟	*When you-arrived?*

Why?

لماذا **li-maadhaa** used before verbs:

لماذا سافرت الى مسقط؟	*Why she-travelled to Muscat?*

2 How to say 'to have'

Arabic has no actual verb meaning *to have*, but uses a combination of a preposition and a noun or pronoun.

Three common prepositions are used:

لـ **li-**	*to, for*
عند **:ind(a)**	*with* (equivalent of French *chez*)

Insight

لدى **ladaa** *with* – this is slightly archaic, though still used. When a pronoun suffix is added, it behaves like **ilaa** (see Unit 10). It has not been used much in this book.

So, to say *Muhammad has a new car* we say:

لمحمد سيارة جديدة	*to mul lammad car new*
عندي كتاب ممتاز	*with-me book excellent* *I have an excellent book*

Insight

li- and **:ind** are more or less interchangeable. The former is considered more elegant, but in spoken Arabic the latter is used almost exclusively.

To say *had*, Arabic uses kaana *was/were* + **li-/:ind**:

كانت لمحمد سيارة جديدة	*was to-muHammad car new*
كان عندي كتاب ممتاز	*was with-me book excellent*

In the first example above, it is not always necessary for the verb **kaana** to agree with its subject (here, **sayyaarah**, f.). **kaana** would be just as acceptable.

To say *will have* use **yakuun** (the present tense of **kaana**) + **li-/:ind.** With this verb the future marker **sa-** or **sawfa** is optional:

سيكون عندكم ضيف غد	*[future marker] he-is with-you guest tomorrow* *You will have a guest tomorrow*

To say *have not* in the present, use the verb **laysa** (see Unit 8) + **li-/:ind**, and in the past and future by applying the appropriate words for *not* (see Unit 10).

3 Thematic sentences

A type of sentence that is often encountered in Arabic is the thematic or topical sentence.

The topic of the sentence, that is, the person or thing the sentence is about, is stated first, followed by what you want to say about the topic. The part of the sentence that comes after you have mentioned the topic must be able to stand independently and very often has a real or implied pronoun, which refers back to that topic.

There are a number of these in the text and we have given below a few examples with literal translation to help you understand the concept. There is no need to spend a lot of time learning how to use this construction, but the Arabs regard it as elegant and you will come across it frequently.

Insight

It is more or less equivalent to English sentences beginning with *as for*, as in *As for Peter, he's rarely at home*. Note that the part of the sentence following the topic (*Peter*) makes complete sense on its own by including the pronoun *he*.

الأول هو العيد الصغير	*the-first he [is] the-festival the-small*
الصوم معناه أن ...	*the-fasting meaning-his [is] that…*

4 The ordinal numbers 1–20

These are adjectives telling you the order things come in. With the exception of *first* and *sixth*, they are easily related to the cardinal numbers, using the root of the number and the word shape **CaaCiC** (see Unit 2). Apart from *first*, they all form the feminine in the usual way by adding ة **-ah**:

first	أول **awwal**, f. أولى **uulaa**
second	ثان، الثاني **thaanin, ath-thaanii****
third	ثالث **thaalith**
fourth	رابع **raabi:**
fifth	خامس **khaamis**
sixth	سادس **saadis**
seventh	سابع **saabi:**
eighth	ثامن **thaamin**
ninth	تاسع **taasi:**

tenth	عاشر **:aashir**
eleventh	حادي عشر **Haadii :ashar** (f. حادية عشرة)
twelfth	ثاني عشر **thaanii :ashar** (f. ثانية عشرة)
thirteenth	ثالث عشر **thaalith :ashar** (f. ثالثة عشرة)

...and so on up to *nineteenth*

twentieth	the cardinal number (عشرون/عشرين) is used.

** For this kind of word, see Unit 17.

أوزان الكلمات **awzáan al-kalimáat** (Word shapes)

🔈 CD2, TR24

The word pattern for this unit is **C¹aC²aa'iC³***, for example, **jaraa'id** جرائد *newspapers*, which sounds like the English *falafel*.

This is another internal plural shape, usually coming from feminine singulars of the shape **CaCiiCah**, e.g. جريدة **jariidah**, singular of the above example. It does not show the accusative marker:

ضرائب from ضريبة **Daríibah, Daráa'ib** *tax*
حقائب from حقيبة **Haqíibah, Haqáa'ib** *bag, suitcase*
حدائق from حديقة **Hadíiqah, Hadáa'iq** *garden, park*

Note: if the singular refers to a female human being, the **-aat** plural is used:

زميلة **zamíilah** (female) *colleague*; pl. زميلات **zamíiláat**

تمرينات tamriináat (Practice)

Exercise 4

Match the questions below with the appropriate answers.

١	من مؤلف هذا الكتاب؟	*a*	ثلاثة: حميد وناصر وسعيد.
٢	أين مدينة الاسكندرية؟	*b*	سأشرحها لك.
٣	ماذا تعمل الآن؟	*c*	في مصر.
٤	متى رجع من جدة؟	*d*	هي هدية لك.
٥	كم ولدا عندك؟	*e*	أذهب إلى المكتب.
٦	لماذا تحب هذه البنت؟	*f*	نجيب محفوظ
٧	كيف تلعب هذه اللعبة؟	*g*	أول بيت على اليمين.
٨	أي بيت بيت فريدة؟	*h*	أقرأ الجرائد.
٩	ما هذا؟	*i*	يوم الجمعة.
١٠	إلى أين تذهبين يا مريم؟	*j*	لأنها جميلة جدا!

مؤلف، ـون **mu'állif, -uun** *author*

شرح **sháraHa S-I a** *explain*

Exercise 5

Rearrange the months of the year into the correct order.

١	سبتمبر	٧	ديسمبر
٢	أبريل	٨	مايو
٣	فبراير	٩	نوفمبر
٤	أكتوبر	١٠	أغسطس
٥	يوليو	١١	يونيو
٦	يناير	١٢	مارس

Exercise 6

Make complete *to have* sentences in the present tense, using either **li-** or **:ind:**

Example: هو .... ثلاثة أولاد ← هو له ثلاثة أولاد

He .... three sons ➔ He has three sons

١ الملك .... قصور كثيرة.

٢ أنت .... أخت طويلة.

٣ أنتم .... أولاد صغار.

٤ أنا .... آلة حاسبة جديدة.

٥ المدرس .... ٥٠ تلميذا

٦ نحن .... سيارة ألمانية.

٧ هم .... حقائب ثقيلة.

٨ الشركة .... ٥ فروع.

٩ محمد .... شقة واسعة.

١٠ سميرة .... فستان جميل.

تلميذ، تلامذة **tilmíidh, taláamidhah** pupil
فرع، فروع **far:, furúu:** *branch* (of a tree, company, etc.)
فستان، فساتين **fustáan, fasaatíin*** *frock, dress*

Now change the sentences 1–5 above into the past tense, using **kaana**.

Exercise 7

Prayer is the second of the five pillars of Islam and Muslims are called to prayer five times a day. The daily calls are:

QUICK VOCAB

الفجر **al-fajr** *dawn*
الظهر **aDH-DHuhr** *midday*
العصر **al-:aSr** *mid-afternoon*
المغرب **al-mághrib** *sunset*
العشاء **al-:isháa'** *late evening*

Prayer times vary according to sunrise and sunset and are always listed in the daily newspapers. Look at the prayer times here from successive days in the month of April. Which day came first?

a

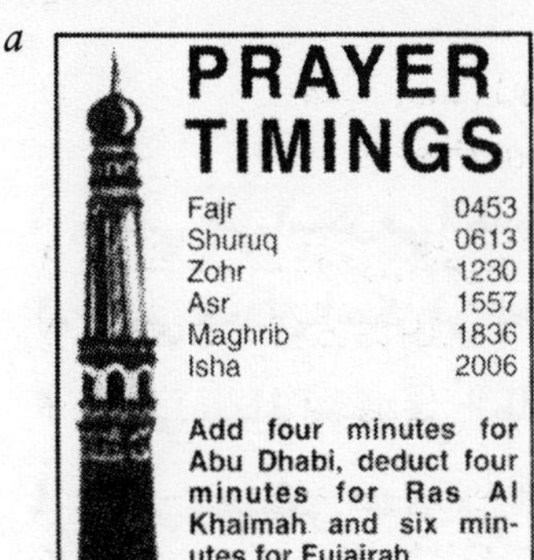

b

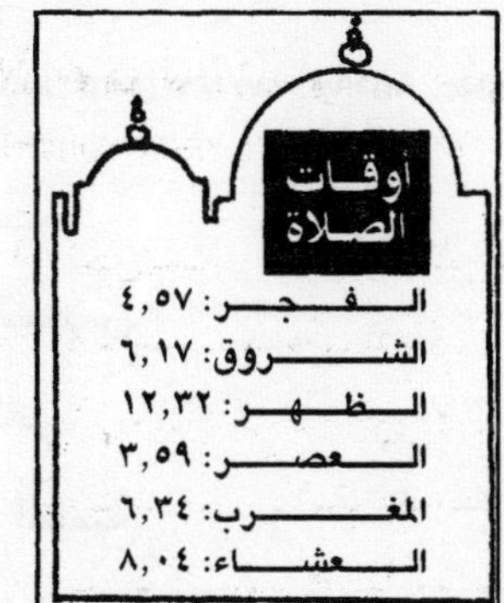

Exercise 8

CD2, TR25

Listen to the recording or read the transcript to find out which floor of the apartment block these people live on.

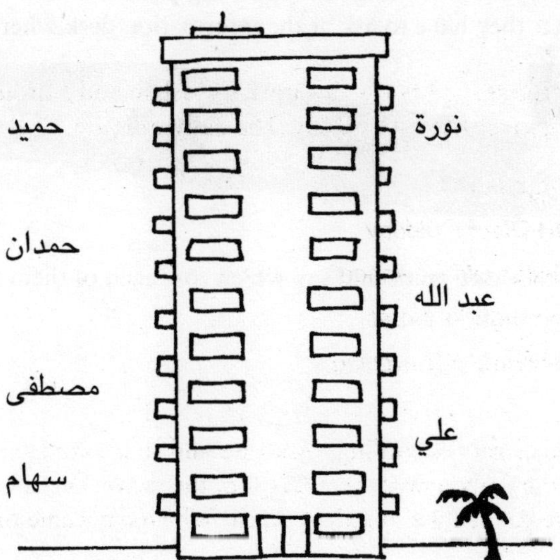

Then record the information about them.

Example: *Ali lives on the third floor.*

١ اسمي علي. أسكن في الطابق الثالث.

٢ اسمي حمدان. أسكن في الطابق السادس.

٣ اسمي سهام. أسكن في الطابق الثاني.

٤ اسمي مصطفى. أسكن في الطابق التاسع.

٥ اسمي عبد الله. أسكن في الطابق الثامن.

٦ اسمي نورة. أسكن في الطابق العاشر.

٧ اسمي حميد. أسكن في الطابق الأول.

Exercise 9

Abdullah takes his family shopping to a large superstore out of town. Everyone is looking for something particular and the store is so big that they have to ask at the information desk where to go.

Look at the store guide and say which row each of them needs to go to.

1 *Household linen*	١ مفارش منزلية
2 *Men's clothing*	٢ ملابس رجالية
3 *Women's clothing*	٣ ملابس نسائية
4 *Children's clothing & shoes*	٤ ملابس وأحذية أطفال
5 *Men's & women's shoes*	٥ أحذية رجالية ونسائية
6 *Baby garments*	٦ ملابس حديثي الولادة
7 *Bicycles*	٧ دراجات
8 *Toys*	٨ لعب
9 *Games/sports accessories*	٩ ألعاب / مستلزمات رياضية
10 *Stationery*	١٠ قرطاسية
11 *Books/greeting cards*	١١ كتب / بطاقات معايدة
12 *Hardware/batteries*	١٢ أدوات / بطاريات
13 *Tables/chairs*	١٣ موائد / كراسي
14 *Home appliances*	١٤ أدوات منزلية
15 *DVDs/CDs*	١٥ أقراص دي في دي / أقراص مدمجة
16 *Electrical accessories/ video games*	١٦ أدوات كهربائية / ألعاب فيديو
17 *Luggage*	١٧ حقائب
18 *Computers/software*	١٨ أجهزة كمبيوتر / برامج
19 *Phones/fax machines*	١٩ هواتف / فاكس
20 *Cameras/DVD recorders*	٢٠ كاميرات / مسجلات دي في دي

Example: *Abdullah needs a pair of shoes and a fax machine:*

يذهب إلى الصف الخامس والصف التاسع عشر.

He goes to the fifth row and the 19th row.

a *Qasim (aged 13) wants a shirt, a video game and batteries.*
b *Nadia needs a greetings card for a friend, some coloured pens and a cassette.*
c *Miriam (17) wants a hair dryer, jeans and a new game.*
d *Ali (18) wants a T-shirt, a CD and a computer.*
e *Sarah wants towels, some chairs for the balcony and clothes for the baby.*

---

10 Things you need to know

1. *Questions are formed in Arabic by using question words like what? etc, or by the question markers* **hal** *and* **a-**.
2. *These question marker words are only used for questions which expect the answer yes or no.*
3. *When more specific answers are required, the question words such as* **maa** *what?,* **man** *who? are used.*
4. *Note that the word* **kam** *how much/many is always followed by a singular noun which takes the accusative marker if appropriate.*
5. *There is no verb to have in Arabic.*
6. *Instead, use the preposition* **li-** *or* **:ind** *followed by a noun or a pronoun suffix.*
7. *To say past (had) place the appropriate part of the verb* **kaan** *before the prepositional phrase.*
8. *To negate (don't have) place the negative verb* **laysa** *before it.*
9. *The past is made negative (didn't have) by the use of* **lam** *or* **maa** *with the appropriate part of the verb* **kaan**.
10. *Future negation is with* **lan** *followed by the appropriate part of* **kaan**.

12

صفحة المرأة
SafHat al-mar'ah
Woman's page

In this unit you will learn:
- ***how to express nationalities such as 'English', 'Lebanese', etc.***

1 صفحة المرأة SafHat al-mar'ah
Woman's page

🔊 CD2, TR26

The following interview was given to a women's magazine by a well-known fashion model, Leila. Look through the vocabulary given below and listen to the interview a few times before answering the questions.

Exercise 1
Say if the following sentences are true or false:

a *Leila comes from Jordan.*
b *She is 28 years old.*
c *She was interested in fashion as a child.*
d *She specialised in literature at university.*

Exercise 2

Listen to the interview again, looking again through the new words underneath and answer the following questions:

a *Does she want to found an agency which:*
i is worldwide? *ii shows world fashions?*
b *Does she hope to employ:*
i male models? *ii female models?*
iii male and female models?
c *What else does she hope to do?*
d *What two things help her to keep slim?*
e *What kind of beauty look does she try to achieve?*
f *How does she feel about make-up?*

الصحفية	أهلا وسهلا.
ليلى	أهلا بك.
الصحفية	أوّلا، ما جنسيتك؟
ليلى	أنا لبنانية من بيروت.
الصحفية	وعمرك؟
ليلى	عمري ٢٨ سنة.
الصحفية	كيف بدأت في مهنة عرض الأزياء؟
ليلى	منذ طفولتي. أحب عرض الأزياء لأنها نوع من أنواع الفن. لذلك دخلت في هذا المجال.
الصحفية	هل درست الفنون؟
ليلى	نعم، درست الفنون في الجامعة وتخصّصت في تصميم الأزياء.
الصحفية	وماذا تطمحين إليه في مهنتك؟
ليلى	طموحي هو إنشاء وكالة عالمية لعرض الأزياء تضم عارضين وعارضات غربيّين وعرب.
الصحفية	وشيء غير هذا؟
ليلى	نعم، تصميم أزياء تحمل ماركة دولية باسمي.
الصحفية	وكيف تحافظين على رشاقتك؟
ليلى	أتبع حمية وأمارس الرياضة الخفيفة.

الصحفية وجمالك؟
ليلى إنّي أفضّل الجمال الطبيعي، ولذلك أترك شعري على طبيعته، ولا أحب وضع الماكياج إلا لضرورات العرض فقط.
الصحفية شكرا لك.
ليلى شكرا.

Exercise 3

Now read the dialogue again and link the English phrases to the Arabic expressions:

a	*How did you begin in the fashion modelling profession?*	١	لذلك دخلت في هذا المجال
b	*because they are a kind of art*	٢	درست الفنون في الجامعة.
c	*that is why I entered this field*	٣	أفضّل الجمال الطبيعي.
d	*I studied arts at university.*	٤	كيف بدأت في مهنة عرض الأزياء؟
e	*male and female western and Arab models*	٥	كيف تحافظين على رشاقتك؟
f	*How do you keep slim?*	٦	عارضين وعارضات غربيّين وعرب
g	*I prefer natural beauty.*	٧	لأنها نوع من أنواع الفن

QUICK VOCAB

صحفي **SúHufii** *reporter/journalist* (f. **SuHufíyyah**)

أوّلا **áwwalan** *first* (adv.)

بدأ **báda' S-I a** *begin*

مهنة، مهن **míhnah, míhan** *job, trade, profession*

عرض **:arD** *showing, displaying*

زي، أزياء **ziyy, azyáa'** *clothes, fashion, style*

منذ **múndhu** *since*

طفولة **Tufúulah** *childhood*

QUICK VOCAB

لأن **li'ánna** *because*
لذلك **li-dháalik** *because of that, for this reason*
مجال، ـات **majáal, -áat** *field, sphere of activity*
تخصّص **takháSSaSa S-V** *specialise*
تصميم **taSmíim** *design, designing*
طمح إلى **TámaHa ilaa S-I a** *aspire to, have the ambition to*
طموح **TumúuH** *aspiration, ambition*
إنشاء **insháa'** *foundation, setting up*
وكالة، ـات **wakáalah, -áat** *agency*
عالمي **:áalamii** *worldwide*
ضم **Dámma D-1 u** *include, comprise*
عارض، ـون **:áariD, -úun** (male) *model*
عارضة، ـات **:áariDah, -áat** (female) *model*
غربي، ـون **ghárbii, -úun** *western*
شيء، أشياء **shay', ashyáa'*** *thing*
غير **ghayr** *other than, apart from*
ماركة **máarkah** *marque, label*
دولي **dúwalii** or **dáwlii** *international*
حافظ على **HáafaDHa :alaa S-III** *keep, preserve*
رشاقة **rasháaqah** *shapeliness, elegance, slim figure*
حمية **Hímyah** *diet*
مارس **máarasa S-III** *practise*
خفيف **khafíif** *light*
جمال **jamáal** *beauty*
ترك **táraka S-I u** *leave, let be*
شعر **sha:r** *hair*
طبيعة **Tabíi:ah** *nature*
وضع **waD:** *putting*
ماكياج **maakyáaj** *make-up*
ضرورة، ـات **Durúurah, -áat** *necessity, requirement*

معلومات ثقافية **ma:luumáat thaqaafíyyah** (Cultural tips)

As is obvious from the interview above, Leila is a thoroughly modern, professional young woman. A role and lifestyle such as hers could only be viable in one of the more liberal Arab states, where a near western attitude prevails.

Indeed every country has its own ideas, running the whole gamut from the above to obligatory veiling and virtual purdah.

The role of women is prescribed to some extent in the Koran and other Islamic texts, and Islamic law (**sharii:ah**) defines many of their rights and privileges. In most Islamic countries, it is still legal for a man to take up to four wives. Westerners are inevitably shocked by this, but the practice is not, in fact, widespread – not least because it is very expensive in terms of dowries and general upkeep. The rules require each wife to be treated equally. Another semi-myth prevalent in the west is that, to obtain a divorce, a man simply has to say to his wife 'I divorce you' three times. This is partly true, but there are numerous conditions in which, in most cases, abuse of this practice is inhibited. For instance, men in many Arab countries have to pay a very large sum of money (dowry) to the bride's family and, depending on the timing and situation of the divorce, some or all of this has to be paid back. This can easily run into tens of thousands of pounds.

الملاحظات **al-mulaaHaDHáat** (Notes)

- **awwalan** *first. For this and other adverbs, see Unit 16.*
- **:umr-ik. :umr** *life is also used for age.*
- **28 sanah**. *For compound numbers see Unit 5. Meanwhile, note that numbers above 10 take the singular noun, not the plural.*
- **uHibb**. *This is a Form IV doubled verb. A doubled verb has the second and third radicals (consonants) the same and some parts of this verb are written with the doubling sign. (See*

Table **D-IV***). Remember that in all Form II, III and IV verbs, the present tense prefixes are vowelled with* **u** *instead of* **a**.

- **li'anna-haa. li'anna** *because is a combination of* **li-** *for and* **'anna** *that (see Unit 8).* **-haa** *refers to the inanimate plural fashions.*
- **naw: min anwaa:.** *An Arabic idiom for one of something.*
- **li-dhaalik** *for that, i.e. for this reason. Another combination with* **li-**.
- **taTmaHiin.** *Feminine verb, as a woman is being addressed.*
- *For the form* **ilay-h**, *see Unit 10.*
- وكالة عالمية لعرض الأزياء تضم... (**wakaalah :aalamiyyah li-:arD al-azyaa' taDumm...**) *An agency for fashion modelling, (which) will include... Arabic does not use a word for which after an indefinite noun (see Unit 13).*
- **gharbiyyiin wa-:arab.** *When adjectives describe a group of mixed males and females, the masculine plurals are used.*
- باسمي *in my name. This is pronounced* **bi-smii.**
- **inn-ii.** *The use of* **inna** + *the suffix pronoun lends a very slight emphasis to the statement (see Unit 8).*

Insight

The four cardinal points of the compass are:

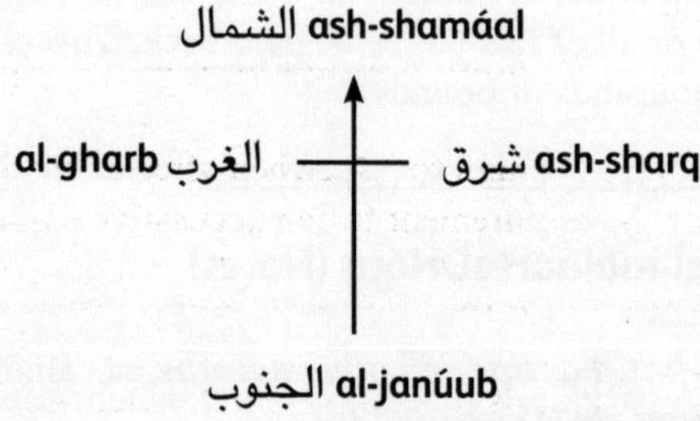

تراكيب اللغة **taraakíib al-lúghah** (Structures)

1 Forming adjectives from nouns

To describe persons or things associated with the noun, English uses a variety of suffixes:

history – historic
man – manly
America – American
Japan – Japanese

Arabic adds the following endings to the noun:

Gender	*Transliteration*	*Arabic*
m. sing.	**-ii**	ـي
f. sing.	**-iyyah**	ـية
m. plural	**-iyyuun/-iyyiin**	ـيون / ـيين
f. plural	**-iyyaat**	ـيات

They should all have the doubling sign over the ي, but this is almost always omitted.

Insight

The ending ـيون changes to ـيين when affected by the possessive or the requirement for an accusative marker (see Unit 14).

There are irregular plurals (masculine only) which will be given with the singulars where required.

The noun sometimes has to be altered slightly:

a If it has **al-** *in front – as in some countries and places – this is dropped:*

المغرب – مغربي *Morocco – Moroccan*

b The feminine ending ـة *and certain other endings are dropped:*

صناعي - صناعة	*industry – industrial*
أمريكي - أمريكا	*America – American*

c Some words change their internal vowelling before the ending:

مدني - مدينة	**madiinah – madanii** *city – urban, civilian*

Insight

Like all Arabic adjectives, these can freely be used as nouns:

إنجليزي *English, an Englishman*

أوزان الكلمات awzáan al-kalimáat (Word shapes)

CD2, TR27

The word pattern for this unit is **taC^{1}C^{2}iiC^3**, for example, **tartíib** ترتيب *arrangement*, which sounds like the French word *tartine*.

This is the verbal noun of all Form II (except the **Lw**, **Ly** types, which have a slightly different form) and therefore always expresses the action of a verb. In English, this can be expressed by adding *-ing* to the verb, but there are often parallel words with a slightly different nuance (e.g. *arranging*, *arrangment*; *presenting*, *presentation*). In these cases, the one Arabic form usually serves for both:

رتب **rattaba S-II** *to arrange, put in order*	➔	ترتيب **tartiib** *arranging, arrangement*
صمم **Sammama S-II** *to design*	➔	تصميم **tasmiim** *designing, design*
مول **mawwala Mw-II** *to finance*	➔	تمويل **tamwiil** *financing*

درس **darrasa S-II** *to teach* ➔ تدريس **tadríis** *teaching*

حول **Hawwala Mw-II** *to convert* ➔ تحويل **tattwíill** *converting, conversion*

تمرينات **tamriináat** (Practice)

Exercise 4

Here are some common word combinations, many of which you will see on road signs, in shops etc.

We give you two nouns, e.g. مركز **markaz**, *centre*, – تجارة **tijaarah**, *commerce*, and your task is to put them together, making the second noun into an adjective: مركز تجاري **markaz tijaarii**, *commercial (shopping) centre*.

Some are given in the definite form:

a منطقة **minTaqah** *area, zone* – زراعة **ziraa:ah** *agriculture*

b المطار **al-maTaar** *the airport* – الدولة **ad-dawlah** *the state*

c قمر **qamar** *moon* – صناعة **Sinaa:ah** *manufacturing***

**Here, the adjective means *artificial*: '*artificial moon*', i.e. *satellite*.

d السوق **as-suuq** *the market* – المركز **al-markaz** *the centre*

e البنك **al-bank** *the bank* – الوطن **al-waTan** *the nation*

f السفارة **as-sifaarah** *the embassy* – الهند **al-hind** *India*

g الشؤون **ash-shu'uun** *the affairs* – الخارج **al-khaarij** *the exterior*

h الأزياء **al-azyaa'** *the fashions* – النساء **an-nisaa'** *the women*

i منطقة **minTaqah** *zone* – صناعة **Sinaa:ah** *industry*

j طبيخ **Tabiikh** *cuisine* – عرب **:arab** *Arabs*

k المتحف **al-matHaf** *the museum* – الشعب **ash-sha:b** *the people, folk*

l البريد **al-bariid** *the post* – الجو **al-jaww** *the air*

m القنصلية **al-qunSuliyyah** *the consulate* – أمريكا **amriikaa** *America*

n الإدارة **al-idaarah** *the administration* – البلد **al-balad** *the town, municipality*

o منطقة **minTaqah** *area, zone* – عسكر **:askar** *army, troops*

p بريد **bariid** *post* – خارج **khaarij** *exterior*

q الآثار **al-aathaar** *the remains* – التاريخ **at-taariikh** *the history*

r الدراسات **ad-diraasaat** *the studies* – الأدب **al-adab** *the literature*

s العلوم **al-:uluum** *the sciences* – الطبيعة **aT-Tabii:ah** *the nature*

t الألعاب **al-al:aab** *the games* – النار **an-naar** *the fire*

u القصر **al-qaSr** *the palace* – الملك **al-malik** *the king*

v المستشفى **al-mustashfaa** *the hospital* – المركز **al-markaz** *the centre*

w بريد **bariid** *post* – داخل **daakhil** *interior*

x الأجهزة **al-ajhizah** *equipment* (pl.) – الكهرباء **al-kahrabaa'** *the electricity*

y الديوان **ad-diiwaan** *diwan, personal office* – الأمير **al-amiir** *the emir*

Things you need to know

1. *A common way to form adverbs from adjectives is to add the indefinite accusative ending* **-an**, *e.g.* **awwal → awwalan** *first.*
2. *To form an adjective from a noun, add the appropriate form of the* **-ii** *suffix (***-ii, -iyyah** *etc).*
3. *Some world areas derived from the points of the compass are* **al-gharb** *the West,* **ash-sharq al-awsaT** *the Middle East,* **ash-sharq al-aqSaa** *the Far East.* **al-maghrib** *is used specifically for Morocco or more generally for North Africa.*

13

الخليج العربي
al-khaliij al-:arabi
The Arabian Gulf

In this unit you will learn:
- ***more about describing places***
- ***how to use the relative pronouns 'who', 'which', 'that', etc.***
- ***about passive verbs***

1 ابتسم، أنت في الشارقة ibtasim, anta fi sh-shaariqah

Smile, you're in Sharjah

CD2, TR28

The passage below is from a tourist brochure about Sharjah, describing its role in the Emirates. Listen to the audio and read the passage carefully several times, referring to the vocabulary given below.

Exercise 1
Now answer these questions:

a *What phrase welcomes the visitor to Sharjah?*
b *Where is Sharjah's geographical location?*
c *What kind of activity is Sharjah a centre for?*

d *How many inhabitants did Sharjah have at the last census?*
e *What capital of the Emirates is Sharjah considered to be?*
f *What does Sharjah have a number of?*
g *What type of programme are transmitted from the television station?*

ابتسم أنت في الشارقة!

بهذه العبارة الترحيبية التي تفيض بكل مشاعر الود الصادق تستقبل الشارقة ضيوفها. وإمارة الشارقة هي إحدى إمارات دولة الإمارات العربية المتحدة التي تحتل موقعا جغرافيا متميزا على الخليج العربي. وهو موقع جعل الشارقة تتمتع على امتداد العصور بدور قيادي بين بلدان الخليج العربي كمركز من أهم مراكز النشاط التجاري.

ويقدر عدد السكان حسب أحدث الإحصاءات التي أجريت عام ١٩٩٥ بحوالي نصف مليون نسمة أي بكثافة تقدر بحوالي ١٩٠ نسمة للكيلومتر المربع.

وتوصف الشارقة بأنها العاصمة الثقافية لدولة الإمارات، وهناك دائرة خاصة ترعى تنفيذ الأنشطة الثقافية بالإمارة، كما تضم الإمارة عددا من المتاحف العلمية والتاريخية الفخمة ومحطة من أحدث محطات الإرسال التلفزيوني تذيع الكثير من البرامج الثقافية والتعليمية.

Exercise 2

Link the English phrases to the Arabic expressions opposite.

a *which expresses the feelings of true friendship*
b *the latest census which was carried out*
c *which looks after the implementation of cultural activities*
d *a number of magnificent scientific and historical museums*
e *Sharjah is described as the cultural capital*
f *190 people to the square kilometre*
g *one of the most important centres for commercial activity*
h *many cultural and educational programmes*

١ التي تفيض بكل مشاعر الود

٢ عددا من المتاحف العلمية والتاريخية الفخمة

٣ ١٩٠ نسمة للكيلومتر المربع

٤ الكثير من البرامج الثقافية والتعليمية

٥ أحدث الإحصاءات التي أجريت

٦ من أهم مراكز النشاط التجاري

٧ ترعى تنفيذ الأنشطة الثقافية

٨ توصف الشارقة بأنها العاصمة الثقافية

QUICK VOCAB

ابتسم **ibtásama [S-VIII]** *smile*
عبارة، ـات **:abáarah, -áat** *phrase, expression*
ترحيبي **tarHíibii** *welcoming* (adj.)
الذي **alládhii** *who, which, that* (f. التي **allátii**)
أفاض ب **afáaDa bi- [My-IV]** *flood, overflow with*
كل **kull** *each, every, all*
مشاعر **masháa:ir*** *feelings, sentiments*
ود **wadd** *love, friendship*
صادق **Sáadiq** *truthful, true*
استقبل **istáqbala [S-X]** *receive, meet*
إحدى **íHdaa** one (f. of أحد **áHad**)
دولة، دول **dáwlah, dúwal** *country, state*
الإمارات العربية المتحدة **al-imaaráat al-:arabíyyah al-muttáHidah** *the United Arab Emirates*
احتل **iHtálla [D-VIII]** *occupy* (a place or position)
موقع، مواقع **máwqi:, mawáaqi:*** *site, situation, place*
جغرافي **jughráafii** *geographical*
متميز **mutamáyyiz** *distinctive, prominent*
الخليج العربي **al-khalíij al-:árabii** *the Arabian Gulf*

جعل **já:ala [S-I a]** *cause, make do something*
تمتع بـ **tamátta:a bi- [S-V]** *enjoy*
على امتداد العصور **:ala imtidáad al-:uSúur** *over the ages*
دور، أدوار **dawr, adwáar** *role, turn*
قيادي **qiyáadii** *leading*
بين **báyna** *among, between*
كـ **ka-** *as, like*
مركز، مراكز **márkaz, maráakiz*** *centre*
أهم **ahámm** *more/most important*
نشاط **nasháaT** *activity*
تجاري **tijáarii** *commercial*
يقدر **yuqáddar** (passive of **S-2**) *is estimated*
عدد، أعداد **:ádad, a:dáad** *number*
ساكن، سكان **sáakin, sukkáan** *inhabitant, resident*
حسب **Hasb** *according to*
أحدث **áHdath** *newest, latest*
إحصاء، ـات **iHSáa', -áat** *count, census*
أجريت **újriyat** *was carried out* (passive of **Ly-IV**)
عام، أعوام **:aam, a:wáam** *year*
نصف، أنصاف **niSf, anSáaf** *half*
نسمة **násamah** *individual* (used in population counts only)
أي **ay** *that is*
كثافة **katháafah** *density*
مربع **murábba:** *square* (adj.)
توصف ... بأنها **túuSaf ... bi-ánna-haa ...** *is described as*
دائرة، دوائر **dáa'irah, dawáa'ir*** *department, directorate* (government)
خاص **khaaSS** *special; private*
رعى **rá:aa [Lh-I]** *take care of, look after*
تنفيذ **tanfíidh** *implementation, execution*
كما **ka-maa** *just as, also*

QUICK VOCAB

تاريخي **taaríikhii** *historical*
إرسال **irsáal** *transmission, sending*
أذاع **adháa:a [My-IV]** *to broadcast*
الكثير من... **al-kathíir min...** *many, a great number of...*
برنامج، برامج **barnáamij, baráamij*** *programme*
ثقافي **thaqáafii** *cultural*
تعليمي **ta:líimii** *educational*

QUICK VOCAB

معلومات ثقافية ma:luumáat thaqaafíyyah (Cultural tips)

The literary Arabic form of the name Sharjah is **ash-shaariqah.** The English version omits the Arabic definite article and the **j** comes from a local pronunciation of the Arabic letter **q.**

The United Arab Emirates (UAE) was formed in December 1971 as a federation of seven sheikhdoms, of which Sharjah ranks third in size and wealth (after Abu Dhabi and Dubai). Although their economies are ultimately based on oil production, all the Emirates have made efforts to diversify. Sharjah has concentrated on promoting and encouraging social, educational and cultural projects, resulting in its being named Arab City of Culture in 1998.

الملاحظات al-mulaaHaDHáat (Notes)

- **ja:ala** *The original meaning of this verb is to put. However, it is very frequently used with a following imperfect verb (here* **yatamatta:**) *to express to cause, to make do something, also sometimes to begin.*
- **yuqaddar** *is estimated, evaluated. This is a passive verb (see grammar section below). Other examples in the text are the feminine form of the same verb –* **tuqaddar, ujriyat** *were carried out and* **tuuSaf** *is described.*

- **nasamah** *a person, individual. This is is a special word used only in population counts.*
- **kamaa**, *literally just as, is often used to join sentences and can usually be translated simply as also.*

Insight

baraamij. The singular **barnaamij** has – according to the Arab interpretation – five root letters (**b-r-n-m-j**). Such words are rare and almost always of foreign derivation. Since the Arabic internal plural system cannot cope with five-consonant words, one is arbitrarily ignored in the plural formation.

تعبيرات رئيسية **ta:biiráat ra'iisíyyah** (Key phrases)

قابلت رجلا يعمل في مصنع الأجهزة الكهربائية

qaabalt rajulan ya:mal fii maSna: al-ajhizah al-kahrabaa'iyyah

I-met a-man he-works in factory [of] the-equipments the-electrical

I met a man who works in the electrical appliances factory

الصديق الذي زرته أمس يسكن في تونس

aS-Sadiiq alladhii zurt-uh ams yaskun fii tuunis

the-friend who I-visited-him yesterday he-lives in Tunisia

The friend whom I visited yesterday lives Tunisia

الضابط الذي سيارته هناك جالس في المقهى

aD-DaabiT alladhii sayyaarat-uh hunaak jaalis fi l-maqhaa

the-officer who his-car [is] there [is] sitting in the-café

The officer whose car is there is sitting in the café

البذلة الجديدة التي اشتريتها مصنوعة في الصين

al-badhlah al-jadiidah allatii ishtarayt-haa maSnuu:ah fi S-Siin

the-suit the-new which I-bought-it [is] manufactured in the-China

The new suit which I bought is made in China

تراكيب اللغة **taraakíib al-lúghah** (Structures)

1 Relative clauses

Relative clauses in English are the second half of sentences such as: *I replied to the letter which arrived last week.*

They are usually introduced by linking words such as *which*, *who*, *whom*, *whose*, *that*, called relative pronouns. The person or thing which the relative clause describes (here *letter*) is called the *antecedent.*

There are two important things to decide in Arabic:

1 *Whether the antecedent is:*
a) definite (with the *or the name of a person or place):*
The train that we were supposed to catch was cancelled.
Mr Smith, who lives next door, lent me his lawn mower.
Muscat, which was once a small town, is now a large metropolis.

b) indefinite (usually with a*):*
He is a character who always has an answer to everything.
Books that you have already read should be thrown out or given away.

Arabic has two different structures, according to the indefinite/definite status of the antecedent.

2 *The antecedent's role in the first part of the sentence, i.e. whether:*
*a) it is doing something (*subject*);*
*b) something is being done to it (*object*);*
*c) it belongs to someone or something (*possessive*).*

English makes slight alterations to some of the relative pronouns:

- *who shows that the antecedent is the subject;*

- *whom shows that the antecedent is the object, or having something done to it;*
- *whose shows a possessive relationship.*

Sometimes the relative pronoun is omitted in informal speech:

The woman [whom] I love...
The films [that] I like...

Forming relative clauses in Arabic

a *those with definite antecedents require the use of relative pronouns (the equivalents of who, which, whom etc.)*
b *those with indefinite antecedents do not use relative pronouns.*

Otherwise, the methods of forming both types are identical.

Arabic relative pronouns

Form	*Arabic pronoun*	*Used with antecedent types*
masc. sing.	الّذي **alládhii**	one male one object of m. gender
fem. sing.	الّتي **allátii**	one female one object of f. gender plural objects of either gender
masc. plur.	الّذين **alladhíina**	plural males only
fem. plur.	الاتي **alláatii**	plural females only
dual (masc.)	اللذان **alladháani**	two men
dual (fem.)	اللتان **allatáani**	two women/objects

Notes:
1 Duals change their endings to ـين **-ayni** when they are governed by another word. (See Unit 14.)
2 In most varieties of spoken Arabic, all the above are reduced to **illi**.

Insight

There is no distinction in Arabic between *who*, *whom* or *which* as there is in English. The relative pronouns agree only in number and gender with the antecedent.

As well as deciding whether to put the relative pronoun in or not, the Arabic relative clause differs from that of English in two ways:

a *it must constitute a complete and independent sentence on its own. English ones do not; which I bought yesterday does not make independent sense.*

b *it must contain some stated or implied pronoun that refers back to the antecedent. This pronoun is called the* referent.

DEFINITE ANTECEDENT

English: *The film that I saw…*

Arabic: *The film* (m. sing.) + *that* (antecedent is definite, so relative pronoun required; select from box) + *I saw* (referent required to show that what you saw refers to the film).

This gives the model:

The film – that – I saw it

Because *film* is masculine in Arabic, it requires the appropriate masculine relative and it is expressed by masculine **-uh** *him*.

So in Arabic we say:

الفيلم – الذي – شاهدته

al-fiilm – alladhii – shaahadt-uh

In both English and Arabic, the relative clause makes independent sense. The relative pronoun is simply a joining word.

INDEFINITE ANTECEDENT

For indefinite antecedents the process is identical, except that there is no relative pronoun:

A film which I saw
A film – I saw it (him)

فيلم – شاهدته

fiilm – shaahadt-uh

RELATIONSHIP BETWEEN VERB AND ANTECENDENT

In the above examples, the antecedent *film* is the object of the verb, i.e. the action of the verb is being applied to it. There are three other possible common relationships between the antecedent and the verb:

1 *Subject. The antecedent is performing the action of the verb.*

The official who works in the customs ➔
The official – who – he-works in the customs *(definite, so needs relative pronoun)*
الموظف – الذي – يعمل في الجمارك
al-muwaDHDHaf – alladhii – ya:mal fi l-jamaarik

An official who works in the customs… ➔
(an) official – he-works in the customs *(indef. – no relative pronoun)*
موظف – يعمل في الجمارك
muwaDHDHaf – ya:mal fi l-jamaarik

Insight

Remember that in Arabic, all verbs are regarded as having built-in pronoun subjects. **yaktub** does not just mean *writes*, it means *he writes*.

2 *Possessive. This is almost always expressed with the relative pronoun whose in English.*

Maryam, whose sister lives in London
Maryam – who – her sister lives in London *(relative pronoun required after proper name, in this case feminine)*
مريم – التي – تسكن أختها في لندن
maryam – allatii – taskun ukht-haa fii landan

A girl whose sister lives in London
(a) girl – her sister lives in London
بنت – تسكن أختها في لندن
bint – taskun ukht-haa fii landan

3 *Prepositional phrases.*

The contractors to whom I paid a large sum
The contractors – who – I-paid to-them a large sum
المقاولون – الذين – دفعت لهم مبلغا كبيرا
al-muqaawiluun – alladhiina – dafa:t la-hum mablaghan kabiiran

Contractors to whom I paid a large sum
Contractors – I-paid to-them a large sum
مقاولون – دفعت لهم مبلغا كبيرا
muqaawiluun – dafa:t la-hum mablaghan kabiiran

All the above examples have verb sentences as the relative clause, but similar combinations are possible with *is/are* verbless sentences. The same rules regarding inclusion or omission of the relative pronoun apply.

The manager, whose name is Qasim…
The manager – who – his-name Qasim
المدير – الذي – اسمه قاسم
al-mudiir – alladhii – ism-uh qaasim

An official whose name is Muhsin
Official – his-name Muhsin
موظف – اسمه محسن
muwaDHDHaf – ism-uh muHsin

2 Passive verbs

A passive verb is one whose subject suffers the action, rather than carries it out (known as an active verb). English uses the auxiliary verb *to be* for the passive:

Active: *A bolt of lightning struck the tree*
Passive: *The tree was struck by a bolt of lightning*

The use of the passive is much more restricted in Arabic than in English. In many verbs, it is identical in writing to the active, as the only changes are in the vowelling, which is not shown.

The rules for forming it for the various verb types are given in the Verb tables.

There are four examples in the text. Two of these look identical to the active forms, but differ in (unseen) vowelling:

يقدر **yuqaddar** (active **yuqaddir**) *is estimated* and its feminine **tuqaddar** [S-II verb]

تعتبر **tu:tabar** (active **tu:tabir)** *is considered* (f. form) [S-VIII]

أجريت **ujriyat** (active أجرت **ajrat**) *was carried out* (f. form) [Ly-IV]

توصف **tuuSaf** (active تصف **taSif**) *is described* (f. form) [Fw-I]

Insight

Some of these verbs are among the most frequently used passive forms in newspaper Arabic, so look out for them. In the case of those that are identical to the active in spelling, your only guideline is the context. For instance (after you have looked up all the words), the subject of the first example is **:adad** *number*. Since numbers may not carry out estimations, the verb must be passive.

أوزان الكلمات **awzáan al-kalimáat** (Word shapes)

CD2, TR29

The word pattern for this unit is **maC¹aaC²iC³***, for example, **maraakiz** مراكز *centres*, which sounds like the English *maracas*.

This is a plural form for many words in Arabic which begin with the prefix **ma-** or (less commonly) **mi-**, some of which have the feminine ending ة.

Insight

One of the few mainly reliable rules for forming internal plurals is that, if the vowel after the middle radical of the root is short, then they will almost invariably take this plural shape, e.g. the example in the box above is the plural of **markaz** (short a after middle radical **k**).

This word pattern does not take the accusative marker.

Another example from the text is:

مواقع **mawaaqi:*** *situations* ← موقع **mawqi:**

Here are a few more common ones:

مدارس **madaaris*** *schools* ← مدرسة **madrasah**

مصانع **maSaani:*** *factories* ← مصنع **maSna:**

مكاتب **makaatib*** *offices, desks* ← مكتب **maktab**

منازل **manaazil*** *residences* ← منزل **manzil**

مناطق **manaaTiq*** *regions* ← منطقة **minTaqah**

تمرينات tamriindownload (Practice)

Exercise 3

There are seven relative clauses in the tourist brochure above, three definite and four indefinite. Can you spot them?

Exercise 4

Rewrite the following sentences, supplying the correct relative pronouns (if any) to put into the gaps.

١ هذا هو البيت .... سنستأجره.

٢ زارني عامل .... يعمل في مصنع.

٣ شاهدت الطبيب .... عيادته في وسط المدينة.

٤ خالد .... قرأت كتابه يدرس في المدرسة الثانوية.

٥ كان الكرسي .... جلست عليه مكسورا.

٦ الطلبة .... يدرسون في الجامعة من الإمارات.

٧ رسالة .... كتبها الأسبوع الماضي وصلت اليوم.

٨ القمصان .... يبيعونها في السوق مصنوعة في الصين.

٩ مغنية .... كانت مشهورة قبل سنوات كثيرة ستزور سورية.

١٠ ابني له صديق .... أصله اسكتلندي.

Translation

1 *This is the house that we are going to rent.*
2 *An employee who works in a factory visited me.*
3 *I saw the doctor whose clinic is in the middle of town.*
4 *Khalid whose book I read teaches at the secondary school.*
5 *The chair that she sat on was broken.*
6 *The students who study at the university are from the Emirates.*

7 *A letter that he sent last week arrived today.*
8 *The shirts that they sell in the souk are made in China.*
9 *A singer (f.) who was famous many years ago will be visiting Syria.*
10 *My son has a friend who is originally* [his origin is] *Scottish.*

استأجر **istá'jara [S-X]** *to rent, be a tenant of*

عيادة، ـات **:iyáadah, -aat** *clinic*

باع **báa:a [My-I]** *sell*

مغنية **mughánniyyah** (female) *singer*

Exercise 5

Read the following excerpts from a Gulf tourist brochure and look out for passive verbs and relative clauses. These are marked in the answer key with bold type and underlining respectively.

١- لقد أعيد بناء منزل الشيخ صقر الكائن في هذه المنطقة.

٢- في هذه المنطقة يمكن مشاهدة أول أشكال تكييف الهواء، البرجيل، الذي كان يستخدم لتبريد البيوت في الخليج. جددت القلعة التي شيدت في القرن الماضي، وحولت إلى متحف.

٣- الطرق الضيقة تأخذ الزائر إلى سوق التوابل التي تنبعث منها روائح أنواع التوابل كلها مثل القرنفل والهال والقرفة التي تباع إلى الزوار من الأكياس التي تحيط المتاجر.

٤- سباقات الهجن رياضة شعبية تقام أيام الجمعة أثناء أشهر الشتاء.

أعاد **a:áada [Mw-IV]** *to repeat, renew*
بناء **bináa'** *building, construction*
كائن **káa'in** *being, existing, situated*
أمكن **ámkana [S-IV]** *to be possible*
مشاهدة **musháahadah** *seeing, viewing*
شكل، أشكال **shakl, ashkáal** *kind, type, form*
هواء **hawáa'** *air*
برجيل، براجيل **barjíil, baráajiil** *traditional wind tower*
تبريد **tabríid** *cooling*
جدد **jáddada [D-II]** *renew, restore*
قلعة، قلاع **qál:ah, qiláa:** *fort, fortress, citadel*
شيد **sháyyada [My-II]** *erect, construct*
قرن، قرون **qarn, qurúun** *century*
ضيق **Dáyyiq** *narrow*
زائر، زوار **záa'ir, zuwwáar** *visitor*
تابل، توابل **táabil, tawáabil** *spice*
رائحة، روائح **ráa'iHah, rawáa'iH*** *smell, scent, perfume*
قرنفل **qurúnful** *cloves*
هال **haal** *cardamom*
قرفة **qírfah** *cinnamon*
كيس، أكياس **kiis, akyáas** *bag, sack*
أحاط **aHáaTa [Mw-IV]** *surround*
متجر، متاجر **mátjar, matáajir*** *trading place, shop, stall*
سباق، ـات **sibáaq, -aat** *race*
هجين، هجن **hajíin, hújun** *racing camel*
شعبي **shá:bii** *folk* (adj.), *popular*
أقام **aqáama [Mw-IV]** (here) *to hold* (of an event)
شتاء **shitáa'**** *winter*

Exercise 6

Link the two sentences together using a relative clause:

١ عمر الشريف ممثل مصري. لعب أدوارا مشهورة كثيرة.

٢ ذهبنا إلى مدينة البتراء القديمة. اكتشفت في سنة ١٨١٢.

٣ في مصر آثار فرعونية مهمة. يزورها سواح كثيرون.

٤ يعمل زوجي في الشارقة. تقع الشارقة في الخليج العربي.

٥ نستأجر شقة في دمشق. يسكن صاحبها في الرياض.

٦ سافروا إلى عدن بطائرة الصبح. وصلت الطائرة الظهر.

QUICK VOCAB

البتراء **al-batráa'** *Petra*

اكتشف **iktáshafa [S-VIII]** *discover* (here passive)

فرعوني **far:úunii** *pharaonic*

دمشق **dimáshq*** *Damascus*

Exercise 7

Many adjectives in Arabic are derived from nouns and there are several examples of them in the text above. See if you can find the nouns in the vocabulary box below in transliteration in the wordsearch.

i	t	a	:	l	ii	m	l	a	d
r	i	a	h	kh	ii	r	aa	t	a
i	j	t	i	m	aa	:	a	l	h
y	aa	u	r	a	d	a	h	h	m
aa	r	m	gh	S	i	i	a	m	:
D	a	a	ii	r	q	f	:	u	i
a	h	t	b	t	aa	b	aa	t	l
h	a	a	i	q	i	f	r	i	m
b	s	S	a	l	S	q	i	H	a
t	aa	th	k	u	t	a	z	y	w
d	h	a	H	aa	y	i	S	i	aa

QUICK VOCAB

جغرافيا *geography*
تاريخ *history*
تجارة *commerce*
علم *science*
اقتصاد *economy*
زراعة *agriculture*
سياحة *tourism*
اجتماع *meeting; sociology*
رياضة *sports*
تعليم *education*
ثقافة *culture*

10 things you need to know

1 *Relative clauses supply supplementary information about preceding nouns in a sentence. In English these are usually introduced by words like* which, that, who etc. *– although these*

are sometimes omitted in informal style, e.g. the flat (which/ that) I live in.

2 *The person or thing about which this information is supplied is known as the* antecedent.

3 *In Arabic, it is very important to recognise whether this is definite or indefinite.*

4 *This is because definite antecedents require a word for* which, who *etc. after them, called the relative pronoun.*

5 *Indefinite antecedents do not have any relative pronoun.*

6 *In all cases, the relative clause must contain something that refers back to the antecedent. This is usually a pronoun (often implicit in a verb), or a pronoun suffix, called by the Arabs a* **raaji:** *– something which returns, refers back.*

7 *Both the relevant pronoun and the* **raaji:** *must agree in number and gender with the antecedent.*

8 *The word 'passive' comes from the Latin word* to suffer. *Passive verbs are those which 'suffer' the action (have it done to them), rather than carry it out (active verbs).*

9 *In unvowelled Arabic, many passive verbs are written in a fashion identical to that of the active, but the correct interpretation is usually obvious from the context.*

10 *The plural pattern of words like* **markaz → maraakiz** *is especially worth learning as it can be predicted quite confidently for a large number of words which have the prefix* **ma-** *and a short vowel after the second radical of the root.*

14

السمع والطاعة
as-sam: wa T-Taa:ah
Hearing is obeying (The Arabian Nights)

In this unit you will learn:

- ***how to follow a recipe***
- ***how to tell people to do something***
- ***more ways of addressing people or attracting their attention***
- ***about duals and masculine plurals in possessive constructions***

---

1 الكشري **al-kushari** Koshari

CD2, TR30

Koshari is a popular Egyptian dish of lentils and rice, often sold from carts in the streets. Look at the Key phrases below and read through the recipe. It will help if you listen to the recording at the same time.

Exercise 1
Now answer these questions:

a How many people does the koshari serve?

b What proportion of rice is used to lentils?
c How long must the lentils be soaked?
d How long do they cook with the rice?
e What else is layered with the rice, lentils and macaroni?
f What is added to the dish before it is served?

(الكمية تكفي ٦ أشخاص)

المقادير

- ٤ أكواب ونصف أرز، يغسل ويصفى
- كوب عدس أسود
- نصف كوب زيت
- ملح حسب الرغبة
- ٧ أكواب ونصف الكوب ماء للأرز
- ١٠ أكواب ماء لسلق المعكرونة
- كوبا معكرونة
- ملعقتا طعام زيت للمعكرونة
- ٦ بصلات مقطعة الى شرائح طويلة

الصلصة

- ملعقتا طعام سمن
- ٦ حبات طماطم مقشرة ومفرومة
- ملعقة صغيرة فلفل حمر حار مطحون
- ملعقتا طعام من معجون الطماطم
- ملح حسب الرغبة

ا لطريقة

١ انقعي العدس بالماء لمدة ٦ ساعات وصفيه.

٢ حمري البصل بالزيت ثم ارفعيه واتركيه جانبا. اسكبي الماء فوقه واتركيه حتى يغلي قليلا، ثم أضيفي الأرز والعدس واتركيه على نار هادئة لمدة ٤٠
دقيقة.

٣ اسلقي المعكرونة بالماء ثم أضيفي الزيت.

٤ حمري الطماطم في الزيت، ثم أضيفي الفلفل ومعجون الطماطم والملح.

٥ أثناء التقديم ضعي خليط الأرز والعدس أولا، ثم طبقة من المعكرونة ثم طبقة من البصل، ورشي فوقه الصلصة الحارة أو قدميها إلى جانب الطبق.

Exercise 2

Link the English phrases to their Arabic equivalents:

a	*fry the onions in the oil*	أضيفي الفلفل ومعجون الطماطم	١
b	*leave them on a low heat*	رشي فوقه الصلصة الحارة	٢
c	*add the pepper and the tomato paste*	ثم أضيفي الأرز والعدس	٣
d	*then add the rice and lentils*	حمري البصل بالزيت	٤
e	*pour the hot sauce over it*	اتركيه على نار هادئة	٥

QUICK VOCAB

كشري **kúshari** name of an Egyptian dish

كمية، ـات **kammíyyah, -aa**t *amount*

كفى **káfaa [Ly-I]** *to suffice, be sufficient for*

شخص، أشخاص **shakhS, ashkháaS** *person*

مقدار، مقادير **miqdáar, maqáadiir*** *quantity, measure*

كوب، أكواب **kuub, akwáab** *glass, cup* (in recipes)

أرز **arúzz** *rice*

غسل **ghásala [S-I i]** *wash*

صفى **Sáffaa [Ly-II]** *drain, strain*

عدس: **ads** *lentils*

أسود **áswad*** *black*, here meaning *brown* (lentils)

زيت **zayt** (edible) *oil*

ملح **milH** *salt*

رغبة، ـات **rághbah, -áat** *desire, wish*

ماء **maa'*** *water*

سلق **salq** *boiling, the action of boiling something*

معكرونة **ma:karúunah** *macaroni*

ملعقة، ملاعق **mil:áqah, maláa:iq*** *spoon, spoonful*

طعام **Ta:áam** *food*

ملعقة طعام **mil:áqat Ta:áam** *tablespoon*

بصل **báSal** *onions*

مقطع **muqáTTa:** *chopped*

شريحة، شرائح **sharíiHah, sharáa'iH*** *slice*

صلصة **SálSah** *sauce*

سمن **sámn** *ghee, clarified butter*

حبة، ـات **Hábbah, -áa**t *grain, seed*; also used for counting units of certain fruits and vegetables

طماطم **TamáaTim*** *tomatoes*

مقشر **muqáshshar** *peeled, skinned*

مفروم **mafrúum** *minced, ground*

فلفل **fúlful/fílfil** *pepper*

أحمر **áHmar*** *red*

حار **Haarr** *hot*

مطحون **maT-Húun** *ground, milled*

معجون **ma:júun** *paste*

طريقة، طرائق **Taríiqah, Taráa'iq*** *method, way*

نقع **náqa:a [S-I a]** *to soak, steep*

مدة **múddah** (period of) *time*

حمر **Hámmara [S-II]** *to brown, fry*

ثم **thúmma** *then*

رفع **ráfa:a [S-I a]** *raise, lift*

جانبا **jáaniban** *aside, to one side*

سكب **sákaba [S-I u]** *to pour out*

فوق **fáwqa** *above, over*

حتى **Háttaa** *until*

غلى **ghálaa [Ly-I]** *to boil, come to the boil*

أضاف **aDáafa [My-IV]** *to add*

نار **naar** *fire* (f.)

هادئ **háadi'** *gentle, quiet*

دقيقة، دقائق **daqíiqah, daqáa'iq*** *minute*

QUICK VOCAB

QUICK VOCAB

أثناء **athnáa'(a)** *during, while*

تقديم **taqdíim** *presentation, serving*

وضع **wáDa:a [Fw-I a]** *to put, place*

خليط **khalíiT** *mixture*

طبقة، ـات **Tábaqah, -áat** *layer*

رش **ráshsha [D-I u]** *sprinkle, spray*

أو **aw** *or*

قدم **qáddama [S-II]** *to present, serve*

جانب، جوانب **jáanib, jawáanib*** *side*

طبق، أطباق **Tábaq, aTbáaq** *plate*

معلومات ثقافية ma:luumáat thaqaafíyyah (Cultural tips)

Arabic cookery

The recipe given is for koshari, a simple, nutritious (vegetarian) dish from Egypt. Instructions in Arabic recipes are usually written in the feminine singular, on the assumption that Arab men stay out of the kitchen!

Although all Arab countries have their delicacies, the most highly regarded are those of the Lebanon and Syria, which have much in common with the cuisines of other eastern Mediterranean countries.

North Africa has many tasty dishes, many of them long-simmered stews eaten with couscous (polenta).

Cookery in the Gulf is much influenced by Indian cuisine, with the extensive use of spices. The staple in the Gulf is rice and there is a wonderful selection of freshly caught fish and shellfish available from local souks at reasonable prices.

There are many good books on Middle Eastern cookery, but those by Claudia Roden and Anissa Helou are especially worth seeking out.

تعبيرات رئيسية **ta:biiráat ra'iisíyyah** (Key phrases)

Describing how to prepare the ingredients
The ingredients should be…

مقشر **muqashshar** *peeled*
مقطع **muqaTTa:** *chopped*
مطحون **maT-Huun** *milled, ground*

Quantities

ملعقة طعام **mil:aqat Ta:aam** *tablespoon*
ملعقة شاي **mil:aqat shaay** *teaspoon*
كوب **kuub** *glass, cup* (in recipes)
مئة غرام **mi'at ghraam** *100 grams*
ليتر **liitir** *litre*

Instructions
All instructions are feminine singular (see above):

انقعي **inqa:ii** *soak*
صفي **Saffii** *strain*
اخلطي **ikhliTii** *mix*
حمري **Hammirii** *brown, fry*
اسلقي **usluqii** *boil*
ارفعي **irfa:ii** *lift*
اتركي **utrukii** *leave*
اسكبي **uskubii** *pour*

أضيفي **aDiifii**	*add*
رشي **rushshii**	*sprinkle*
غطي **ghaTTii**	*cover*
قدمي **qaddimii**	*serve*

تراكيب اللغة **taraakíib al-lúghah** (Structures)

1 Giving instructions and directions

The type of verb used for giving someone instructions or directions is called the *imperative*. In English, this does not usually differ from the ordinary present tense verb:

Present tense: *You work hard*
Imperative: *Work hard!*

Arabic uses a special adaptation of the variant form of the present tense called the *jussive*, which you can find in the Verb tables at the end of this book.

Forming the imperative
This is also explained in the section on verbs at the end of the book, but it is simply constructed as follows:

a *Look up in the verb tables the you form, or 2nd person singular, jussive form of the present tense, e.g.:*

تقدم **tuqaddim**	*you present, serve*

b *Remove the prefix* **ta-** *or* **tu-**, *to get* قدم **qaddim.**

c *If the result, as in the above example, begins with:*
- *a consonant followed by any of the vowels, you have formed the imperative masculine singular* (قدم **qaddim** *serve!*)

- *two consonants (Arabic letters* **dh** *(ذ),* **kh** *(خ), etc. counting as only one consonant), supply an* **alif** *at the beginning and pronounce it in most cases as the vowel* **i**.

تستعلم **tasta:lim**	*you enquire*
→ ستعلم **sta:lim**	
→ استعلم **ista:lim**	*enquire!*

d *Form I verbs, as usual, show vowel variation. With sound Form I verbs (see Table S-I), removing the prefix always results in a two-consonant beginning, so an* **alif** *must be prefixed. Note the vowel following the second consonant, which can be* **a**, **i** *or* **u**.

- *If it is* **a** *or* **i**, *the above rules for two consonants apply:* تغسل **taghsil** *wash* → غسل **ghsil** → اغسل **ighsil** *Wash!*

- *If it is* **u**, *the* **alif** *must also be given a* **u**-*vowel:* تترك **tatruk** *leave (aside)* → ترك **truk** → اترك **utruk** *Leave!*

In practice, this is not too important, as these vowels are very often elided unless the imperative comes at the beginning of a sentence.

Insight

The one exception to the above rules is the Form IV verb (all types; see tables). In these verbs, an **alif** with an **a** vowel is always prefixed to the shortened jussive form, whether this begins with two consonants or not. This initial **a** vowel is never elided, and is often written with a **hamzah** as below:

ترسل **tursil** (from أرسل S-IV *to send*) → رسل **rsil** → أرسل **arsil** *Send!*

تضيفي **tuDiifii** (f. sing. from أضاف·My-IV *to add*) → ضيفي **Diifii** → أضيفي a **Diifii** *Add!* (f. sing.). The **alif** is added even though the shortened jussive begins with a consonant followed by a vowel.

Irregular imperatives

The following irregular imperatives occur very frequently:

تعال **ta:aal** *Come!* (no phonetic relation to the verb جاء **jaa'a**)

خذ **khudh** *Take!* from أخذ **akhadha** *to take*

هات **haat** *Give!*, probably from the verb أتى **ataa**

كل **kul** *Eat!*, from أكل **akala** *to eat*

Feminine and plural imperatives

Feminine and plural imperatives obey the rules above, using the relevant parts of the jussive:

ـي **-ii** f. sing. (addressed to one female)
ـوا **-uu** m. pl.
ـن **-na** f. pl.

For *Come!* these same endings are added to تعال giving تعالي، تعالوا etc. The same is true for the other irregular imperatives listed above.

> ## Insight
>
> The dual imperatives for addressing two people occur rarely and have been omitted from this section. However, they can be deduced from the jussive form in exactly the same way.

Negative imperatives

Use the negative word لا **laa**, not followed by the appropriate part of the jussive, retaining its prefix:

لا تترك **laa tatruk**	*don't leave* (to a man)
لا تغسلي **laa taghsilii**	*don't wash* (to a woman)
لا تستعلموا **laa tasta:limuu**	*don't enquire* (to several men)

معلومات ثقافية **ma:luumáat thaqaafíyyah** (Cultural tips)

A situation in which you often see imperatives are road signs telling you to do something (*slow down*, *stop*, etc.)

Insight

Many common signs are expressed in a different way, for instance with the word الرجاء **ar-rijaa'** which means *the request*, i.e. *it is requested, please do/don't do something*. This is followed by a noun indicating the action requested. Such signs often feature the word عدم **:adam** *lack of*, *absence of* when the request is a negative one, i.e *not to do something*.

2 More ways to address people

As we have already seen, all forms of Arabic use the vocative particle يا **yaa** when addressing people or attracting attention:

يا سامي! **yaa saamii** *Sami!*

A slightly different form is used when the person addressed has the definite article:

يا ايها الأمير! **yaa ayyuhaa al-amiir!** *O Emir!*

This construction is commonly found in political and other emotive speeches with a plural noun:

يا ايها الإخوة العرب! *O Arab brothers!*
yaa ayyuhaa l-ikhwah al-:arab

يا ايتها السيدات! *Ladies!*
yaa ayyatuhaa (f.) **as-sayyidaat**

3 Masculine plurals and duals in possessive constructions

As you know these endings all end in the letter **nuun** ن:

Masculine plural:

ـون **-uun** (subject)
ـين **-iin** (object, possessives amd after all prepositions)

Dual:

ـان **-aan** (f. ـتان **-ataan**) (subject)
ـين **-ayn** (f. ـتين **-atayn**) (object, possessives and after all prepositions)

However, when any of these types of word form the first part of a possessive construction, the letter **nuun** of the endings is dropped. There are several examples of such duals in the recipe:

كوبا معكرونة	*two cups of macaroni*
ملعقتا طعام زيت	*two tablespoons of oil*

(this is a double possessive, the Arabic literally reading two-spoons [of] food [of] oil)

Examples of the masculine plural are:

حضر موظفو الحكومة **HaDara muwaDHDHafuu l-Hukuumah**	*The officials of the government attended*
تطلب الشركة مندوبي مبيعات **aTlub ash-sharikah manduubii mabii:aat**	*The company is seeking sales representatives*

أوزان الكلمات **'awzáan al-kalimáat** (Word shapes)

CD2, TR31

The word pattern for this unit is **istiC¹C²aaC³**, for example, **istinkaar** استنكار *rejection*, which sounds like the English *(m)ist in car* (omitting first letter):

This is the verbal noun of S-X verbs.

استخدام **istikhdaam**	*using, usage, use*
استعمال **isti:maal**	same meaning as above
استعلام **isti:laam**	*enquiring, enquiry*
استقبال **istiqbaal**	*reception* (of guests, etc.)
استثناء **istithnaa'**	*excepting, exception*

تمرينات **tamriináat** (Practice)

Exercise 3

You are in an aeroplane and are served a meal. Match each of these packs of food and seasoning to the appropriate English word.

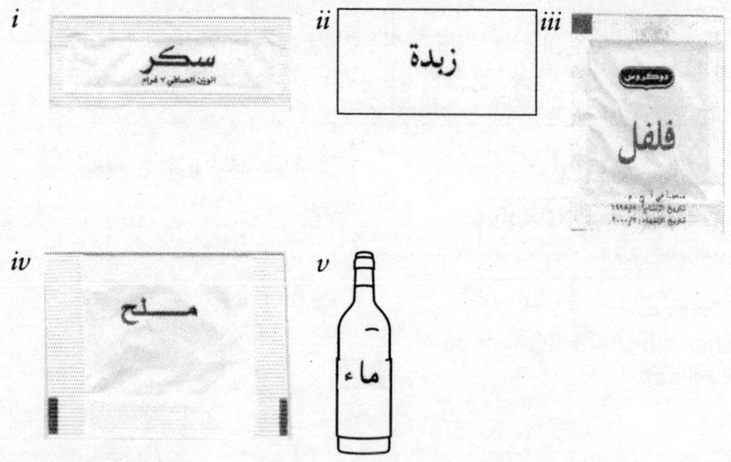

a salt *b pepper* *c sugar* *d butter* *e water*

Exercise 4

Look at these road signs and match them with the English.

a Turn left *b Stop* *c Slow down* *d Turn right*

Exercise 5

You are in a car park in Dubai and have to pay the parking fee. Read the instructions on the ticket machine and answer the questions that follow.

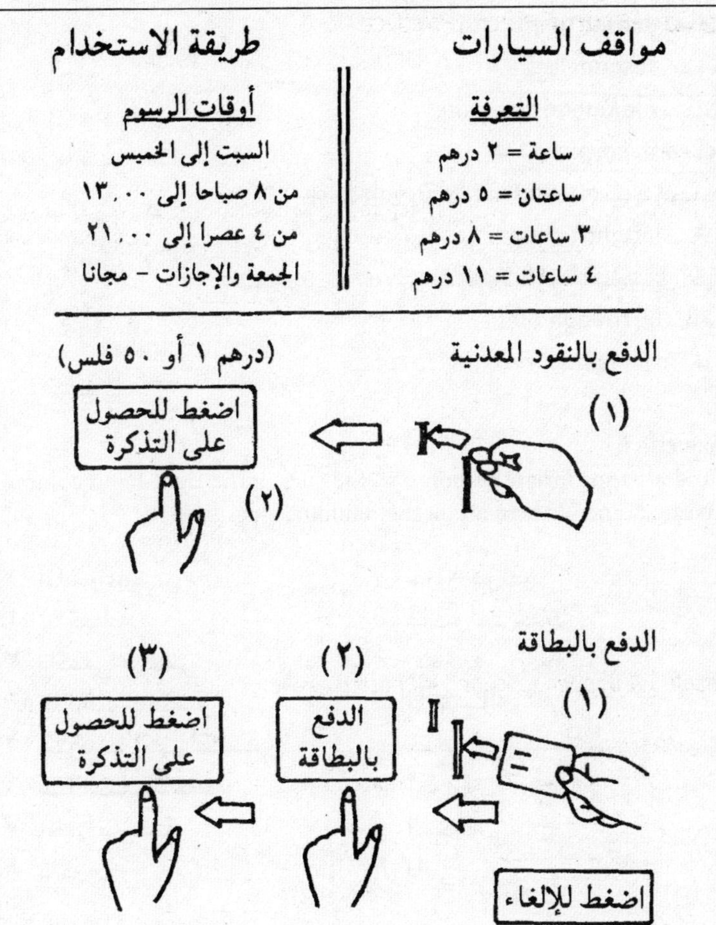

a *Match the following English with the Arabic:*

i Payment by coins	1 الدفع بالبطاقة
ii Payment by card	2 الدفع بالنقود المعدنية

b *Which coins can you use?*

c *On what days do you not need to pay a fee?*

d *What is the longest time you can park?*

e *How much does it cost to park for two hours?*

f *Find the word for* press

QUICK VOCAB

تعرفة **ta:rífah** *tariff*

رسوم **rusúum** *fees*

مجانا **majáanan** *free, gratis*

دفع **daf:** *payment*

نقود معدنية **nuqúud ma:daníyyah** *coins*

اضغط **íDghaT** *press!*

للحصول على **li-l-HuSúul :ála** *(in order) to obtain*

بطاقة **buTáaqah** *card*

للإلغاء **li-l-ilgháa'** *(in order) to cancel*

Exercise 6

Find an appropriate response to the cues in the right-hand column. (Note: Some of these are in the feminine singular.)

١	أنا جوعان	*a*	جربه، هو لذيذ
٢	أنا تعبانة	*b*	هات واحد جديد
٣	تاكسي! تاكسي	*c*	رده إليه
٤	هذا الكوب مكسور	*d*	كل شيئا!
٥	عمري ما أكلت الكسكس	*e*	خذها إلى المستشفى
٦	هذا الكتاب لأحمد	*f*	اجري!
٧	أختي مريضة	*g*	المحطة
٨	تأخرت!	*h*	نامي

QUICK VOCAB

عمري ما... **:úmrii maa...** *I have never...*

جرب **járraba [S-II]** *try out, taste*

رد إلى **rádda [D-I u]** *return something to someone*

جرى **járaa [Ly-I]** *run*

نام **náama [Ma-I]** *sleep*

Exercise 7

CD2, TR32

A local supermarket has special offers on some food items that are announced over the loudspeaker. Listen to the recording and answer the questions.

a *How much is the minced lamb per kilo?*
b *What do they want you to see?*
c *What do they suggest you make for a meal?*
d *How long does the cheese offer last?*
e *Listen to the recording again, and select an appropriate word from the box to put into the gaps below, putting it into the imperative form.*

.... إلى قسم اللحوم! .... بأسعار مذهلة! تنزيلات في لحم الغنم

المفروم الكيلو بـ ٨ دراهم.

.... تشكيلة الجبن من فرنسا وإيطاليا. .... وجبة معكرونة للعائلة اليوم.

.... جبنة الحلوم اللذيذة. أسعار خاصة لليوم فقط

اشتروا	أطبخوا	تعالوا	جربوا	شاهدوا

QUICK VOCAB

قسم، أقسام **qism, aqsáam** *section, division*
لحم، لحوم **laHm, luHúum** *meat*
مذهل **múdh-hil** *amazing*
غنم **ghánam** *sheep* (collective)
جبنة **jubnah** *cheese*
طبخ **Tabakh(a) [S1 u]** *to cook*
تشكيلة، ـات **tashkíilah, -áat** *selection*
وجبة، ـات **wájabah, -áat** *meal*
جبنة الحلوم **júbnat al-Hallúum** *Halloumi cheese*

Exercise 8

a *Read the following exchange between Fawzi and his assistant Karim. (Note that where English says* shall I…, *Arabic uses the simple present tense.)*

كريم أفتح هذه الرسالة؟
فوزي نعم، افتحها.

Instruct Karim to do what he offers to do, using an imperative verb (with suffix pronoun if necessary):

١ أرسل الفاكس الآن؟
٢ أكتب الرسالة فورا؟
٣ اتصل بالمكتب؟

b *Fatimah's new maid is helping her with the lunch. Can you tell her to do what she is offering?*

١ أضع الماء على الطاولة؟
٢ أترك الأرز في المطبخ؟
٣ أغسل الصحون؟

الآن **al-áan** *now*
أرسل **ársala [S-IV]** *send*
فورا **fáwran** *immediately*

10 things you need to know

1. *The imperative form of the verb is that which is used when telling someone to do something. Since it is always used when addressing someone, it is a type of you-form.*
2. *In Arabic, it is derived from the appropriate part of the jussive variant of the present tense.*
3. *First, the prefix (always* **ta-** *or* **tu-***) is removed.*
4. *If the resulting word begins with two consonants, an initial vowel must be supplied.*
5. *This is because Arabic will not accept words beginning with an unvowelled consonant, e.g.* **taktub** *with the* **ta-** *removed would result in the impossible form* **ktub.**
6. *Thus an* **alif** *is prefixed to the word, nominally vowelled according to the rules given, although this is rarely shown in print.*
7. *For negative commands (don't...), use* **laa** *followed by the jussive variant of the full you-form of the present tense.*
8. *When you are addressing someone directly, it is obligatory to use the word* **yaa** *before naming the person. For the sake of clarity, we have translated this as the rather archaic 'O…'.*
9. *If the following word has the definite article, this must be extended to the phrase* **yaa ayyu-haa l-** *– a form much favoured by politicians when haranguing the masses.*
10. *The masculine plural and dual suffixes of the noun* **-uun** *and* **-aan** *are changed to* **-iin** *and* **-ayn** *respectively if they are the object of a verb, the second element of a possessive phrase, or after all prepositions. If they are the first element of a possessive phrase, the final* **nuun** *is also omitted.*

15

العرب في هوليوود
al-:arab fii huuliiwuud
Arabs in Hollywood

In this unit you will learn:

- ***to make comparisons***
- ***to say how things are done***
- ***more about shopping***

1 العرب في هوليوود al-:arab fii huuliiwuud

The Arabs in Hollywood

CD2, TR33

The best-known Arab actor to have achieved stardom in the western cinema is the Egyptian-born Omar Sharif, famous for his celebrated roles in the films *Lawrence of Arabia* and *Dr Zhivago*. However, in the 1990s, competition came along in the shape of Salma Hayek.

Read the magazine article about Salma, looking carefully through the new vocabulary.

Exercise 1

Now answer the questions:

a *What was Salma Hayek the first Arab woman to do?*
b *What aspect of her beauty appeals particularly to the west?*
c *Which stars does she compete with in Hollywood?*
d *When was she born?*
e *Where does her mother come from originally?*
f *How old was she when she was spotted by producers?*
g *What film did she work in with Quentin Tarantino?*
h *What will her most recent film give her?*

سلمى... العربية التي قهرت هوليوود

في الشرق نعتبرها سفيرة الجمال العربي التي استطاعت ان تكون أول امرأة تخترق أسوار هوليوود وتفرض نفسها على أعلى قائمة نجمات السينما.

وفي الغرب يعتبرونها رمزا لسحر الشرق بما تحمله من ملامح شرقية غاية في الجمال الذي يناظر السحر. ولهذا أعطوها البطولات في أكبر أفلامهم مفضلينها على أكثر نجمات هوليوود جمالا. وإذا سلمى الحايك اليوم تزاحم شارون ستون وديمي مور وغيرهما من نجمات هوليوود.

وسلمى الحايك، أو اسطورة الشرق في الغرب، المولودة سنة ١٩٦٦، هي ابنة مهاجر لبناني مقيم بالمكسيك والدتها اسبانية الأصل. وإذا اجتمع الجمال اللبناني والاسباني تكون الثمرة في حلاوة سلمى الحايك. ولأنها جميلة جدا فقد رصدتها عين المنتجين وهي في الثالثة عشر من عمرها واختيرت وقتها كأجمل الوجوه التلفزيونية. ثم أخذها المنتج تارانتينو إلى لوس انجليس لتشترك في الفيلم «ديسبيرادو» الى جانب انطونيو بانديراس وأعطت للفيلم مذاقا خاصا جدا جلب لها اهتمام شركات الإنتاج الكبرى وسرعان ما قدموا لها العقود الكثيرة بل إنها أخذت مؤخرا دورا كان من المفترض أن يسند لمغنية شهيرة امريكية ولكن منتجي هوليوود فضلوا سلمى عليها ومن الأكيد أن هذا الفيلم سيعطي لسلمى انطلاقه أكثر قوة وانتشارا.

Exercise 2

Match the English phrases to the Arabic expressions:

a	*the first woman*	١	أكثر نجمات هوليوود جمالا
b	*the leads in their greatest films*	٢	انطلاقة أكثر قوة وانتشارا
c	*most of the stars of Hollywood in terms of beauty*	٣	أول امرأة
d	*the most beautiful television personality*	٤	أجمل الوجوه التلفزيونية
e	*greater eminence as regards power and popularity*	٥	البطولات في أكبر أفلامهم

QUICK VOCAB

قهر **qáhara [S-1 a]** *to conquer*

اعتبر **i:tábara [S-VIII]** *to consider, regard*

سفيرة، ـات **safíirah, -áat** *ambassador* (female)

استطاع **istaTáa:a [Mw-X]** *to be able*

امرأة، نساء **imrá'ah, nisáa'** (irregular plural) *woman*

اخترق **ikhtáraqa [S-VIII]** *to breach* (wall, defences, etc.)

سور، أسوار **suur, aswáar** *wall, fence*

فرض **fáraDa [S-I i]** *impose*

نفس، نفوس **nafs, nufúus** *self; soul* (f.)

اعلى **á:laa** *highest; the highest point, top*

قائمة، قوائم **qáa'imah, qawáa'im** *list*

نجمة، ـات **nájmah, -áat** *star*, (female) *film star*

رمز، رموز **ramz, rumúuz** *symbol, code*

سحر **siHr** *magic*

ملامح **maláamiH*** *features*

غاية **ghaayah** *extreme, most*

ناظر **náaDHara [S-III]** *to equal, compete with*

أعطى **á:Taa [Ly-IV]** *to give*

بطولات **buTúulaat** *leading roles*

فيلم، افلام **fiilm, afláam** *film*

مفضل **mufáDDil** *preferring*

زاحم **záaHama [S-III]** *to jockey for position with*

غير **ghayr** *other than*

اسطورة، اساطير **usTúurah, asáaTiir*** *legend*

مولود **mawlúud** *born*

ابنة، بنات **íbnah, banáat** *daughter* (alternative to **bint**)

مهاجر، ـون **muháajir, -úun** *emigrant*

مقيم **muqíim** *residing, resident*

المكسيك **al-maksíik** *Mexico*

اسباني **isbáanii** *Spanish*

أصل، أصول **aSl, uSúul** *origin, basis*

إذا **ídhaa** *if*

اجتمع **ijtáma:a [S-VIII]** *meet, come together*

ثمرة **thámrah** *fruit*

حلاوة **Haláawah** *sweetness;* also *beauty*

رصد **ráSada [S-I u]** *observe, watch, monitor*

عين، عيون **:ayn, :uyúun** *eye;* also *spring* (of water) (f.)

منتج، ـون **múntij, -úun** *producer*

اختار **ikhtáara [My-VIII]** *to choose*

وقتها **waqt-haa** *then, at that time*

أجمل **ájmal*** *more/most beautiful*

وجه، وجوه **wajh, wujúuh** *face,* (media) *personality*

تلفزيوني **tilifizyúunii** *television* (adj.), *televisual*

أخذ **ákhadha [S-I u**] *to take*

لـ **li-** *for, in order to*

اشترك **ishtáraka [S-VIII]** *to participate, subscribe*

مذاق **madháaq** *flavour*

جلب **jálaba [S-I i]** *attract, bring*

اهتمام **ihtimáam** *attention, concern, interest*

QUICK VOCAB

QUICK VOCAB

انتاج **intáaj** *production*

الكبرى **al-kúbraa** *the largest* (see grammar notes)

سرعان ما **sur:áan maa** *quickly, before long*

عقد **:aqd** *contract*

بل **bal** *rather;* (here) *in fact, indeed*

مؤخرا **mu'ákhkhiran** *recently, lately*

مفترض **muftáraD** *assumed, supposed*

أسند ل **ásnada [S-IV]** *entrust to, vest in*

مغنية، ـات **mughánniyah, -áat** (female) *singer*

شهير **shahíir** *famous*

أكيد **akíid** *certain*

انطلاقة **inTiláaqah** (here) *eminence, brightness*

أكثر **ákthar*** *more/most*

قوة، ـات **qúwwah, -áat** *force, power, strength*

انتشار **intisháar** *spread, currency;* (here) *popularity*

الملاحظات al-mulaaHaDHáat (Notes)

- **awwal imra'ah** *the first woman.* **awwal** *first is treated in Arabic as a superlative adjective. See below.*
- **imra'ah** *woman is an irregular noun:*
  1 When it has the definite article, it drops both the initial **alif**; *(*المرأة*) and the vowel after the* **r** *and is pronounced* **al-mar'ah**
  2 It has the phonetically-unrelated plural **nisaa'**, *also with the variant* **niswaan** *(*نساء، نسوان*).*
- **an takuun.** *Although no verb to be is used in simple statements equating to is/are, certain conjunctions, including* **an** *that, require the present subjunctive after them. See below.*
- **bi-maa** *is a common conjunction, usually translated as for, in that, as, because.*
- **salmaa (al-)Haayik.** *The Arab press seems to be unsure*

whether Salma's family name should have the article or not. Both usages appear.

- **ghayr-humaa** *lit., and other than them-two. The dual suffix is used because two people (Stone and Moore) have been named.*
- **ibnah** *is used for daughter in isolation. If you say daughter of Rashid, the form is* **bint**, *which also means girl.*
- **takuun** *will/would be. When the present tense of* **kaana** *is used, it implies future or uncertainty instead of straight fact.*
- **fa-qad** *This is* **fa-** *so with the past marker* **qad** *(see Unit 8)*
- **ath-thaalithah :asharah min :umr-haa.** *This phrase is feminine to agree with the unstated word* **sanah** *year. See section on ordinal numbers in Unit 11.*
- **ukhtiirat.** *Past tense passive of a My-VIII verb. See Verb tables.*
- **waqt-haa** *soon, quickly. Lit., her time means then with a sense of immediacy, there and then*
- **wujuuh** *faces also has the extended meaning of (show business) personalities.*
- **bal** *is an emphatic word, meaning not only this but…*
- **muntijii huuliiwuud.** *For the dropping of the final* **nuun** *of the first word, see Unit 14.*

تعبيرات رئيسية **ta:biiráat ra'iisíyyah** (Key phrases)

Comparatives and superlatives

محمود أطول من ناصر	*Mahmoud is taller than Nasir*
هذه هي المشكلة الأصعب	*This is the hardest problem*
هل شاهدت البرنامج الأول؟	*Did you see the first programme?*
هي أجمل امرأة في هوليوود	*She is the most beautiful woman in Hollywood*

تراكيب اللغة **taraakíib al-lúghah** (Structures)

1 Forming comparatives and superlatives

Comparative adjectives in English usually end in *-er* and are followed by the word *than*: *larger than life*.

Superlatives usually end in *-(e)st*: *the greatest show on earth*.

Comparatives

Because they involve internal changes, true comparatives in Arabic can only be formed from simple adjectives with three root consonants, often plus a long vowel (usually **aa, ii**, e.g. **waasi:**, **kabiir**). The comparative of such adjectives can be constructed taking the following steps:

a Identify the three root consonants, e.g.: **kabiir ➔ k-b-r.**
b Prefix an **alif** *(pronounced* **a***) and re-vowel the root letters as follows:*
1st radical – no vowel
2nd radical – an **a***-vowel.*
e.g. كبير ➔ *radicals* ك-ب-ر ➔ أكبر **akbar**

Insight

Note: Although it is not always written, the prefixed **alif** technically has a **hamzah** on it (أ), so the **a** vowel is never elided.

This form does not change and is used for all genders and numbers.

The word for *than* is من **min**:

الفيل أكبر من الفأر **al-fiil akbar min al-fa'r**	*The elephant is bigger than the mouse*

Look at the following common adjectives and their comparatives:

طويل *tall*	أطول *taller*
قصير *short*	أقصر *shorter*
كبير big	أكبر *bigger/older* (humans)
صغير *small*	أصغر *smaller/younger* (humans)
قديم *old*	أقدم *older* (things)
رخيص *cheap*	أرخص *cheaper*
جميل *beautiful*	أجمل *more beautiful*

طارق سليم

أمي اختي

سليم أطول من طارق

saliim aTwal min Taariq

Salim is taller than Tariq

اختي اقصر من أمي

ukht-ii aqSar min umm-ii

My sister is shorter than my mother

PRONUNCIATION NOTES

1 *If the adjective has the same second and third root letters, the* **a***-vowel is shifted back from the second radical to the first and the second and third radicals are written as one (technically with the doubling sign* **shaddah***, but this is usually omitted):*

شديد **shadiid** *strong, violent* → radicals ش–د–د → أشد **ashadd**

هام **haamm** *important* → radicals هـ م م → أهم **ahamm**

2 *If it ends in one of the weak letters* و *or* ي*, this becomes a long aa (written* ى*) in the comparative:*

حلو **Hulw** *sweet, beautiful* ➔ radicals ح–ل–و ➔ أحلى **aHlaa**

الغالي **al-ghaalii**** *expensive* ➔ radicals غ–ل–ي ➔ أغلى **aghlaa**

*** given here with the definite article, as indefinites of this type have an irregular spelling (see Unit 17).*

3 *For polysyllabic words that cannot conform to the above system, Arabic uses* أكثر **akthar** *more and* أقل **aqall** *less followed by an adverbial accusative (see below), ending in a marked or unmarked* **-an.**

Superlatives

Superlatives are formed in exactly the same way as comparatives, but take different sentence structures. All of the examples below are taken from the article above.

1 SUPERLATIVE + INDEFINITE SINGULAR NOUN (TECHNICALLY IN THE GENITIVE)

أول امرأة **awwal imra'ah**	*the first woman*

First is regarded as a superlative.

2 SUPERLATIVE + DEFINITE PLURAL NOUN

أجمل الوجوه التلفزيونية **ajmal al-wujuuh at-tilifizyuuniiya**	*the most beautiful television personality*

This equates with the English parallel *the most beautiful of [the] television personalities.*

3 DEFINITE NOUN + DEFINITE SUPERLATIVE

شركات الانتاج الكبرى **sharikaat al-intaaj al-kubraa**	*the biggest production companies*

In the last example, the first word **sharikaat** is definite because it is the first term in a possessive (see Unit 6).

This is actually more of an intensive than a superlative, probably better translated as *the great production companies.*

A few common adjectives have a feminine form when required by agreement (here for a neuter plural). This is derived from the three root letters and vowelled and spelled as in **kubraa**. This is the least common of the three constructions, but is often encountered in set phrases, e.g.:

الشرق الأوسط *the Middle East* (m.)
ash-sharq al-awsaT

بريطانيا العظمى *Great Britain* (f., from عظيم *mighty*)
briiTaanyaa l-:uDHmaa

Note also that أول **awwal** *first* functions exactly as a superlative. When used after the noun, as in construction 3 above, it takes the feminine form أولى **uulaa**, e.g. أول مرة or المرة الأولى *[for] the first time.*

Insight

Note that none of these comparatives or superlatives takes the **alif** accusative marker.

2 The adverbial accusative

The adverbial accusative is often associated with the comparative or superlative, and there are several examples in the article above. We will look at adverbs themselves in more detail in Unit 16.

Use of the adverbial accusative

The adverbial accusative tells us to what respect or characteristic the comparative refers. In English we might say:

He is better off than me in terms of/as regards possessions, but he is worse off for money.

Modern colloquial English often uses the suffix -wise:

She has done less well career-wise, but her personal life is more satisfying.

Formation

The adverbial accusative is always indefinite and is formed from a noun or adjective with the ending **-an** (marked by an **alif** on most masculines; unmarked in the feminine). This ending is usually pronounced, even in informal spoken Arabic.

Therefore, you need only remember to put in the **alif** when required. Examples from the passage are:

أكثر نجمات هوليوود جمالا

lit., *the greatest of the Hollywood stars in terms of beauty* (marked accusative **jamaalan**)

انطلاقة أكثر قوة وانتشارا

prominence greater in terms of strength and popularity (unmarked **quwwatan**, marked **intishaaran**)

This construction is frequently used with the two words **akthar** *more, most*, and **aqall** *less* to form comparatives and superlatives where the adjective is too long or complex to use the direct formation. In this case, the equivalent noun of the adjective is used. This takes experience, but here are two examples:

a *The adjective* مجتهد **mujtahid** *diligent, hard working, has far too many letters to form a direct comparative. The equivalent noun is* اجتهاد **ijtihaad** *diligence. Adding the accusative ending, we get:*

أكثر اجتهادا **akthar ijtihaadan** *more diligent* [lit., more in terms of diligence]

b *The adjective* مفيد **mufiid** *beneficial comes from the noun* افادة **ifaadah** *benefit:*

اقل افادة **aqall ifaadatan** *less beneficial, of less benefit*

Here the noun has a feminine ending, so there is no **alif**.

3 Conjunctions

Conjunctions join parts of sentences, explaining the relationship of one part to another. Common examples are *and* expressing a direct link and *or*, which expresses an alternative. These are used in much the same way as their English equivalents. Others express a more complex link, for instance, purpose, reason and so on.

These last in Arabic fall into two distinct categories, depending on the type of word that comes after them. Here are some examples of the most commonly encountered conjunctions from the interview above:

1 Conjunctions followed by verbs

أن **an** *that*. The verb following is usually in the present subjunctive (see Verb tables):

استطاعت أن تكون أول امرأة [lit., she was able that she be…]	*she was able to be the first woman…*
كان من المفترض أن يسند لمغنية شهيرة [lit., …was of the supposed that it be entrusted]	*… should have been entrusted to a famous singer*

ل **li** *to, in order that*. The verb following is always in the subjunctive:

لتشترك في الفيلم	*(in order) to take part in the film*

Insight

Note that this should be distinguished from the identical word meaning *to*, for use with nouns, which is a preposition, not a conjunction.

Other conjunctions in this category will be pointed out as we come across them.

2 Conjunctions followed by nouns or pronouns

These are technically in the accusative.

أن **anna** *that*:

ومن الأكيد أن هذا الفيلم *and it is certain that this film…*

(followed by a noun with the demonstrative pronoun)

لأن **li'anna** *because*:

ولأنها جميلة جدا *and because she is very beautiful*

(followed by the suffix – i.e. accusative – pronoun)

ولكن، لكن **walaakinna**, **laakinna** *but* (no difference in meaning):

ولكن منتجي هوليوود… *but the Hollywood producers…*

(lit., *producers of Hollywood*) showing accusative masculine plural noun with final **nuun** dropped (see Unit 14)

Insight

Although not really a conjunction, the slightly emphatic particle إن **inna** also belongs to this category (see Unit 8).

أوزان الكلمات **awzáan al-kalimáat** (Word shapes)

🔊 **CD2, TR34**

The word pattern for this unit is **C¹aC²aaC³iiC⁴***, for example, **maqaadíir** مقادير *quantities*, which sounds like the English *magazine* (accent on last syllable).

This is another internal plural shape. This one derives from singulars that have four consonants, with a long vowel between the third and the fourth. The accent is always on the last syllable. Presence of the feminine suffix ة **-ah** makes no difference.

Insight

This is a pretty safe bet for any such word, but there are a few exceptions. These plurals do not take the accusative marker. In the text for this unit we have:

اسطورة، اساطير **usTuurah, asaaTiir*** *legend*

(the **hamzah** counts as a radical)

Here are some other examples. Watch for the long vowels (any of them) between the third and the fourth radicals:

مفتاح **miftaaH** *key* ➔ مفاتيح **mafaatiiH***

مقدار **miqdaar** *amount, quantity* ➔ مقادير **maqaadiir***

منديل **mandiil** *handkerchief* ➔ مناديل **manaadiil***

صندوق **Sunduuq** *box, chest* ➔ صناديق **Sanaadiiq***

عصفور **:uSfuur** *sparrow, small bird* ➔ عصافير **:aSaafiir***

There are not many exceptions to this rule. Some adjectives take the ـون **-uun** ending, and note the following nouns:

أستاذ، أساتذة **ustaadh, asaatidhah** *professor*

تلميذ، تلامذة **tilmiidh, talaamidhah** *pupil* (but also تلاميذ **talaamiidh**)

معلومات ثقافية ma:luumáat thaqaafíyyah (Cultural tips)

There are quite a few English words deriving ultimately from Arabic, often via Spanish and hence French (the Arabs ruled most of Spain for about 500 years). *Magazine* – originally in the military sense – is one of them. It comes from مخازن **makhaazin***, plural of مخزن **makhzan** *storehouse* (a slightly different Word shape from that given above). Here are a few others:

- *both* zero *and* cypher *ultimately derive from* صفر **Sifr** zero, *the concept of which the Arabs passed to the West*
- calibre *derives from* قالب **qaalib** mould *(for bullets, etc.)*
- algorithm *derives from the name of a famous Arab philosopher* الخوارزمي **al-khawaarizmii**
- algebra *is from Arabic* الجابر **al-jaabir** resetting
- chemise *is from* قميص **qamiiS**, *mentioned in the Koran (7th century* AD*)*
- *more subtle is* arsenal *from* دار الصناعة **daar aS-Sinaa:ah**, *and* admiral *from* أمير البحر **amiir al-baHr** *(with the last word omitted).*

تمرينات **tamriináat** (Practice)

Exercise 3

The adverts below all offer bargains to the shopper. Look at the ads and answer the questions about each one that follow. The key vocabulary is given after the questions.

a

b

c

d

e

WESTERN UNION ويسترن يونيون
أسرع طريقة لإرسال الأموال حول العالم
نقودكم تصلكم في دقائق
من أي مكان في العالم
خبرة أكثر من ١٢٥ عاماً
خدمة سريعة: نقودكم تصلكم في دقائق
خدمة سهلة: لا يتطلب حساب بنكي
خدمة تعتمدون عليها: الملايين حول العالم يثقون بنا
خدمة عملية: ٥٠٠,٠٠٠ موقع في أكثر من ١٦٠ دولة

f

a *What do you have to do to win a prize?*
b *How long has the Co-op been serving its customers?*
c *What do you get free if you buy the oil?*
d *What are the two main prizes to be won?*
e *What does Western Union promise you?*
f *How do you obtain the discount offered at Bou Khalil?*

QUICK VOCAB

ربح **rábaHa [S-I a]** *to win, gain, profit*
فاضل **fáaDil** *favourable, good*
عرض، عروض **:arD, :urúuD** *offer, deal*
زبون، زبائن **zabúun, zabáa'in*** *customer, client*
مجانا **majjáanan** *free, gratis*
نقد، نقود **naqd, nuqúud** *cash, money*
مكان، أمكنة **makáan, ámkinah** *place*
حسم **Hasm** *discount*
بطاقة، ـات **buTáaqah, -áat** *card*
امتياز **imtiyáaz** *distinction, privilege*

Exercise 4

You are thinking of buying a laptop, and have narrowed the choice down to two possibilities. Look at the two specifications below.

A

- شاشة ١٣ بوصة
- مشغل القرص الثابت ٨٠ غيغابيت
- ذاكرة وصول عشوائي ١ غيغابيت
- موديم ٤٤ ك
- سهل الاستعمال
- ٥٩٩٩ درهم

B

- شاشة ١٥ بوصة
- مشغل القرص الثابت ١٦٠ غيغابيت
- ذاكرة وصول عشوائي ٣ غيغابيت
- موديم ٥٦ ك
- ٨٤٩٩ درهم

a *Select appropriate adjectives from the box to fill in the gaps, changing them to the comparative form.*

١ هذا الكمبيوتر له شاشة ....

٢ له موديم ....

٣ له ذاكرة ....

٤ له قرص ثابت ....

٥ هو .... استعمالا.

٦ هو ....

QUICK VOCAB

سهل **sahil** *easy*
حسن **Hasan** *good*
رخيص **rakhiiS** *cheap*
سريع **sarii:** *fast*
صغير **Saghiir** *small*
كبير **kabiir** *big*
شاشة **sháashah** *screen*
موديم **múudiim** *modem*
ذاكرة **dháakirah** *memory*
قرص ثابت **qurS tháabit** *hard disk*
استعمال **isti:máal** *use, usage*

b *Which computer does each of the specifications in part* **a** *above refer to?*

---

10 things you need to know

1 *The comparative of adjectives which consist of only three consonants – ignoring any long vowels present – are formed according to the formula* **aC¹C²aC³**, *so* **kabiir** *becomes* **akbar.**

2 *This shape remains the same for all genders and numbers.*
3 *It does not take the accusative marker.*
4 Than *is expressed by* **min** *(which usually means* from*).*
5 *The pattern is slightly modified if the root has the second and third consonants the same, or if the third consonant is a* **waaw** *or a* **yaa'**.
6 *Superlatives are formed in exactly the same way as comparatives, but are used in a different way.*
7 *Again this does not change for gender, except for a few common adjectives which have a feminine form of the superlative, having the shape* **$C^1uC^2C^3aa$** *when used after a definite noun.*
8 **awwal** first *is regarded as a superlative in Arabic and has the feminine form* **uulaa** *(أولى).*
9 *Adjectives with more than three consonants cannot be fitted into these patterns and use a different construction.*
10 *Conjunctions are joining words which connect two parts of a sentence. Apart from the simple* and *and* or *they fall into two types in Arabic: those which are followed by a verb and those followed by a noun or pronoun.*

16

صفحة الرياضة
SafHat ar-riyaaDah
Sports page

In this unit you will learn:

- ***about sports and leisure activities***
- ***about colours***
- ***to describe how or when you have done something***

1 الليلة السوداء al-laylah s-sawdaa'

The black night

CD2, TR35

Listen to the recording of this report of a football match between Morocco and Tunisia. The vocabulary is given for you below, so look through that carefully first and then attempt the exercises.

Exercise 1

a *For which side is it a black night?*
i Morocco *ii Tunisia*
b *Which round of the competition is it?*
i the first *ii the fourth* *iii the final*
c *Where did the match take place?*
d *How many spectators were there?*

Listen to the recording again and answer these questions.

e By how many goals did Tunisia win?
f Which side scored first?
g Who scored at the end of the first half?

Listen to the recording one more time.

h When was the last goal scored?
i What happened to Suleiman al-Fasi?
j Which team was he playing for?

ليلة سوداء للكرة المغربية

تأهل الفريق التونسي للدور النهائي من مسابقة كأس العرب لكرة القدم في ليلة سوداء للكرة المغربية. وعلى ملعب الزمالك في القاهرة امس، وأمام ٤٢ الف متفرج قاد محمود التركي الفريق التونسي الى الفوز. وسجل التركي شخصياً ثلاثة اهداف في المباراة التي انتهت ٥-١.

وافتتح الفريق التونسي التسجيل عن طريق لاعب وسطه جعفر ابو عادل بتسديدة رائعة من خارج المنطقة خدعت الحارس المغربي في الدقيقة التاسعة من المباراة. وكانت نتيجة الفرصة الاولى للفريق المغربي هدفهم الوحيد في اخر الشوط الأول عندما سدد طارق الأحمر كرة قوسية دخلت ركن المرمى التونسي وأدرك التعادل.

ولكنه بدا ان اللاعبين المغاربة قد رفعوا الراية البيضاء في الشوط الثاني وسيطر التونسيون على اللعب سيطرة تامة. وجاءت الأهداف بسرعة فظيعة، آخرها في الدقيقة الأخيرة من مباراة عندما أودع القائد التونسي الكرة في الشبكة المغربية للمرة الثالثة بعد ما احتسب الحكم ركلة ركنية وطرد المدافع المغربي سليمان الفاسي لنيله البطاقة الصفراء الثانية.

Exercise 2

Link the English phrases below with the Arabic expressions:

a	*a black night for Moroccan football*	١	... اللاعبين المغاربة قد رفعوا الراية البيضاء
b	*al-Turki himself scored three goals*	٢	للمرة الثالثة
c	*the Moroccan players raised the white flag*	٣	لنيله البطاقة الصفراء الثانية
d	*for the third time*	٤	ليلة سوداء للكرة المغربية
e	*the referee awarded a corner kick*	٥	احتسب الحكم ركلة ركنية
f	*for getting his second yellow card*	٦	سجل التركي وحده ثلاثة أهداف

QUICK VOCAB

ليلة، ـات، ليال **láyla, -áat, layáalin** *night*

أسود، سوداء **áswad***, fem. **sawdáa'*** *black*

كرة، ـات **kúrah, -áat** *ball*, also used as a shortened form of كرة القدم **kúrat al-qádam** *football*

مغربي، مغاربة **mághribii, magháaribah** *Moroccan*

تأهل **ta'áhhala [S-V]** *to qualify* (لـ **li-** *for*)

فريق، فرق **faríiq, fíraq** *team*

نهائي **niháa'ii** *final* (adj.)

مسابقة، ـات **musáabaqah, -áat** *competition*

كأس، كؤوس **ka's, ku'úus** *cup, trophy*

الزمالك **az-zamáalik** *Zamalek* (an area of Cairo)

ألف، آلاف **alf, áalaaf** *thousand*

متفرج، ـون **mutafárrij, -úun** *spectator*

قاد **qáada [Mw-I]** *to lead*

فوز **fawz** *victory*

QUICK VOCAB

سجل **sájjala [S-II]** *to score, to register*

وحده **wáHd-uh** *himself*

هدف، أهداف **hádaf, ahdáaf** *goal, target, aim*

مباراة، مباريات **mubáaraah, mubaarayáat** *match* (sport)

انتهى **intáhaa [Ly-VIII]** *to come to an end, finish*

افتتح **iftátaHa [S-VIII]** *to commence, open*

تسجيل **tasjíil** *registration, scoring*

عن طريق **:an Taríiq** *by way of*

لاعب، ـون **láa:ib, -úun** *player*

لاعب وسط **láa:ib wasT** *midfield player* (football)

تسديدة، ـات **tasdíidah, -áat** *shot* (football)

رائع **ráa'i:** *splendid, brilliant, marvellous*

خارج **kháarij** *outside*

منطقة، مناطق **mínTaqah, manáaTiq*** *area* (football: *penalty area*)

خدع **kháda:a [S-I a]** *to deceive*

حارس، حراس **Háaris, Hurráas** *guard* (football: *goalkeeper*)

تاسع **táasi:** *ninth*

نتيجة، نتائج **natíijah, natáa'ij*** *result, outcome*

فرصة، فرص **fúrSah, fúraS** *chance, opportunity*

وحيد **waHíid** *sole, only, singular*

شوط، أشواط **shawT, ashwáaT** *half* (football), *heat* (athletics, etc.), *race*

عندما **:índamaa** *when*

سدد **sáddada [S-II]** *to aim* (football: *shoot*)

قوسي **qáwsii** *curved, bowed*

دخل **dákhala [S-I u]** *to enter*

ركن، أركان **rukn, arkáan** *corner*

مرمى **mármaa** *goal, goalmouth*

أدرك **ádraka [S-IV]** *to attain, achieve*

تعادل **ta:áadul** *balance, equality* (football: *draw, equal score*)

بدا **bádaa [Lw-I]** *to appear, seem, show*

رفع **rafa:(a) [S1 a]** *raise, hoist*

راية، ـات **ráayah, -áat** *flag, banner*

أبيض، بيضاء **ábyaD***, f. **bayDáa'*** *white*

الثاني **ath-tháani** *the second*

سيطر على **sáyTara :álaa [Q-I]** *to dominate*

العب **a:b** *play, game*

سيطرة **sáyTarah** *domination*

تام **taamm** *complete*

سرعة **súr:ah** *speed*

اخير **akhíir** *last*

أودع **áwda:a [Fw-IV]** *to place*

شبكة، شباك **shábaka, shibáak** *net, netting*

مرة، ـات **márrah, -áat** *time, occasion*

بعد ما **ba:d maa** *after* (before a verb)

احتسب **iHtásaba [S-VIII]** *to award, grant*

حكم، حكام **Hákam, Hukkáam** *referee, umpire*

ركلة، ـات **ráklah, -áat** *kick*

ركني **rúknii** *corner* (adj.)

طرد **Tárada [S-I u]** *to banish, drive away* (football: *send off*)

مدافع، ـون **mudáafi:, -úun** *defender*

نيل **nayl** *getting, receiving*

بطاقة، ـات **buTáaqah, -áat** *card*

أصفر، صفراء **áSfar***, f. **Safráa'*** *yellow*

QUICK VOCAB

الملاحظات **al-mulaaHaDHáat** (Notes)

- **sawdaa'** black, *f. For this and other basic colour adjectives, see grammar notes below.*
- **sajjala** scored. *This and other words take on special meanings in football contexts. Its usual meaning is to* register, record.

- **ahdaaf**, *pl. of* **hadaf** *goals scored. The word for the physical goal (posts and net) is* **marmaa** *which occurs later in the text.*
- **sayTara ... sayTarah taammah** *dominated ... completely. See section on adverbs below.*
- **akhiir** *and* **aakhir** *both mean last, but they are used differently:*
  – **akhiir** *is a normal adjective coming after the noun:*

  الفصل الأخير **al-fasl al-akhiir** *the last section.*

  – **aakhir** *is a noun meaning the last part of something and is usually used as the first term of a possessive construction:*

  آخرها **aakhir-haa** *the last of them, i.e. the goals.*
- **ba:d maa** *after. When* **ba:d, qabl** *before and certain other words relating to time are followed by a verb, it is necessary to interpose this (meaningless)* **maa.**
- **li-nayl-uh** *getting, obtaining.* **nayl** *here is a verbal noun, and the phrase can be paraphrased because of his getting, for getting. This type of construction is quite common in Arabic.*

تعبيرات رئيسية **ta:biiráat ra'iisíyyah** (Key phrases)

السيارة الحمراء **as-sayyaarah l-Hamraa'** *the red car*
قميص أزرق **qamiiS azraq** *a blue shirt*
زهرة صفراء **zahrah Safraa'** *a yellow flower*
الجبل الأخضر **al-jabal al-akhDar** *the green mountain*

تراكيب اللغة **taraakíib al-lúghah** (Structures)

1 Irregular adjectives

As you learned in Unit 3, most Arabic adjectives form their feminine by adding ة **-ah** to the masculine form.

There is an important set of adjectives that behave differently. The most common of these refer to the basic colours, and some physical disabilities.

These adjectives have three forms:

a *masculine singular*
b *feminine singular*
c *plural for human beings.*

a) Masculine singular
Identical in all respects to the comparative adjective (see Unit 15) and following the same rules regarding doubled and weak radicals.

Does not take the **alif** accusative marker.

b) Feminine singular
The first radical takes an **a** vowel, the second no vowel and the suffix **-aa'** ـاء is added after the third radical.

Again this does not take the accusative marker.

c) Plural form
Used only when referring to several human beings. The first radical takes **u-** and the second no vowel.

This form does take the accusative marker when required.

English	*Masculine*	*Feminine*	*Plural*
black	أسود **aswad**	سوداء **sawdaa'**	سود **suud**
white	أبيض **abyaD**	بيضاء **bayDaa'**	بيض **biiD**[1]
red	أحمر **aHmar**	حمراء **Hamraa'**	حمر **Humr**
green	أخضر **akhDar**	خضراء **khaDraa'**	خضر **khuDr**
yellow	أصفر **aSfar**	صفراء **Safraa'**	صفر **Sufr**

blue	أزرق **azraq**	زرقاء **zarqaa'**	زرق **zurq**
lame	أعرج **a:raj**	عرجاء **:arjaa'**	عرج **:urj**
blind	أعمى **a:maa**[2]	عمياء **:amyaa'**	عميان **:umyaan**[3]

1 Arabic will not accept the combination **uy** so the vowel changes to **ii**.
2 Root ends with ى (See rules for comparatives in Unit 15.)
3 An alternative form, usually used with this adjective.

2 Other colours

The above rules apply only to what Arabic regards as the basic colours. Other colours are formed from nouns with the adjectival ending ـي **-ii** (see Unit 12) and behave normally:

Noun	*Adjective*
برتقال **burtuqaal** *orange*	برتقالي *orange*
بن **bunn** *coffee beans*	بني *brown*
بنفسج **banafsaj** *violet*	بنفسجي *violet*
ورد **ward** *roses*	وردي *pink*

Examples from the text are:

ليلة سوداء	*a black night*
الراية البيضاء	*the white flag*
البطاقة الصفراء	*the yellow card*
طارق الأحمر	*Taariq al-aHmar* (here used as a proper name)

3 Adverbs

Adverbs describe how, when or where the action of a verb is performed. In both English and Arabic, there are two ways to form them.

Accusative marker

In English, we add the suffix *-ly* to the adjective: *She sings beautifully*. The Arabic equivalent of this is to add the accusative marker to an adjective or sometimes a noun. This is written with an **alif** unless the word has the feminine ending and is always pronounced **-an**. Such common words as *very*, *always*, *never* are also formed in this way.

So we have شخصيا **shakhSiyyan** *personally*, from **shakhSii** *personal*, which is itself derived from **shakhS** *person*.

Here are some other common examples:

a) From adjectives	*b) From nouns*
كثيرا **kathiiran** *frequently, a lot, often*	عادة **:aadatan** *usually*
نادرا **naadiran** *rarely*	فجأة **faj'atan** *suddenly*
قريبا **qariiban** *promptly, soon*	صدفة **Sudfatan** *by chance, fortuitously*
سريعا **sarii:an** *quickly*	جدا **jiddan** *very*
يوميا **yawmiyyan** *daily*	أبدا **abadan** *never*
شهريا **shahriyyan** *monthly*	أحيانا **aHyaanan** *sometimes*
أولا **awwalan** *first* (also the other ordinal numerals:)	فورا **fawran** *immediately*
ثانيا **thaaniyan** *second*	مباشرة **mubaasharatan** *directly*
ثالثا **thaalithan** *third*, etc.	طبعا **Tab:an** *naturally, of course*
أخيرا **akhiiran** *lastly, at last*	حقا **Haqqan** *really, truly, in fact*
دائما **daa'iman** *always*	
رسميا **rasmiyyan** *officially*	

Prepositional

The second way to form adverbs in English is to use a preposition (usually *with*, *in* or *by*) plus a noun: *I am writing this in haste.*

The same applies to Arabic, the usual preposition being **bi-**: بالضبط **bi-DH-DHabT** *with exactness, exactly.*

In Arabic, as in English, both methods can be used, often with a slight change in meaning – *hastily/in haste.* سريعا **sarii:an** *quickly* can also be expressed as بسرعة **bi-sur:ah** *with speed.*

Common examples of this type are:

ببطء **bi-buT'**	*slowly*
بجد **bi-jadd**	*seriously*
بوضوح **bi-wuDuuH**	*clearly*

Verbal nouns

A common adverbial construction in Arabic is *verb + its verbal noun* (accusative) + *an adjective* (also accusative) qualifying the verbal noun.

Insight

This will be familiar to readers of the King James Bible where phrases like *They rejoiced a great rejoicing* are quite frequent in the Old Testament (presumably because it was translated from Hebrew, a sister Semitic language to Arabic). This has exactly the same meaning as *They rejoiced greatly.*

There is one example in the text:

سيطر التونسيون على اللعب سيطرة تامة

The Tunisians dominated the play completely
(lit., a complete domination)

أوزان الكلمات **awzáan al-kalimáat** (Word shapes)

CD2, TR36

The word pattern for this unit is **C¹aC²C³aC⁴ah**, for example, **barbarah** بربرة *barbarism*, which sounds like the English *Barbara*.

This is the verbal noun shape from QI-verbs (see Verb tables). In the football text we have:

سيطرة **sayTarah**	*domination*

Here are a few more:

ترجم Q-I → ترجمة **tarjamah**	*translating, translation*
فلسف Q-I → فلسفة **falsafah**	*philosophising, philosophy*
زلزل Q-I → زلزلة **zalzalah**	*quaking, earthquake* (also sometimes زلزال **zilzaal**)
تلفز Q-I → تلفزة **talfazah**	*televising, television*

تمرينات **tamriináat** (Practice)

Exercise 3

See if you can work out which of these sports corresponds to the pictures that follow:

١ ايروبيك	٧ التزلج على الثلج
٢ تنس الطاولة	٨ بولينغ
٣ كرة اليد	٩ الغوص بالسكوبا
٤ كرة القدم	١٠ صيد السمك
٥ جولف	١١ التزلج على الماء
٦ باليه	١٢ الزوارق الشراعية

ثلج **thalj** *ice*

زورق، زوارق **záwraq, zawáariq*** *boat*

معلومات ثقافية ma:luumáat thaqaafíyyah (Cultural tips)

Some of the sports mentioned in the exercise are transliterations into Arabic of English terms. If these contain the letter *g*, which Arabic does not have, various spellings arise. جولف *golf* is written with a ج. Most Egyptians pronounce ج as a hard *g* and this spelling is fairly general. However, in بولينغ *bowling* we have a spelling with the nearest Arabic sound غ **gh**.

Insight

There are, unfortunately, no hard and fast rules. It seems to be down to the whim of the writer/typesetter. In fact, you often even see the same word spelled in two different ways (ج and غ) in the same document. More rarely, ق is used, as this is pronounced hard *g* in the spoken dialects of many Arab countries, including nearly the whole of the Arabian Peninsula.

The other (main) letters which Arabic lacks, *p* and *v*, are usually transcribed as ب **b** and ف **f**, respectively. Occasionally you will see the adopted Persian letters پ **p** and ڤ **v** with three dots, but this is not very common.

Foreign words in Arabic often have a liberal sprinkling of long vowels, as their word shapes do not conform to the usual guidelines.

Exercise 4

Read the prospectus for this women's club and answer the questions.

a *How much does annual membership cost?*
b *Up to how many children may accompany a mother free?*
c *Until what age are boys allowed to accompany their mothers?*
d *The club is open from:*
i 9am   ii 10am
e *The club closes at:*
i 9pm   ii 10pm
f *How much does monthly membership of the Library cost?*
g *Name three facilities which are free for members.*

نادي الفتيات

العضوية في النادي مفتوحة لكافة جنسيات للسيدات والأطفال.

(البنات من جميع الأعمار أما الأولاد الذكور حتى ١٠ سنوات فقط)

عضوية نادي الفتيات:

عضوية فردية .... ٧٢٠٠ درهم سنويا

عضوية عائلية (الأم + ٣ أبناء)................ ٧٣٠٠ درهم سنويا

عضوية المكتبة................................ ٦٢٠ درهم شهريا

عضوية يومية للزوار

الكبار (أكثر من ١٣ سنة)............................ ٥٠ درهم

الصغار (حتى ١٢ سنة) .... ٢٠ درهم

تسهيلات النادي:

- حجرة الألعاب الرياضية
- سونا
- الأيروبيك*
- المسبح*
- المكتبة*
- منتجع الصحة*
- قاعة التزلج*
- كافتريا*
- مركز الفن
- ملاعب التنس

* الاستخدام للعضوات مجانا

النادي مفتوح طوال اليوم من الساعة ٩ صباحا حتى الساعة ١٠ مساء.

QUICK VOCAB

نادي، أندية **naadii, andiyah** *club* (social)

فتاة فتيات **fataah, fatayaat** *young woman*

عضوية **:uDuwiyyah** *membership*

كافة **kaafat** *all*

سيدة سيدات **sayyidah, sayyidaat** *lady*

طفل أطفال **Tifl, aTfaal** *child, baby*

أما **ammaa** *as for, with regard to*

ذكور **dhukuur** *males*

فقط **faqaT** *only*

فردي **fardii** *single*

سنويا **sanawiyyan** *annually*

عائلي **:aa'ilii** *family* (adj.)
مكتبة **maktabah** *library, bookshop*
شهرياً **shahriyyan** *monthly*
يومي **yawmii** *daily*
زائر زوار **zaa'ir, zuwwaar** *visitor*
كبار **kibaar** *adults*
صغار **aSghaar** *children*
تسهيل ـات **tas-hiil, -aat** *facilities*
حجرة الألعاب الرياضية **Hujrat al-al:aab ar-riyaaDiyyah** *sports/games room*
مسبح **masbaH** *swimming pool*
منتجع الصحة **muntaja: aS-SiHHah** *fitness centre*
قاعة التزلج **qaa:at at-tazalluj** *ice rink*
مركز الفن **markaz al-fann** *art/craft centre*
ملاعب التنس **malaa:ib at-tanis** *tennis courts*
استخدام **istikhdaam** *use* (noun)
عضوة ـات **:uDuwwah, -aat** (female) *member*
طوال اليوم **Tiwaal al-yawm** *all day*
الجنسيات **al-jinsiyyaat** *(the) nationalities*

QUICK VOCAB

Exercise 5

CD2, TR37

Five people are talking about how often they take part in sporting activities. Listen to the recording and write down in the columns below who likes to do what and how often. We've done the first one for you.

سؤال: ماذا تحب من الرياضات؟
جواب: ألعب كرة القدم كثيرا

يوميا	كثيرا	أحيانا	نادرا	أبدا
Example	*football*			
١				
٢				
٣				
٤				
٥				

مارس **máarasa [S-III]** *to practise, carry out, perform*

Exercise 6

Select an appropriate adverb from the box to fill in the gaps in the sentences. You may only use each adverb once.

١ افتح الباب .... عندنا ضيف.

٢ ذهبت إلى السوق وقابلت أحمد هناك.......... .

٣ كان ذلك البرنامج مهما ....

٤ كنا جالسين في البيت، وقام زيد .... وخرج.

٥ تسافر هذه الطائرة إلى الرياض.......... .

٦ يا أولاد، العبوا .... ، الوالد نائم.

صدفة	فجأة	بسرعة	بهدوء	مباشرة	جدا

نائم **náa'im** *sleeping, asleep*

Exercise 7

You are shopping for clothes with some Arabic-speaking friends. How would you say what they are looking for? Make up complete sentences like this one:

Yunis – *blue coat* يحتاج يونس إلى معطف أزرق.

a Ali – black shoes
b Sonia – yellow dress
c Saeed – green shirt
d Khalid – white socks
e Faridah – red trousers
f Hamed – brown belt
g Anisa – pink handbag

10 things you need to know

1 *There is a special set of adjectives which denote the main colours and certain physical disabilities.*
2 *These have three forms: masculine singular, feminine singular and a plural.*
3 *The masculine singular is the same shape as the comparative, i.e.* **aC¹C²aC³** *eg* **aSfar** yellow. *(Think saffron)*
4 *The feminine singular shape is* **C¹aC²C³aa'**: **Hamraa'** *(this the origin of the Alhambra in Granada).*
5 *The plural form is* **C¹uC²C³**: **Humr.**
6 *As with the comparatives, there is a slightly different form for roots ending in* **waaw** *or* **yaa'**: **aC¹C²aa**, *e.g.* **a:maa** blind *(written أعمى).*
7 *Of these, only the plural form takes the accusative marker.*
8 *Other colours use the names of natural objects with the adjective ending* **-ii**, *e.g.* **bunnii** brown, *from* **bunn** coffee beans.
9 *There are two ways of forming adverbs. One is to add* **-an** *(written with an* **alif** *except for words with the feminine ending) to a noun or adjective, e.g.* **sarii:an** quickly.
10 *The other is to prefix a noun with the preposition* **bi-**, *here rendered* with, *e.g.* **bi-sur:ah** with speed, quickly *(a more common alternative to the above).*

17

من كل بلد خبر
min kull balad khabar
News from every country

In this unit you will learn:

- ***to talk about 'each', 'every', 'all' and 'some'***
- ***to use some irregular nouns and adjectives***

1 مصر miSr Egypt

CD2, TR38

Exercise 1
Read the passage and answer the questions:

a *Who made a statement welcoming the UN resolution?*
b *What has been smuggled abroad?*
c *Which famous Egyptian pieces are in the British Museum?*

مصر

الآثار المصرية في الخارج

اعرب رئيس دائرة الاثار المصرية أمس عن ترحيبه بقرار الجمعية العمومية للأمم المتحدة بالسماح للدول التي لها آثار مهربة في الخارج باستردادها. وقال

إنه هناك حوالي ٢١ مليون قطعة أثرية مصرية مسروقة في الغرب أشهرها ذقن أبو الهول وحجر رشيد الموجودان في المتحف البريطاني في لندن.

Exercise 2

Now find the Arabic for the following expressions:

a *the head of the department of Egyptian antiquities*
b *approximately 21 million*
c *the beard of the Sphynx*
d *the Rosetta Stone*

QUICK VOCAB

أثر، آثار **áthar, aatháar** sing. *track, trace*, pl. also *archaeological remains, antiquities*

الخارج **al-kháarij** *abroad, the outside*

أعرب عن **á:raba :an [S-IV]** *to state, express*

ترحيب **tarHíib** *welcome, welcoming* (noun)

قرار، ـات **qaráar, -áat** *decision, resolution*

جمعية، ـات **jam:íyyah, -áat** *group, assembly, society*

عمومي **:umúumii** *general*

أمة، أمم **úmmah, úmam** *nation*

متحد **muttáHid** *united*

سماح **samáaH** *permission*

مهرب **muhárrab** *smuggled*

استرداد **istirdáad** *getting back, reclaiming*

قطعة، قطع **qíT:ah, qíTa:** *piece*

أثري **átharii** *archaeological*

مسروق **masrúuq** *stolen*

الغرب **al-gharb** *the west*

أشهر **ásh-har*** *more/most famous*

ذقن، ذقون **dhaqn, dhuqúun** (f.) *beard*

أبو الهول **abuu l-hawl** *the Sphynx* [lit., Father of Terror]

حجر، أحجار **Hájar, aHjáar** *stone*

رشيد **rashíid** *Rosetta*, a town in Egypt; *Rashid* (man's name)

موجود **mawjúud** *found, situated, existing*

الملاحظات al-mulaaHaDHáat (Notes)

- **a:raba** *to express requires the preposition* **:an.**
- **tarHiib** *and its verb* **raHHab** *to welcome require* **bi-.**
- **samaaH** *permission also requires* **bi-.**
- **inna-h(u).** *The verb* **qaala** *to say uniquely is followed by* **inna** *for that. All other verbs use* **anna** *(see Unit 8).*
- **ash-har** *is the comparative/superlative of* **mash-huur.** *This is an irregular formation, actually taken from another word. (See Unit 15.)*
- **abuu l-hawl** *the Sphynx. For the irregular noun* **abuu,** *see below.*
- **al-mawjuudaan.** *The adjective here is in the dual as it refers to two objects (the Sphinx's beard and the Rosetta Stone).*

---

2 اليمن al-yaman The Yemen

CD2, TR39

Exercise 3
Read the passage and answer the questions

a *What arrived in the port of Aden?*
b *Who was it carrying?*
c *What do the tourists hope to visit?*

اليمن

٤٥٠ سائح أوروبي في عدن

استقبل ميناء عدن أمس الأول سفينة سياحية ألمانية تحمل أكثر من ٤٠٠ سائح وسائحة من مختلف الجنسيات الأوروبية. وسيزور هؤلاء السواح بعض المدن اليمنية التاريخية.

Exercise 4

Find the Arabic for the English expressions:

a *of various nationalities*
b *the tourists will visit some Yemeni towns*

QUICK VOCAB

اليمن **al-yáman** *Yemen*
سائح، سواح **sáa'iH, suwwáaH** *tourist*
أوروبي، ـون **urúubii** *European*
عدن **:ádan** *Aden*
ميناء، المواني **miináa', al-mawáanii** (sometimes f.) *harbour, port*
أمس الأول **ams al-áwwal** *the day before yesterday*
سفينة، سفن **safíinah, súfun** *ship*
سياحي **siyáaHii** *tourist* (adj.), *touristic*
ألماني **almáanii** *German*
مختلف **mukhtálif** *different, various*
تاريخي **taaríikhii** *historical, historic*

الملاحظات al-mulaaHaDHáat (Notes)

- **miinaa'** *harbour. The plural of this word is a defective noun (see below).*
- **ams al-awwal** *lit., yesterday the-first. Also occurs in the form* **awwal ams,** *both meaning the day before yesterday.*
- **mukhtalif** *various when, as here, used as the first part of a possessive construction. When used as an ordinary adjective, it means different.*
- **ba:D** *some. See below.*

3 أمريكا amriikaa America

CD2, TR40

Exercise 5

Read the passage and answer the questions:

- a *How old is the millionaire's prospective bride?*
- b *How old is he?*
- c *What aids does he need?*
- d *How much does he love his fiancée?*

أمريكا

أعلن مليونير أمريكي من ولاية كاليفورنيا في الأسبوع الماضي أنه سيتزوج فتاة في الخامسة والعشرين من عمرها. وهذا بعد احتفاله بعيد ميلاده المئوي بأيام قليلة. وهو يستخدم منظما لضربات القلب ويتنقل على كرسي بعجلات. وقال انه يحبها من كل قلبه وهي تبادله الحب.

Exercise 6

Find the Arabic for the following English expressions:

- a *he will marry a girl*
- b *he said that he loves her*
- c *with all his heart*

QUICK VOCAB

أعلن **á:lana [S-IV]** *to announce, state*

مليونير **malyoonáyr** *millionaire*

ولاية، ـات **wiláayah, -aat** *administrative division of a country*; here *state*

تزوج **tazáwwaja [Mw-V]** *to marry*

فتاة، فتيات **fatáah, fatayáat** *girl, young woman*

احتفال، ـات **iHtifáal, -áat** *celebration*

مئوي **mí'awii** *centennial, hundredth*

منظم، ـات **munáDHDHim, -áat** *regulator*

ضربة، ـات **Dárbah, Darabáat** *a beat, blow*

QUICK VOCAB

قلب، قلوب **qalb, qulúub** *heart*

تنقل **tanáqqala [S-V]** *to be transported*

كرسي، كراسي **kúrsii, karáasii** *chair*

عجلة، ـات **:ájalah, -áat** *wheel*

بادل **báadala [S-III]** *to return, reciprocate to someone*

الملاحظات al-mulaaHaDHáat (Notes)

- **al-maaDii** *the past. Defective adjective. See Structure, Section 3.*
- **al-khaamisah wa-l-:ishriin** *the 25th. Note that in compounds of tens and units, only the unit takes the ordinal form. For basic rules, see Unit 11. The adjective applies to the implied/ understood feminine noun* **sanah** *year.*
- **iHtifaal** *celebration and its verb require* **bi-**.
- **mi'awii** *hundredth. This is not a true ordinal number, rather an adjective meaning centennial from* مئة **mi'ah** – *irregular but most common spelling – or* مائة **hundred.**
- **munaDHDHim(an) li-Darabaat al-qalb** *regulator for beats of the heart, i.e. a pacemaker.*
- **min kull qalb-uh** *with all his heart. For* **kull,** *see grammar section below.*
- **tubaadil-uh** *she reciprocates [to him]. Many of such Form III verbs take a direct object, where in English a preposition is required. See Verb tables.*

---

4 أبو ظبي abuu DHabii Abu Dhabi

CD2, TR41

Exercise 7
Read the passage and answer the questions:

a Who is Fairuz?

b Why is she in Abu Dhabi?

أبو ظبي

وصلت إلى الإمارات اليوم المطربة اللبنانية المشهورة فيروز في زيارة خاصة، ستزور خلالها أخاها الذي يقيم في أبو ظبي.

Exercise 8

Now find the Arabic for the following English expressions:

a She arrived in the Emirates today.
b She will visit her brother.

QUICK VOCAB

أبو ظبي **abuu DHábi** *Abu Dhabi*

وصل **wáSala [Fw-I i]** *to arrive* (إلى **ilaa** *at*)

مطربة، ـات **múTribah, -aat** (female) *singer, musician*

فيروز **fayrúuz** *Fairuz* (female name); *turquoise* (gem)

زيارة، ـات **ziyáarah, -áat** *visit*

خلال **khaláal** *during*

أخ، إخوان/ إخوة **akh, ikhwáan** or **íkhwah** *brother*

الملاحظات al-mulaaHaDHáat (Notes)

- **abuu DHabii.** *Lit., 'father of gazelle'. For* **abuu**, *see grammar section below.*
- **waSal** *to arrive requires the preposition* **ilaa.**
- **akhaa-haa** *her brother. See grammar section below.*

---

5 نيو يورك nyuu yuurk New York

CD2, TR42

Exercise 9

Read the passage and answer the questions:

a *What special day has UNESCO chosen to commemorate on 21 March?*
b *Who is Ali al-Allaq?*
c *What is poetry greater than?*

نيو يورك

اختارت منظمة اليونسكو يوم ٢١ مارس يوما عالميا للشعر. ورحب الشعراء العرب بهذا، بينهم الشاعر العراقي علي جعفر العلاق الذي قال إنه «مؤمن إيمانا لا حدود له أن الشعر أكبر من الزمان كله، وأكثر اتساعا من الأمكنة جميعا. إنه مالئ اللحظات والفصول والقرون بجمال المعنى ومعنى الجمال».

Exercise 10

Find the Arabic for the following English expressions:

a *Arab poets welcomed this.*
b *Poetry is greater than all time.*
c *It fills the moments … with the beauty of meaning.*

QUICK VOCAB

أقام **aqáama [Mw-IV]** *to reside*

منظمة، ـات **munáDHDHamah, -áat** *organisation*

شعر **shi:r** *poetry*

رحب بـ **ráHHaba [S-II]** *to welcome* (requires **bi-**)

شاعر، شعراء **sháa:ir, shu:aráa'*** *poet*

عراقي **:iráaqii** *Iraqi*

مؤمن، ـون **mú'min, -úun** *believing, a believer* (in something)

إيمان **iimáan** *belief, faith*

حد، حدود **Hadd, Hudúud** *limit, border*

زمان، أزمنة **zamáan, azmínah** *time*

اتساع **ittisáa:** *extent, compass*

مكان، أمكنة **makáan, amkínah** *place*

جميعا **jamíi:an** *all together*

مالئ **máali'** *filling, filler*

لحظة، ـات **láHDHah, laHaDHáat** *moment*

فصل، فصول **faSl, fuSúul** *section, season* (of the year)

قرن، قرون **qarn, qurúun** *century*

معنى، المعاني **má:naa, al-ma:áanii** *meaning*

الملاحظات al-mulaaHaDHáat (Notes)

- **yawman :aalamiyyan** *as a world day. Adverbial accusative of respect. (See Unit 15.)*
- **mu'min iimaanan.** *Adverbial accusative. (See Unit 15.)*
- **laa Huduud la-h(u)** *Lit., no limits to it. Here the word* **laa** *is used to negate a noun. For its other uses, see Unit 10.*
- **ittisaa:an** *in extent and* **jamii:an** *all together are examples of the adverbial accusative. See also below.*

تعبيرات رئيسية ta:biiráat ra'iisíyyah (Key phrases)

كل يوم **kull yawm**	*every day*
كل عام وأنت بخير **kull :aam wa-anta bi-khayr**	*Happy Birthday/Eid, etc.*
من كل قلبي **min kull qalb-ii**	*with all my heart*
بعض الناس **ba:D an-naas**	*some of the people*

تراكيب اللغة taraakíib al-lúghah (Structures)

1 'Each', 'every' and 'all'

All these English words are expressed using the Arabic كل **kull,** but with different constructions according to the specific meaning required.

each, every	**kull** + indefinite singular
all	**kull** + definite plural def. plural + **kull** + suffix pronoun

Each, every

The construction used for both of these is the same: **kull** followed by an indefinite singular noun (without the definite article **al-**):

من كل بلد خبر	*from every country news*
كل عام وأنت بخير	lit., *every year and you in well-being*

The Arabic congratulatory phrase in the second example is used in connection with all anniversaries, particularly birthdays.

خير **khayr** (state of) *well-being*

كل مشكلة لها حل	*every problem has a solution* [lit., every problem for it a solution]

مشكلة، مشاكل **múshkilah, masháakil*** *problem*
حل، حلول **Hall, Hulúul** *solution*

All

a) **kull** followed by a noun with the definite article, usually plural. This is a possessive construction and obeys the rules given in Unit 6.

كل المتاحف مقفولة يوم الجمعة	*all [of] the museums are closed on Friday*
كان كل العساكر يحملون أسلحة	*all [of] the soldiers were carrying arms*
كل البنات حاضرات	*all [of] the girls are present*
عسكري، عساكر **:askárii, :asáakir**	*soldier*
سلاح، أسلحة **siláaH, aslíHah**	*weapon, arm*

حاضر **HáaDir** *present, here*

The noun can be replaced by a suffix pronoun:

كلهم أخذوا قطعة كعك	*all of them (they all) took a piece of cake*

كعك **ka:k** *cake*

b) A plural noun with the definite article, followed by **kull** with a suffix pronoun agreeing with the noun. This construction is slightly more common. To make it clear, here are the same examples as above in the new format. The meaning is exactly the same.

المتاحف كلها مقفولة يوم الجمعة	*the museums all-of-them are closed on Friday*
كان العساكر كلهم يحملون أسلحة	*the soldiers all-of-them were carrying arms*
البنات كلهن حاضرات	*the girls all-of-them are present*

When used with a singular noun or pronoun suffix, the translation can be *all* or *the whole*, e.g. from the text:

الزمان كله	*all time, the whole of time*
أكلت الكعك كله	*She ate all the cake, the whole cake.*

An alternative word for *all* is جميع **jamii:**, used either with a plural in the same way as **kull** or, as we have in the text, with the accusative marker as an adverb (see Unit 16):

وأكثر اتساعا من الأمكنة جميعا	*and greater in compass than all places*

Some

The word for *some* is بعض **ba:D**, a noun meaning *a part of something*. This is used in the same way as **kull** when it means *all* as explained above:

بعض المدن اليمنية التاريخية — *some of the historic Yemeni towns*
بعضهم عرب وبعضهم إنجليز — *some of them are Arabs, and some English*

Summary
kull is a noun meaning *the whole*, *totality* of something.

ba:D is a noun meaning *a part* of something. They are both sometimes used independently:

قال البعض إنها مجنونة — *some said that she was mad*
من كل قلبه — *with all his heart*

مجنون، مجانين **majnúun, majaaníin*** *mad*

2 Irregular nouns

There are two classes of irregular nouns and adjectives which must be mentioned as the variations in their endings show up in print, i.e. they do not consist entirely of unmarked vowel endings.

Insight

Remember that literary Arabic recognises three cases of the noun/adjective, depending on its function in the sentence:

Nominative, *used for the subject of all sentences and the complement of verbless sentences; also for the complement of* **inna**-*type sentences (see Unit 8).*

Accusative, *used for the object of verb sentences, the subject of* **inna**, *the complement of* **kaana** *sentences (Unit 8) and for many adverbial expressions (Unit 16).*

Genitive, *used for the second part of possessive constructions (i.e. for the possessor) and after all prepositions.*

Two common nouns behave differently when they form the first part of a possessive phrase, either with another noun or a pronoun suffix:

أب، آباء **ab, aabaa'**	*father*
أخ، إخوان\إخوة **akh, ikhwaan** or **ikhwah**	*brother*

These behave normally when they do not form the first part of a possessive:

له أخ واحد	*he has one brother*

In possessives, they show the nominative case with a و, the accusative with an ا, and the genitive with a ي.

For example, take *her brother/father*, using the possessive suffix **-haa.**

Case	*her father*	*her brother*
Nominative	أبوها **abuu-haa**	أخوها **akhuu-haa**
Accusative	أباها **abaa-haa**	أخاها **akhaa-haa**
Genitive	أبيها **abii-haa**	أخيها **akhii-haa**

Here is an example from the article above:

ستزور خلالها أخاها	*during which she will visit her brother* (accusative, object of a verb)

Examples of the other two cases are:

يعمل أبوهم في شركة كبيرة	*their father works in a big company* (nominative, subject of a verb)
نسكن مع أبينا	*we live with our father* (genitive after a preposition)

المـلاحظات al-mulaaHaDHáat (Notes)

- *When the suffix* ـي **-ii** *my is added to these words, the various long vowel endings are omitted and all cases are* أبي **ab-ii** *and* أخي **akh-ii.**
- *Technically, in formal Standard Arabic, the same varying forms should be used before another noun, but this seems to be dropping out of modern press Arabic and the nominative* **-uu** *form is used in all contexts. This is important, as* **abuu**, *especially, occurs in many personal and place names. For instance, in the text we have* في أبو ظبي *in Abu Dhabi, which should technically be* أبي **abii** *after the preposition* في *in.*
- **abuu** *is frequently used to express a possessor of something, rather than a strictly biological father, e.g.* أبو الهول *possessor of terror; that which holds terror, i.e. the Sphynx (see also below).*
- *A common word* ذو، ذا، ذي **dhuu, dhaa, dhii** *possessor is only used with a following noun, e.g.* كان رجلا ذا شأن *he was a man of importance [lit., possessor of importance].*

Insight

You can avoid using **abuu** etc. in many situations by substituting the regular noun والد **waalid**, which also means *father*, but this is not permissible in proper names. You can't do anything about **akh**, though.

3 Defective nouns and adjectives

Another class of irregular words are the so-called defective nouns and adjectives. The defect is that, in certain cases as explained below, they lose their final letter, which is always ي. These are perfectly regular in the definite, but the indefinite works as follows, using the word **qaaDii** *judge* as a model:

Definite	all cases:	القاضي **al-qaaDii**
Indefinite	Nominative	قاض **qaaDin**
	Accusative:	قاضيا **qaaDiyan**
	Genitive:	قاض **qaaDin**

The class also includes adjectives such as الماضي، ماض، ماضيا **al-maaDii, maaDin, maaDiyan** *past, former.*

Insight

These words are a common source of error to Arabs when writing, perhaps because in spoken Arabic, the final **-ii** is always pronounced and native speakers feel instinctively that there is something missing or unnatural if they drop it.

Important note: To save confusion, and because they look peculiar in isolation in their truncated form, words of this class have been given in the vocabularies and glossaries with the definite article, e.g.:

القاضي، قضاة **al-qaaDii, quDaah** *judge*

الماضي **al-maaDii** *past* (adj.)

Note that it can be the singular which is defective, as in the examples above, or the plural as in the following examples:

معنى، المعاني **ma:naa, al-ma:aanii** *meaning*

ميناء، الموانى **miinaa', al-mawaanii** *harbour*

Here are another couple of common defective adjectives:

ماء صاف **maa' Saafin** *pure water*

السد العالي **as-sadd al-:aali** *the High Dam* (in Egypt)

QUICK VOCAB

ماء، مياه **maa, miyaah** *water*
الصافي **aS-Saafii** *pure, clear*
سد، سدود **sadd, suduud** *dam*
العالي **al-: aalii** *high*

أوزان الكلمات awzáan al-kalimáat (Word shapes)

Exercise 11

The following is a revision exercise, covering the word shapes given in all the previous units. You are given an Arabic root, along with its basic meaning. Refer back to the relevant unit and create the required word shape. The answers, along with their meanings, are given in the key and on the recording:

Unit 1 و–ح–د *to be one, unique*
Unit 2 ب–ر–د *being cold*
Unit 3 ض–ب–ط *being exact, accurate*
Unit 4 ل–ع–ب *playing*
Unit 5 ف–ط–ر *breaking one's fast*
Unit 6 ط–ب–ع *printing, typing*
Unit 7 ف–هـ–م *understanding*
Unit 8 ر–س–م *drawing*
Unit 9 ع–ل–م *knowing*
Unit 10 ع–ل–م *knowing*
Unit 11 ف–ض–ل *being preferable, good, excellent*
Unit 12 ف–س–ر *explaining, elucidating*
Unit 13 ن–ظ–ر *seeing, looking at*
Unit 14 ك–ش–ف *uncovering, discovering*
Unit 15 ف–ت–ح *opening*
Unit 16 ل–خ–ب–ط *being mixed up, in a mess*

تمرينات tamriináat (Practice)

Exercise 12
Find the odd one out:

١ أخي - عمي - أمي - أبي

٢ أب - مطرب - مدير - شاعر

٣ أبو صالح - أبو ظبي - أبو الهول

٤ كرسي - طاولة - غسالة - رئيس

٥ ميناء - قلب - سفينة - ماء

غسالة، ـات **ghassáalah, -áat** *washing machine*

Exercise 13
Here is part of a hotel guide for Algiers. Look at the key to the hotel facilities and decide whether these statements referring to the four hotels described below are true or false.

١ كل غرفة في فندق الخليج فيها تلفزيون وراديو وعرض أفلام.

٢ بعض الفنادق فيها ملعب تنس.

٣ كل الفنادق تقبل بطاقات التسليف.

٤ بعض الفنادق لها مواقف سيارات.

٥ كل فندق فيه تكييف.

٦ كل الفنادق فيها صالون تجميل.

٧ كلها فيه مسبح.

٨ بعض الغرف في فندق «اللؤلؤة» فيها حمام.

٩ في كل فندق خدمة تنظيف الملابس.

١٠ ليس في كل الغرف في فندق «سبلنديد» هاتف.

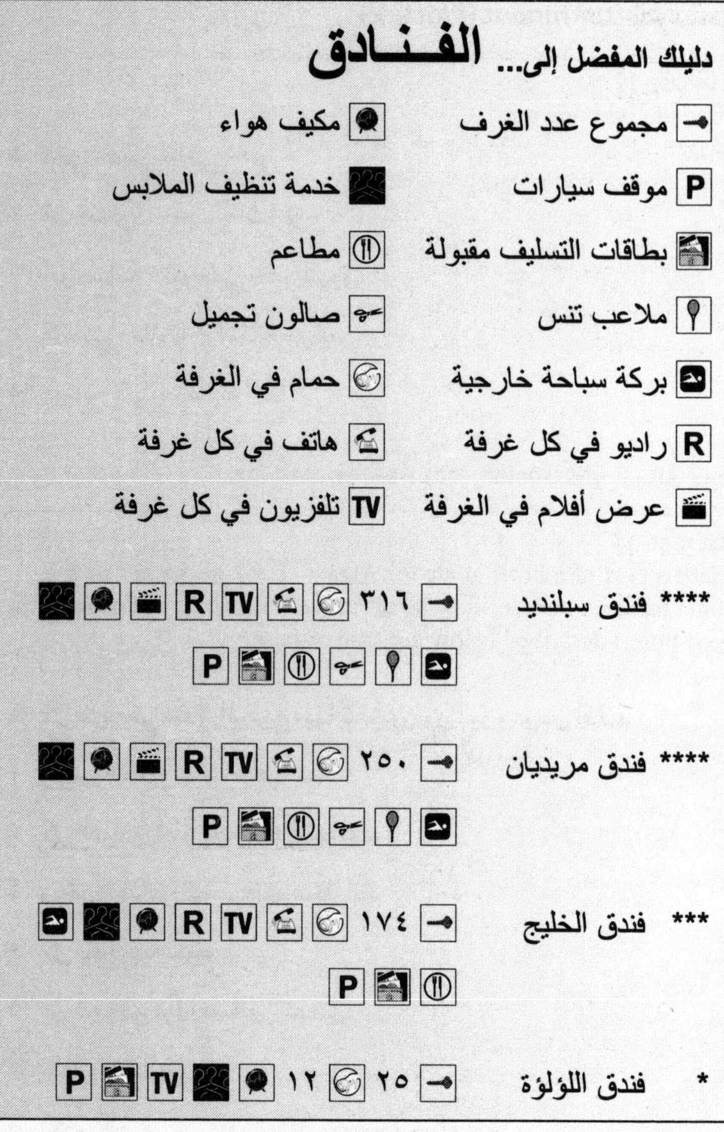

دليلك المفضل إلى... الفنــادق

مجموع عدد الغرف	مكيف هواء
P موقف سيارات	خدمة تنظيف الملابس
بطاقات التسليف مقبولة	مطاعم
ملاعب تنس	صالون تجميل
بركة سباحة خارجية	حمام في الغرفة
R راديو في كل غرفة	هاتف في كل غرفة
عرض أفلام في الغرفة	TV تلفزيون في كل غرفة

**** فندق سبلنديد ٣١٦ TV R
P

**** فندق مريديان ٢٥٠ TV R
P

*** فندق الخليج ١٧٤ TV R
P

* فندق اللؤلؤة ٢٥ ١٢ TV P

قبل **qábila [S-I a]** *to accept*

بطاقة التسليف **buTáaqat at-tasliif** *credit card*

تكييف **takyíif** *air conditioning*

صالون تجميل **Sáaluun tajmíil** *beauty salon*

خدمة، ـات **khídmah, -áat** *service*

تنظيف **tanDHíif** *cleaning*

ملابس **maláabis** *clothes*

QUICK VOCAB

Exercise 14

Add the word *all* to the plural nouns (underlined) in the following sentences, using **kull** with a suffix pronoun agreeing with the noun.

Example:

لعب الأولاد في الحديقة	*The children played in the garden.*
لعب الأولاد كلهم في الحديقة	*All the children played in the garden.*

١ درس الطلبة للامتحانات.

٢ وصل السواح من ألمانيا.

٣ تفتح الدكاكين في المساء.

٤ رحب الموظفون بتقرير المدير.

٥ استقبلته أخواته في المطار.

٦ وضعت الكتب على الرف.

1 *The students studied for their examinations.*
2 *The tourists arrived from Germany.*
3 *The shops open in the evening.*
4 *The employees welcomed the director's report.*
5 *His sisters met him in at the airport.*
6 *I put the books on the shelf.*

10 things you need to know

1 *The word* **kull** *is used for* each, every *and* all, *the meaning depending on the structure of the sentence.*

2 *For* each *and* every, *use* **kull** *followed by an indefinite noun:* **kull yawm** every day.

3 *To express* all, *there are two possible constructions:* **kull** *followed by a definite plural, e.g.* **kull al-mataaHif** all the museums.

4 *The second and more common alternative is a definite plural, followed by* **kull** *with a pronoun suffix agreeing with the noun:* **al-mataaHif kull-haa**, *lit., 'the-museums all-them'.*

5 *The word for* some *is* **ba:D** *which is used in the same way as* **kull** *when it means* all. **ba:D al-mudun** some of the towns.

6 *There is a set of five irregular nouns – all common as first terms of a possessive phrase – which show their case ending by means of a long (and therefore visible) vowel.*

7 *Only three of these are in common use:* **abuu** father, **akhuu** brother *and* **dhuu** possessor of.

8 *These become* **abaa, akhaa** *and* **dhaa** *in the accusative:* **qaabalt akhaa-k** I met your brother.

9 *They become* **abii, akhii** *and* **dhii** *in the genitive (second terms of possessives and after all prepositions):* **bayt abii-naa** our father's house.

10 *Another set of irregular nouns (and adjectives) are those of the shape* **C^{1}aaC^{2}ii** *where the final* **yaa'** *is dropped in the nominative and genitive of the indefinite, e.g.* **qaaDin** *nominative and genitive, but* **qaaDiyan** *accusative.*

Key to the exercises

Script and pronunciation guide

1 Volvo, Honda, Jeep, Toyota, Chrysler, IKEA

Unit 1

1 a عليكم b السلام
2 السلام عليكم
3 a الخير b صباح c مساء d النور
4 a صباح الخير b مساء النور c مساء الخير d السلام عليكم
e وعليكم السلام
5 a حالك b وأنت؟ الحمد لله. c أهلا بك/أهلا وسهلا d كيف حالكم
e أهلا وسهلا
6 1 c; 2 b; 3 a
7 1 c; 2 b; 3 a
8 a شاي بسكر b المصباح c الأهرام d سندوتش
9 Aladdin and the magic lamp
10 Sun: a, c, d, e, g; Moon: b, f
12 i d; ii b; iii e; iv c; v a
13 ١ g; ٢ a; ٣ b; ٤ c; ٥ i; ٦ j; ٧ h; ٨ d; ٩ e; ١٠ f
a Rabat; b Algiers or Algeria; c Cairo; d Riyadh; e Manamah; f Baghdad; g The Middle East; h Saudi Arabia; i (The) Sudan; j Jordan
14 a coffee; b lemon; c small Coca-Cola; d chocolate ice-cream; e the cinema; f the bank
15 a **as-sandwíitsh**; b **at-tilifúun**; c **al-bayt**; d **aT-TamáaTim**;

e **as-síinima**; f **al-bíirah aS-Saghiirah**; g **al-bárgar al-kabíir**; h **ar-ráadyo al-jadíid**

16 1 g; 2 d; 3 h; 4 c; 5 e; 6 b; 7 a; 8 f

17 ١ السينما الجديدة ٢ بنت صغيرة ٣ كتاب جميل٤ فيلم طويل ٥ البيت الكبير الواسع

18 ١ ص–غ–ر ٢ ط–و–ل ٣ ب–ع–د ٤ ق–ر–ب ٥ ج–د–د ٦ ق–د–م ٧ ج–م–ل ٨ ل–ط–ف ٩ ك–ر–م ١٠ ص–ح–ح

1 S-gh-r; 2 T-w-l; 3 b-:-d; 4 q-r-b; 5 j-d-d; 6 q-d-m; 7 j-m-l; 8 l-T-f; 9 k-r-m; 10 S-H-H

Unit 2

Dialogue 1* min áyna ánta? *Where are you from?

Translation:

Suad Well. My name is Suad. What's your name?
Michael My name is Michael.
Suad Welcome, Michael. Where are you from?
Michael I am from Manchester, in England. And you?
Suad I am from Alexandria, in Egypt.

Transliteration:

su:áad Hásanan. ána ísm-ii su:áad. maa ísm-ak?
máaykal ána ísm-ii máaykal
su:áad áhlan wa-sáhlan yaa máaykal. min áyna anta?
máaykal ána min manshastar fii inglatárra. wa-ánti?
su:áad ána min al-iskandaríyyah fii miSr.

1 a Suad; b Michael
2 a Manchester; b Alexandria
3 a أنا من مانشستر b وأنت؟

Dialogue 2 miSr jamíilah *Egypt is beautiful*

Translation:

Egypt is very beautiful. Cairo is a big city and it is very old. The Egyptian Museum is in Tahrir Square close to the Nile Hotel. There is an excellent restaurant in the Nile Hotel in Tahrir Square. And, of course, there are the pyramids in Geezah.

Transliteration:

miSr jamíilah jíddan. al-qáahirah madíinah kabíirah, wa-híya qadíimah jíddan. al-mátHaf al-míSrii fii maydáan at-taHríir qaríib min fúnduq al-níil. hunáaka máT:am mumtáaz fii fúnduq al-níil fii maydáan at-taHríir. wa-Táb:an hunáaka l-ahráam fi l-gíizah.

4 a that it is big, beautiful and very old; b in Tahrir Square; c an excellent restaurant

Dialogue 3 raqm tilifóon-ak kam? *What's your phone number?*

Translation:

Zaki What's your phone number, Hamid?
Hamid My phone number is 6347211. And your phone number?
Zaki My phone number is 6215500. Marie, what's your phone number?
Marie My phone number is 6207589.

Transliteration:

zákii ráqam tilifóon-ak kam, yaa Háamid?
Háamid ráqam tilifóon-ii síttah thaláathah árba:ah sáb:ah ithnáyn wáaHid wáaHid. wa-ráqam tilifóon-ak ánta?
Zaki ráqam tilifóon-ii síttah ithnáyn wáaHid khámsah khámsah Sifr Sifr. yaa maarii, ráqam tilifóon-ik kam?
maarii ráqam tilifóon-ii síttah ithnáyn Sifr sáb:ah khámsah thamáanyah tís:ah

5 a 6215500 b 6207589 c رقم تلفون d رقم تلفوني ...
6 عـ–ـد–ـل/ل–ز–مـ/ن–شـ–ـفـ/ك–مـ–ـل/ن–ـفـ–ع/ص–ـل–ح/س–ـل–ـم

7 a السكرتير الجديد b السيارة الجميلة c الولد الطويل
d المدير المشغول e البيت الصغير
8 a السكرتير جديد b السيارة جميلة c الولد طويل d البيت صغير e
المدير مشغول
9 a هو جديد b هي جميلة c هو طويل d هو صغير e هو مشغول
10 ١ أأنت من مصر؟ ٢ هل محمد في دبي؟ ٣ أهي أمريكية؟
٤ هل الكتاب جديد؟ ٥ هل يتكلم عربي؟
11 ١ السيارة جديدة ٢ هي مشغولة ٣ الفندق قريب من الأهرام
٤ محمد هنا ٥ هو مشغول
12 1 Tunis; 2 Lebanon; 3 Paris; 4 Scotland; 5 Abu Dhabi; 6 Italy
13 a Dubai; b Ras al-Khaimah; c Abu Dhabi
14 a 973; b 20; c 1; d 974; e 966; f 39

Unit 3

Dialogue 1 **á-ánta suudáani?** *Are you Sudanese?*

Translation:
Husáam Hello! Are you Egyptian?
Záki No, I'm Sudanese, from Khartoum. And you?
Husáam I'm Egyptian, from Tanta.
Záki Where is Tanta?
Husáam Tanta is near Cairo.

Transliteration:
Husáam márHaban. 'a-ánta míSrii?
záki laa, ána suudáanii min al-kharTúum. wa-ánta?
Husáam ána míSrii min TánTaa
záki áyna TánTaa?
Husáam TánTaa qaríibah min al-qáahirah

1 a Sudanese; b Khartoum
2 a Egypt; b England; c Australia; d the Lebanon; e France

Translation:
Suad I am Egyptian, and you, Mike?
Michael I am English.
Kylie I am Australian.
Yuunis I am Lebanese. I am from Beirut.
Marie I am French.

Transliteration:
su:áad ána miSríyyah, wa-ánta yaa máayk?
máayk ána inglíizii
káaylii ána ustraalíyyah
yúunis ána lubnáanii. ána min bayrúut
maarii ána faransíyyah

Dialogue 2* hal tatakállam inglíizii? *Do you speak English?

Translation:
Passenger Excuse me. Where are you from?
Julie I am from England. And you?
Passenger I am from Amman. I am Jordanian.
Julie Do you speak English?
Passenger No, I am sorry, I don't speak English. I only speak Arabic.

Transliteration:
ráakib :an ídhn-ik. min áyna ánti?
júulii ána min ingiltárra. wa-ánta?
ráakib ána min :ammáan. ána úrdunii
júulii hal tatakállam inglíizii?
ráakib laa, má:a l-ásaf, laa atakállam inglíizii. atakállam :árabi fáqaT

3 a English; b Arabic

Translation:
Passenger You speak Arabic fluently!
Julie No, only a little

Transliteration:
ráakib tatakallamíin al-:arabíyyah bi-Taláaqah!
júulii laa, qalíilah fáqaT

4 a هل تتكلم إنجليزي؟ b قليلة
5 true

Dialogue 3 maa :ámal-ak? *What is your occupation?*

Translation:
Passenger What is your occupation?
Julie I am a student, at London University. And you?
Passenger I am a doctor in Amman.

Transliteration:
ráakib maa :ámal-ik?
júulii ána Táalibah fii jáami:at lándan. wa-anta?
ráakib ána Tabíib fii :ammáan

6 a student; b in Amman
7 a ما عملك؟ b أنا طبيب

Dialogue 4 hal lándan madíinah kabíirah? *Is London a big city?*

Translation:
Passenger Is London a big city?
Julie Yes, it is a very big city. There are many big museums and bridges and shops.
Passenger Where is the university?
Julie It is in the middle of the town, near the British Museum.

Transliteration:
ráakib hal lándan madíinah kabíirah?
júulii ná:am híya madíinah kabíirah jíddan. hunáaka matáaHif kabíirah kathíirah wa-jusúur wa-maHalláat
ráakib áyna l-jáami:ah?
júulii híya fii wasT al-madíinah, qaríibah min al-mátHaf al-bríiTáanii

8 a museums/ bridges/ shops; b the university

9 a Morocco; b Jordan; c Oman; d Bahrain; e Kuwait

10 a 4E; b 7C; c 6A; d 2G; e 1B; f 3D; g 5F

11 a Salma; b Damascus, Syria
c اسمها سلمى d تتكلم اللغة العربية

Translation:
... her name is Salma and she is Syrian, from Damascus. She speaks Arabic, English and French. She is a teacher.

Transliteration:
... ísm-haa sálmaa wa-híya suuríyyah min dimáshq. tatakállam al-lughah al-:arabíyyah wa l-ingliizíyyah wa l-faransíyyah. híya mudárrisah.

12

١ اسمي مارتن رومانو
٢ أنا أمريكي
٣ أنا طالب
٤ قليل
٥ نعم، طبعا!
٦ نعم، اللغة الإيطالية ... بطلاقة.

Translation:
Martin Romano is American. He is a student. He speaks English, fluent Italian, and a little Arabic.

Transliteration:
máartin ruumáanuu min amríikaa. huwa Táalib. yatakállam inglíizii, wa-iiTáalii bi-Taláaqah wa :árabi qalíilan.

13 ١ مشغولة ٢ المصرية، مشهورة ٣ جديد ٤ الكبيرة، أمريكية ٥ جديدة ٦ الانجليزية، نافعة ٧ جديدة، كثيرة ٨ واحدة ٩ سعيدة

14 a هي مدرسة b هي طالب c هو مهندس d هو مديرة e هي طالبة f هي طبيبة

Unit 4

Dialogue 1 **áyna l-matáaHif?** *Where are the museums?*

Translation:
Hassan This is the map of Sharjah. This is the Old Town and this is the fish market.
Jim Where are the museums?
Hassan These are the museums here and here. This is the Arts Museum and this is the Natural History Museum, on the airport road.
Bridget That museum is far away.
Jim Yes, that's true. Look, the Fort Museum is here, in Tower (Burj) Street. It's an excellent museum and maybe afterwards we can go to the Old Town.
Bridget Good. We'll go to the Fort Museum.

1 a The Old Town; b It's too far; c The Fort Museum
2 a 4; b 2; c 3; d 1

Dialogue 2 **yáqfil as-sáa:ah kam?** *What time does it close?*

Translation:
Hassan Good morning. At what time does the museum close?
Attendant Good morning. It closes at one o'clock and opens at four o'clock in the afternoon.
Bridget What is the time now?
Hassan It's a quarter past ten.
Bridget Good. We have plenty of time.
Attendant Welcome, come in. This is a brochure of the museum.
Hassan Thank you.

3 a 1pm; b 4pm; c 10:15 am; d a brochure
4 a 4; b 1; c 6; d 2; e 5; f 3
5 a Wednesday evenings; b Monday; c 8:30pm; d 9am; e Friday; f 5

Dialogue 4* bi-kam...? *How much does it cost?

Translation:
Hassan Hello!
Female attendant Hello!
Hassan How much is a ticket, please?
Female attendant Adults are six dirhams and children three dirhams.
Hassan Three tickets at six dirhams please.
Female attendant Eighteen dirhams please. Thank you. Here are the tickets.
Hassan Thank you.

6 a 6 Dhs; b 3Dhs; c 18 Dhs
7 a 4; b 1; c 2; d 3
8 a 1:30; b 6:55; c 10:15; d 5:00; e 9:00am
9 see transcript
10 ١ يوم؛ ٢ يوم الأربعاء؛ ٣ أمس؛ ٤ يوم الأحد؛ ٥ بعد غد؛ ٦ يوم الجمعة
11 ١ هذا؛ ٢ هذه؛ ٣ أولائك؛ ٤ هذه؛ ٥ أولائك؛ ٦ تلك
12 3/12/1952; 19/11/1967; 1/1/2000; 28/2/1990; 17/4/1836
13

١ مساء الخير	٤ تفضل.
٢ التذكرة بكم؟	٥ المسرح يفتح الساعة كم؟
٣ أربعة تذاكر من فضلك.	٦ شكرا

a 4 dinars; b 7 o' clock; c half past seven
14 see transcript

Unit 5

Dialogue 1* háadhihi híya záwjat-ii *This is my wife

Translation:
Hamed Tom, come in, please.
Tom Thank you, Hamed.
Hamed This is my wife, Salma. Salma, this is Tom, from the office.

Tom Good evening, Salma, how are you?
Salma I'm well, praise God. Welcome. And how are you?
Tom Praise God. This is a present for you. *(He gives Salma some flowers)*
Salma Thank you, Tom. This is my father and this is my mother... and this is our son, Tamiim. Please, sit down.
Tom How old is Tamiim?
Salma He is 15 years old and our daughter Farida is 21.
Hamed How old are your children, Tom?
Tom Our children are small – our son is 5 and our daughter is 3 years old.

1 a Salma; b 15; c 21; d younger
2 a هذا والدي b تفضل إجلس c هذا ابننا d أولادك أنت، كم عمرهم؟ e بنتنا عمرها ٣ سنوات
3 33 thaláathah wa-thalaathiín; 40 ٤٠ ; 44 árba:ah wa-arba:iín; 57 sáb:ah wa-khamsiín; 68 thamáanyah wa-sittiín; 76 síttah wa-sab:iín; 85 khámsah wa-thamaaniín; 99 tís:ah wa-tis:iín.
4 ١٤ ٢٤ ٢٨ ٣١ ٤٢ ٥٣ ٥٨ ٧ ٨٨ ٩٦
5 a Lantern Dhs.99; b Barbecue Dhs.89; c Relax chair Dhs.65; d Tow rope Dhs.50; e Sleeping bag Dhs.42; f Ice chest Dhs.79; g Charcoal Dhs.25
6 a 4; b 1; c 3; d 6; e 5; f 2
7 ١ قميصك وسخ ٢ والدتي إيطالية ٣ هرمي هو الكبير
٤ هذه أختي مريم ٥ ليست هذه السيارة سيارتي
٦ أهذا مكتبه الجديد؟ ٧ جدهم من تونس ٨ أين حقائبنا ؟
8 i a خالد b مريم c سلمان وفهد وخميس
ii a ابنه b بنته c والده d أخته
iii a بنت عمته b زوج عمته c جدهم

Unit 6

Dialogue 1* áyna wásT al-madiinah? *Where is the town centre?

Translation:
Andy Excuse me, where is the centre of town?

Man Straight ahead. Where are you going to?
Andy I'm going to the office of Ali al-Mabrouk. Do you know it? Here is a map of the town. *(Andy produces a map of the town)*
Man Yes, I know it. Let me think. Yes, it's here. *(He shows Andy on the map)* After the big mosque, turn left at the traffic lights. This is King Hussein Street. Go straight ahead for about 100 metres.
Andy Yes, I understand.
Man The office of Ali al-Mabrouk is on the right, beside the petrol station, opposite the Plaza cinema.
Andy Oh, yes. Thank you. Is there a car park there?
Man Yes, there is a big car park behind the office of Ali al-Mabrouk.
Andy Thank you very much.
Man You're welcome.

1 a عن اذنك! b i; c left; d 100m; e petrol station; f iii
2 a ٧; b ٢; c ٥; d ٣; e ٦; f ١; g ٤
3 a hotel; b mosque; c fish market; d post office; e park; f old fort
4 a 4; b 5; c 7; d 2; e 3; f 1; g 6
5 see transcript
6 see transcript
7 ١ مدير البنك ٢ وسط المدينة ٣ عاصمة البلاد ٤ مكتب الشركة ٥ أخت راشد
8 ١ شوارع أبو ظبي عريضة ٢ جامعة القاهرة كبيرة ٣ حدائق القصر جميلة ٤ غرف الشقة واسعة ٥ طبيخ المغرب لذيذ ٦ دكاكين السوق صغيرة
9 a حزامي b جوارب تميم c منديلي d نظارتي e بنطلون تميم

Unit 7

Dialogue 1 **ákhii fahd** *My brother Fahd*

Translation:
He travelled to Amman in March and worked in the Jordanian office of his company. He stayed with my uncle. We wrote a letter to him every week. He returned to Kuwait in September.

1 a False b False c True
2 a 3; b 1; c 2

Dialogue 2 máadhaa fa:ált ams? *What did you do yesterday?*

Translation:
Zaki What did you do yesterday?
Sonya Yesterday I went to the house of Ahmed.
Zaki How did you go there?
Sonya I went by taxi. He and his family live in Zamalek.
Zaki What did you do?
Sonya I met his father and his mother and his sisters. His mother cooked lunch. After lunch we drank Arabic coffee.
Zaki And did you like it?
Sonya Yes, it is delicious.
Zaki Did you return by taxi?
Sonya No, I didn't come back by taxi. Ahmed gave me a lift home in his car.

3 a by taxi; b his family; c i; d ii; e Ahmed's mother; f i; g iii; h ٤; i ١; j ٥; k ٢; l ٣
4 ١ ما تأخرت الطائرة ٢ ما كلم العمال الرئيس٣ ما أكلت الخبز
5 a ٥; b ١; c ٢; d ٣; e ٤
6 a ٨; b ٣; c ١; d ٦; e ٧; f ٥; g ٢; h ٤
7 a سافروا b فتحت c تفرجت d وصلت e طبخت، أكلنا
8 a a ٢; b ٥; c ٦; d ١; e ٤; f ٣
b ١ لعبت؛ ٢ قابلت؛ ٣ جلست؛ ٤ ركبت؛ ٥ شربت؛ ٦ ذهبت
9 ١ كتبتها ٢ أكلتها ٣ كلمهم ٤ سألته ٥ غسلنها ٦ قابلها
10 a ٣; b ٤; c ١; d ٥; e ٢
11 Translation:
Bill and Mary and the children *travelled* from London and *arrived* in Dubai in March 2010. They *stayed* there for a week. They *lived* in a big flat near the sea and *met* many people from the Emirates. On Monday Bill *played* tennis and Mary *went* to the beach. On Tuesday they *went* to the house of their friend Mansour, and his wife *cooked* Arabic food for them.

سافر بيل وميري والأولاد من لندن ووصلوا إلى دبي في شهر مارس سنة ٢٠١٠. قعدوا هناك لمدة أسبوع. سكنوا في شقة كبيرة قريبة من البحر، وقابلوا ناسا كثيرين من الإمارات. يوم الاثنين لعب بيل تنس، وذهبت ميري إلى الشاطئ. يوم الثلثاء ذهبوا إلى بيت صديقهم منصور، وطبخت لهم زوجته طعاما عربيا.

12

١ محمد سافر إلى القاهرة
٢ الأولاد رجعوا من المدرسة
٣ المهندسون حضروا المؤتمر
٤ البنات طبخن طعاما عربيا
٥ الصحون وقعت من المائدة

Unit 8

Dialogue 1 kaan yaa maa kaan *Once upon a time*

Translation:
In the days of the Caliph Harun al-Rashid there was, in Baghdad, a poor porter whose name was Hindbad. One day this Hindbad was carrying a heavy load to the house of a merchant in the market. And that was in the summer and the heat of the sun was very strong. Hindbad became tired and thirsty. So he stopped in the road at the gate of a magnificent palace to rest from his work. He put his burden on the ground and sat down. And while he was sitting like that, he heard beautiful music emanating from inside the palace. And there was a servant standing in front of the gate of the palace, so Hindbad asked him: Who is the owner of this magnificent palace?

1 a ii; b to a merchant's house in the market;
c he was tired and thirsty; d ii; e Whose palace is this?
2 a 5; b 6; c 1; d 3; e 2; f 4

Dialogue 2 as-sindibaad al-baHrii *Sindbad the sailor*

Translation
And the servant said to him: Verily it is the palace of Sindbad the Sailor. And the porter said: And who is he? And the servant was astonished

and said: You are living in Baghdad and you have not heard of Sindbad the Sailor? Hindbad said: No. The servant said: He is the one who has travelled the seven seas and has seen all the wonders of the world. And the porter became sad and asked himself, saying: Why is this Sindbad rich and I am not rich? And Sindbad heard this from inside the palace and despatched another servant to the gate. This servant came out of the palace gate and said to Hindbad: Come with me. So the porter followed him inside the palace and he saw there a tall man, sitting in the midst of a group of people, and this man was Sindbad. And the Sailor said to the porter: Greetings and welcome. And he seated him next to himself and offered him many kinds of delicious food. And after that he told him about his amazing voyages and Sindbad had already ordered his servants to take Hindbad's load to the merchant's house.

3 a because Hindbad hadn't heard of Sindbad the Sailor; b ii; c i; d iii; e ii; f to deliver the load to the merchant

4 a 6; b 4; c 2; d 8; e 1; f 7; g 3; h 5

5 ١ كانت؛ ٢ كانت؛ ٣ كانوا؛ ٤ كان

6 ١ كان ذلك الطعام لذيذا ٢ كانت حدائق الفندق واسعة
٣ كانت شركتنا مشهورة في الخليج
٤ كان عمر الشريف ممثلا مصريا ٥ كان الأولاد سعداء

7 ١ لا، ليست الساعة ١٠,٣٠ الصبح ٢ لا، ليس محمود في البهو
٣ لا، ليست في مطعم البستان ٤ لا، لسن في المسبح ٥ نعم، هو في مركز الأعمال ٦ نعم، هي في ملعب الجولف
٧ لا، ليست أرقام الغرف ٥١١، ٥١٢ و ٥١٣
٨ نعمٍ، هم في ملعب التنسٍ

8 ليس الفهد مخططا وليس النمر منقطا

9 ١ ليس علي طالبا كسلانا ٢ لست تعبانا بعد رحلتي
٣ ليست الفنادق الكبيرة في وسط المدينة ٤ ليست مشهورة جدا
٥ ليس الطبيب مشغولا في المستشفى
٦ ليست هذه القصة من ألف ليلة وليلة طويلة جدا

10 ١ كانت شهرزاد روت قصة جديدة كل ليلة ٢ كان الخدام قد خرجوا من القصر ٣ كان البحري خبر الحمال عن رحلاته العجيبة
٤ كانت الخادمات قد تبعنه الى داخل القصر
٥ كان الناس قد أكلوا الأكل اللذيذ

Unit 9

1 waDHáa'if shaághirah Situations vacant

1 iii
2 i c; ii a; iii b
3 1 viii; 2 iii; 3 vii; 4 i; 5 x; 6 v; 7 iv; 8 ii
4 1: ii, iv, vi, vii, ix; 2: iv, vi; 3: iv, vii, ix, x
5 3 years' experience in UAE food sales; good English; valid residence permit; aged 24–28 years; Emirates' driving licence

2 li-l-iijaar For rent

6 a ٣ ; b ٤; c ١; d ٥; e ٦; f ٢
7 a iv; b v; c ii; d i; e iv; f vii; g iii
8 a 3; b 4; c 1; d 2
9 ١ هولاء الأولاد أذكياء ٢ بناتك جميلات ٣ القمصان مخططة
٤ قرأنا الجرائد الإنجليزية ٥ البنوك مقفولة بعد الظهر
٦ الرجال المصريون نشاط
10 ١ وجدنا مطاعم جيدة في القاهرة ٢ حضر المدراءَ الاجتماع
٣ هل أنتم جوعى؟ ٤ السكرتيرات مشغولات
٥ بناتها طالبات في الجامعة ٦ هم ممثلون كويتيون
٧ الأفلام طويلة
11 ١ وصل العمال الجدد ٢ أين الكتب الفرنسية؟ ٣ وجدته المدرسات
على الرف ٤ أصبح الأولاد سمانا ٥ خرج الضيوف من الفنادق
12 ١ c; ٢ b; ٣ d; ٤ a
13 ١ المكتبان مقفولان ٢ ليس الفنيان حاضرين ٣ الحمامان واسعان
٤ عمل الموظفان في الوزارتين ٥ كلمت المديرتان العاملين
14 ١ جون باركر ٢ ٣٢ سنة ٣ إنجليزي ٤ متزوج ٥ ص ب ٥٦٧، أبو
ظبي ٦ ١٢٣٤٥٦٧ ٧ الإنجليزية، العربية ٨ نعم ٩ نعم ١٠ ٥ سنوات

Unit 10

Dialogue 1 **maadhaa ta:mal kull yawm?** *What do you do every day?*

Translation

Fawzia What do you eat in the morning?

Kamal I always eat fruit and sometimes bread and cheese and I drink coffee. I usually telephone my son. He lives in America.

Fawzia And then what do you do?

Kamal I go to the office – my driver takes me at eight thirty and I talk with him in the car about the day's news.

Fawzia And then?

Kamal The secretary types letters for me while I read financial reports. This takes two to three hours.

Fawzia Do you use a computer?

Kamal Yes, of course. I learned the use of a computer at the College of Commerce.

Fawzia And what do you do in the afternoon?

Kamal In the afternoon I sit with the general manager and we discuss company affairs and I attend daily meetings with the employees.

1 a fruit; b i; c i; d ii; e the general manager; f daily

2 a ٣; b ١; c ٥; d ٤; e ٢

Dialogue 2 **maadhaa ta:mal fii awqaat al-faraagh?** *What do you do in your free time?*

Translation:

Ali What do you do in your leisure time, Hisham?

Hisham I play golf and I swim. When we lived in Amman I used to play tennis, but I don't play now. I read a lot.

Ali I read a lot too. I like modern poetry. Do you like poetry, Ruhiyyah?

Ruhiyyah No, I prefer novels. I watch television a lot and I like the Egyptian serials.

Ali I don't like them.

Hisham Me neither. I really hate them. I prefer cultural programmes or sports, but Ruhiyyah doesn't like sport.

Ruhiyyah But we both like the cinema. We are going to the cinema this evening. Will you come with us, Ali?

3 a tennis; b reading a lot; c Ruhiyyah; d Go to the cinema; e i
4 a ١; e ٢; d ٣; b ٤; c ٥
5 Hameed, 3
6 ١ ليس هذا الجمل قبيحا ٢ ليست البيوت رخيصة في الرياض ٣ لن نسافر إلى الهند في الشهر القادم ٤ ما ذهبنا/لم نذهب إلى المسبح يوم الجمعة ٥ أختي لا تعمل في صيدلية ٦ ما درس/لم يدرس صالح في أمريكا
7 ١ لها ٢ معه ٣ علينا ٤ مني ٥ إليه
8 حميد يلعب كرة وسكواش. يحب التنس والسباحة لا يحب القراءة والكتب. يكره السينما والتلفيزيون
9 ١ يتعلمون ٢ تتصل ٣ نشرب ٤ أكتب ٥ يكلمنا ٦ تعرفين ٧ تقفل ٨ يصلن ٩ يلعبن ١٠ يكسبون
10 ١ يسأل ٢ تحمل ٣ يفحص ٤ يقدم ٥ (لا) أفهم ٦ تذهب
11 a March; b price reductions and valuable prizes; c cultural events/artistic events/sporting events/horse races/fireworks; d above the famous Dubai creek

---

Unit 11

al-a:yaad al-islaamiyyah *Islamic festivals*

Literal translation:
Jack how-many festival with the-muslims?
Ahmad the-festivals the-important with-us [are] two
Fran and-what [are] they-two?
Ahmad the-first he [is] the-festival the-small and-name-his [is] festival [of] the-fast-breaking
Jack and in which month he?
Ahmad festival [of] the-fast-breaking he [is] in first day [of] month [of] Shawal
Fran and what [is] occasion-his?
Ahmad occasion-his [is] that [the] month [of] Shawal he-follows [the]

month [of] Ramadan the-holy, and-he [the] month [of] the-fasting with the-Muslims

Jack and what [is] meaning [of] the-fasting with-you?

Ahmad the-fasting, his-meaning [is] that the-people not they-eat and-not they-drink in the-daytime. This he [is] meaning of the-fasting

Fran and what [is] he the-festival the-other?

Ahmad he [is] the-festival the-great or festival [of] the-sacrifice

Jack and what [is] occasion-his?

Ahmad occasion-his [is] the-pilgrimage and he-begins in last day of [the] days [of] the pilgrimage. And the-pilgrimage, meaning-his [is] that the-people they-travel to Mecca the-Holy and-they-visit the-Kaabah

Fran and how they-celebrate (for) this the-festival?

Ahmad they they-slaughter in-him [i.e. it] sacrifice (animals)

Jack and what [is] she the-sacrifice(animal)?

Ahmad the sacrifice (animal) she [is a] sheep [which] they-slaughter-him and-they-eat-him in [the] end [of] the-pilgrimage. And he [i.e. it] [is a] custom with the-muslims

Fran so festivals-your two only then?

Ahmad no, in some [of] the-regions they celebrate (with) festival third

Jack and what [is] he?

Ahmad he [is] birthday [of] the-prophet PBUH* in [the] month [of] Rabii the-first

Fran yes, this [is] like [the] festival [of] the-birth with-us we the Christians

* Peace and Prayers be Upon Him (said after the name of the Prophet)

1 a two; b Ramadan; c eating and drinking in the daytime
2 a ii; b i; c i; d they sacrifice a sheep; e the Prophet's birthday
3 a ٦; b ١٠; c ١; d ٤; e ٨; f ٢; g ٩; h ٧; i ٣; j ٥
4 a ٥; b ٧; c ٢; d ٩; e ١٠; f ١; g ٨; h ٣; i ٤; j ٦
5 ٧, ٩, ٤, ١, ١٠, ٥, ١١, ٨, ٢, ١٢, ٣, ٦
6 ١ الملك له قصور كثيرة ٢ أنت عندك أخت طويلة ٣ أنتم عندكم أولاد صغار ٤ أنا عندي آلة حاسبة جديدة ٥ المدرس عنده ٥٠ تلميذا ٦ نحن عندنا سيارة ألمانية ٧ هم عندهم حقائب ثقيلة ٨ الشركة لها ٥ فروع ٩ محمد عنده شقة واسعة ١٠ سميرة عندها فستان جميل

١ الملك كانت له قصور كثيرة ٢ أنت كانت عندك أخت طويلة

٣ أنتم كان عندكم أولاد صغار ٤ أنا كانت عندي آلة حاسبة جديدة
٥ المدرس كان عنده ٥٠ تلميذا

7 b (The days are getting longer)

8 ١ Ali–3rd; ٢ Hamdan–6th; ٣ Siham–2nd; ٤ Mustafa–9th; ٥ Abdullah–8th; ٦ Noora–10th; ٧ Hameed–1st

9

a يذهب إلى الصف الرابع، والصف السادس عشر والصف الثاني عشر

b تذهب إلى الصف الحادي عشر والصف العاشر والصف الخامس عشر

c تذهب إلى الصف السادس عشر والصف الثالث والصف التاسع

d يذهب إلى الصف الثاني والصف الرابع عشر والصف الثامن عشر

e تذهب إلى الصف الأول والصف الثالث عشر والصف السادس

Unit 12

1 SafHat al-mar'ah *Woman's page*

Literal translation:

Journalist (female) welcome
Leila welcome to-you
Journalist firstly what [is] nationality-your?
Leila I (am) Lebanese from Beirut
Journalist and-age-your?
Leila age-my 28 year
Journalist how you-began in profession (of) showing the-fashions?
Leila since childhood-my. I-like showing the-fashions because-they (are a) kind (of the) kinds (of) the-art. for-that I-entered into this field
Journalist (?) you-studied the-arts?
Leila yes I-studied the-arts in the-university and-I-specialised in designing (of) the-fashions
Journalist and-what you-aspire to-it in profession-your?
Leila ambition-my he (is the) founding (an) agency world(wide) for-showing the-fashions (which) it-includes (male-)models and (female-) models western and-Arab
Journalist and-thing other-than this?

Leila (the) designing (of) fashions (which) they-carry (a) label international in-name-my
Journalist and-how you-keep slimness-your?
Leila I-follow (a) diet and-I-practise the-exercise the-light
Journalist and-beauty-your?
Leila indeed-I I-prefer the-beauty the-natural, and-for-this (reason) I-leave hair-my to nature-its, and-not I-like putting (on) the-make-up except for-(the)-requirements (of) modelling only
Journalist thanks to-you
Leila thanks

1 a false; b true; c true; d false
2 a i; b iii; c have her own international label; d diet and light exercise; e natural beauty; f she only uses it for work
3 a ٤; b ٧; c ١; d ٢; e ٦; f ٥; g ٣
4 a منطقة زراعية؛ b المطار الدولي؛ c قمر صناعي؛ d السوق المركزي/المركزية؛ e البنك الوطني؛ f السفارةالهندية؛ g الشؤون الخارجية؛ h الأزياء النسائية؛ i منطقة صناعية؛ j طبيخ عربي؛ k المتحف الشعبي؛ l البريد الجوي؛ m القنصلية الأمريكية؛ n الإدارة البلدية؛ o منطقة عسكرية؛ p بريد خارجي؛ q الآثار التاريخية؛ r الدراسات الأدبية؛ s العلوم الطبيعية؛ t الألعاب النارية؛ u القصر الملكي؛ v المستشفى المركزي؛ w بريد داخلي؛ x الأجهزة الكهربائية؛ y الديوان الأميري

Unit 13

1 ibtasim, anta fi sh-shaariqah *Smile, you're in Sharjah*

Literal translation:
With this the-phrase the-welcoming which overflows with-all the-feelings [of] the-friendship the-true she-greets [the-]Sharjah her-guests. And Emirate [of] the-Sharjah she [is] one [of] emirates [of the] state [of] the-Emirates the-Arab the-United which she-occupies [a] situation geographical prominent on the-Gulf the-Arab. And-he [is a] situation [which] has-caused the-Sharjah she-enjoys [i.e. to enjoy] over [the] extent [of] the-ages [a] role leading among [the] countries [of] the-Gulf

the-Arab as [a] centre [of the] most-important [of] centres [of] the-activity the-commercial.
And-he-is-estimated [the] number [of] the-inhabitants according-to [the] latest the-census which was-carried-out [in] year 1995 at-about half million individual that [is] in-density [which] is-estimated at-about 190 individual to-the-kilometre the-square.
And-Sharjah she-is-described by-that-she [is] the-capital the-cultural for-[the] state [of] the-Emirates, and-there [is a] department special [which] she-looks-after [the] implementation [of] the-activities the-cultural in the-Emirate, also she-comprises the-Emirate [a] number [of] the-museums the-scientific and-the-historical the-magnificent and [a] station from [the] most-modern [of] stations [of] the-transmission the-televisual [which] she-broadcasts the-many of the-programmes the-cultural and-the-educational.

1 a Smile you are in Sharjah; b on the Arabian Gulf; c commercial; d half a million; e cultural; f museums; g cultural and educational
2 a ١; b ٥; c ٧; d ٢; e ٨; f ٣; g ٦; h ٤
3 definite:
التي تفيض بكل مشاعر الود.../ التي تحتل موقعا.../ التي أجريت عام ١٩٩٥ ....
indefinite:
دائرة خاصة ترعى.../ موقع جعل الشارقة تتمتع.../ بكثافة تقدر بحوالي ١٩٠ نسمة للكيلومتر المربع.../ تذيع الكثير من البرامج...

4

١ هذا هو البيت الذي سنستأجره
٢ زارني عامل يعمل في مصنع
٣ شاهدت الطبيب الذي عيادته في وسط المدينة
٤ خالد الذي قرأت كتابه يدرس في المدرسة الثانوية
٦ الطلبة الذين يدرسون في الجامعة من الإمارات
٧ رسالة كتبها الأسبوع الماضي وصلت اليوم
٨ القمصان التي يبيعونها في السوق مصنوعة في الصين
٩ مغنية كانت مشهورة قبل سنوات كثيرة ستزور سورية

٥ كان الكرسي الذي جلست عليه مكسورا

١٠ ابني له صديق أصله اسكتلندي

5

١ لقد أعيد بناء منزل الشيخ صقر الكائن في هذه المنطقة

٢ في هذه المنطقة يمكن مشاهدة أول أشكال تكييف الهواء، البرجيل، الذي كان يستخدم لتبريد البيوت في الخليج. جددت القلعة التي شيدت في القرن الماضي، وحولت إلى متحف.

٣ الطرق الضيقة تأخذ الزائر إلى سوق التوابل التي تنبعث منها روائح أنواع التوابل كلها مثل القرنفل والهال والقرفة التي تباع إلى الزوار من الأكياس التي تحيط المتاجر.

٤ سباقات الهجن رياضة شعبية تقام أيام الجمعة أثناء أشهر الشتاء.

6

١ عمر الشريف ممثل مصري لعب أدوارا مشهورة كثيرة

٢ ذهبنا إلى مدينة البتراء القديمة التي اكتشفت سنة ١٨١٨.

٣ في مصر آثار فرعونية مهمة يزورها سواح كثيرون.

٤ يعمل زوجي في الشارقة التي تقع في الخليج العربي.

٥ نستأجر شقة في دمشق يسكن صاحبها في الرياض.

٦ سافروا إلى عدن بطائرة الصبح التي وصلت الظهر.

7

i	t	a	:	l	ii	m	l	a	d
r	i	a	h	kh	ii	r	aa	t	a
i	j	t	i	m	aa	:	a	l	h
y	aa	u	r	a	d	a	h	h	m
aa	r	m	gh	S	i	i	a	m	:
D	a	a	ii	r	q	f	:	u	i
a	h	t	b	t	aa	b	aa	t	l
h	a	a	i	q	i	f	r	i	m
b	s	S	a	l	S	q	i	H	a
t	aa	th	k	u	t	a	z	y	w
d	h	a	H	aa	y	i	S	i	aa

Unit 14

Koshari

Literal translation:
The-Koshari
(the-amount she-suffices 6 persons)
The-quantities
4 cups and-half rice, it-is-washed and-it-is-strained
Cup [of] lentils black
Half cup [of] oil
Salt according-to the-desire
7 cups and-half [of] the-cup [of] water for-the-rice
10 cups [of] water for-boiling [of] the-macaroni
two-cups [of] macaroni
two spoons [of] food (i.e. tablespoons) [of] oil for-the-macaroni
6 onions cut into slices long
The-sauce
two-spoons [of] food [of] ghee

6 fruits [of] tomato peeled and-chopped
[a] spoon small [of] pepper red hot ground
two-spoons [of] food of paste [of] the-tomatoes
salt according-to the-desire
The-method
1- soak the-lentils in-the-water for-period [of] 6 hours and strain-it
2- fry the-onions in-the-oil then lift-them and-leave-them aside. Pour the-water over-them and-leave-them until they-boil a-little, then add the-rice and-the-lentils and-leave-them on fire gentle for-period [of] 40 minute.
3- boil the-macaroni in-the-water then add the-oil
4- fry the-tomatoes in-the-oil, then add the pepper and the paste [of] the-tomatoes and the-salt
5- during the-presenting (i.e. serving) place [the] mixture [of] the-rice and-the-lentils firstly, then [a] layer of the-macaroni then [a] layer of the-onions, and-sprinkle over-it the-sauce the-hot or present-it to [the] side [of] the-plate.

1 a 6; b four and a half times as much; c 6 hours; d 40 minutes; e onions; f tomato sauce
2 a ٤; b ٥; c ١; d ٣; e ٢
3 i c; ii d; iii b; iv a; v e
4 i c; ii a; iii d; iv b
5 a i2/ii1; b 1 Dirham, 50 fils; c Fridays & holidays; d 4 hours; e 5 Dirhams; f اضغط
6 a ٥; b ٤; c ٦; d ١; e ٧; f ٨; g ٣; h ٢;
7 a 8 dirhams; b selection of cheeses; c macaroni; d today only e تعالوا، اشتروا، شاهدوا، اطبخوا. جربوا
8 a ١ ارسله ٢ اكتبها ٣ اتصل
b ١ ضعيه ٢ اتركيه ٣ اغسليها

Unit 15

1 **al-:arab fii huuliiwuud** ***Arabs in Hollywood***

Literal translation:

Salma the-Arab [girl] who she-conquered Hollywood

In the-east we-regard-her [as the] ambassadress [of] the-beauty the-Arab who she-was-able that she-be [the] first woman [who] she-penetrates [the] walls [of] Hollywood and-she-imposes self-her on [the] top [of the] list [of the] stars [of] the-cinema

And-in the-west they-regard-her [as a] symbol of-[the]-magic [of] the-East by-what she-bears-it of features oriental [the] extreme in the-beauty which it-equals the-magic and-for-this they-gave-her the-leads in [the] greatest [of] films-their preferring-her to most [of the] stars [of] Hollywood beauty-wise and-so Salma Hayek today she-competes [with] Sharon Stone and-Demi Moore and-other-[than]-them-two of [the] stars [of] Hollywood

And-Salma al-Hayek, or [the] legend [of] the-East in the-West, the-born [in the] year 1966 she [is the] daughter [of an] emigrant Lebanese residing in-Mexico mother-her Spanish [of] the-origin and-if came-together the-beauty the-Lebanese and-the-Spanish will-be the-fruit in [the] beauty [of] Salma al-Hayek. And-because-she [is] beautiful very so-[past marker] spotted-her [the] eye [of] the-producers and-she in the-thirteenth [year] of age-her and-she-was-chosen at-that-time as-[the]-most-beautiful [of] the-faces the-television. Then he-took-her the-producer Tarantino to-Los Angeles so-she-participates in the-film Desperado at [the] side [of] Antonio Banderas and-she-gave to-the-film [a] flavour special very [which] it-attracted to-her [the] interest [of the] companies [of] the-production the-great and-soon they-offered to-her the-contracts the-many in-fact indeed-she she-took recently [a] part it-was of the-assumed that it-be-entrusted to-[a]-singer famous American but [the] producers [of] Hollywood they-preferred Salma to-her and-[it is]-of the-certain that this the-film it-will-give to-Salma eminence greater power-wise and-popularity-wise

1 a breach the walls of Hollywood; b her oriental features; c Sharon Stone and Demi Moore; d 1966; e Spain; f 13; g Desperado; h Power and popularity

2 a ٣; b ٥ ; c ١; d ٤; e ٢
3 a spend more than 250 Dirhams; b ii more than 20 years; c spaghetti; d gold and cash; e your money will arrive in minutes; f use the Privilege card
4 a

١	هذا الكمبيوتر له شاشة أكبر	٤	له قرص ثابت أحسن.
٢	له موديم أسرع.	٥	هو أسهل استعمالا.
٣	له ذاكرة أصغر.	٦	هو أرخص.

b 1B; 2B; 3A; 4B; 5A; 6A

Unit 16

1 al-laylah s-sawdaa' *The black night*

Literal translation:
Night black for-the [foot]ball the-Moroccan
Qualified the-team the-Tunisian for the-round the-final of (the) competition (of the) Cup (of) the-Arabs in night black for-the [foot]ball the-Moroccan. And-on (the) pitch of the-Zamalek in the-Cairo yesterday, and-before 42 thousand spectator led Mahmoud al-Turki the-team the-Tunisian to the-victory. And-scored al-Turki personally three goals in the-match which ended 5-1
And-opened the-team the-Tunisian the-scoring by way (of) its-centre Jaafar Abu Adil with (a) shot splendid from outside the-area (which) deceived the-goalkeeper the-Moroccan in the-minute the-ninth of-the-match. And-was (the)-result of the-opportunity the-first for-the-team the-Moroccan their-goal the-sole in (the) end (of) the-half the-first when shot Tariq al-Ahmar (a) ball curved (which) entered (the) corner (of) the-goal the-Tunisian and gained the-equality
But-it appeared that the-players the-Moroccan [past marker] raised the-flag the-white in the-half the-second and-dominated the-Tunisians [on] the-play domination complete. And-came the-goals with-speed horrific, (the) last-(of)-them in the-minute the-last of-the-match when placed the-captain the-Tunisian the-ball [in] the-net the-Moroccan for-the-time the-third after awarded the-referee kick corner and-sent-off

the-defender the-Moroccan Suleiman al-Fasi for-his-getting the-card the-yellow the-second

1 a i; b iii; c Cairo; d 42,000; e four; f Tunisia; g Tariq al-Ahmar (Morocco); h the last minute of the match; i he got a second yellow card and was sent off; j Morocco.
2 a ٤; b ٦ ; c ١; d ٢; e ٥; f ٣
3 1 g; 2 e; 3 d; 4 l; 5 a; 6 j; 7 h; 8 f; 9 c; 10 k; 11 b; 12 i
4 a Dhs. 2700; b 3; c 10yrs; d i; e ii; f Dhs. 260; g any three of: gym, aerobics, library, swimming pool, ice-skating, café
5 see transcript

	Never	Rarely	Sometimes	Frequently	Daily
1			*tennis*	*golf*	
2					*gym*
3		*swim*		*skating*	
4			*swim, sail*		
5		*sail*		*aerobics*	

6

١ افتح الباب بسرعة. عندنا ضيف.
٢ ذهبت إلى السوق وقابلت أحمد هناك صدفة.
٣ كان ذلك البرنامج مهما جدا.
٤ كنا جالسين في البيت، وقام زيد فجأة وخرج.
٥ تسافر هذه الطائرة إلى الرياض مباشرة.
٦ يا أولاد، العبوا بهدوء، الوالد نائم.

7

١ يحتاج علي إلى جزمة سوداء.
٢ تحتاج سونية إلى فستان أصفر.
٣ يحتاج سعيد إلى قميص أخضر.
٥ تحتاج فريدة إلى بنطلون أحمر.
٦ يحتاج حامد إلى حزام بني.
٧ تحتاج أنيسة إلى حقيبة وردية.

٤ يحتاج خالد إلى جوارب
بيضاء.

Unit 17

1 miSr *Egypt*

Literal translation:
Egypt
The-antiquities the-Egyptian in the-abroad
He-stated head [of the] department [of the] antiquities the-Egyptian yesterday about welcoming-his of-resolution [of] the-assembly the-general to-the-Nations the-United to-the-allowing to-the-states which to-them antiquities smuggled in the-abroad for-reclaiming-them. And-he-said that-it there approximately 21 million piece archaeological Egyptian stolen in the-West most-famous-[of]-them beard [of] Father of Terror [i.e. the Sphynx] and stone [of] Rosetta the-situated in the-Museum the-British in London

1 a the head of the Egyptian Antiquities Department; b antiquities; c the Sphynx's beard and the Rosetta stone
2 a رئيس دائرة الآثار المصرية　c ذقن أبو الهول
b حوالي ٢١ مليون　d حجر رشيد

2 al-yaman *The Yemen*

Literal translation:
the-Yemen
450 tourist European in Aden
Received port [of] Aden yesterday the-first [i.e. the day before yesterday] ship touristic German [which] she-carries more than 400 tourist [male] and-tourist [female] from various [of] the-nationalities the-European. And-[future marker]-visit these the-tourists some [of] the-towns the-Yemeni the-historical

3 a a German tourist ship; b more than 400 tourists; c visit some of Yemen's historical towns

4 a من مختلف الجنسيات b سيزور هؤلاء السواح بعض المدن اليمنية

3 amriikaa America

Literal translation:
America
Announced millionaire American from state [of] California in the-week the-past that-he [future marker] marry [a] girl in the-fifth and-the-twenty of life-her. And-this after celebrating-his of-anniversary [of] birth-his the-hundredth by-days few. And-he he-uses regulator for-beats [of] the-heart and-he- is transported on chair with-wheels. And-he-said that-he he-loves-her from all [of] his-heart and-she returns-him the-love

5 a 25; b 100; c pacemaker, wheelchair; d with all his heart

6 a سيتزوج فتاة c من كل قلبه
b قال انه يحبها

4 abuu DHabii Abu Dhabi

Literal translation:
Abu Dhabi
She-arrived to The-Emirates today the-singer the-Lebanese the-famous Fairuz in visit private, [future marker]- she-visits during-it brother-her who he-resides in Abu Dhabi

7 a Lebanese singer; b for a private visit

8

a وصلت الى الامارات اليوم b ستزور أخاها

5 nyuu yuurk *NEW YORK*

Literal translation:
New York
Chose organisation [of] the-UNESCO [the] day 21 March [as a] day world-wide for-the-poetry. And-welcomed the-poets the-Arab [with]-this, among-them the-poet the-Iraqi Ali Jaafar al-Allaq who he-said that-he [was] "Believing belief not limits to-it that the-poetry [is] bigger than the-time all-[of]-it, and-more extent-wise than the-places totally. Indeed-it [is] filler [of] the-moments and-the-seasons and-the-centuries with-beauty [of] the-meaning and meaning [of] the-beauty"

9 a World Poetry Day; b an Iraqi poet; c all time

10 a رحب الشعراء العرب بهذا c انه مالئ اللحظات بجمال المعنى
b الشعر أكبر من الزمان كله

11 Unit 1: وحيد **waHiid** *unique*
Unit 2: بارد **baarid** *cold*
Unit 3: مضبوط **maDbuuT** *exact*, *accurate*
Unit 4: ملعب **mal:ab** *playing field/court/pitch*
Unit 5: فطور **fuTuur** *breakfast*
Unit 6: طباعة **Tibaa:ah** *printing*, *typing*
Unit 7: تفاهم **tafaahum** *(mutual) understanding*
Unit 8: رسام **rassaam** *artist*
Unit 9: معلم **mu:allim** *teacher*, *instructor*, *master*
Unit 10: علماء: **ulamaa'** *scholars*, *religious leaders*
Unit 11: فضائل **faDaa'il** *advantages*, *good points*
Unit 12: تفسير **tafsiir** *explanation*, *interpretation*
Unit 13: مناظر **manáaDHir** *views*, *sights*
Unit 14: استكشاف **istikshấaf** *discovery*, *act of trying to discover*
Unit 15: مفتاح **miftaaH** *key*
Unit 16: لخبطة **lakhbaTah** *mix up*, *mess*

12 ١ أمي ٣ أبو صالح ٥ قلب
٢ أب ٤ رئيس

13 1 F; 2 T; 3 T; 4 F; 5 T; 6 F; 7 F; 8 T; 9 T; 10 F

14

١ درس الطلبة كلهم للامتحانات.

٢ وصل السواح كلهم من ألمانيا.

٣ تفتح الدكاكين كلها في المساء.

٤ رحب الموظفون كلهم بتقرير المدير.

٥ استقبلته أخواته كلهن في المطار.

٦ وضعت الكتب كلها على الرف.

Listening transcripts

Unit 4

Exercise 9

(all preceded by **as-sáa:ah...**)

a **tis:ah**

b **thalaatha wa-niSf**

c **ithna:shar illaa rub:**

d **arba:ah wa-thulth**

e **ithna:shar wa-:asharah**

f **ithnayn illa khamsah**

Exercise 14

(all preceded by **as-sáa:ah...**)

a **síttah wa-niSf wa-khámsah**

b **thamáanyah wa-:ásharah**

c **tís:ah wa-niSf ílla khámsah**

d **sáb:ah**

e **árba:ah ílla rub:**

f **khámsah wa-niSf**

g **wáaHidah wa-rub:**

h **wáaHidah ílla khámsah**

i **thaláathah wa-thulth**

j **:ásharah wa-khámsah**

Unit 5

Exercise 5

a **tis:ah wa-tis:iin dirham**

b **tis:ah wa-thamaaniin dirham**

c **khamsah wa-sittiin dirham**

d **khamsiin dirham**

e **ithnayn wa-arba:iin dirham**

f **tis:ah wa-sab:iin dirham**

g **khamsah wa-:ishriin dirham**

Unit 6

Exercise 5

a أين البلدية؟
b أين مركز الشرطة؟
c أين مركز التسوق «البستان»؟
d أين شارع الملك فيصل؟
e أين مطعم شهرزاد؟

Exercise 6

a على شمال الميدان، أمام سوق السمك

b وراء الميدان، بين سوق السمك والبنك

c أمام برج الاتصالات على شمال الصيدلية

d بين الكورنيش وشارع جمال عبد الناصر

e وراء مركز الشرطة بين سوق الذهب والفندق

Unit 14

Exercise 7

تعالوا إلى قسم اللحوم! اشتروا بأسعار مذهلة!
تنزيلات في لحم الغنم المفروم الكيلو بـ ٨ دراهم.
شاهدوا تشكيلة الجبن من فرنسا وإيطاليا.
اطبخوا وجبة معكرونة للعائلة اليوم. جربوا جبنة الحلوم اللذيذة.
أسعار خاصة لليوم فقط

Unit 16

Exercise 5

Example:

سؤال ماذا تحب من الرياضات؟

جواب ألعب كرة القدم كثيرا

١ ماذا تلعب يا يونس؟

ألعب تنس أحيانا، لكن ألعب جولف كثيرا

٢ وأنت يا سعيد؟

أذهب إلى القاعة الرياضية يوميا

٣ هل تمارسين السباحة يا فريدة؟

لا، أمارس السباحة نادرا. أفضل التزلج. أمارس التزلج كثيرا

٤ هل تمارس السباحة يا حامد؟

نعم، أسبح أحيانا، وأحيانا أركب الزوارق الشراعية

٥ يا سونية، هل ركبت الزوارق الشراعية؟

لا أبدا. أمارس الايروبيك كثيرا

Glossary of language terms

Accent See *stress*.

Adjectives Adjectives describe a person or thing, e.g. a *huge* building, I am *tired*. In Arabic, these have the same properties as nouns and must agree with them in number, gender and definiteness.

Adverbs Adverbs describe how, when or where the action of a verb occurs or has occurred. In English, they usually end in *-ly*, e.g. *quickly*. In Arabic, they end either in **-an** or are phrases such as *with speed*, i.e. *quickly*.

Agreement This term describing changes in one word caused by another mainly applies to nouns and adjectives and verbs, which must agree with their subjects, e.g. feminine subject requires feminine verb.

Articles The words *a* or *an* (indefinite article), and *the* (definite article). Arabic has no indefinite article, so to say *a book* you just say *book*. The definite article **al-** is attached or prefixed to the following word.

Comparative Adjectives that compare two things. In English, they often end in *-er* or are preceded by the word *more*, e.g. *brighter/more intelligent*.

Conjunctions Words that join parts of sentences, e.g. *and*, *or*, *but*.

Consonants The non-vowel letters, e.g. **b, d, g, dh, DH**.

Demonstratives See *pronouns*.

Dual A special form in Arabic to refer to *two* of anything, as opposed to one (singular) and more than two (plural).

Elision Where part of a word – usually a vowel – is omitted to smooth speech.

Gender Masculine or feminine. See *adjectives* and *nouns*.

Hidden t The feminine ending of a noun **-ah**, which in certain contexts changes to **-at**.

Imperative The form of a verb used when telling someone to do something.

Interrogatives Question words. See also *pronouns*.

Negatives These are words used to negate or deny something, e.g. *no*, *not*. Arabic uses different words with nouns/adjectives and verbs.

Nouns A noun is the name of a person, thing, place or an abstract concept, e.g. *Hassan*, *boy*, *book*, *Dubai*, *economics*. In Arabic a noun has three important properties:

1 It is either *masculine* or *feminine*. There is no 'neuter', or *it*, used in English to describe inanimate objects or abstracts. This is called *gender*.

2 It is either *singular* (one only), *dual* (two only) or *plural* (more than two). English does not have a dual. This is called *number*.

3 It is either *definite* or *indefinite*. The noun refers either to an unspecified person or thing or to a specific one. In English, indefinites are often preceded by *a* or *an*, but this is omitted in Arabic. Definites are often preceded by *the*, *this*, *that* etc., or *his*, *her*. Names of people and places (words with capital letters in English) are automatically definite, e.g. *Ahmed*, *Bahrain*. The concept of definiteness is very important in Arabic as it affects other words in the sentence. (Note that pronouns are always definite.)

Number See *adjectives* and *nouns*.

Numbers The numbers or numerals divide into two sets, *cardinal*, e.g. *one*, *two*, *three* and *ordinal*, e.g. *first*, *second*, *third*.

Object The object of a verb is the thing or person which the action of the verb affects. It contrasts with the subject, e.g. *the dog* (subject) *chased the cat* (object).

Phrase A phrase is a part of a sentence, not necessarily making sense on its own, but useful for describing features of a language, e.g. *the big house*.

Plural More than one. See *adjectives* and *nouns*.

Possessive When something owns or possesses something else. In English, we either add *'s* to the noun, e.g. *Charlie's aunt*, or use a possessive pronoun, e.g. *my father*, or the word *of*, e.g. *the manager of the company*.

Prefix A short part of a word added to the beginning of a noun or verb, e.g. English *un-*, *dis-* or *pre-*.

Prepositions Usually short words relating a noun to its place in space or time, e.g. *in*, *on*, *with*. In Arabic, a few common prepositions are prefixed to the following word.

Pronouns Pronouns are used as substitutes for nouns. The English personal pronoun *he* has three forms: subject *he*, object *him*, and possessive *his* (in other pronouns such as *you* some of these forms have fused together), e.g. *He* isn't at home (subject pronoun), We saw *him* (object pronoun) and It is *his* house (possessive pronoun). Subject pronouns have equivalent words in Arabic. *Object* pronouns and *possessive* pronouns share the same form in Arabic and are not separate words, but endings or suffixes attached to their verbs or nouns.

Other types of pronoun are demonstratives, e.g. *this*, *that*, relatives, e.g. *who*, *which*, *that* (in phrases like *the one that I like best*) and interrogatives *who*, *what* and *which* (used in questions like *who goes there?*).

Relatives See *pronouns*.

Sentence A sentence is a complete utterance making sense on its own, e.g. *he is in his room*. In English, these must contain a verb, but sentences with *is* and *are* do not have a verb in Arabic. For instance, the sentence above would be *he in his room* in Arabic.

Stem See *verbs*.

Stress Also called *accent*. This is the part or syllable of a word that is most emphasised, e.g. the first *o* in English *photograph*. In the first few units of this book, stress has been marked with an accent: **á**, **ú** etc.

Subject The subject of a sentence is the person or thing that is carrying out the action. It can be a noun, pronoun or a phrase as in: *Bill* lives in Abu Dhabi, *He* works for the oil company, *The best picture* will win the prize.

Suffix An ending attached to a word that alters its meaning.

Superlative Applied to adjectives when they express the highest level of a quality. In English, they end in *-est* or are preceded by *most*, e.g. *the brightest/most intelligent boy*. See also *comparative*.

Tense See *verbs*.

Verbs 'Doing' words expressing action, e.g. *He reads* the newspaper every day. Its most important features are:

1 *Tense*. This tells us when the action is/was performed. In Arabic, there are only two tenses, present (*I go*, *am going*) and past (*I went*, *I have gone*). The future (*I shall go*) is the same as the present with a special prefix.

2 *Inflections*. This means that the prefix and/or suffix of the verb changes according to who is doing the action. For instance, in English, most verbs in the present tense change, e.g. *I go*, *they go*, but *he/she/it goes*. In Arabic there is a different verb part for each person, singular and plural. The part of the verb that remains constant in the middle of all the prefixes and suffixes is called the *stem*. This is an important concept in learning Arabic and may be compared to the *go-* part of goes in the example above.

Note a) that the verb *is/are* is omitted in Arabic, and b) the English verb *to have* is not a real verb in Arabic, but a combination of a preposition and a noun or pronoun.

Vowels The sounds equivalent to *a*, *e*, *i*, *o*, *u* or combinations of them in English. Arabic has **a**, **i**, **u** and their long equivalents **aa**, **ii**, **uu**. See also *consonants*.

Word order In Arabic, adjectives usually follow their nouns, e.g. *good man* becomes *man good*. Possessive pronouns are also suffixed to their nouns: *my book* becomes *book-my*.

Grammar summary

This grammar summary is intended to be used as a reference and does not cover all the language given in the course.

1 Definite and indefinite

In Arabic, all nouns and adjectives are either *definite* or *indefinite.*

The definite article

A definite noun is specific and can be a proper noun (e.g. *Cairo, Mohammed*), a pronoun (e.g. *I, you, they*) or preceded by the word **al-**, the, called the definite article. **al-** never changes for gender or number and is *always* attached to the following noun or adjective, e.g. البيت **al-bayt**, *the house.*

al- is always the same in written Arabic. In pronunciation, if the preceding word ends in a vowel or **-ah**, the **a** of **al-** is omitted, e.g. القهوة اللذيذة **al-qáhwah l-ladhíidhah**, *the delicious coffee.*

If the word begins with one of the following Arabic letters:

t ت **th** ث **d** د **dh** ذ **r** ر **z** ز **s** س **sh** ش **S** ص **D** ض
T ط **DH** ظ **l** ل **n** ن

the **l** of the **al-** is omitted in pronunciation and the following letter is *clearly doubled.*

Written	*Pronounced after a consonant*	*Pronounced after a vowel*
الرَجُل	**ar-rajul**	**r-rajul** *the man*
الشمس	**ash-shams**	**sh-shams** *the sun*
النور	**an-nuur**	**n-nuur** *the light*

The indefinite article

There is no *indefinite article* or word for *a* in Arabic. **bayt** in Arabic means *a house.*

---

2 Nouns

Masculine and feminine

In Arabic, all nouns are either masculine or feminine in gender. Nouns ending in **-ah** are usually feminine, but there are a few feminine nouns that do not have this ending, e.g. أم **umm** *mother*, and a handful of masculine nouns end in **-ah**, e.g. خليفة **khalíifah** *caliph.*

Singular and plural

Arabic plural formations should be learned at the same time as the singular.

The plural in Arabic refers to more than two (2+). For just two of anything, we need to use the *dual* (see the following section on this).

The *external masculine plural*, used in words for male human beings, is formed by adding ون **-uun** to the singular noun, e.g.

مدرس، مدرسون **mudarris ➔ mudarrisuun** (m.) *teachers*. (For the accusative form, add ين **-iin** to the singular.)

The *external feminine/neuter plural*, used for the plural of most females and some other nouns, is formed by dropping the ة **-ah** (if there is one) and adding ات **-aat** to the singular word, e.g. مدرسة، مدرسات **mudarrisah ➔ mudarrisaat** (f.) teachers. (There is no special accusative form.)

The *internal plural*, used mainly for males and things, is formed by altering the internal vowelling of the word and/or by adding prefixes or suffixes. Although there is no general relationship between the singular word shape and the plural word shape, short words are more likely to take an internal plural, e.g. كتاب، كتب **kitaab ➔ kutub** *books*.

All plurals of things are regarded in Arabic as *feminine singular* for the purposes of agreement of adjectives and verbs.

The dual

The *dual* must be used when talking about two of anything and is mostly regular for both nouns and adjectives. It is formed by adding an external suffix, similar to the masculine external plural, to the majority of nouns and adjectives.

Case	*Suffix*	*Example*
Subject	**-aan** ـان	**SaaHibaan** صاحبان
Other cases	**-ayn** ـين	**SaaHibayn** صاحبين

If a word has the feminine **-ah** ending, this changes to **-at** (spelled with an ordinary ت), and the suffix **-aan** is added to it.

Adjectives must take the appropriate masculine or feminine dual ending and also agree with the noun in case, e.g. السيارتان كبيرتان

as-sayyaarataan kabiirataan, which means *the two cars are big*. It is not usually necessary to insert the numeral word.

As with the masculine plural ending ون/ـين **-uun/-iin**, the final ن is *omitted* if the word has a pronoun suffix or is the first term of a possessive construction, e.g. كوبا ماء **kuubaa maa'** *two cups of water*.

In spoken Arabic, the ending **-ayn** is used in all contexts.

---

3 Adjectives

Agreement of adjectives

Adjectives must agree in number, gender and definiteness with the nouns they describe, e.g.:

الفيلم الممتاز **al-fiilm al-mumtaz**	*the excellent film*
جريدة جيدة **jariidah jayyidah**	*a good newspaper*

In most cases, the feminine of an adjective is formed by adding ة **-ah** to the masculine, e.g. طويل، طويلة **Tawiil, Tawiilah** *tall, long*.

If there is more than one adjective, it is added after the first one, agreeing with it and the noun, e.g.:

الفندق الكبير الجديد **al-funduq al-kabiir al-jadiid**	*the big new hotel*
بنت جميلة صغيرة **bint jamiilah Saghiirah**	*a beautiful young girl*

Adjectives of nationality

Adjectives indicating nationality are formed by adding ي **-ii**/ية **-íyyah** to the name of the country, e.g. مصر **miSr** *Egypt*, مصري/مصرية **míSrii/miSríyyah** *Egyptian*.

Where the name of a country ends in **-aa** or **-ah**, this is omitted before the ending is added:

بريطانيا **briiTáanya**	*Britain*
بريطاني/بريطانية **briiTáanii/briiTaaníyyah**	*British*

If the Arabic place name has the word **al-** *the* in front of it, this is omitted from the nationality adjective:

المغرب **al-mághrib**	*Morocco*
مغربي/مغربية **mághribii/maghribíyyah**	*Moroccan*

Singular and plural adjectives

The plurals of Arabic adjectives follow the same rules as nouns, adding the **-uun** (m.) or the **-aat** (f.) ending, or by means of internal plurals, which are given in the vocabulary with their singulars.

All plurals of things are regarded in Arabic as feminine singular, e.g. الكتب الطويلة **al-kútub aT-Tawíilah** *the long books*.

Noun		*Adjective*
Male human beings	*either* *or*	internal plural if it has one + **-uun**
Female human beings		+ **-aat**
Things/abstracts		+ **-ah** (f. sing.)

The primary colours are an exception (see Unit 16).

Word order

The adjective comes after the noun. In sentences with verbs, the verb usually (but not always) comes first.

4 Pronouns

Subject or personal pronouns

Subject pronouns are always definite.

Singular	*Plural*
أنا **ána** *I*	نحن **náHnu** *we*
أنت **ánta** *you* (m.)	أنتم **ántum** *you* (m. pl.)
أنت **ánti** *you* (f.)	أنتن **antúnna** *you* (f. pl.)
هو **húwa** *he*	هم **hum** *they* (m.)
هي **híya** *she*	هن **húnna** *they* (f. pl.)

The final **alif** of أنا **ana** is pronounced short and the first syllable is accented. Most final **-aa** sounds in informal modern Arabic are pronounced short unless they bear the stress.

The male and female singular *you* forms are identical in writing, but the context usually makes clear which one is intended.

English *it* is translated into Arabic as *he* or *she*, depending on the gender of the word to which it refers.

Possessive pronoun suffixes

There is no equivalent in Arabic to English *mine*, *yours* etc. The words *my*, *your*, *his* etc. are expressed in Arabic as suffixes joined on to the object that is possessed, e.g. بيتهم **báyt-hum** *their house*.

Singular	*Plural*
ي **-ii** *my*	نا **-na(a)** *our*
ك **-ak** *your* (m.)	كم **-kum** *your* (m.)
ك **-ik** *your* (f.)	كن **-kúnna** *your* (f.)
ه **-uh** *his*	هم **-hum** *their* (m.)
ها **-ha(a)** *her*	هن **-húnna** *their* (f.)

Object pronoun suffixes

Arabic uses the same pronoun suffixes as the possessive pronoun suffixes, with the exception of *me*, which is ني **-nii** after verbs.

The suffixes are added to the verb to express the object of the sentence, e.g.:

كلمته أمس **kallamt-uh ams**	*I spoke to him yesterday*
خبرني ناصر **khabbar-nii naaSir**	*Nasser told me*

5 Saying *to have*

There is no verb *to have* in Arabic. Instead, this is expressed by using one of the prepositions لـ **li-** *to/for* or عند **:ind(a)** *with* (cf. French *chez*) with a noun or pronoun, e.g. للولد كتاب **li-l-walad kitaab** *the boy has a book*.

The object of the English verb then becomes the subject of the Arabic sentence, e.g. *he has a car* ➔ عنده سيارة **:ind-uh sayyaarah** (lit., *with him (is) a car*).

---

6 Accusative marker

Arabic cases

Formal Arabic has three varying case endings showing the part played by a word in a sentence, most of which are omitted in modern Arabic.

The only case ending appearing in print in contemporary written Arabic – except for a few special types of noun – is the *accusative* case of *indefinite unsuffixed* nouns or adjectives. It is written by placing an **alif** after the noun/adjective and pronounced **-an**. This ending is generally ignored in spoken Arabic except in many adverbs and some traditional Arabic greetings, e.g. طبعا **Tab:an** *naturally*, أهلا وسهلا **ahlan wa sahlan** *hello, welcome*.

The few unsuffixed nouns and adjectives that do not add the **alif** include the main colours, some forms of the internal plural and many proper nouns. These are all marked in the vocabulary boxes and the glossaries with an asterisk (*).

كان الكلب أبيض **kaana l-kalb abyaD**	*the dog was white*
قرأنا جرائد كثيرة أمس **qara'naa jaraa'id kathiirah ams**	*we read many newspapers yesterday*
قابلنا أحمد في السوق **qaabalnaa aHmad fi s-suuq**	*we met Ahmed in the souq*

Uses of the accusative marker

In Arabic, the accusative marker is used where the second noun is the *object* of the sentence: شاهدوا قصرا فخما **shaahaduu qaSran fakhman** *they saw a magnificent castle.*

It is also used after the verbs كان **kaana** *was, were/to be*, ليس **laysa** *is not, are not/not to be*, أصبح **aSbaHa** *to become* and a few other similar verbs.

It is also used in some common expressions and adverbs (see earlier) and also after certain short words or particles, such as إنّ **inna** and أنّ **anna.**

---

7 Verbs

'Is/are' sentences

There is no Arabic equivalent to the English *is/are.* Instead, a definite concept is simply followed by an indefinite one, e.g. **al-bayt kabiir** *the house is big.*

Past tense

All Arabic verbs are derived from a root, usually a three-letter one, e.g. ك-ت-ب **k-t-b**, which has the meaning of *writing*. Most verbs are formed from either a past or a present *stem*, with a standard set of *prefixes* and *suffixes*. The same prefixes and suffixes apply to every Arabic verb.

The Arabic past tense is used when the action of the verb is complete. To form the past tense, suffixes are added to the past stem, e.g. **katab**, as follows:

Singular	*Plural*
kátab-a *he wrote*	**kátab-uu** *they* (m.) *wrote*
kátab-at *she wrote*	**katáb-na** *they* (f.) *wrote*
katáb-t(a) *you* (m.) *wrote*	**katáb-tum** *you* (m.) *wrote*
katáb-ti *you* (f.) *wrote*	**katab-túnna** *you* (f.) *wrote*
katáb-t(u) *I wrote*	**katáb-na(a)** *we wrote*

If the subject is not stated as a noun, it is usually unnecessary to use a subject pronoun, since the suffix distinguishes the subject, e.g. **katabat** *she wrote.*

If the subject is a noun, the normal (but not exclusive) word order in Arabic is V–S–O:

1 Verb 2 Subject 3 Object/the rest

Verbs that come at the beginning of the sentence in Arabic can only have the *he* or *she* form, i.e. always singular, never plural, e.g. زار الوزراء البيوت الجديدة **zaara l-wuzaaraa' al-buyuut al-jadiidah** *the ministers visited the new houses.*

Verb	*Subject*
he form for ...	1 one male being
	2 two or more male beings
	3 one object (grammatically m.)
she form for ...	1 one female being
	2 two or more female beings
	3 one object (grammatically f.)
	4 *two or more* of any object

If the sentence has two verbs, the word order is V1–S–O–V2:

1 1st Verb   2 Subject   3 Object (if any)   4 2nd Verb

The first verb is in the *he/she* form and the second verb follows the subject and agrees fully with it, e.g. ذهب الأولاد إلى السينما وشاهدوا الفيلم **dhahaba l-awlaad ilaa s-siinamaa wa-shaahaduu l-fiilm** *the boys went to the cinema and watched the film.*

A verb that for any reason comes *after* its subject must agree fully in number and gender.

Saying 'was' and 'were'

Although there is no verb in Arabic for *is/are*, the verb كان **kaana** is necessary for *was/were*.

The suffix endings are the same past tense ones used on all Arabic verbs.

Singular	*Plural*
كان **kaan-a** *he was*	كانوا **kaan-uu** *they* (m.) *were*
كانت **kaan-at** *she was*	كنّ **kun-na** *they* (f.) *were*
كنت **kun-t(a)** *you* (m.) *were*	كنتم **kun-tum** *you* (m.) *were*
كنت **kun-ti** *you* (f.) *were*	كنتن **kun-tunna** *you* (f.) *were*
كنت **kun-t(u)** *I was*	كنا **kun-naa** *we were*

The final vowels in parentheses are omitted in informal speech.

Since the last letter of the root of this verb is **-n**, the doubling sign is used when the suffix also begins with an **-n**, e.g **kunna** *they* (f.) and **kunnaa** *we*, e.g كنّا في تونس في الصيف **kunnaa fii tuunis fi S-Sayf** *we were in Tunisia in the summer.*

The doubling sign does not usually appear in printed Arabic.

After the verb **kaana** the accusative marker must be used with unsuffixed indefinite nouns or adjectives.

kaana usually comes first in the sentence, e.g كان جمال عبد الناصر قائدا عظيما **kaana jamaal :abd an-naaSir qaa'idan :aDHiiman** *Jamaal Abd al-Nasir was a great leader.*

Present tense

The Arabic present tense is used if the action of the verb is incomplete. To form the present tense, prefixes – and suffixes for certain parts – are added to the present tense stem, e.g. **ktub**, as follows:

Singular	*Plural*
ya-ktub *he writes, is writing*	**ya-ktub-uun** *they* (m.) *write*
ta-ktub *she writes*	**ya-ktub-na** *they* (f.) *write*
ta-ktub *you* (m.) *write*	**ta-ktub-uun** *you* (m.) *write*
ta-ktub-iin *you* (f.) *write*	**ta-ktub-na** *you* (f.) *write*
a-ktub *I write*	**na-ktub** *we write*

A full explanation of how to find the present stem of the verb is given in the verb tables.

Expressing the future

Arabic expresses what you will do in the future by placing the word سوف **sawfa** before the present tense verb or the prefix سـ **sa-**, which is joined to the verb that follows it, e.g. سوف يصل الوزير غدا **sawfa yaSil al-waziir ghadan** *the minister will arrive tomorrow;* سيلعب الأولاد في الشارع **sa-yal:ab al-awlaad fi-sh-shaari:** *the children will play in the street.*

Pluperfect tense

The pluperfect tense is formed by using the verb كان **kaana** with the *past tense*.

The word قد **qad** emphasises that the action is completely over and done with.

The word order is always:

1 **kaana** 2 Subject 3 **qad** (optional) 4 Main verb 5 The rest

The same rules of agreement must be followed as those given above. The pluperfect tense is used to say what you had done, e.g. كان المدير (قد) وصل يوم السبت **kaana al-mudiir (qad) waSal yawm as sabt** *the manager had arrived on Saturday.*

The past continuous

The past continuous is formed with **kaana** and the present tense verb. It is used to say what used to happen or what was habitual, e.g. كنا نذهب إلى السوق كل يوم **kunnaa nadhhab ilaa s-suuq kull yawm** *we used to go to the market every day.*

Verb tables

The Arabic Verb

The Arabic verb is best considered from three distinct points of view: grammatical, phonetic and stem modification.

1 Grammatical

The grammatical variations of the verb are there for two main reasons:

a *to tell us who is carrying or has carried out the action. This is important as, unlike English, Arabic commonly omits the subject pronouns I, you, he, etc. so the verb itself has to carry this information;*

b *to tell us the timing of the action, i.e. when it takes (has taken/will take etc.) place.*

Subject markers

The grammatical term for who is responsible for the action of a verb is called *person*.

Like English, Arabic verbs have three persons:

- *the person(s) speaking (I, we), called the first person*
- *the person(s) spoken to (you), called the second person*
- *the person(s) spoken about (he, she, it, they) called the third person.*

However, Arabic makes finer distinctions in some cases:

- *The second person has to indicate the sex of the person spoken to. This is called* gender.
- *The Arabic verb has a set of parts referring to two people known as the* dual. *English only distinguishes between* one *and* more than one.

Note: Traditionally, the Arabic verb is tabled in the reverse order of persons, i.e. starting with the third. This is because the third person *he* part is regarded as the simplest, most basic form of the verb. This convention has been employed throughout this book.

	Singular	*Dual*	*Plural*
third person	*he* *she**	*they two* (m) *they two* (f.)	*they* (m.) *they (f.)*
second person	*you* (m.) *you* (f.)	*you two* (m. & f.)	*you* (m.) *you* (f.)
first person	*I* (m. & f.)		*we* (m. & f.)

* Since Arabic has no neuter gender, English *it* must be rendered *he* or *she* according to the grammatical gender of the Arabic noun.

Tense

The tense of a verb refers to when the action takes/took/will take place. Arabic has only two true tenses, *present* and *past*.

Other grammatical characteristics

The present tense – but not the past – of the Arabic verb has three variants called *moods*. The normal form of the present tense is called the *indicative* and the other two forms are the *subjunctive* and the *jussive*. These are not so important in Modern Arabic, as often all three look identical. However, in some types of verb, the jussive, especially, shows changes in spelling and so all three have been included in the tables. The subjunctive and the jussive are mainly used with certain conjunctions. These are dealt with in the main body of the book.

The *imperative* is a special form of the jussive, used in issuing commands. This is not included in the tables, as its formation from the jussive is explained in Unit 14.

Another distinction is that technically known as *voice*. Normal verbs where the subject is responsible for the action are called *active*: *He ate the cake*. So-called *passive* verbs are those where the grammatical subject has the action of the verb performed on it: *The cake was eaten*.

For technical reasons, passives are much less important in Arabic than in English, but they have been included for the sake of completeness.

2 Phonetic

The Arabic verb is relatively regular. Virtually all verbs take the same prefixes and suffixes and those that vary do so in a minor way. There are, for example, no so-called irregular or strong verbs as proliferate in European languages, such as English *go*, *went*, *has gone/is*, *was*, *has been*, and so on.

However, there are several phonetic factors which affect verbs:

a *The presence of one of the letters* و *or* ي *as a root letter in any position. These letters tend to be elided or smoothed out into vowels.*
b *Verb roots where the third consonant is the same as the second, e.g.* **d-l-l**, **m-r-r**, *etc. This causes contracted verb forms.*
c *The letter* ء **hamzah** *causes some spelling difficulties when it occurs in a root. However, these are learned by experience and observation and no tables have been given.*

Note: Verbs that do not have any of the above features have been termed *sound* (abbreviation **S**) in this book.

3 Stem modification

The tenses of the Arabic verb are formed by attaching prefixes and suffixes to the 'heart' or 'nucleus' of the verb, called the *stem*. An approximate English parallel would be to take *talk* as the stem of that verb. In language instruction, we can then say that, for instance, you add the suffix *-s* for the *he* form – *he talks* – and *-ed* to form the past tense – *talked*.

A significant feature of the Arabic verb is *stem modification*, which means that the stems themselves are modified in a finite number of ways to give different meanings. The nearest we get to this in English is *to fall* and *to fell* (a tree) i.e. *cause it to fall*, but, in Arabic, the phenomenon is very widespread.

Every Arabic verb has the potential to modify its stem in nine different ways, which, by western (but not Arab) convention are referred to as *derived forms* and indicated using the Roman numerals I–X, Form I being the base form. It is doubtful if any verb possesses the total of 10 derived forms, but it is essential to learn them all, as many basic everyday verbs are up in the high numbers.

Table 1: Prefixes and suffixes of the verb

This table gives all the prefixes and suffixes which, when applied to the relevant present or past stem, give all the parts of the Arabic verb. It should be studied in conjunction with the following notes.

The table in transliteration follows English order, from left to right:

Hyphen + letter = suffix (e.g. **-at**)

Letter + hyphen = prefix (e.g. **ya-**)

	Past	*Present*	*Subjunctive/ Jussive*
Singular			
he	stem-**a**	**ya**-stem	no written change in sound verbs except for parts given
she	stem-**at**	**ta**-stem	
you (m.)	stem-**ta**	**ta**-stem	
you (f.)	stem-**ti**	**ta**-stem-**iina**	**ta**-stem-**ii**
I	stem-**tu**	**a**-stem	
Dual			
they two (m.)	stem-**aa**	**ya**-stem-**aani**	**ya**-stem-**aa**
they two (f.)	stem-**ataa**	**ta**-stem-**aani**	**ta**-stem-**aa**
you two (m. & f.)	stem-**tumaa**	**ta**-stem-**aani**	**ta**-stem-**aa**
Plural			
they (m.)	stem-**uu**	**ya**-stem-**uuna**	**ya**-stem-**uu**
they (f.)	stem-**na**	**ya**-stem-**na**	
you (m.)	stem-**tum**	**ta**-stem-**uuna**	**ta**-stem-**uu**
you (f.)	stem-**tunna**	**ta**-stem-**na**	
we	stem-**naa**	**na**-stem	

Tip: Make a habit while learning these verb parts of noting which suffixes begin with a vowel and which with a consonant.

Here is an Arabic example, using the verb *to write*. In order to highlight the prefixes and suffixes, lengthened ligatures (lines joining the letters) have been used and the vowelling of the past and present stems (كَتَب and كْتُب respectively) has been omitted.

	Past	*Present*	*Subjunctive/ Jussive*
Singular			
he	كتبَ	يَـكتب	no written change in sound verbs except for parts given
she	كتبَـتْ	تَـكتب	
you (m.)	كتبْـتَ	تَـكتب	
you (f.)	كتبْـتِ	تَـكتبِـينَ	تَـكتبِي
I	كتبْـتُ	أكتب	
Dual			
they two (m.)	كتبَـا	يَـكتبَـانِ	يَـكتبَـا
they two (f.)	كتبَـتَـا	تَـكتبَـانِ	تَـكتبَـا
you two (m. & f.)	كتبْـتُـمَـا	تَـكتبَـانِ	تَـكتبَـا
Plural			
they (m.)	كتبُـوا	يَـكتبُـونَ	يَـكتبُـوا
they (f.)	كتـبْـنَ	يَـكتبْـنَ	
you (m.)	كتبْـتُـمْ	تَـكتبُـونَ	تَـكتبُـوا
you (f.)	كتبْـتُـنَّ	تَـكتبْـنَ	
we	كتبْـنَـا	نَـكتب	

Tip: The Arabic version of the tip given above is to note which stems end with a **sukuun** (no vowel sign) on the last consonant of the root and which do not.

Notes

a *The above tables give all the prefixes and suffixes which, when applied to the appropriate stems, give all the parts of any Arabic verb, with the following minor exceptions:*

- *with derived stems II, III and IV (see Table S) and* all *passive stems (Table S) the prefixes of the present tense are vowelled with* **u**, *i.e.* يُـ، تُـ، أُ، نُـ.
- *in certain stems whose final radical is* و or ي *certain of the endings are slightly modified in pronunciation, but not in writing. These changes are of little importance in practice, but are dealt with in the appropriate tables.*

b *Certain short final vowels are habitually omitted in speech:*

- *Past tense: final vowel of* he, you masculine *(but not feminine), and I in the singular. Any resulting ambiguity is usually cleared up by context.*
- *Present tense:* **-i** *of the dual forms ending in* **-aani**, *and* **-a** *of the second person singular feminine and the plural forms ending in* **-uuna** *(but not the* **-a** *of the feminine plural* **-na** *ending).*

c *Note carefully the (unpronounced)* **alif** *written after plural forms ending in* **-uu** *in both tenses. This is a spelling convention which applies only to this verb suffix.*

d *The moods. Where no written changes are indicated in the table, the unsuffixed parts of the indicative originally ended in* **-u**, *those of the subjunctive in* **-a** *and the jussive with no vowel. These are unmarked in Modern Arabic and have thus been ignored in this book, only parts which differ in spelling having been noted. You will note that verb parts ending in* **-uuna** *and* **-aani** *lose their* ن *in the subjunctive and jussive – see also note c) above. The feminine plural* **-na** *ending is not affected.*

Verb tables

Introduction

So that you can identify each verb and cross-reference it with the Verb tables, we have devised the following system and tagged all the verbs in the vocabularies and glossaries accordingly.

The verb entries are given as in the following example:

كتب **kataba [S-1 u]** *to write*

Reading from left to right these represent:

1 كتب *The he form of the past tense in the Arabic script (see note in section 1 above). This also in most cases constitutes the past stem.*
2 **kataba** *This is the transliteration of the Arabic in 1 above and provides the vowel of the middle radical (especially relevant to Form I verbs).*
3 **[S-1 u]** *This identifies the verb type so that you can look it up in the tables. This example is an S type, Form I [S-I]. The following lower case letter (here* **u***) is the vowel to be used in the present stem. It is only necessary to give this vowel for Form I verbs as other types show no variation.*
4 *to write The meaning.*

Reminder: In virtually all Arabic verbs, it is only the stem that changes. Once you have learned the prefixes and suffixes given in the table above, you can apply them to all verbs. So, although there appear to be a lot of tables, you only have to learn between two and four stem parts for each verb. Your task will therefore be much lighter if you spend some time now mastering the prefixes and suffixes thoroughly.

Table S, Sound verbs [S-I to S-X]

'Sound' in this context means 'without weakness'. The definition in relation to the Arabic verb is simple: a sound verb is one which:

- *does NOT have* و *or* ي *as any of its radicals (root consonants)*
- *does NOT have the same letter for its middle and last radical (such as* ر-د-د*, for example).*

If a root does not display either of the above two features, it is sound (**S**).

Important note: Since it is impossible to find a verb that occurs in all the derived forms (II–X), we have followed the convention of using the root ف-ع-ل **f-:-l** in the following table. Although not particularly user friendly because of the difficult middle consonant, this has the advantage of being the system that the Arabs use. You will, therefore, be able to seek advice from native speakers.

Verbs in these categories are marked in the glossaries S-I to S-X (but see special notes on Forms I and IX below).

The following table gives the past and present stems. To construct the required verb part, simply add the prefixes and/or suffixes given in Table 1 (above) to the appropriate stem, observing the Form I vowellings where necessary.

Active	Past stem	Present stem
S-I	فَعَل	فْعَل
S-II	فَعَّل	فَعِّل
S-III	فَاعَل	فَاعِل
S-IV	أَفْعَل	فْعِل
S-V	تَفَعَّل	تَفَعَّل
S-VI	تَفَاعَل	تَفَاعَل
S-VII	اِنْفَعَل	نْفَعِل
S-VIII	اِفْتَعَل	فْتَعِل
S-IX	see notes below	
S-X	اِسْتَفْعَل	سْتَفْعِل

Passive	Past stem	Present stem
S-I	فُعِل	فْعَل
S-II	فُعِّل	فَعَّل
S-III	فُوعِل	فَاعَل
S-IV	أُفْعِل	فْعَل
S-V	تُفُعِّل	تَفَعَّل
S-VI	تُفُوعِل	تَفَاعَل
S-VII	none	
S-VIII	اُفْتُعِل	فْتَعَل
S-IX	see notes below	
S-X	اُسْتُفْعِل	سْتَفْعَل

General notes

- *The passive is given in full for the sake of completeness, but it is not worth devoting a lot of time to learning it as it is much more restricted in use than its English equivalent. Form VII does not have a passive, and in some other forms it is rare.*
- *Form IX. For technical reasons, this comparatively rare form is given below along with the Doubled Verb (Table D).*

Form S-I

This is the only form that has more than one vowel pattern. In the glossaries, the past stem vowelling can be obtained from the transliteration (e.g. **kataba**), while the present stem vowelling is given after the verb type (e.g. **S-I u**). So the verb فَعَلَ فْعَل **fa:ala f:al** given in the table would be marked **S-I a**. As there is no reliable way to predict these vowellings they have to be learned along with their verbs. The vowels in the passive of Form I, however, do not change.

Form S-II

This is formed by doubling the middle radical and vowelling according to the table. It often has a causative meaning, e.g. **fahima** (**I**) *to understand*, **fahhama** (**II**) *to make someone understand, explain*. The present tense prefixes take a **u** vowel (see above).

Form S-III

Formed by interposing an **alif** between the first and middle radicals. Again, the present tense prefixes take a **u** vowel.

Form S-IV

Formed by prefixing أ to the root in the perfect. This disappears in the present, which again takes a **u** vowel. Like Form II, this often has a causative meaning.

Form S-V

Formed by prefixing **ta-** and doubling the middle radical. (Note: the past and present stems of Forms V and VI are identical. All the other derived forms above Form I alternate a middle radical vowel of **a** in the past with **i** in the present.)

Form S-VI
Formed by prefixing **ta-** and introducing an **alif** after the first radical. Again, both stems are identical.

Form S-VII
Formed by prefixing إنـ **in-** to the stem and following the vowel pattern given. Like all other forms beginning with **alif**, this disappears in the present.

Form S-VIII
Formed by prefixing **alif** and introducing ت after the first radical. Some assimilations occur in this form when certain letters occur as the first radical. These will be pointed out as they occur.

Form S-IX
Because its formation involves the reduplication of the last radical, this behaves like a doubled verb and is therefore given in Table D.

Form S-X
Formed by prefixing إسْتـ **ist-** to the root. The **alif** disappears in the present.

Summary
Study this table carefully, as it comprises the bones of the Arabic verb system. Pay attention in particular to the vowel on the middle radical. Remember that you have only two things to learn:

- *the prefixes and suffixes given in Table 1*
- *the variations in the stem vowel of Form I, i.e. that on the middle radical.*

Table Q, Quadriliteral verbs [Q-I and Q-II]

These are verbs that have four consonant roots instead of the usual three consonants. They normally only exist in two derived forms, called I and II although they differ from the normal patterns for those categories (see below).

We use the root **z-l-z-l**, which means *to shake something* in Form I and *to be shaken* in Form II.

Active	*Past stem*	*Present stem*
Q-I	زَلْزَل	زَلْزِل
Q-II	تَزَلْزَل	تَزَلْزَل

Although conventionally known as Forms Q-I and Q-II, these actually work like S-II and S-V verbs, respectively. If you remember that the **shaddah** (doubling sign) used on these represents a letter without a vowel followed by one with a vowel (in this case its twin, e.g. **bb**, **kk**, and so on) you will see that the verbs above show the same sequence of unvowelled letter followed by vowelled letter (in the case of our example, **lz**). Q-I and Q-II therefore form exact parallels to SII and SV. QI, uniquely among Form I verbs, shows no variations in vowelling and the present prefix takes a **u** vowel.

Table D, Doubled verbs [D-I to D-X]

Introduction

Doubled verbs are those whose middle and last root letters are the same (**d-l-l**, **m-r-r** and the like). Because Form IX involves the doubling of this radical, it is included here rather than in Table S.

All doubled verbs (including Form IX) have two stems for each tense (past and present). It will help you to to understand this if you think along the lines of suffixes that begin with a vowel as opposed to those that begin with a consonant (prefixes don't matter). These two factors determine the stems used.

To put it another way:

- *Past tense. All parts except he, she, they (m.) in the past tense use the normal stem (i.e. like the sound verb, Table S).*

▸ *Present tense. All parts except the (comparatively rare) second and third person feminine plural use the normal stem.*

Apart from those verb parts mentioned above, a contracted stem is used, contracted in this context meaning that the middle and final radicals are reduced to one letter and written with the doubling sign **shaddah**. To illustrate this type of verb, we use the root م–د–د **m-d-d**. Form I means *to extend*, *stretch*. Not all the derived forms given here exist, but the same root is used throughout the table for the sake of uniformity.

Note: Forms D-II and D-V behave like sound verbs as the middle radical is doubled and therefore cannot contract.

NS = normal stem (i.e. as in Table S)
CS = contracted stem

Active	*Past stem*	*Present stem*
I NS	مَدَد	مْدُد
CS	مَدّ	مُدّ
II	مَدَّد	مَدِّد
III NS	مَادَد	مَادِد
CS	مَادّ	مَادّ
IV NS	أَمْدَد	مْدِد
CS	أَمَدّ	مِدّ
V	تَمَدَّد	تَمَدَّد
VI NS	تَمَادَد	تَمَادَد
CS	تَمَادّ	تَمَادّ
VII NS	اِنْمَدَد	نْمَدِد

CS	اِنْمَدّ	نْمَدّ
VIII NS	اِمْتَدَد	مْتَدِد
CS	اِمْتَدّ	مْتَدّ
X NS	اِسْتَمْدَد	سْتَمْدِد
CS	اِسْتَمَدّ	سْتَمْدّ

The passives are given only for forms that occur reasonably frequently.

Passive	*Past stem*	*Present stem*
I NS	مُدِد	مْدَد
CS	مُدّ	مَدّ
IV NS	أُمْدِد	مْدَد
CS	أُمِدّ	مَدّ
VIII NS	أُمْتُدِد	مْتَدَد
CS	أُمْتُدّ	مْتَدّ
X NS	أُسْتُمْدِد	سْتَمدَد
CS	أُسْتُمِدّ	سْتَمدّ

Form S-IX

The comparatively rare Form S-IX is not a true doubled verb in terms of root. However, as its construction involves doubling the last radical, it behaves like a doubled verb and has been included here. In Modern Arabic, it is only used with the special adjective roots given in Unit 16 and has no passive. We shall use here **iHmarra** *to become red, to blush*.

Active	*Past stem*	*Present stem*
IX NS	اِحْمَرَر	حْمَرَر
CS	اِحْمَرّ	حْمَرّ

Form D-I

Like all Form I verbs, the doubled roots admit various vowellings. These are given in the usual way, e.g. **D-I u** (the vowelling of the example in Table D). However, in the past tense, the contracted stem always takes an **a** vowel and the 'true' vowel only appears in the normal stem. In the present, the vowel given goes on the second radical in the normal stem and the first radical in the contracted stem. Here, for example, are the stems of the **D-I** a verb from the root **DH-l-l**:

Active	*Past stem*	*Present stem*
I NS	ظَلِل	ظْلَل
CS	ظَلّ	ظَلّ

Forms II and V

These behave like S verbs, as the doubling of the middle radical inhibits any contraction.

Table Fw, Verbs with first radical w [Fw-I to Fw-X]

We use the root **w-S-l** *to arrive* in Form I as the model for this type of verb.

Active	*Past stem*	*Present stem*
I	وَصَل	صِل
IV	أَوْصَل	وصِل
VIII	اِتَّصَل	تَّصِل
Passive	*Past stem*	*Present stem*
I	وُصِل	وصَل
IV	أَوْصَل	وصَل
VIII	أُتُّصِل	تَّصَل

Forms not given are regular (Table S) or do not occur.

Form I

The main feature of this is that the present stem loses its و altogether. Also, the middle radical of Form I has varying vowels, indicated in the vocabularies by the usual convention. The example verb in the table is **Fw i**.

Form IV

The only slightly unusual feature here is that, in the present, the و combines with the **u** vowel of the prefix to form a long vowel **uu**. So, for instance, **yu- + wSil** is pronounced **yuuSil**.

Form VIII

The و becomes assimilated to the following ت, giving **ittaSala**, **yattaSil**.

Tip: This is because Arabic will not allow the sequence **iw**. The same goes for **ui**, so if you concoct a verb form – or any word for that matter – containing such a sequence, it is going to be wrong (see also Table Fy).

Passive
Again, when the و is preceded by a **u** vowel, the two combine into a long **uu**.

Note: Doubled verbs beginning with و do not drop the letter, but behave like normal doubled verbs (see Table D).

Table Fy, Verbs with first radical y [Fy-I to Fy-X]

Such verbs are not common. We use the example **yabisa** *to be* or *become dry*.

Active	*Past stem*	*Present stem*
I	يَبِس	يْبَس
IV	أَيْبَس	وبِس
Passive	*Past stem*	*Present stem*
IV	أَيْبَس	وبِس

Forms not given are regular (Table S) or do not occur.

Form I
The ي does not drop out in the present.

Form IV
In the present of IV active and passive, the theoretical combination **ui** is replaced by **uu** (see Table Fw above).

Table Mw, Verbs with middle radical w [Mw-I to Mw-X]

Like the doubled verb, these have two stems for each tense. In this case, it is better to call them long stem (LS) and short stem (SS). The rules for their use are identical in principle to those applying to the doubled verb: LS before a suffix beginning with a vowel and SS before one beginning with a consonant. Please see under doubled verb for a more detailed explanation.

We use the root **q-w-l** *to say* in Form I.

Active	*Past stem*	*Present stem*
I LS	قَال	قُول
SS	قُل	قُل
IV LS	أقَال	قِيل
SS	أَقل	قِل
VII LS	اِنْقَال	نْقَال
SS	اِنْقَل	نْقَل
VIII LS	اِقْتَال	قْتَال
SS	اِقْتَل	قْتَل
X LS	اِسْتَقَال	سْتَقِيل
SS	اِسْتَقَل	سْتَقِل

Jussive

In this type of verb, the jussive differs from the normal present tense and the subjunctive. The prefixes and suffixes are given in Table 1 and Table S, but note that in Mw verbs the short stem is used in all parts of the jussive that do not have a vowel in the last radical, e.g. يَقُل، تَقُل **yaqul, taqul** *he, you*, etc. but يَقُولُوا، تَقُولُوا، تَقُولِي **yaquuluu, taquuluu, taquulii** *they, you* pl., *you* f. sing.

Passive

In the passive, the vowelling of the stems is as follows:

Passive	*Past stem*	*Present stem*
I LS	قِيل	قَال
SS	قِل	قَل
IV LS	أُقِيل	قَال
SS	أُقِل	قَل
VII	none	
VIII LS	اُقْتِيل	قْتَال
SS	اُقْتِل	قْتَل
X LS	اُسْتُقِيل	سْتَقَال
SS	اُسْتُقِل	سْتَقَل

Derived forms

As usual, the forms not mentioned are regular and behave like sound verbs, the و behaving like a consonant.

Table My, Verbs with middle radical y [My-I to My-X]

Apart from Form I, these behave in an identical way to Mw verbs in the table above. We use the root **S-y-r** *to become*.

Active	*Past stem*	*Present stem*
I LS	صَار	صِير
SS	صِر	صِر

Jussive

See Table Mw above. The same principle applies here: يَصِر، تَصِر

yaSir, **taSir** *he*, *you*, etc. but يَصِيرُوا، تَصِيرُوا، تَصِيرِي **yaSiiruu**, **taSiiruu**, **taSiirii** *they*, *you* pl., *you* f. sing.

Passive
Same as Table Mw above.

Derived forms
See Table Mw above. These verbs behave in the same way.

Table Ma

This is a slight misnomer, in that these verbs actually have either **w** or **y** as the middle radical. However, as the present tense takes an **a** vowel, the code **Ma** has been used.

This is a small group of verbs, but it includes some very common ones. We use the root **n-w-m** *to sleep*.

Active	*Past stem*	*Present stem*
I LS	نَام	نَام
SS	نِم	نَم

Jussive
See Table Mw above. The same principle applies here: يَنَم، تَنَم **yanam**, **tanam** *he*, *you*, etc. but يَنَامُوا، تَنَامُوا، تَنَامِي **yanaamuu**, **tanaamuu**, **tanaamii** *they*, *you* pl., *you* f. sing.

Passive
See Table Mw above.

Derived forms
See Table Mw above. These verbs behave in the same way.

Table Lw-I, Verbs with last radical 'w'

Notes

- *This type of verb and those in the following tables do not lend themselves easily to a reduction into a convenient number of stems, so their conjugations are given in a fuller form and are best learned by heart.*
- *The derived forms are the same for all types, so these are given separately below.*

We use the root **n-d-w** *to call, invite.*

Active	*Past*	*Present*	*Subjunctive* as present except parts given	*Jussive* as subj. except parts given
Singular				
he	نَدَا	يَنْدُو		يَنْدُ
she	نَدَتْ	تَنْدُو		تَنْدُ
you (m.)	نَدَوْتَ	تَنْدُو		تَنْدُ
you (f.)	نَدَوْتِ	تَنْدِينَ	تَنْدِي	
I	نَدَوْتُ	أَنْدُو		أَنْدُ
Plural				
they (m.)	نَدَوْا	يَنْدُونَ	يَنْدُوا	
they (f.)	نَدَوْنَ	يَنْدُونَ		
you (m.)	نَدَوْتُمْ	تَنْدُونَ	تَنْدُوا	
you (f.)	نَدَوْتُنَّ	تَنْدُونَ		
we	نَدَوْنَا	نَنْدُو		نَنْدُ

Summary

There are many phonetic factors at work here, which cause different sorts of elisions and changes. To list all these would defeat the purpose so, as has been suggested, it is better to learn these verbs by heart, spending more time on the most commonly occurring parts.

Active	*Past*	*Present*	*Subjunctive* as present except parts given	*Jussive* as subj. except parts given
Singular				
he	نُدِيَ	يُنْدَى		يُنْدَ
she	نُدِيَتْ	تُنْدَى		تُنْدَ
you (m.)	نُدِيتَ	تُنْدَى		تُنْدَ
you (f.)	نُدِيتِ	تُنْدَيْنَ	تُنْدَيْ	
I	نُدِيتُ	أُنْدَى		أُنْدَ
Plural				
they (m.)	نُدُوا	يُنْدَوْنَ	يُنْدَوْا	
they (f.)	نُدِينَ	يُنْدَوْنَ		
you (m.)	نُدِيتُمْ	تُنْدَوْنَ	تُنْدَوْا	
you (f.)	نُدِيتُنَّ	تُنْدَيْنَ		
we	نُدِينَا	نُنْدَى		نُنْدَ

Table Ly-I, Verbs with last radical 'y'

This is by far the most common of this type of verb. We shall use the root **r-m-y** *to throw*, and, again, give the verb in full.

Active	Past	Present	Subjunctive as present except parts given	Jussive as subj. except parts given
Singular				
he	رَمَى	يَرْمِي		يَرْمِ
she	رَمَتْ	تَرْمِي		تَرْمِ
you (m.)	رَمَيْتَ	تَرْمِي		تَرْمِ
you (f.)	رَمَيْتِ	تَرْمِي	تَرْمِينَ	
I	رَمَيْتُ	أَرْمِي		أَرْمِ
Plural				
they (m.)	رَمَوْا	يَرْمُونَ	يَرْمُوا	
they (f.)	رَمَيْنَ	يَرْمِينَ		
you (m.)	رَمَيْتُمْ	تَرْمُون	تَرْمُوا	
you (f.)	رَمَيْتُنَّ	تَرْمِينَ		
we	رَمَيْنَا	نَرْمِي		نَرْمِ

Passive
Identical to Lw type. See table above.

Table La-I

Again, a slight misnomer. These verbs actually have third radical **w** or **y**, but the past has an **i** vowel and the present an **a** vowel on the middle radical. We use the root **l-q-y** *to meet with*, *find*.

Active	*Past*	*Present*	*Subjunctive* as present except parts given	*Jussive* as subj. except parts given
Singular				
he	لَقِيَ	يَلْقَى		يَلْقَ
she	لَقِيَتْ	تَلْقَى		تَلْقَ
you (m.)	لَقِيتَ	تَلْقَى		تَلْقَ
you (f.)	لَقِيتِ	تَلْقَي	تَلْقَيْنَ	
I	لَقِيتُ	أَلْقَى		أَلْقَ
Plural				
they (m.)	لَقُوا	يَلْقَوْنَ	يَلْقَوْا	
they (f.)	لَقِينَ	يَلْقَيْنَ		
you (m.)	لَقِيتُمْ	تَلْقَوْنَ	تَلْقَوْا	
you (f.)	لَقِيتُنَّ	تَلْقَيْنَ		
we	لَقِينا	نَلْقَى		نَلْقَ

Passive

Identical to Lw type. See table above.

Table Lh-I

The **h** here stands for *hybrid*. A few verbs conjugate like **r-m-y** in the past (Table Ly) and **l-q-y** in the present (Table La). We shall give merely a few sample parts, using the root **s-:-y** *to hurry*, *make an effort at something*.

Active	*Past*	*Present*	*Subjunctive* as present except parts given	*Jussive* as subj. except parts given
Singular				
he	سَعَى	يَسْعَى		يَسْعَ
she	سَعَتْ	تَسْعَى		تَسْعَ

Passive

As usual, the same as all the L-type verbs (see tables above).

L-type verbs, derived forms [Lw/y/a, etc. II–X]

The derived forms are the same for all three types of verb with و or ي as the last radical.

Although a table is given below, there is a shortcut to learning these:

- *Forms II, III, IV, VII, VIII and X (there is no Form IX) conjugate like* **r-m-y** *(Table Ly) in both tenses.*
- *V and VI conjugate like* **r-m-y** *(Table Ly) in the past and* **l-q-y** *(Table La) in the present.*

The following table, therefore, only gives two parts (the *he* form of the past and the present). The rest of the parts can be found by referring to the two tables mentioned above.

Again we use the root **l-q-y**, which exists in quite a number – but not all – of the derived forms.

Active	*Past stem*	*Present stem*
II	لَقَّى	يُلَقِّي
III	لاقَى	يُلاقِي
IV	أَلْقَى	يُلْقِي
V	تَلَقَّى	يَتَلَقَّى
VI	تَلاقَى	يَتَلاقَى
VII	اِنْلَقَى	يَنْلَقِي
VIII	اِلْتَقَى	يَلْتَقِي

Passive	*Past stem*	*Present stem*
X	اِسْتَلْقَى	يَسْتَلْقِي
II	لُقِّيَ	يُلَقَّى
III	لُوقِيَ	يُلاقَى
IV	أُلْقِيَ	يُلْقَى
V	تُلُقِّيَ	يُتَلَقَّى
VIII	اُلْتُقِيَ	يُلْتَقَى
X	اُسْتُلْقِيَ	يُسْتَلْقَى

The forms not given are either non-existent or extremely rare.

Some irregularities

The only really irregular verb in Arabic is لَيْسَ *not to be*, used for negation. This is given in full in Unit 8. It only exists in one tense, which is past in form, but present in meaning.

The verb رَأَى *to see* conjugates in the past like رَمَى (Table Ly), but has the irregular present form يَرَى where the **hamzah** and its supporting **alif** are dropped. This tense is vowelled like the present of La verbs, e.g. يَرَى، تَرَى **yaraa, taraa**, etc.

The verb رَأَى has no imperative, that of the alternative verb نَظَرَ *to look, see* being used instead (اُنْظُرْ).

Verbs with **hamzah** as one of their radicals are mainly regular, but are sometimes difficult to spell. The rules for this are too complex to be practically useful and it is better to learn by experience.

There are a number of 'doubly weak' verbs, showing the characteristics of two different types. These and certain other phonetic variations – especially of Form VIII verbs – have been noted in the text.

Arabic–English vocabulary

This glossary relates mainly to the texts in the units and the key vocabulary boxes. It is arranged according to the order of the Arabic alphabet (see pages 3–4) as opposed to the root system used by most dictionaries. This should enable you to find words more easily. The Arabic definite article (*the* الـ) has been included with words that always have it (e.g. الدنيا **ad-dunyaa** *the world*), but left out where you are more likely to be looking for the word in its non-definite form (e.g. *Sharjah*, Arabic الشارقة **ash-shaariqah**). Words that do not take the accusative marker are marked with an asterisk (*).

ا

آلة حاسبة **aalah Haasibah** *computer*

أب **ab** *father*

أحاط بـ **aHaaTa bi- [My-IV]** *surround*

احتفال، ات **iHtifaal, -aat** *party, celebration*

ابتسم **ibtasama [S-VIII]** *smile*

ابن، أبناء **ibn, abnaa'*** *son*

ابنة، بنات **ibnah, banaat** *daughter*

أبو الهول **abuu l-hawl** *the Sphynx*

أبو ظبي **abuu DHabi** *Abu Dhabi*

أبيض، بيضاء **abyaD***, f. **bayDaa'*** *white*

أثر، آثار **athar, aathaar** sing. *track, trace*, pl. also *archaeological remains*

أثري **atharii** *archaeological*

اتساع **ittisaa:** *extent, compass*

اجتمع **ijtama:a [S-VIII]** *meet, come together*

أجمل **ajmal*** *more/most beautiful*

أحب، يحب **aHabba [D-IV]** *like, love*

احتسب **iHtasaba [S-VIII]** *to award*

احتفل ب **iHtafala bi- [S-VIII]** *celebrate*

احتل **iHtalla [D-VIII]** *occupy*

أحدث **aHdath** *newest, latest*

إحصاء، ات **iHSaa', -aat** *count, census*

أحمر **aHmar*** *red*

أخ، إخوان/ إخوة **akh, ikhwaan** or **ikhwah** *brother*

أخت، أخوات **ukht, akhawaat** *sister*

اختار **ikhtaara [My-VIII]** *to choose*

اخترق **ikhtaraqa [S-VIII]** *to breach*

أخذ **akhadha [S-I u]** *to take*

آخر **aakhar*** (f. أخرى **ukhraa**) *other*

آخر **aakhir** *end, last part of something*

أخضر **akhDar*** *green*

أخير **akhiir** *last*

أدرك **adraka [S-IV]** *to attain, achieve*

إذا **idhaa** *if*

إذا **idhan** *so, therefore*

أذاع **adhaa:a [My-IV]** *to broadcast*

أذن **udh(u)n** (f.) *ear*

أربعة **arba:ah** *four*

أردني **urduni** *Jordanian*

أرز **aruzz** *rice*

إرسال **irsaal** *transmission, sending*

أرسل **arsala [S-IV]** *send*

أرض **al-arD** (f.) *the ground, the earth*

اسباني **isbaanii** *Spanish*

استأجر **ista'jara [S-X]** *to rent, be a tenant of*

استخدام **istikhdaam** *use, employment*

استخدم **istakhdama [S-X]** *to use, employ*

استرداد **istirdaad** *demanding back, reclaiming*

استطاع **istaTaa:a [Mw-X]** *to be able*

استعمال **isti:maal** *use, usage*

استغرق **istaghraqa [S-X]** *take, use up, occupy* (of time)

استقبل **istaqbala [S-X]** *receive, meet*

أسطورة، أساطير **usTuurah, asaaTiir*** *legend*

اسم، أسماء **ism, asmaa'** *name*

أسند ل **asnada [S-IV]** *entrust to, vest in*

أسود، سوداء **aswad***, f. **sawdaa'*** *black*

إشارة، ات **ishaarah, -aat** (traffic) *signal*

اشترك **ishtaraka [S-VIII]** *to participate, take part*

أشكرك **ashkur-ak/ik** *thank you* (to a man/woman)

أشهر **ash-har*** *more/most famous*

أصاب **aSaaba** *hit, strike*

أصبح **aSbaHa [S-IV]** *become*

أصفر، صفراء **aSfar***, f. **Safraa'*** *yellow*

أصل، أصول **aSl, uSuul** *origin, basis*

أضاف **aDaafa [My-IV]** *to add*

أعاد **a:aada [Mw-IV]** *to repeat, renew*

اعتبر **i:tabara [S-VIII]** *to consider, regard*

أعرب عن **a:raba :an [S-IV]** *to state, express*

أعزب **a:zab*** *bachelor, single*

أعطى **a:Taa [Ly-IV]** *to give*

أعلن **a:lana [S-IV]** *to announce, state*

اعلى **a:laa** *highest; the highest point, top*

أفاض ب **afaaDa bi- [My-IV]** *flood, overflow with*

افتتح **iftataHa [S-VIII]** *to commence, open*

أقام **aqaama [Mw-IV]** *to reside; to hold* (an event, etc.)

اكتشف **iktashafa [S-VIII]** *discover*

أكثر **akthar*** *more/most*

أكل **akl** *things to eat, food*

أكل، يأكل **akala, ya'kul [S-I u]** *eat*

أكيد **akiid** *certain, definite*

الـ **al-** *the*

الآن **al-'aan** *now*

الاسكندرية **al-iskandariyyah** *Alexandria*

الإمارات العربية المتحدة **al-imaaraat al-:arabiyyah al-muttaHidah** *the United Arab Emirates*

الأهرام **al-ahraam** *the pyramids*

الحمد لله **al-Hamdu li-l-laah** *praise God*

الحين **al-Hiin** *now*

الذي **alladhii** *who, which, that* (f. التي **allatii**)

السعودية **as-sa:udiyyah** *Saudi Arabia*

السلام عليكم **as-salaamu-alaykum** *hello*

العالم **al-:aalam** *the world*

الغد **al-ghad** *tomorrow*

ألف، آلاف **alf, aalaaf** *thousand*

إلا **illaa** *except*

الله **Al-laah** *God, Allah*

ألماني **almaanii** *German*

المغرب **al-maghrib** *sunset; Morocco*

اليوم **al-yawm** *today*

أمّا **ammaa** *as for*

أمة، أمم **ummah, umam** *nation*

أمام **amaam** *in front of*

امتياز **imtiyaaz** *distinction, privilege*

امرأة، نساء **imra'ah, nisaa'** (irregular plural) *woman*

أمريكا **amriika** *America*

أمس **ams** *yesterday*

أمس الأول **ams al-awwal** *the day before yesterday*

أمكن **amkana [S-IV]** *to be possible*

إن **in** *if*

أنا **ána** *I*

انبعث **inba:atha [S-VII]** *emanate, be sent out*

أنت **anta/anti** *you* (m./f.)

انتاج **intaaj** *production*

انتشار **intishaar** *spread, currency; popularity*

انتهى **intahaa [Ly-VIII]** *to come to an end, finish*

إنجلترا **ingiltarra** (with *g* as in *garden*) *England*

إنجليزي **ingliizi** *English*

انسان، ناس **insaan, naas** *human being*; pl. = *people*

إنشاء **inshaa'** *foundation, setting up*

أنظري **unDHurii** *look!* (to a woman)

اهتمام **ihtimaam** *attention, concern, interest*

أهلا وسهلا **ahlan wa-sahlan** *welcome*

أهم **ahamm** *more/most important*

أو **aw** *or*

أودع **awda:a [Fw-IV]** *to place*

أوروبي، ون **uruubii** *European*

أول **awwal** *first*

أولا **awwalan** *first* (adv.)

أي **ay** *that is*

أيّ **ayy** *which*

أيس كريم **ays kriim** *ice cream*

أيضاً **ayDan** *also*

إيمان **iimaan** *belief, faith*

أين **ayna** *where*

ب

بـِ **bi-** *with*

باب، أبواب **baab, abwaab** *gate, door*

بادل **baadala [S-III]** *to swap, exchange with someone*

بارد **baarid** *cold* (adj.)

باع **baa:a [My-I]** *to sell*

بالغ، ون **baaligh, baalighuun** *adult*

بجانب **bi-jaanib** *next to, beside*

بحر، بحار **baHr, biHaar** *sea, large river*

بدأ **bada' [S-I a]** *begin*

بدا **badaa [Lw-I]** *to appear, seem, show*

بدون **bi-duun** *without*

برج، أبراج **burj, abraaj** *tower*

برجيل، براجيل **barjiil, baraajiil** *traditional wind tower*

برغر، ات **barghar, -aat** *hamburger*

برنامج، برامج **barnaamij, baraamij*** *programme*

بريطانيا العظمى **briiTaanyaa l-:uDHmaa** *Great Britain*

بريطاني **briiTaanii** *British*

بصل **baSal** *onions*

بطاقة، ات **buTaaqah, -aat** *card*

بطاقة التسليف **buTaaqat at-tasliif** *credit card*

بطلاقة **bi-Talaaqah** *fluently*

بطولات **buTuulaat** *leading roles*

بعد **ba:d** *after*

بعد الظهر **ba:d aDH-DHuhr** *(in the) afternoon*

بعد ما **ba:d maa** *after* (before a verb)

بعض **ba:D** *some, part of something*

بعيد **ba:iid** *far away, distant*

بكم **bi-kam** *how much*

بل **bal** *rather*; here *in fact, indeed*

بلد، بلاد/بلدان **balad, bilaad/ buldaan** *country*

بناء **binaa'** *building, construction*

بنت، بنات **bint, banaat** *girl, daughter*

بنزين **banziin** *petrol*

بهو **bahw** *lobby* (hotel)

بنك، بنوك **bank, bunuuk** *bank*

بيت، بيوت **bayt, buyuut** *house*

بيرة **biirah** *beer*

بين **bayna** *between, among*

بينما **baynamaa** *while*

ت

تابل، توابل **taabil, tawaabil** *spice*

تاجر، تجار **taajir, tujjaar** *merchant*

تاريخ **taariikh** *history*

تاريخي **taariikhii** *historical*

تاكسي **taaksi** *taxi*

تاسع **taasi:** *ninth*

تام **taamm** *complete*

تأهل إلى **ta'ahhala [S-V]** *qualify* (لـ **ilaa** *for*)

تبريد **tabriid** *cooling*

تبع **tabi:a** *follow*

تجارة **tijaarah** *trade, commerce*

تجاري **tijaarii** *commercial*

تخصص **takhaSSaS [S-V]** *specialise*

تذكرة، تذاكر **tadhkirah, tadhaakir*** *ticket*

ترحيب **tarHiib** *welcome, welcoming* (noun)

ترحيبي **tarHiibii** *welcoming* (adj.)

ترك **taraka [S-I u]** *leave, let be*

تزوج **tazawwaja [Mw-V]** *to marry*

تسجيل **tasjiil** *registration, scoring*

تسديدة، ات **tasdiidah, -aat** *shot* (football)

تسهيلات **tas-hiilaat** *facilities*

تسوق **tasawwuq** *shopping*

تشكيلة، ات **tashkiilah, -aat** *selection*

تصميم **taSmiim** *design, designing*

تعادل **ta:aadul** *balance, equality* (football: *draw, equal score*)

تعبان **ta:baan** *tired*

تعلم **ta:allama [S-V]** *learn*

تعليمي **ta:liimii** *educational*

تفاحة، تفاح **tufaaHah, tufaaH** *apple*

تفرج على **tafarraja :ala [S-V]** *watch, look at*

تفضل **tafaDDal** *come in* (to a man)

تقديم **taqdiim** *presentation*

تقرير، تقارير **taqriir, taqaariir*** *report*

تكلم **takallama [S-V]** *speak*

تكييف **takyiif** *air conditioning*

تلفون **tilifuun** *telephone*

تلفزيوني **tilifizyuunii** *television* (adj.), *televisual*

تمتع بـ **tamatta:a [S-V]** *enjoy*

تنس **tanis** *tennis*

تنظيف **tanDHiif** *cleaning*

تنفيذ **tanfiidh** *implementation, execution*

تنقل **tanaqqala [S-V]** *to be carried, transported*

ث

ثالث **thaalith** *third* (adj.)

ثالثة عشر **thaalithah :ashar** *thirteenth*

ثقافي **thaqaafii** *cultural*

ثقيل **thaqiil** *heavy*

ثلاثة **thalaathah** *three*

ثلج **thalj** *ice*

ثم **thumma** *then*

ثمرة **thamrah** *fruit*

ج

جاء، يجيء **jaa'a, yajii' [My-I]** *come*

جار، جيران **jaar, jiiraan** *neighbour*

(الـ) جاري **al-jaarii** *the current*

جالس **jaalis** *sitting, seated*

جامع، جوامع **jaami:, jawaami:*** *large mosque*

جامعة، ات **jaami:ah** *university*

جانب، جوانب **jaanib, jawaanib*** *side*

جانبا **jaaniban** *aside, to one side*

جبنة **jubnah** *cheese*

جدا **jiddan** *very*

جدد **jaddada [D-II]** *renew, restore*

جديد **jadiid** *new*

جرب **jarraba [S-II]** *try out, taste*

جرى **jaraa [Ly-I]** *to run*

جريدة، جرائد **jariidah, jaraa'id*** *newspaper*

جسر، جسور **jisr, jusuur** *bridge*

جعل **ja:ala [S-I a]** *cause, make do something; place, put*

جغرافي **jughraafii** *geographical*

جلب **jalaba [S-I i]** *attract*

جلس **jalasa [S-I i]** *sit, sit down*

جماعة، ات **jamaa:ah, -aat** *group, gathering*

جمال **jamaal** *beauty*

جائزة؛ جوائز **jaa'izah, jawaa'iz*** *prize, reward*

جمرك، جمارك **jumruk, jamaarik*** *customs, excise*

جميع **jamii:** *all*

جمعية، ات **jam:iyyah, -aat group,** *assembly, society*

جمل، جمال **jamal, jimaal** *camel*

جميعا **jamii:an** *all together*

جميل **jamiil** *beautiful*

جنسية، ات **jinsiyyah, -aat** *nationality*

جنيه، ات **junayh, -aat** *pound* (money)

جوعان، جوعى **jaw:aan*, jaw:aa*** *hungry*

جولف **guulf** *golf*

جيب، جيوب **jayb, juyuub** *pocket*

جيد **jayyid** *of good quality*

(الـ)جيزة **al-jiizah** *Geezah*, a district of Cairo

ح

حار **Haarr** *hot*

حارس، حراس **Haaris**, **Hurraas** *guard* (football: *goalkeeper*)

حاضر، ون **HaaDir**, **-uun** *present, here*

حافظ على **HaafaDHa :alaa [S-III]** *keep, preserve*

حبة، ات **Habbah**, **-aat** *grain, seed;* also used for counting units of certain fruits and vegetables

حتى **Hattaa** *until, even*

(الـ)حج **al-Hajj** *the pilgrimage*

حجر، أحجار **Hajar**, **aHjaar** *stone*

حجرة **Hujrah** *room*

حد، حدود **Hadd**, **Huduud** *limit, border*

حديث **Hadiith** *modern, up-to-date*

حديقة، حدائق **Hadiiqah**, **Hadaa'iq*** *garden, park*

حرارة **Haraarah** *heat*

حزين **Haziin** *sad*

حسب **Hasb** *according to*

حسم **Hasm** *discount*

حسنا **Hasanan** *well, right, OK*

حصن، حصون **HiSn**, **HuSuun** *fort, fortress*

حضر **HaDara [S-I u]** *attend*

حقيبة، حقائب **Haqiibah**, **Haqaa'ib*** *bag, suitcase*

حكم، حكام **Hakam**, **Hukkaam** *referee, umpire*

حل، حلول **Hall**, **Huluul** *solution*

حلاوة **Halaawah** *sweetness, beauty*

حمال، ون **Hammaal**, **-uun** *porter*

حمام، ات **Hammaam**, **-aat** *bathroom*

حمر **Hammara [S-II]** *to brown, fry*

حمل، أحمال **Himl**, **aHmaal** *load, burden*

حمل **Hamala [S-I i]** *carry*

حمية **Himyah** *diet*

حوالي **Hawaalii** *about, approximately*

خ

خادم، خدام **khaadim**, **khuddaam** *servant*

خادمة، ات **khaadimah**, **-aat** (female) *servant*

(الـ)خارج **al-khaarij** *the outside, abroad*

خارج **khaarij** *outside*

خاص **khaaSS** *special; private*

خال **khaal** *uncle* (on mother's side)

خالة **khaalah** *aunt* (on mother's side)

خامس **khaamis** *fifth*

خبر، أخبار **khabar**, **akhbaar** *news* (sing. = *an item of news*)

خبز **khubz** *bread*

خدع **khada:a [S-I a]** *to deceive*

خدمة، ات **khidmah**, **-aat** *service*

خروف، خرفان **kharuuf**, **khirfaan** *sheep*

خريطة، خرائط **khariiTah**, **kharaa'iT*** *map*

خفيف **khafiif** *light* (adj.)

خلال **khilaal** *during*

(الـ)خليج العربي **al-khaliij al-:arabii** *the Arabian Gulf*

خليط **khaliiT** *mixture*

خليفة، خلفاء **khaliifah**, **khulafaa'*** *Caliph*, head of the Islamic state

خور **khawr** *creek*

خير **khayr** (state of) *well-being*

د

دائرة، دوائر **daa'irah**, **dawaa'ir*** *(government) department*

داخل **daakhil** *inside, the inside of something*

دخل **dakhala [S-I u]** *to enter*

دراسة، ات **diraasah**, **-aat** *study*

درجة الحرارة **darajat al-Haraarah** *temperature*

درس **darasa [S-I u]** *study*

درهم، دراهم **dirham**, **daraahim*** *dirham* (unit of currency)

دش **dushsh** *shower*

دقيقة، دقائق **daqiiqah**, **daqaa'iq*** *minute*

دكان، دكاكين **dukkaan**, **dakaakiin*** *small shop, stall*

دمشق **dimashq*** *Damascus*

دهش **dahisha [S-1 a]** *be surprised, astonished*

دور، أدوار **dawr**, **adwaar** *role, turn*

دولة، دول **dawlah**, **duwal** *country, state*

دولي **duwalii** or **dawlii** *international*

دينار، دنانير **diinaar**, **danaaniir** *dinar* (currency)

ذ

ذاكرة **dhaakirah** *memory*

ذلك **dhaalik(a)** *that* (m.)

ذبح **dhabaHa [S-I a]** *slaughter*

ذبيحة، ذبائح **dhabiiHah**, **dhabaa'iH*** *sacrificial animal*

ذقن، ذقون **dhaqn**, **dhuquun** (f.) *beard, chin*

ذكور **dhukuur** *males*

ذهب **dhahab** *gold*

ذهب **dhahaba**, **[S-I a]** *go*

الذي **alladhii** *who, which, that* (f. التي **allatii**)

ر

رائحة، روائح **raa'iHah**, **rawaa'iH*** *smell, scent, perfume*

رائع **raa'i:** *splendid, brilliant, marvellous*

راديو، رواديو **raadyo**, **rawaadyo** *radio*

راكب ، ركاب **raakib**, **rukkaab** *passenger*

راية، ات **raayah**, **-aat** *flag, banner*

رئيس، رؤساء **ra'iis**, **ru'asaa'*** *boss, chief*

ربح **rabaHa [S-I a]** *to win, gain, profit*

ربع **rub:** *quarter*

رجع **raja:a [S-I i]** *return, come back*

رجل **rijl** *foot* (f.)

رجل، رجال **rajul**, **rijaal** *man*

رحب ب **raHHaba [S-II]** *to welcome* (requires **bi-**)

رحلة، ات **riHlah**, **-aat** *journey, voyage*

رد **radda [D-I u]** *return something to someone*

رسالة، رسائل **risaalah**, **risaa'il*** *letter, message*

رش **rashsha [D-I u]** *sprinkle, spray*

رشاقة **rashaaqah** *shapeliness, elegance*

رشيد **rashiid** *Rashid* (man's name); also *Rosetta*, a town in Egypt

رصد **raSada [S-I u]** *observe, watch*

رعى **ra:aa [Lh-I]** *take care of, look after*

رغبة، ات **raghbah**, **-aat** *desire, wish*

رف، رفوف **raff**, **rufuuf** *shelf*

رفع **rafa:a [S-I a]** *to lift, raise*

رقم تلفون **raqm tilifuun** *telephone number*

ركلة، ات **raklah**, **-aat** *kick*

ركن، أركان **rukn**, **arkaan** *corner*

ركني **ruknii** *corner* (adj.)

رمز، رموز **ramz**, **rumuuz** *code, symbol*

رواية، ات **riwaayah**, **-aat** *novel, story*

رياضة، ات **riyaaDah**, **-aat** *sport, exercise*

ز

زائر، زوار **zaa'ir**, **zuwwaar** *visitor*

زاحم **zaaHama [S-III]** *to compete with*

زار **zaara [Mw-I]** *visit*

زبون، زبائن **zabuun**, **zabaa'in*** *customer, client*

زمان، أزمنة **zamaan**, **azminah** *time*

زوج **zawj** *husband*

زوجة، ات **zawjah**, **-aat** *wife*

زورق، زوارق **zawraq**, **zawaariq*** *boat*

زي، أزياء **ziyy**, **azyaa'*** *clothes, fashion, style*

زيارة، ات **ziyaarah**, **-aat** *visit*

زيت **zayt** (edible) *oil*

س

سائح، سواح **saa'iH**, **suwwaaH** *tourist*

سائق،ون/ساقة **saa'iq**, **-uun/ saaqah** *driver*

سؤال، أسئلة **su'aal**, **as'ilah** *question*

سادس **saadis** *sixth*

ساعة، ات **saa:ah**, **-aat** *hour, time, watch, clock*

سافر **saafara [S-III]** *to travel*

ساكن **saakin** *living, residing*

ساكن، سكان **saakin**, **sukkaan** *inhabitant, resident*

سالم **saalim** *safe, sound*

سباحة **sibaaHah** *swimming*

سباق، ات **sibaaq**, **-aat** *race*

سبح **sabaHa [S-I a]** *swim*

ستة **sittah** *six*

سجل **sajjala [S-II]** *to register, to score*

سحر **siHr** *magic*

سد، سدود **sadd**, **suduud** *dam*

سدد **saddada [S-II]** *to aim;* (football) *shoot*

سرعان ما **sur:aan maa** *quickly, before long*

سرعة **sur:ah** *speed*

سعر، أسعار **si:r**, **as:aar** *price*

سعيد، سعداء **sa:iid**, **su:adaa'*** *happy*

سفيرة، ات **safiirah**, **-aat** (female) *ambassador*

سفينة، سفن **safiinah**, **sufun** *ship*

سكب **sakaba [S-I u]** *to pour out*

سكر **sukkar** *sugar*

سكن **sakana [S-I u]** *live, reside*

سلاح، أسلحة **silaaH**, **asliHah** *weapon, arm*

سلق **salq** (the action of) *boiling something*

سماح **samaaH** *permission*

سمع **sami:a [S-I a]** *to hear, listen*

سمك **samak** *fish* (collective)

سمن **samn** *ghee, clarified butter*

سندويتش، ات **sandawiitsh**, **-aat** *sandwich*

سنة، سنوات **sanah**, **sanawaat** *year*

سور، أسوار **suur**, **aswaar** *wall*

سوق، أسواق **suuq**, **aswaaq** (usually f.) *market*

سونا **sawnaa** *sauna*

سيارة، ات **sayyaarah**, **-aat** *car*

سيدة، ات **sayyidah**, **-aat** *lady*

سيطر على **sayTara :alaa [Q-I]** *to dominate*

سيطرة **sayTarah** *domination*

سينما، سينمات **siinamaa**, **siinamaat** (f.) *cinema*

ش

شارع، شوارع **shaari:**, **shawaari:*** *street, road*

(الـ)شارقة **ash-shaariqah** *Sharjah*

شاشة **shaashah** *screen*

شاطئ **shaaTi'** *shore, beach*

شاعر، شعراء **shaa:ir**, **shu:araa'*** *poet*

شأن، شؤون **sha'n**, **shu'uun** *affair, important matter*

شاهد **shaahada [III]** *see, look at*

شاي **shaay** *tea*

شبكة، شباك **shabaka**, **shibaak** *net, netting*

شتاء **shitaa'*** *winter*

شجرة، أشجار **shajarah**, **ashjaar** *tree*

شخص، أشخاص **shakhS**, **ashkhaaS** *person*

شديد **shadiid** *strong, mighty*

شرب **shariba [S-I a]** *drink*

شرح **sharaHa [S-I a]** *explain*

شركة، ات **sharikah**, **-aat** *company, firm*

شريحة، شرائح **shariiHah**, **sharaa'iH*** *slice*

شعب، شعوب **sha:b**, **shu:uub** *people, folk*

شعبي **sha:bii** *folk, popular*

شعر **sha:r** *hair*

شعر **shi:r** *poetry*

شقة، شقق **shaqqah**, **shiqaq** *flat, apartment*

شكراً **shukran** *thank you*

شكراً جزيلاً **shukran jaziilan** *thank you very much*

شكل، أشكال شكراً جزيلًا **shukr** **shakl**, **ashkaal** *type, shape*

شكلاتة **shokolaatah** *chocolate*

شمال **shamaal** *left*

شمس **shams** *sun*

شهير **shahiir** *famous*

شوط، أشواط **shawT**, **ashwaaT** *heat, race*; football: *half*

شيء، اشياء **shay'**, **ashyaa'*** *thing, something*

شيد **shayyada [My-II]** *erect, construct*

ص

صاحب، أصحاب **SaaHib**, **aS-Haab** *owner, master;* also sometimes *friend*

صادق **Saadiq** *truthful, true*

(الـ)صافي **(aS-Saafii** *pure, clear*

صالح **SaaliH** *doing right*

صالة **Saalah** *sitting-room, lounge*

صالون تجميل **Saaluun tajmiil** *beauty salon*

صباح الخير **SabaaH al-khayr** *good morning*

صبح **SubH** *morning*

صحن، صحون **SaHn**, **SuHuun** *dish*

صحيح **SaHiiH** *correct, right*

صديق، أصدقاء **Sadiiq**, **aSdiqaa'*** *friend*

صغير **Saghiir** *young* (person), *small* (thing)

صف، صفوف **Saff**, **Sufuuf** *class* (school)

صفى **Saffaa [Ly-II]** *drain, strain*

صلصة **SalSah** *sauce*

صلى الله عليه وسلم **Sallaa l-Laaahu :alay-hi wa-sallam** *Prayers and Peace be Upon Him* (said after mentioning the name of the Prophet)

صندوق بريد **Sanduuq bariid** *post office box*

صوم **Sawm** *fast, fasting*

صيدلية، ات **Saydaliyyah, -aat** *pharmacy*

صيف **Sayf** *summer*

ض

ضربة، ات **Darbah, Darabaat** *a blow, beat*

ضرورة، ات **Duruurah, -aat** *necessity, requirement*

ضم **Damma [D-I u]** *include, comprise*

ضيف، ضيوف **Dayf, Duyuuf** *guest*

ضيق **Dayyiq** *narrow*

ط

طائرة، ات **Taa'irah, -aat** *aeroplane*

طالب، طلاب/طلبة **Taalib, Tullaab/ Talabah** *student*

طالبة، طالبات **Taalibah, -aat** *female student*

طبخ **Tabakha [S-I u]** *cook*

طبع **Taba:a [S-I a]** *print, type*

طبعا **Tab:an** *naturally, of course*

طبق، أطباق **Tabaq, aTbaaq** *plate, dish*

طبقة، ات **Tabaqah, -aat** *layer*

طبيب، أطباء **Tabiib, aTibbaa'*** *doctor*

طبيب أسنان **Tabiib asnaan** *dentist*

طبيخ **Tabiikh** *cooking, cuisine*

طبيعة **Tabii:ah** *nature*

طبيعي **Tabii:ii** *natural*

طرد **Tarada [S-I u]** *to banish, drive away* (football: *send off*)

طريق، طرق **Tariiq, Turuq** *road, way*

طريقة، طرائق **Tariiqah, Taraa'iq*** *method, way*

طعام **Ta:aam** *food*

طفل، أطفال **Tifl, aTfaal** *child*

طفولة **Tufuulah** *childhood*

طماطم **TamaaTim*** *tomatoes*

طمح إلى **TamaHa ilaa [S-I a]** *aspire to*

طموح **TumuuH** *aspiration, ambition*

طنطا **TanTaa** *Tanta* (town in Egypt)

طوال اليوم **Tiwaal al-yawm** *all day*

طويل **Tawiil** *tall (person), long (thing)*

ظ

ظهر **DHuhr** *noon*

ع

عائلة،ات **:aa'ilah, -aat** *family*

عادة، ات **:aadah, -aat** *custom, habit*

عادل **:aadil** *just, upright*

عارض، ون **:aariD, -uun** (male) *model*

عارضة، ات **:aariDah, -aat** (female) *model*

عاش **:aasha [My-I]** *live*

عاصمة، عواصم **:aaSimah, :awaaSim*** *capital* (city)

عالمي **:aalamii** *worldwide*

(الـ)عالي **al-: aalii** *high*

عام **:aamm** *general*

عام، أعوام **:aam, a:waam** *year*

عامل، عمال **:aamil, :ummaal** *workman*

عبارة، ات **:abaarah, -aat** *phrase, expression*

عجلة، ات **:ajalah, -aat** *wheel, bicycle*

عجيب **:ajiib** *wonderful*

عجيبة، عجائب **:ajiibah, :ajaa'ib*** (object of) *wonder*

عدد، أعداد **:adad, a:daad** *number*

عدس **:ads** *lentils*

عدن **:adan** *Aden*

عراقي **:iraaqii** *Iraqi*

عربي، عرب **:arabii** *Arabic, Arab*

عرض **:arD** *showing, displaying*

عرض، عروض **:arD, :uruuD** *offer, deal*

عرف **:arafa [S-I i]** *to know*

عريض **:ariiD** *wide*

عسكري، عساكر **:askarii, :asaakir*** *soldier*

عشاء **:ishaa'** *late evening* (prayer time)

عشرة **:ashrah** *ten*

عصر **:aSr** *mid-afternoon*

عضوة، عضوات **:uDwah, :uDuwaat** *member* (f.)

عضوية **:uDwiyyah** *membership*

عطشان **:aTshaan** *thirsty*

عفوا **:afwan** *you're welcome, don't mention it* (reply to *thanks*)

عقب **:aqaba [S-I u]** *come after, follow*

عم **:amm** *uncle* (on father's side)

عمة **:ammah** *aunt* (on father's side)

عمان **:ammaan** *Amman* (capital of Jordan); **:umaan** *Oman* (Sultanate of)

عمر **:umr** *life, age*

عمل، أعمال **:amal, a:maal** *work, job, business*

عمل **:amila [S-I a]** *do, work*

عمومي **:umuumii** *general*

عن **:an** *about, concerning*

عند **:inda** *at, with*

عندما **:indamaa** *when*

عنوان، عناوين **:unwaan, :anaawiin*** *address*

عيادة، ات **:iyaadah, -aat** *clinic*

عيد، أعياد **:iid, a:yaad** *festival*

عيد الأضحى **:iid al-aD-Haa** *Festival of the Sacrifice*

عيد الميلاد **:iid al-miilaad** *Christmas*

عين، عيون **:ayn, :uyuun** (f.) *eye; also spring* (of water)

غ

غاية **ghaa yah** *extreme, most*

(الـ)غرب **al-gharb** *the west*

غربي، ون **gharbii**, **-uun** *western*

غرفة، غرف **ghurfah**, **ghuraf** *room*

غسالة، ات **ghassaalah**, **-aat** *washing machine*

غسل **ghasala [S-I i]** *wash*

غلى **ghalaa [Ly-I]** *to boil, come to the boil*

غنم **ghanam** *sheep* (collective)

غني، أغنياء **ghanii**, **aghniyaa'*** *rich, rich person*

غير **ghayr** *other than, apart from*

ف

فاضل **faaDil** *favourable, good*

فاكهة، فواكه **faakihah**, **fawaakih*** *fruit*

فاهم **faahim** *understanding*

فتاة، فتيات **fataah**, **fatayaat** *girl, young woman*

فتح **fataHa [S-I a]** *open*

فترة، ات **fatrah**, **-aat** *period, time, spell*

فجر **fajr** *dawn*

فحص **faHaSa [S-1 a]** *to examine*

فخم **fakhm** *magnificent*

فراغ **faraagh** *leisure*

فردي **fardii** *single*

فرنسا **faransaa** *France*

فرنساوي **faransaawi** *French*

فرصة، فرص **furSah**, **furaS** *chance, opportunity*

فرض **faraDa [S-I i]** *impose*

فرع، فروع **far:**, **furuu:** *branch* (of a tree, company, etc.)

فرعوني **far:uunii** *pharaonic*

فريق، فرق **fariiq**, **firaq** *team*

فستان، فساتين **fustaan**, **fasaatiin*** *frock, dress*

فصل، فصول **faSl**, **fuSuul** *section, season* (of the year)

فضل **faDDala [S-II]** *prefer*

فطر **fiTr** *breaking of a fast*

فظيع **faDHii:** *shocking, awful*

فعل **fa:ala [S-I a]** *to do, make*

فعلا **fi:lan** *really, actually, in fact*

فقط **faqaT** *only*

فقير، فقراء **faqiir**, **fuqaraa'*** *poor, poor person*

فلفل **fulful/filfil** *pepper*

فن، فنون **fann**, **funuun** *art, craft, technique*

فني **fannii** *artistic, technical*

فندق، فنادق **funduq**, **fanaadiq*** *hotel*

فهد، فهود **fahd**, **fuhuud** *leopard*

فهم **fahima [S-I a]** *to understand*

فورا **fawran** *immediately*

فوز **fawz** *victory*

فوق **fawqa** *above, over*

في **fii** *in*

فيروز **fayruuz** *Fairuz* (female name); *a turquoise* (gem)

فيلا، فيلل **fiilla**, **fiilal** *villa*

فيلم، افلام **fiilm**, **aflaam** *film*

ق

قائمة، قوائم **qaa'imah, qawáa'im** *list*

قابل **qaabala [S III]** *encounter, meet*

قاد **qaada [Mw-I]** *to lead*

قارب، قوارب **qaarib, qawaarib*** *(small) boat*

قال **qaala [Mw-I]** *to say*

القاهرة **al-qaahirah** *Cairo*

قبل **qabila [S-I a]** *to accept*

قبيح **qabiiH** *ugly*

قدم **qaddama [S-II]** *to present, serve*

قديم **qadiim** *old, ancient* (of things)

قرأ، يقرأ **qara'a, yaqra' [S-I a]** *read*

قرار، ات **qaraar, -aat** *decision, resolution*

قرص ثابت **qurS thaabit** *hard disk*

قرفة **qirfah** *cinnamon*

قرن، قرون **qarn, quruun** *century*

قرنفل **qurunful** *cloves*

قريب **qariib** *near*

قسم، أقسام **qism, aqsaam** *section, division*

قصة، قصص **qiSSah, qiSaS** *story, tale*

قصر، قصور **qaSr, quSuur** *palace*

قطر، أقطار **quTr, aqTaar** *region, area*

قطعة، قطع **qiT:ah, qiTa:** *piece*

قفل **qafala [S-1 i]** *close, shut*

قلب، قلوب **qalb, quluub** *heart*

قلعة، قلاع **qal:ah, qilaa:** *fort, fortress, citadel*

قلم، أقلام **qalam, aqlaam** *pen, pencil*

قليل **qaliil** *little, few* (quantity, number)

قليلاً **qaliilan** *slightly, a little*

قمر **qamar** *moon*

قميص، قمصان **qamiiS, qumSaan** *shirt*

قهر **qahara [S- a]** *to conquer*

قهوة **qahwah** *coffee*

قوة، ات **quwwah, -aat** *force, power, strength*

قوسي **qawsii** *curved, bowed*

قيادي **qiyaadii** *leading*

قيم **qayyim** *valuable*

ك

ك **ka-** *as, like*

كائن **kaa'in** *being, existing,*

كأس، كؤوس **ka's, ku'uus** *cup, trophy*

كافة **kaafat** *all*

كامل **kaamil** *complete, whole*

كبير **kabiir** *big, old* (of people)

كتاب، كتب **kitaab, kutub** *book*

كتب **kataba [S-I-u]** *to write*

كتيب **kutayyib** *booklet, brochure*

كثافة **kathaafah** *density*

كثير **kathiir** *much, many*

كرة، ات **kurah**, **-aat** *ball*; also used as a shortened form of كرة القدم **kurat al-qadam** *football*

كرسي، كراسي **kursii**, **karaasii** *chair*

كره **kariha [S-I a]** *hate*

كريم **kariim** *noble, generous*

كسلان **kaslaan** *lazy*

كشري **kushari** name of an Egyptian lentil dish

الكعبة **al-ka:bah** *The Kaabah* (Holy Shrine in Mecca)

كعك **ka:k** *cake*

كفى **kafaa [Ly-I]** *to suffice, be sufficient for*

كل **kull** *each, every, all*

كلام **kalaam** *speech*

كلية، ات **kulliyyah**, **-aat** *college, faculty*

كم **kam** *how many, how much*

كما **ka-maa** *just as, also*

كمية، ات **kammiyyah**, **-aat** *amount*

كوب، أكواب **kuub**, **akwaab** *glass, cup*

كيس، أكياس **kiis**, **akyaas** *bag, sack*

كيف **kayf(a)** *how*

ل

لِـ **li-** *to, for*

لا **laa** *not, no*

لازم **laazim** *necessary*

لاعب، ون **laa:ib**, **-uun** *player*

لأن **li'anna** *because*

لحظة، ات **laHDHah**, **laHaDHaat** *moment*

لحم، لحوم **laHm**, **luHuum** *meat*

لذلك **li-dhaalik** *because of that, for this reason*

لذيذ **ladhiidh** *delicious, tasty*

لطيف **laTiif** *pleasant, nice*

لعب، ألعاب **la:b**, **al:aab** *playing, game*

لعب **la:iba [S-I a]** *play*

لماذا **li-maadha(a)** *why*

لمدة **li-muddat** *for the period of...*

لندن **landan** *London*

ليلة، ات، ليال **layla**, **-aat**, **layaalin** *night*

ليمون **laymoon** *lemon*

م

ما **maa** (before nouns and pronouns) *what?*; (before verbs) *not*

ماء، مياه **maa'**, **miyaah** *water*

مائدة، موائد **maa'ida**, **mawaa'id*** *table*

مؤتمر، ات **mu'tamar**, **-aat** *conference*

مؤخرا **mu'akhkhiran** *recently*

ماذا **maadhaa** (before verbs) *what?*

مارس **maarasa [S-III]** *to practise, carry out, perform*

ماركة **maarkah** *marque, label*

ماكياج **maakyaaj** *make-up*

مالئ **maali'** *filling, filler*
مالي **maalii** *financial*
مؤلف، ون **mu'allif, -uun** *author*
مؤمن، ون **mu'min, -uun** *believing, a believer* (in something)
مئوي **mi'awii** *centennial, hundredth*
مباراة، مباريات **mubaaraah, mubaarayaat** *match* (sport)
مباشرةً **mubaasharatan** *directly*
مبسوط **mabsuuT** *contented, happy*
مبلغ، مبالغ **mablagh, mabaaligh*** *sum of money*
متجاور **mutajaawir** *adjacent, adjoining*
متجر، متاجر **matjar, mataajir*** *trading place, shop, stall*
متحد **muttaHid** *united*
متحف، متاحف **matHaf, mataaHif*** *museum*
متر، أمتار **mitr, amtaar** *metre*
متزوج **mutazawwaj** *married*
متفرج، ون **mutafarrij, -uun** *spectator*
متميز **mutamayyiz** *distinctive, prominent*
متى **mataa** *when*
مجتهد **mujtahid** *diligent, hard-working*
مثل **mithl** *like*
مجال، ات **majaal, -aat** *field, sphere of activity*
مجانا **majjaanan** *free, gratis*
مجنون، مجانين **majnuun, majaaniin*** *mad*
محطة، ات **maHaTTah, -aat** *station*
محل، محلات **maHall, maHallaat** *shop, store*
مخرج، مخارج **makhraj, makhaarij** *exit*
مخطط **mukhaTTaT** *striped*
مدافع، ون **mudaafi:, -uun** *defender*
مدخل، مداخل **madkhal, madaakhil** *entrance*
مدة **muddah** (period of) *time*
مدرس، ون **mudarris, -uun** *teacher*
مدير، مدراء **mudiir, mudaraa'** *manager*
مدينة، مدن **madiinah, mudun** *town, city*
مذاق **madhaaq** *flavour*
مربع **murabba:** *square* (adj.)
مرة، ات **marrah, -aat** *time, occasion*
مرحبا **marHaban** *welcome*
مركز الشرطة **markaz ash-shurTah** *police station*
مركز الفنون **markaz al-funuun** *craft centre*
مرمى **marmaa** *goal, goalmouth*
مريض، مرضى **mariiD, marDaa** (adj.) *ill*; (noun) *patient*
مساء **masaa'** *evening*
مساء الخير **masaa' al-khayr** *good evening*

مسابقة، ات **musaabaqah**, **-aat** *competition*

مسؤول، ون **mas'uul**, **-uun** *official*

مسبح، مسابح **masbaH**, **masaabiH*** *swimming pool*

مستشفى، مستشفيات **mustashfaa**, **mustashfayaat** *hospital*

مسرح، مسارح **masraH**, **masaariH*** *theatre*

مسرحية، ات **masraHiyyah**, **-aat** *play* (theatrical)

مسروق **masruuq** *stolen*

مسلسل، ات **musalsal**, **-aat** *serial, series*

مسلم، ون **muslim**, **-uun** *Muslim*

مسموح **masmuuH** *permitted*

مسيحي، ون **masiiHii**, **-uun** *Christian*

موسيقى **muusiiqaa** (f.) *music*

مشاهدة **mushaahadah** *seeing, viewing*

مشغول **mashghuul** *busy*

مشكلة، مشاكل **mushkilah**, **mashaakil*** *problem*

مشهور **mashhuur** *famous*

مصباح، مصابيح **miSbaaH**, **maSaabiiH** *lamp*

مصر **miSr*** *Egypt*

مطار، ات **maTaar**, **-aat** *airport*

مطبخ، مطابخ **maTbakh**, **maTaabikh*** *kitchen*

مطحون **maT-Huun** *ground, milled*

مطربة، ات **muTribah**, **-aat** (female) *singer, musician*

مطعم، مطاعم **maT:am**, **maTaa:im*** *restaurant*

مع **ma:a** *with, together with*

مع الأسف **má:a l-asaf** *sorry*

معجون **ma:juun** *paste*

معكرونة **ma:karuunah** *macaroni*

معنى، المعاني **ma:naa**, **al-ma:aanii** *meaning*

مغربي، مغاربة **maghribii**, **maghaaribah** *Moroccan*

مغنية، ات **mughanniyah**, **-aat** (female) *singer*

مفتاح، مفاتيح **miftaaH**, **mafaatiiH*** *key*

مفترض **muftaraD** *assumed, supposed*

مفروض **mafruuDH** *necessary, obligatory*

مفروم **mafruum** *chopped, ground*

مفضل **mufaDDil** *preferring*

مقدار، مقادير **miqdaar**, **maqaadiir*** *quantity, measure*

مقشر **muqashshar** *peeled, skinned*

مقطع **muqaTTa:** *chopped*

مقيم **muqiim** *residing, resident*

مكان، أمكنة **makaan**, **amkinah** *place*

مكة المكرمة **makkah l-mukarramah** *Holy (City of) Mecca*

مكتب، مكاتب **maktab, makaatib*** *office*

مكتبة، ات **maktabah, -aat** *library, bookshop*

مكتوب **maktuub** *written*

مكتوم **maktuum** *concealed*

المكسيك **al-maksiik** *Mexico*

ملابس **malaabis*** *clothes*

ملامح **malaamiH*** *features*

ملح **milH** *salt*

ملعب، ملاعب **mal:ab, malaa:ib*** *sports ground, pitch*

ملعقة، ملاعق **mil:aqah, malaa:iq*** *spoon, spoonful*

ملك، ملوك **malik, muluuk** *king*

مليونير **malyoonayr** *millionaire*

ممتاز **mumtaaz** *excellent*

ممثل، ون **mumaththil, -uun** *actor, representative*

ممنوع **mamnuu:** *forbidden*

من **man** *who?* (in questions)

من **min** *from*

من الممكن **min al mumkin** *maybe*

من فضلك **min faDlak** *please*

مناسبة، ات **munaasabah, -aat** *occasion*

منتج، ون **muntij, -uun** *producer*

منتجع صحة **muntaja: SiHHah** *fitness centre*

منذ **mundhu** *since*

منطقة، مناطق **minTaqah, manaaTiq*** *region, area* (football: *penalty area*)

منظم، ات **munaDHDHim, -aat** *regulator*

منظمة، ات **munaDHDHamah, -aat** *organisation*

منقط **munaqqaT** *spotted*

منبعث **munba:ith** *emanating*

مهاجر، ون **muhaajir, -uun** *emigrant*

مهرب **muharrab** *smuggled*

مهرجان ؛ ات **mahrajaan, -aat** *festival*

مهم **muhimm** *important*

مهنة، مهن **mihnah, mihan** *job, trade, profession*

مهندس، ون **muhandis, -uun** *engineer*

مواقيت **mawaaqíit** *opening hours*

موجود **mawjuud** *found, situated, existing*

موديم **muudiim** *modem*

موقع، مواقع **mawqi:, mawaaqi:*** *site, situation, place*

موقف، مواقف **mawqif, mawaaqif*** *stopping, parking place*

مولد النبي **mawlid an-nabii** (festival of) *the Prophet's Birthday*

مولود **mawluud** *born*

ميدان **maydaan** *square* (in a town)

ميناء، المواني **miinaa', al-mawaanii** (sometimes f.) *harbour, port*

ن

نائم **naa'im** *sleeping, asleep*

نادي، أندية **naadi, andiyah** *club* (social)

نار **naar** (f.) *fire*

ناس **naas** *people*

ناشف **naashif** *dry*

ناظر **naaDHara [S-III]** *to equal, compete with*

نافع **naafi:** *useful*

نام **naama [Ma-I]** *sleep*

نتيجة، نتائج **natiijah, nataa'ij*** *result, outcome*

نجمة، ات **najmah, -aat** *star,* (female) *film star*

نساء **nisaa'*** (pl.) *women*

نسمة **nasamah** *individual* (used in population counts only)

نشاط **nashaaT** *activity*

نصف، أنصاف **niSf, anSaaf** *half*

نظيف **naDHiif** *clean*

نفس، نفوس **nafs, nufuus** (f.) *self, soul*

نقد، نقود **naqd, nuquud** *cash, money*

نقع **naqa:a [S-I a]** *to soak, steep*

نقل **naql** *transport, transportation*

نمر، نمور **namir, numuur** *tiger*

نهائي **nihaa'ii** *final* (adj.)

نهار **nahaar** *daytime, hours of daylight*

نهاية **nihaayah** *end*

نور **nuur** *light* (noun)

نوع، أنواع **naw:, anwaa:** *kind, sort, type*

نيل **nayl** *getting, receiving*

هـ

هادئ **haadi'** *quiet, gentle*

هال **haal** *cardamom*

هجين، هجن **hajiin, hujun** *racing camel*

هدف، أهداف **hadaf, ahdaaf** *target, aim, goal*

هدية، هدايا **hadiyah, hadaayaa*** *gift, present*

هذا/هذه **haadha/haadhihi** *this* (m./f.)

هرم، أهرام **haram, ahraam** *pyramid*

هنا **hunaa** *here*

هناك **hunaaka** *there, there is/are*

الهند **al-hind** *India*

هو **huwa** *he*

هو،هي **huwa/hiya** *it* (lit., *he/she*)

هواء **hawaa'** *air*

هواية، ات **hawaayah, -aat** *hobby*

هي **hiya** *she, it*

و

و **wa-** *and*

واحد **waaHid** *one*

واسع **waasi:** *roomy, spacious*

واقف **waaqif** *standing, stationary*

والد **waalid** *father*

والدة **waalidah** *mother*

وجبة، ات **wajabah**, **-aat** *meal*

وجه، وجوه **wajh**, **wujuuh** *face, (media) personality*

وحيد **waHiid** *sole, only, singular*

ود **wadd** *love, friendship*

وراء **waraa'(a)** *behind*

وسخ **wasikh** *dirty*

وسط **wasT** *middle, centre* (of town, etc.)

وصل **waSala [Fw-I i]** *to arrive*

وصل **waSSal [S-II]** *connect, transport*

وضع **waD:** *putting*

وضع **waDa:a [Fw-I a]** *to put, place*

وقت، أوقات **waqt**, **awqaat** *time*

وقع **waqa:a [Fw-I a]** *fall*

وقف **waqafa [Fw-I i]** *stop, stand*

وكالة، ات **wakaalah**, **-aat** *agency*

ولا **wa-laa** *and not, nor*

ولاية، ات **wilaayah**, **-aat** *administrative division of a country; state*

ولد، أولاد **walad**, **awlaad** *boy* (pl. also *children*)

ولكن **walaakin**, **walaakinna** *but*

ى

يا **yaa** *O!* (used before the name when addressing someone directly)

يقام **yuqaam** *is held, takes place* (passive verb)

يد **yad** (f.) *hand*

اليمن **al-yaman** *Yemen*

يمين **yamiin** *right (hand)*

يوم، أيام **yawm**, **ayyaam** *day*

يومي **yawmii** *daily* (adj.)

English–Arabic vocabulary

This is again based on the words in the vocabulary boxes, which relate directly to the texts.

about, approximately حوالي **Hawaalii**

about, concerning عن **:an**

above, over فوق **fawqa**

Abu Dhabi أبو ظبي **abuu DHabi**

accept قبل **qabila [S-I a]**

according to حسب **Hasb**

activity نشاط **nashaaT**

actor, representative ممثل، ون **mumaththil, -uun**

add أضاف **aDaafa [My-IV]**

address عنوان، عناوين **:unwaan, :anaawiin***

Aden عدن **:adan**

adjacent, adjoining متجاور **mutajaawir**

adult بالغ، ون **baaligh, baalighuun**

aeroplane طائرة، ات **Taa'irah, -aat**

affair, important matter شأن، شؤون **sha'n, shu'uun**

after بعد **ba:d** (before nouns), بعد ما **ba:d maa** (before verbs)

afternoon; (in the) afternoon بعد الظاهر **ba:d aDH-DHuhr**

agency وكالة، ات **wakaalah, -aat**

aim, shoot سدد **saddada [S-II]**

air هواء **hawaa'**

air conditioning تكييف **takyiif**

airport مطار، ات **maTaar, -aat**

Alexandria الاسكندرية **al-iskandariyyah**

all جميع **jamii:**

all day طوال اليوم **Tiwaal al-yawm**

all together جميعا **jamii:an**

also أيضاً **ayDan**

ambassador (female) سفيرة، ات **safiirah, -aat**

America أمريكا **amriika**

Amman عمان **:ammaan**

amount كمية، ات **kammiyyah, -aat**

and و **wa-**

announce, state أعلن **a:lana [S-IV]**

appear, seem, show بدا **badaa [Lw-I]**

apple تفاحة، تفاح **tufaaHah, tufaaH**

approximately حوالي **Hawaalii**

Arab, Arabic عربي، عرب **:arabii**

Arabian Gulf الخليج العربي **al-khaliij al-:arabii**

archaeological أثري **atharii**

arrive وصل **waSala [Fw-I i]**

art, craft, technique فن، فنون **fann, funuun**

artistic, technical فني **fannii**

as, like ك **ka-**

as for أمّا **ammaa**

aside, to one side جانبا **jaaniban**

ask سأل **sa'ala [S-I a]**

aspiration, ambition طموح **TumuuH**

aspire, have the ambition طمح إلى **TamaHa ilaa [S-I a]**

assembly, society مفترض **jam:iyyah, -aat**

assumed, supposed مفترض **muftaraD**

at, with عند **:inda**

attain, achieve أدرك **adraka [S-IV]**

attend حضر **HaDara [S-I u]**

attention, concern, interest اهتمام **ihtimaam**

attract جلب **jalaba [S-I i]**

aunt (on father's side) عمة **:ammah**

aunt (on mother's side) خالة **khaalah**

author مؤلف، ون **mu'allif, -uun**

award, grant احتسب **iHtasaba [S-VIII]**

baby طفل، أطفال **Tifl, aTfaal**

bachelor, single أعزب **a:zab***

bag, sack كيس، أكياس **kiis, akyaas**

bag, suitcase حقيبة، حقائب **Haqiibah, Haqaa'ib***

balance, equality تعادل **ta:aadul**

ball, football كرة، ات **kurah, -aat**

banish, drive away (football: *send off*) طرد **Tarada [S-I u]**

bank بنك، بنوك **bank, bunuuk**

bathroom حمام، ات **Hammaam, -aat**

be able استطاع **istaTaa:a [Mw-X]**

be carried, transported تنقل **tanaqqala [S-V]**

be surprised, astonished دهش **dahisha [S-1 a]**

beard ذقن، ذقون **dhaqn, dhuquun** (f.)

beautiful جميل **jamiil**

beauty جمال **jamaal**

beauty salon صالون تجميل **Saaluun tajmiil**

because لأن **li'anna**

because of that, for this reason لذلك **li-dhaalik**

become أصبح **aSbaHa [S-IV]**

beer بيرة **biirah**

begin بدأ **bada' [S-I a]**

behind وراء **waraa'(a)**

being, existing, situated كائن **kaa'in**

belief, faith إيمان **iimaan**

believing, a believer (in something) مؤمن، ون **mu'min, -uun**

beside, next to بجانب **bi-jaanib**

between, among بين **bayna**

bicycle عجلة، ـات **:ajalah, -aat**

big, old كبير **kabiir**

black أسود، سوداء **aswad***, f. **sawdaa'***

boat زورق، زوارق **zawraq, zawaariq***, قارب، قوارب **qaarib, qawaarib***

boil, come to the boil غلى **ghalaa [Ly-I]**

boiling, the action of boiling something سلق **salq**

book كتاب، كتب **kitaab, kutub**

booklet, brochure كتيب **kutayyib**

born مولود **mawluud**

boss, chief رئيس، رؤساء **ra'iis, ru'asaa'***

boy ولد، أولاد **walad, awlaad** (pl. also *children*)

branch فرع، فروع **far:, furuu:**

breach اخترق **ikhtaraqa [S-VIII]**

bread خبز **khubz**

breaking of a fast فطر **fiTr**

bridge جسر، جسور **jisr, jusuur**

British بريطاني **briiTaanii**

broadcast أذاع **adhaa:a [My-IV]**

brochure كتيب **kutayyib**

brother أخ، إخوان/ إخوة **akh, ikhwaan** or **ikhwah**

brown, fry حمر **Hammara [S-II]**

building, construction بناء **binaa'**

busy مشغول **mashghuul**

but ولكن **walaakin, walaakinna**

Cairo القاهرة **al-qaahirah**

cake كعك **ka:k**

Caliph خليفة، خلفاء **khaliifah, khulafaa'***

camel جمل، جمال **jamal, jimaal**

camel (for racing) هجين، هجن **hajiin, hujun**

capital (city) عاصمة، عواصم **:aaSimah, :awaaSim***

car سيارة، ات **sayyaarah, -aat**

card بطاقة **buTaaqah**

cardamom هال **haal**

carry حمل **Hamala [S-I i]**

cash, money نقد، نقود **naqd, nuquud**

cause, make do something; place, put جعل **ja:ala [S-I a]**

celebrate احتفل ب **iHtafala bi- [S-VIII]**

centennial, hundredth مئوي **mi'awii**

century قرن، قرون **qarn, quruun**

certain, definite أكيد **akiid**

chair كرسي، كراسي **kursii, karaasii**

chance, opportunity فرصة، فرص **furSah, furaS**

cheese جبنة **jubnah**

child طفل، أطفال **Tifl, aTfaal**

childhood طفولة **Tufuulah**

chocolate شكلاتة **shokolaatah**

choose اختار **ikhtaara [My-VIII]**

chopped مقطع **muqaTTa:**

chopped, ground مفروم **mafruum**

Christian مسيحي، ون **masiiHii, -uun**

Christmas عيد الميلاد **:iid al-miilaad**

cinema سينما، سينمات **siinamaa, siinamaat** (f.)

cinnamon قرفة **qirfah**

city مدينة، مدن **madiinah, mudun**

class, row, line صف، صفوف **Saff, Sufuuf**

clean نظيف **naDHiif**

cleaning تنظيف **tanDHiif**

clinic عيادة، ات **:iyaadah, -aat**

close, shut قفل **qafala [S-1 i]**

clothes ملابس **malaabis***

cloves قرنفل **qurunful**

club (social) نادي، أندية **naadi, andiyah**

code, symbol رمز، رموز **ramz, rumuuz**

coffee قهوة **qahwah**

cold بارد **baarid**

college, faculty كلية، ات **kulliyyah, -aat**

come جاء، يجيء **jaa'a, yajii' [My-I]**

come after, follow عقب **:aqaba [S-I u]**

commence, open افتتح **iftataHa [S-VIII]**

commercial تجاري **tijaarii**

company, firm, business شركة، ات **sharikah, -aat**

compete with زاحم **zaaHama [S-III]**

competition مسابقة، ات **musaabaqah, -aat**

complete تام **taamm**

complete, whole كامل **kaamil**

computer آلة حاسبة **aalah Haasibah**

concealed مكتوم **maktuum**

conference مؤتمر، ات **mu'tamar, -aat**

connect, transport وصل **waSSal [S-II]**

conquer قهر **qahara [S- a]**

consider, regard اعتبر **i:tabara [S-VIII]**

contented, happy مبسوط **mabsuuT**

cook طبخ **Tabakha [S-I u]**

cooking, cuisine طبيخ **Tabiikh**

cooling تبريد **tabriid**

corner (adj.) ركني **ruknii**

corner ركن، أركان **rukn, arkaan**

correct, right صحيح **SaHiiH**

count, census إحصاء، ات **iHSaa', -aat**

country بلد، بلاد/بلدان **balad, bilaad/buldaan**

country, state دولة، دول **dawlah, duwal**

craft centre مركز الفنون **markaz al-funuun**

credit card بطاقة تسليف **buTaaqat tasliif**
creek خور **khawr**
cultural ثقافي **thaqaafii**
cup, trophy كأس، كؤوس **ka's, ku'uus**
curved, bowed قوسي **qawsii**
custom, habit عادة، ات **:aadah, -aat**
customer, client زبون، زبائن **zabuun, zabaa'in***
customs, excise جمرك، جمارك **jumruk, jamaarik***
daily (adj.) يومي **yawmii**
dam سد، سدود **sadd, suduud**
Damascus دمشق **dimashq***
daughter ابنة، بنات **ibnah, banaat**
dawn فجر **fajr**
day يوم، أيام **yawm, ayyaam**
daytime, hours of daylight نهار **nahaar**
deceive خدع **khada:a [S-I a]**
decision, resolution قرار، ات **qaraar, -aat**
defender مدافع، ون **mudaafi:, -uun**
delicious, tasty لذيذ **ladhiidh**
demanding back, reclaiming استرداد **istirdaad**
density كثافة **kathaafah**
dentist طبيب أسنان **Tabiib asnaan**
department (government) دائرة، دوائر **daa'irah, dawaa'ir***
design, designing تصميم **taSmiim**
desire, wish رغبة، ات **raghbah, -aat**
diet حمية **Himyah**
diligent, hard-working مجتهد **mujtahid**
dinar (currency) دينار، دنانير **diinaar, danaaniir***
directly مباشرةً **mubaasharatan**
director, manager مدير، مدراء **mudiir, mudaraa'***
dirham درهم، دراهم **dirham, daraahim***
dirty وسخ **wasikh**
discount حسم **Hasm**
discover اكتشف **iktashafa [S-VIII]**
discuss ناقش **naaqasha [S-III]**
dish صحن، صحون **SaHn, SuHuun**
distinction, privilege امتياز **imtiyaaz**
distinctive, prominent متميز **mutamayyiz**
division of a country; state ولاية، ات **wilaayah, -aat**
do, make فعل **fa:ala [S-I a]**
do, work عمل **:amila [S-I a]**
doctor طبيب، أطباء **Tabiib, aTibbaa'***
dominate سيطر على **sayTara :alaa [Q-I]**
domination سيطرة **sayTarah**

door, gate باب، أبواب **baab, abwaab**

drain, strain صفى **Saffaa [Ly-II]**

drink شرب **shariba [S-I a]**

driver سائق،ون/ساقة **saa'iq, -uun/saaqah**

dry ناشف **naashif**

each, every, all كل **kull**

ear أذن **udh(u)n (f.)**

eat أكل، يأكل **akala, ya'kul [S-I u]**

educational تعليمي **ta:liimii**

Egypt مصر **miSr***

emanate, be sent out انبعث **inba:atha [S-VII]**

emanating منبعث **munba:ith**

emigrant مهاجر، ون **muhaajir, -uun**

encounter, meet قابل **qaabala [S III]**

end نهاية **nihaayah**

end, last part of something آخر **aakhir**

engineer مهندس، ون **muhandis, -uun**

England إنجلترا **ingiltarra**

English, Englishman إنجليزي **ingliizi**

enjoy تمتع بـ **tamatta:a [S-V]**

enter دخل **dakhala [S-I u]**

entrance مدخل، مداخل **madkhal, madaakhil***

entrust, vest in أسند ل **asnada [S-IV]**

equal, compete with ناظر **naaDHara [S-III]**

erect, construct شيد **shayyada [My-II]**

European أوروبي، ون **uruubii**

evening مساء **masaa'***

every, each, all كل **kull**

excellent ممتاز **mumtaaz**

except إلا **illaa**

exit مخرج، مخارج **makhraj, makhaarij***

explain شرح **sharaHa [S-I] a**

extent, compass اتساع **ittisaa:**

extreme, most غاية **ghaa yah**

eye; also *spring* (of water) عين، عيون **:ayn, :uyuun (f.)**

face, (media) personality وجه، وجوه **wajh, wujuuh**

facilities تسهيلات **tas-hiilaat**

fall, happen وقع **waqa:a [Fw-I a]**

family عائة، ـات **:aa'ilah, -aat**

famous شهير **shahiir** مشهور **mashhuur**

far away, distant بعيد **ba:iid**

fashion, style زي، أزياء **ziyy, azyaa'***

fast, fasting صوم **Sawm**

father أب **ab** ، والد **waalid**

favourable, good فاضل **faaDil**

features ملامح **malaamiH***

festival, anniversary عيد، أعياد **:iid, a:yaad**

festival (event) مهرجان ؛ ات **mahrajaan, -aat**

field, sphere of activity مجال، ات **majaal, -aat**

fifth خامس **khaamis**

filling, filler مالئ **maali'**

film فيلم، افلام **fiilm, aflaam**

final (adj.) نهائي **nihaa'ii**

financial مالي **maalii**

finish, come to an end انتهى **intahaa [Ly-VIII]**

fire نار **naar** (f.)

first أول **awwal**

first (adv.) أولا **awwalan**

fish (collective) سمك **samak**

fitness centre منتجع صحة **muntaja: SiHHah**

flag, banner راية، ات **raayah, -aat**

flat, apartment شقة، شقق **shaqqah, shiqaq**

flavour مذاق **madhaaq**

flood, overflow with أفاض ب **afaaDa bi- [My-IV]**

fluently بطلاقة **bi-Talaaqah**

folk, pertaining to the people شعبي **sha:bii**

follow تبع **tabi:a**

food طعام **Ta:aam**

food, things to eat أكل **akl**

foot رجل **rijl**

football كرة القدم **kurat al-qadam**

for the period of... لمدة **li-muddat**

forbidden ممنوع **mamnuu:**

force, power, strength قوة، ات **quwwah, -aat**

fort, fortress حصن، حصون **HiSn, HuSuun** قلعة، قلاع **qal:ah, qilaa:**

found, situated, existing موجود **mawjuud**

foundation, setting up إنشاء **inshaa'***

four أربعة **arba:ah**

France فرسا **faransaa**

free, gratis مجانا **majjaanan**

French فرنساوي **faransaawi**

friend صديق، أصدقاء **Sadiiq, aSdiqaa'***

frock, dress فستان، فساتين **fustaan, fasaatiin***

from من **min**

fruit فاكهة، فواكه **faakihah, fawaakih***

game, playing لعب، ألعاب **la:b, al:aab**

garden, park حديقة، حدائق **Hadiiqah, Hadaa'iq***

Geezah (district of Cairo) الجيزة **al-jiizah**

general عام **:aamm** عمومي **:umuumii**

geographical جغرافي **jughraafii**

German ألماني **almaanii**

getting, receiving نيل **nayl**

ghee, clarified butter سمن **samn**

gift, present هدية، هدايا **hadiyah, hadaayaa***

girl, daughter بنت، بنات **bint, banaat**

girl, young woman فتاة، فتيات **fataah**, **fatayaat**

give أعطى **a:Taa [Ly-IV]**

glass, cup كوب، أكواب **kuub**, **akwaab**

go ذهب **dhahaba**, **[S-I a]**

goal, goalmouth مرمى **marmaa**

God, Allah الله **Al-laah**

gold ذهب **dhahab**

golf جولف **guulf**

good جيد **jayyid**

good evening مساء الخير **masaa' al-khayr**

good morning صباح الخير **SabaaH al-khayr**

grain, seed حبة، ات **Habbah**, **-aat**

Great Britain بريطانيا العظمى **briiTaanyaa l-:uDHmaa**

green أخضر **akhDar***

ground (sports), *pitch* ملعب، ملاعب **mal:ab**, **malaa:ib***

ground, earth أرض **al-arD** (f.)

ground, milled مطحون **maT-Huun**

group, gathering جماعة، ات **jamaa:ah**, **-aat**

guard (football: *goalkeeper*) حارس، حراس **Haaris**, **Hurraas**

guest ضيف، ضيوف **Dayf**, **Duyuuf**

hair شعر **sha:r**

half نصف، أنصاف **niSf**, **anSaaf**

hamburger برغر، ات **barghar**, **-aat**

hand يد **yad** (f.)

happy, joyful سعيد، سعداء **sa:iid**, **su:adaa'***

harbour, port ميناء، الموانى **miinaa'**, **al-mawaanii** (sometimes f.)

hard disk قرص ثابت **qurS thaabit**

hate كره **kariha [S-I a]**

he هو **huwa**

heart قلب، قلوب **qalb**, **quluub**

heat حرارة **Haraarah**

heat, race (football: *half*) شوط، أشواط **shawT**, **ashwaaT**

heavy ثقيل **thaqiil**

hello السلام عليكم **as-salaamu-alaykum**

here هنا **hunaa**

high العالي **al-: aalii**

historical تاريخي **taariikhii**

history تاريخ **taariikh**

hit, strike أصاب **aSaaba**

hobby هواية، ات **hawaayah**, **-aat**

hospital مستشفى، مستشفيات **mustashfaa**, **mustashfayaat**

hot حار **Haarr**

hotel فندق، فنادق **funduq**, **fanaadiq***

hour, time, watch, clock ساعة، ات **saa:ah**, **-aat**

house بيت، بيوت **bayt**, **buyuut**

how كيف **kayf(a)**

how many, how much كم **kam**

how much? بكم **bi-kam**

human being; pl. = *people* انسان، ناس **insaan**, **naas** *hungry* جوعان، جوعى **jaw:aan*, jaw:aa***

husband زوج **zawj**

I أنا **ána**

ice ثلج **thalj**

ice-cream أيس كريم **ays kriim**

if إن **in**, إذا **idhaa**, لو **law**

ill مريض، مرضى **mariiD, marDaa**

immediately فورا **fawran**

implementation, execution تنفيذ **tanfiidh**

important مهم **muhimm**

impose فرض **faraDa [S-I i]**

in في **fii**

in front of أمام **amaam**

include, comprise ضم **Damma [D-I u]**

India الهند **al-hind**

individual (used in population counts only) نسمة **nasamah**

inhabitant, resident ساكن، سكان **saakin, sukkaan**

inside داخل **daakhil**

international دولي **duwalii** or **dawlii**

Iraqi عراقي **:iraaqii**

is held, takes place (passive verb) يقام **yuqaam**

it هو،هي **huwa/hiya** (lit., *he/she*)

Jordanian أردني **urduni**

journey, voyage رحلة، ات **riHlah, -aat**

just, upright عادل **:aadil**

just as, also كما **ka-maa**

Kaabah الكعبة **al-ka:bah**

keep, preserve حافظ على **HaafaDHa :alaa [S-III]**

key مفتاح، مفاتيح **miftaaH, mafaatiiH***

kick ركلة، ات **raklah, -aat**

kind, sort, type نوع، أنواع **naw:, anwaa:**

king ملك، ملوك **malik, muluuk**

kitchen مطبخ، مطابخ **maTbakh, maTaabikh***

know عرف **:arafa [S-I i]**

lady سيدة، ات **sayyidah, -aat**

lamp مصباح، مصابيح **miSbaaH, maSaabiiH**

last أخير **akhiir**

late evening (prayer time) عشاء **:ishaa'**

layer طبقة، ات **Tabaqah, -aat**

lazy كسلان **kaslaan**

lead قاد **qaada [Mw-I]**

leading قيادي **qiyaadii**

leading roles بطولات **buTuulaat**

learn تعلم **ta:allama [S-V]**

leave, let be ترك **taraka [S-I u]**

left شمال **shamaal**

legend أسطورة، أساطير **usTuurah, asaaTiir***

leisure فراغ **faraagh**

lemon ليمون **laymoon**

lentils عدس **:ads**

leopard فهد، فهود **fahd, fuhuud**

letter, message رسالة، رسائل **risaalah, risaa'il***

library, bookshop مكتبة، ات **maktabah, -aat**

life, age عمر **:umr**

lift, raise رفع **rafa:a [S-I a]**

light (adj.) خفيف **khafiif**

light (noun) نور **nuur**

like مثل **mithl**

like, love أحب، يحب **aHabba [D-IV]**

limit, border حد، حدود **Hadd, Huduud**

list قائمة، قوائم **qaa'imah, qawaa'im***

little, few (quantity, number) قليل **qaliil**

live عاش **:aasha [M-y I]**

live, reside سكن **sakana [S-I u]**

load, burden حمل، أحمال **Himl, aHmaal**

lobby (hotel) بهو **bahw**

London لندن **landan**

look! (to a woman) أنظري **unDHurii**

love, friendship ود **wadd**

macaroni معكرونة **ma:karuunah**

mad مجنون، مجانين **majnuun, majaaniin***

magic سحر **siHr**

magnificent فخم **fakhm**

make-up ماكياج **maakyaaj**

males ذكور **dhukuur**

man رجل، رجال **rajul, rijaal**

manager مدير، مدراء **mudiir, mudaraa'**

map خريطة، خرائط **khariiTah, kharaa'iT***

market سوق، أسواق **suuq, aswaaq** (usually f.)

marque, label ماركة **maarkah**

married متزوج **mutazawwaj**

marry تزوج **tazawwaja [Mw-V]**

match (sport) مباراة، مباريات **mubaaraah, mubaarayaat**

matter, affair شأن، شؤون **sha'n, shu'uun**

maybe من الممكن **min al mumkin**

meal وجبة، ات **wajabah, -aat**

meaning معنى، المعاني **ma:naa, al-ma:aanii**

meat لحم، لحوم **laHm, luHuum**

meet, come together اجتمع **ijtama:a [S-VIII]**

member (f.) عضوة، عضوات **:uDwah, :uDuwaat**

membership عضوية **:uDwiyyah**

memory ذاكرة **dhaakirah**

merchant تاجر، تجار **taajir, tujjaar**

method, way طريقة، طرائق **Tariiqah, Taraa'iq***

metre متر، أمتار **mitr, amtaar**

Mexico المكسيك **al-maksiik**

mid-afternoon عصر **:aSr**

middle وسط **wasT**

millionaire مليونير **malyoonayr**

minute دقيقة، دقائق **daqiiqah, daqaa'iq***

mixture خليط **khaliiT**

model (male) عارض، ون **:aariD, -uun**; (female) عارضة، ات **:aariDah, -aat**

modem موديم **muudiim**

modern, up-to-date حديث **Hadiith**

moment لحظة، ات **laHDHah, laHaDHaat**

moon قمر **qamar**

more/most أكثر **akthar***

morning صبح **SubH**

Moroccan مغربي، مغاربة **maghribii, maghaaribah**

mosque (large) جامع، جوامع **jaami:, jawaami:***

mother والدة **waalidah**

much, many كثير **kathiir**

museum متحف، متاحف **matHaf, mataaHif***

music موسيقى **muusiiqaa** (f.)

Muslim مسلم، ون **muslim, -uun**

name اسم، أسماء **ism, asmaa'****

narrow ضيق **Dayyiq**

nation أمة، أمم **ummah, umam**

nationality جنسية، ات **jinsiyyah, -aat**

natural طبيعي **Tabii:ii**

naturally, of course طبعا **Tab:an**

nature طبيعة **Tabii:ah**

near (to) قريب من **qariib min**

necessary لازم **laazim**

necessary, obligatory مفروض **mafruuDH**

necessity, requirement ضرورة، ات **Duruurah, -aat**

neighbour جار، جيران **jaar, jiiraan**

net, netting شبكة، شباك **shabaka, shibaak**

new جديد **jadiid**

newest, latest أحدث **aHdath***

news خبر، أخبار **khabar, akhbaar**

newspaper جريدة، جرائد **jariidah, jaraa'id***

nice لطيف **laTiif**

night ليلة، ات، ليال **layla, -aat, layaalin**

ninth تاسع **taasi:**

no, not لا **laa**

noble, generous كريم **kariim**

noon ظهر **DHuhr**

nor ولا **wa-laa**

not (before verbs) ما **maa**

novel, story رواية، ات **riwaayah, -aat**

now الآن **al-'aan**, الحين **al-Hiin**

number عدد، أعداد **:adad, a:daad**

O! (when addressing someone directly) يا **yaa**

observe, watch رصد **raSada [S-I u]**

occasion مناسبة، ات **munaasabah, -aat**

occupation, work عمل، أعمال **:amal, a:maal**

occupy احتل **iHtalla [D-VIII]**

offer, deal عرض، عروض **:arD, :uruuD**

office مكتب، مكاتب **maktab, makaatib***

official مسؤول، ون **mas'uul, -uun**

oil (edible) زيت **zayt**

old, ancient (of things) قديم **qadiim**

Oman (Sultanate of) عمان **:umaan**

one واحد **waaHid**

onions بصل **baSal**

only فقط **faqaT**

open فتح **fataHa [S-I a]**

opening hours مواقيت **mawaaqiit***

or أو **aw**

organisation منظمة، ات **munaDHDHamah, -aat**

origin, basis أصل، أصول **aSl, uSuul**

other آخر **aakhar*** (f. أخرى **ukhraa**)

other than, apart from غير **ghayr**

outside خارج **khaarij**

owner, master; also sometimes *friend* صاحب، أصحاب **SaaHib, aS-Haab**

palace قصر، قصور **qaSr, quSuur**

participate, take part اشترك **ishtaraka [S-VIII]**

passenger راكب، ركاب **raakib, rukkaab**

past (noun) الماضي **al-maaDii**

paste معجون **ma:juun**

patient (sick person) مريض، مرضى **mariiD, marDaa***

peeled, skinned مقشر **muqashshar**

pen, pencil قلم، أقلام **qalam, aqlaam**

people ناس **naas**

people, folk شعب، شعوب **sha:b, shu:uub**

pepper فلفل **fulful/filfil**

period, time, spell فترة، ات **fatrah, -aat**

permission سماح **samaaH**

permitted مسموح **masmuuH**

person شخص، أشخاص **shakhS, ashkhaaS**

petrol بنزين **banziin**

pharaonic فرعوني **far:uunii**

pharmacy صيدلية، ات **Saydaliyyah, -aat**

phrase, expression عبارة، ات **:abaarah, -aat**

piece قطعة، قطع **qiT:ah, qiTa:**

pilgrimage الحج **al-Hajj**

pitch, course, playing field ملعب، ملاعب **mal:ab, malaa:ib***

place مكان، أمكنة **makaan, amkinah**

place أودع **awda:a [Fw-IV]**

plate, dish طبق، أطباق **Tabaq, aTbaaq**

play, game لعب **la:b**

play (theatrical) مسرحية، ات **masraHiyyah, -aat**

play لعب **la:iba [S-I a]**

player لاعب، ون **laa:ib, -uun**

pleasant, nice لطيف **laTiif**

please (go ahead, sit down, enter etc.) تفضل **tafaDDal**

please (when asking for something) من فضلك **min faDlak**

pocket جيب، جيوب **jayb, juyuub**

poet شاعر، شعراء **shaa:ir, shu:araa'***

poetry شعر **shi:r**

police station مركز الشرطة **markaz ash-shurTah**

poor, poor person فقير، فقراء **faqiir, fuqaraa'***

porter حمال، ون **Hammaal, -uun**

possible, to be أمكن **amkana [S-IV]**

post office box صندوق بريد **Sanduuq bariid**

pound (money) جنيه، ات **junayh, -aat**

pour out سكب **sakaba [S-I u]**

practise, carry out, perform مارس **maarasa [S-III]**

praise God الحمد لله **al-Hamdu li-l-laah**

prefer فضل **faDDala [S-II]**

preferring مفضل **mufaDDil**

present, gift هدية، هدايا **hadiyah, hadaayaa***

present, here حاضر، ون **HaaDir, -uun**

present, serve قدم **qaddama [S-II]**

presentation تقديم **taqdiim**

price سعر، أسعار **si:r, as:aar**

print, type طبع **Taba:a [S-I a]**

prize, reward جائزة، جوائز **jaa'izah, jawaa'iz***

problem مشكلة، مشاكل **mushkilah, mashaakil***

producer منتج، ون **muntij, -uun**

production انتاج **intaaj**

programme برنامج، برامج **barnaamij, baraamij***

pupil تلميذ، تلامذة/تلاميذ **tilmiidh, talaamidhah/talaamiidh***

pure, clear الصافي **aS-Saafii**

put, place وضع **waDa:a [Fw-I a]**

putting وضع **waD:**

pyramids الأهرام **al-ahraam**

qualify تأهل **ta'ahhala [S-V]** (لـ **li-** *for*)

quantity, measure مقدار، مقادير **miqdaar, maqaadiir***

quarter ربع **rub:**

question سؤال، أسئلة **su'aal, as'ilah**

quickly, before long سرعان ما **sur:aan maa**

quiet, gentle هادئ **haadi'**

race سباق، ات **sibaaq, -aat**

radio راديو، روداديو **raadyo, rawaadyo**

raise رفع **rafa:a [S-I a]**

read قرأ، يقرأ **qara'a, yaqra' [S-I a]**

really, actually, in fact فعلا **fi:lan**

receive, meet استقبل **istaqbala [S-X]**

recently مؤخرا **mu'akhkhiran**

red أحمر **aHmar***

referee, umpire حكم، حكام **Hakam, Hukkaam**

region, area (football: *penalty area*) منطقة، مناطق **minTaqah, manaaTiq***

region, zone, area قطر، أقطار **quTr, aqTaar**

register, score سجل **sajjala [S-II]**

registration, scoring تسجيل **tasjiil**

regulator منظم، ات **munaDHDHim, -aat**

renew, restore جدد **jaddada [D-II]**

rent, be a tenant of استأجر **ista'jara [S-X]**

repeat, renew أعاد **a:aada [Mw-IV]**

report تقرير، تقارير **taqriir, taqaariir***

reside; hold (an event, etc.) أقام **aqaama [Mw-IV]**

residing, living مقيم **muqiim**

restaurant مطعم، مطاعم **maT:am, maTaa:im***

result, outcome نتيجة، نتائج **natiijah, nataa'ij***

return something to someone رد **radda [D-i u]**

return, come back رجع **raja:a [S-I i]**

rice أرز **aruzz**

rich, rich person غني، أغنياء **ghanii, aghniyaa'****

right (hand) يمين **yamiin**

right, correct صالح **SaaliH**

road, street شارع، شوارع **shaari:, shawaari:***

road, way طريق، طرق **Tariiq, Turuq**

role, turn دور، أدوار **dawr, adwaar**

room حجرة **Hujrah**

room غرفة، غرف **ghurfah, ghuraf**

roomy, spacious واسع **waasi:**

row, class (in school) صف، صفوف **Saff, Sufuuf**

run جرى **jaraa [Ly-I]**

sacrificial animal ذبيحة، ذبائح **dhabiiHah, dhabaa'iH***

sad حزين **Haziin**

safe, sound سالم **saalim**

salt ملح **milH**

sandwich سندويتش، ات **sandawiitsh, -aat**

sauce صلصة **SalSah**

Saudi Arabia السعودية **as-sa:udiyyah**

sauna سونا **sawnaa**

say قال **qaala [Mw-I]**

screen شاشة **shaashah**

sea, large river بحر، بحار **baHr, biHaar**

section, division قسم، أقسام **qism, aqsaam**

section, season (of the year) فصل، فصول **faSl, fuSuul**

see, look at شاهد **shaahada [III]**

seeing, viewing مشاهدة **mushaahadah**

selection تشكيلة، ات **tashkiilah, -aat**

self, soul نفس، نفوس **nafs, nufuus** (f.)

sell باع **baa:a [My-I]**

send أرسل **arsala [S-IV]**

serial, series مسلسل، ات **musalsal, -aat**

servant خادم، خدام **khaadim, khuddaam**; (f.) خادمة، ات **khaadimah, -aat**

service خدمة، ات **khidmah, -aat**

shape, kind, type شكل، أشكال **shakl, ashkaal**

shapeliness, elegance, slim figure رشاقة **rashaaqah**

Sharjah الشارقة **ash-shaariqah**

she, it هي **hiya**

sheep خروف، خرفان **kharuuf, khirfaan**; (collective) غنم **ghanam**

shelf رف، رفوف **raff, rufuuf**

ship سفينة، سفن **safiinah, sufun**

shirt قميص، قمصان **qamiiS, qumSaan**

shocking, awful فظيع **faDHii:**

shop, stall دكان، دكاكين **dukkaan, dakaakiin***

shop, store محل، محلات **maHall, maHallaat**

shopping تسوق **tasawwuq**

shore, beach شاطئ **shaaTi'**

shot (football) تسديدة، ات **tasdiidah, -aat**

shower دش **dushsh**

showing, displaying عرض **:arD**

side جانب، جوانب **jaanib, jawaanib***

signal إشارة، ات **ishaarah, -aat**

since منذ **mundhu**

singer (female) مغنية، ات **mughanniyah, -aat**

singer, musician (female) مطربة، ات **muTribah, -aat**

single فردي **fardii**

sister أخت، أخوات **ukht, akhawaat**

sit, sit down جلس **jalasa [S-I i]**

site, situation, place موقع، مواقع **mawqi:, mawaaqi:***

sitting, seated جالس **jaalis**

sitting-room, lounge صالة **Saalah**

six ستة **sittah**

sixth سادس **saadis**

slaughter ذبح **dhabaHa [S-I a]**

sleep نام **naama [Ma-I]**

sleeping, asleep نائم **naa'im**

slice شريحة، شرائح **shariiHah, sharaa'iH***

slightly, a little قليلاً **qaliilan**

small, young صغير **Saghiir**

smell, scent, perfume رائحة، روائح **raa'iHah, rawaa'iH***

smile ابتسم **ibtasama [S-VIII]**

smuggled مهرب **muharrab**

so, therefore إذا **ídhan**

soak, steep نقع **naqa:a [S-I a]**

soldier عسكري، عساكر **:askarii, :asaakir***

sole, only, singular وحيد **waHiid**

solution حل، حلول **Hall, Huluul**

some, part of something بعض **ba:D**

son ابن، أبناء **ibn, abnaa'***

sorry مع الأسف **má:a l-asaf**

Spanish اسباني **isbaanii**

speak تكلم **takallama [S-V]**

special; private خاص **khaaSS**

specialise تخصص **takhaSSaS [S-V]**

spectator متفرج، ون **mutafarrij, -uun**

speech كلام **kalaam**

speed سرعة **sur:ah**

Sphynx أبو الهول **abuu l-hawl**

spice تابل، توابل **taabil, tawaabil***

splendid, brilliant, marvellous رائع **raa'i:**

spoon, spoonful ملعقة، ملاعق **mil:aqah, malaa:iq***

sport, exercise رياضة، ات **riyaaDah, -aat**

spotted منقط **munaqqaT**

spread, currency انتشار **intishaar**

sprinkle, spray رش **rashsha [D-I u]**

square (adj.) مربع **murabba:**

square (in a town) ميدان **maydaan**

standing, stationary واقف **waaqif**

star, (female) *film star* نجمة، ات **najmah, -aat**

state, express أعرب عن **a:raba :an [S-IV]**

station محطة، ات **maHaTTah, -aat**

step, degree درجة، ات **darajah, -aat**

stolen مسروق **masruuq**

stone حجر، أحجار **Hajar, aHjaar**

stop, stand وقف **waqafa [Fw-I i]**

stopping, parking place موقف، مواقف **mawqif, mawaaqif***

story, tale قصة، قصص **qiSSah, qiSaS**

street, road شارع، شوارع **shaari:, shawaari:***

striped مخطط **mukhaTTaT**

strong, mighty شديد **shadiid**

student طالب، طلاب/طلبة **Taalib, Tullaab/Talabah** (f. طالبة، طالبات **Taalibah, -aat**)

study, studying (noun) دراسة، ات **diraasah, -aat**

study درس **darasa [S-I u]**
suffice, be sufficient for كفى **kafaa [Ly-I]**
sugar سكر **sukkar**
sum (of money) مبلغ، مبالغ **mablagh, mabaaligh***
summer صيف **Sayf**
sun شمس **shams**
sunset; Morocco المغرب **al-maghrib**
surround أحاط بـ **aHaaTa bi- [My-IV]**
sweetness حلاوة **Halaawah**
swim سبح **sabaHa [S-I a]**
swimming سباحة **sibaaHah**
swimming pool مسبح، مسابح **masbaH, masaabiH***
table مائدة، موائد **maa'ida, mawaa'id***
take أخذ **akhadha [S-I u]**
take care of, look after رعى **ra:aa [Lh-I]**
take, use up, occupy (of time) استغرق **istaghraqa [S-X]**
tall, long طويل **Tawiil**
target, aim, goal هدف، أهداف **hadaf, ahdaaf**
taxi تاكسي **taaksi**
tea شاي **shaay**
teacher مدرس، ون **mudarris, -uun**
team فريق، فرق **fariiq, firaq**
telephone تلفون **tilifuun**
telephone number رقم تلفون **raqm tilifuun**
television (adj.), *televisual* تلفزيوني **tilifizyuunii**
temperature درجة الحرارة **darajat al-Haraarah**
ten عشرة **:ashrah**
tennis تنس **tanis**
thank you شكراً **shukran**
thank you (to a man/woman) أشكرك **ashkur-ak/ik**
thank you very much شكراً جزيلاً **shukran jaziilan**
that ذلك **dhaalik**
that is أي **ay**
the الـ **al-**
theatre مسرح، مسارح **masraH, masaariH***
then ثم **thumma**
there, there is/are هناك **hunaaka**
thing, something شيء، اشياء **shay', ashyaa'***
third ثالث **thaalith**
thirsty عطشان **:aTshaan**
thirteenth (f.) ثالثة عشر **thaalithah :ashar**
this هذا/هذه **haadha/haadhihi** (m./f.)
thousand ألف، آلاف **alf, aalaaf**
three ثلاثة **thalaathah**
ticket تذكرة، تذاكر **tadhkirah,tadhaakir***
tiger نمر، نمور **namir, numuur**
time زمان، أزمنة **zamaan, azminah**
time وقت، أوقات **waqt, awqaat**

time (period of) مدة **muddah**

time, occasion مرة، ات **marrah, -aat**

tired تعبان **ta:baan**

to, for لِـ **li-**

today اليوم **al-yawm**

tomatoes طماطم **TamaaTim***

tomorrow الغد **al-ghad**

tourist سائح، سواح **saa'iH, suwwaaH**

tower برج، أبراج **burj, abraaj**

town, city مدينة، مدن **madiinah, mudun**

track, trace أثر، آثار **athar, aathaar**

trade, commerce تجارة **tijaarah**

trade, profession مهنة، مهن **mihnah, mihan**

trading place, shop, stall متجر، متاجر **matjar, mataajir***

transmission, sending إرسال **irsaal**

transport, take, give a lift وصل **waSSala [II]**

transport, transportation نقل **naql**

travel سافر **saafara [S-III]**

tree شجرة، أشجار **shajarah, ashjaar**

truthful, true صادق **Saadiq**

try out, taste جرب **jarraba [S-II]**

ugly قبيح **qabiiH**

uncle (on father's side) عم **:amm**

uncle (on mother's side) خال **khaal**

understand فهم **fahima [S-I a]**

understanding فاهم **faahim**

united متحد **muttaHid**

United Arab Emirates الإمارات العربية المتحدة **al-imaaraat al-:arabiyyah al-muttaHidah**

university جامعة، ات **jaami:ah**

until, even حتى **Hattaa**

upright, honest صالح **SaaliH**

use, employ استخدم **istakhdama [S-X]**

use, employment استخدام **istikhdaam**

use, usage استعمال **isti:maal**

useful نافع **naafi:**

valuable قيم **qayyim**

very جدا **jíddan**

victory فوز **fawz**

villa فيلا، فيلل **fiilla, fiilal**

visit زار **zaara [Mw-I]**

visit زيارة، ات **ziyaarah, -aat**

visitor زائر، زوار **zaa'ir, zuwwaar**

wall سور، أسوار **suur, aswaar**

wash غسل **ghasala [S-I i]**

washing machine غسالة، ات **ghassaalah, -aat**

watch, look at تفرج على **tafarraja :ala [S-V]**

water ماء، مياه **maa', miyaah**

weapon, arm سلاح، أسلحة **silaaH, asliHah**

welcome مرحبا **marHaban**; أهلا وسهلا **ahlan wa-sahlan**

welcome رحب ب **raHHaba bi- [S-II]**

welcome, welcoming (noun) ترحيب **tarHiib**

welcoming (adj.) ترحيبي **tarHiibii**

well, right, OK حسنا **Hasanan**

well-being (state of) خير **khayr**

west الغرب **al-gharb**

western غربي، ون **gharbii, -uun**

what? (before nouns and pronouns) ما **maa**; (before verbs) ماذا **maadhaa**

wheel, bicycle عجلة، ات **:ajalah, -aat**

when متى **mataa** (in questions); *when* عندما **:indamaa**

where أين **ayna**

which أيّ **ayy**

while بينما **baynamaa**

white أبيض، بيضاء **abyaD***, f. **bayDaa'***

who? (in questions) من **man**

who, which, that الذي **alladhi** (f. التي **allatii**)

why لماذا **li-maadha(a)**

wide عريض **:ariiD**

wife زوجة، ات **zawjah, -aat**

win, gain, profit ربح **rabaHa [S-I a]**

wind tower برجيل، براجيل **barjiil, baraajiil***

winter شتاء **shitaa'***

with, together with مع **ma:a**

without بدون **bi-duun**

woman امرأة، نساء **imra'ah, nisaa'** (irregular plural)

wonder, wonderful thing عجيبة، عجائب **:ajiibah, :ajaa'ib***

wonderful عجيب **:ajiib**

work, job, business عمل، أعمال **:amal, a:maal**

workman عامل، عمال **:aamil, :ummaal**

world الدنيا **ad-dunya(a)** (f.), العالم **al-:aalam**

worldwide عالمي **:aalamii**

written مكتوب **maktuub**

year سنة، سنوات **sanah, sanawaat**; عام، أعوام **:aam, a:waam**

yellow أصفر، صفراء **aSfar***, f. **Safraa'***

Yemen اليمن **al-yaman**

yesterday أمس **ams**

you أنت **anta/anti** (m./f.)

you're welcome (in reply to *thank you*) عفوا **:afwan**

Grammar index

The numbers refer to the units.

Credits

Front cover: © ImageState Media

Back cover and pack: © Jakub Semeniuk/iStockphoto.com, © Royalty-Free/Corbis, © agencyby/iStockphoto.com, © Andy Cook/iStockphoto.com, © Christopher Ewing/iStockphoto.com, © zebicho – Fotolia.com, © Geoffrey Holman/iStockphoto.com, © Photodisc/Getty Images, © James C. Pruitt/iStockphoto.com, © Mohamed Saber – Fotolia.com

Pack: © Stockbyte/Getty Images